*Insiders and Outsiders*

# Insiders and Outsiders

## Jewish and Gentile Culture in Germany and Austria

Edited by Dagmar C. G. Lorenz
and Gabriele Weinberger

WAYNE STATE UNIVERSITY PRESS
Detroit, Michigan 48202

Copyright © 1994 by Wayne State University Press, Detroit, Michigan 48202. All rights are reserved. No part of this book may be reproduced without formal permission. Manufactured in the United States of America.

99 98 97 96 95 94      5 4 3 2 1

**Library of Congress Cataloging-in-Publication Data**

Insiders and outsiders : Jewish and Gentile culture in Germany and Austria / edited by Dagmar C. G. Lorenz and Gabriele Weinberger.
   p. cm.
   Includes index.
   ISBN 0-8143-2497-5 (alk. paper). — ISBN 0-8143-2498-3 (pbk., alk. paper)
   1. Jews—Germany—Identity.  2. Jews—Austria—Identity.  3. Jews—Germany—Intellectual life.  4. Jews—Austria—Intellectual life.  5. Germany—Civilization—Jewish influences.  6. Austria—Civilization—Jewish influences.  7. Germany—Ethnic relations.  8. Austria—Ethnic relations.     I. Lorenz, Dagmar C. G., 1948-.  II. Weinberger, Gabriele.

DS135.G33I48   1994

305.892'4043—dc20                                        93-46000

*This book is dedicated to*
*Annemarie Weinberger*
*and*
*Mohsin Abdou*

# Contents

**Contributors** ix

**Introduction**
 Dagmar C. G. Lorenz 3

**Historical Perspectives: Emancipation and Assimilation**

*Chicken Soup*, or the Penalties for Sounding Too Jewish
 Sander L. Gilman 15

Residues of Otherness: On Jewish Emancipation
during the Age of German Enlightenment
 Barbara Fischer 30

The Wandering Jew's Rhine Journey: Heine's *Lorelei*
 Jost Hermand 39

Jews and Anti-Semitism in Fin-de-Siècle Vienna
 Egon Schwarz 47

Historical Visions: Anna Seghers on the Revolution in Haiti
 Sima Kappeler 66

Jean Améry and Austria
 Ruth Beckermann 73

**Jewish Languages and Discourses**

Structure, Standardization, and Diglossia: The Case of Courland Yiddish
 Neil G. Jacobs 89

Alsatian Yiddish Theater at the Turn of the Century
 Astrid Starck 100

The Debate about Hebrew, in German: The *Kulturfrage*
in the Zionist Congresses, 1897–1914
 Michael Berkowitz 109

Babylon or Jerusalem: Berlin as the Center
of Jewish Modernism in the 1920s
 Delphine Bechtel 116

Authors of German Language in Israel
 Margarita Pazi 124

**Nationalism, Symbiosis, and Anti-Semitism**

Thomas Mann's *Wälsungenblut* in the Context
of the Intermarriage Debate and the "Jewish Question"
 Alan Levenson 135

The Negative German–Jewish Symbiosis
 Jack Zipes 144

Historical Consciousness and Jewish Identity:
Stefan Zweig and Wilhelm Speyer on the Way to Themselves
    Luke Springman      155

*Bezwingt des Herzens Bitterkeit:* Hilde Burger's Return from "Paradise"
    Roslyn Abt Schindler      175

## The Legacy of the Holocaust

"You Who Live Safe in Your Warm Houses":
Your Role in the Production of Holocaust Testimony
    Irene Kacandes      189

Social Darwinism and Edgar Hilsenrath's Ghetto Novel *Nacht*
    Dagmar C. G. Lorenz      214

Politics to Pulp a Novel: The Fate of the First Edition
of Edgar Hilsenrath's *Nacht*
    Susann Moeller      224

The Case of Jakob Littner: Authors, Publishers,
and Jewish History in Unified Germany
    Dagmar C. G. Lorenz      235

The Glory of Austrian Resistance and the Forgotten Jews
    Ruth Beckermann      251

## Gender and Ethnicity in Films of the 1980s

Ethnicity, Sexuality, and Politics in
István Szabó's *Colonel Redl* and *Mephisto*
    Dagmar C. G. Lorenz      263

Rosa von Praunheim's Celebration of the Victim
as Survivor: Jews and Gays in *Anita, Dances of Vice*
    Gabriele Weinberger      280

## The Tenuous Continuity: Contemporary German Jewish Culture

The Legacy of Jewish Vienna
    Dagmar C. G. Lorenz      293

Beyond the Bridges
    Ruth Beckermann      301

Identity Problems of Postwar Generation Jews in Germany:
A Historical Perspective
    Lea Fleischmann      308

Lea Fleischmann and Wolf Biermann: Like Strangers in Their Own House
    Peter Werres      313

Barbara Honigmann: A Preliminary Assessment
    Guy Stern      329

**Conclusion**: The New Germany and the Future of a Negative Symbiosis
    Gabriele Weinberger      347

**Indexes of Names and Titles**      352

# Contributors

**DELPHINE BECHTEL** received her M.A. from the Ecole Normale Supérieure and Sorbonne (Paris) in 1981 and her Ph.D. from Columbus University in 1989. She taught Yiddish language and literature at Columbia University. She is Associate Professor of German and Jewish Literature at the University of Paris, the Sorbonne Nouvelle. She is the author of *Der Nister's Work 1907–1929: A Study of a Yiddish Symbolist* (1990).

**RUTH BECKERMANN** is the author of *Die Mazzesinsel. Juden in der Wiener Leopoldstadt* (1984), *Unzugehörig. Österreicher und Juden nach 1945* (1989), and director, producer, and writer of the films *Wien Retour* (1983), *Die papierene Brücke* (1987), and *Nach Jerusalem* (1991). She was born in Vienna and lives and works as a journalist, filmmaker, and author in Vienna and Paris.

**MICHAEL BERKOWITZ** is Assistant Professor of History at Ohio State University. He published *Berlin Zionist Culture and West European Jewry before World War I* (1993). His field of specialization is German Jewry, in particular Zionism. He is a member of the Executive Board of the Melton Center for Jewish Studies, Ohio State University.

**BARBARA FISCHER** received her Ph.D. in German Literature from the University of California at San Diego. She is currently Assistant Professor at the Institute of German Studies, Concordia College, Minnesota. Her research interests center on eighteenth-century German literature and philosophy and minority discourse in German.

**LEA FLEISCHMANN** was born in Ulm, Germany, the daughter of Polish Holocaust survivors. She spent her childhood in several DP camps until her family settled in Frankfurt am Main in 1957. In 1973 she graduated with a degree in pedagogy from Johann Wolfgang Goethe University and taught in Wiesbaden and Offenbach. In 1979 she resigned her position as *Studienrätin* and emigrated to Israel. Her major publications are *Dies ist nicht mein Land. Eine Jüdin verläßt die Bundesrepublik* (1980), *Ich bin Israelin—Erfahrungen in einem orientalischen Land* (1982), and *Gas—Tagebuch einer Bedrohung. Israel während des Golfkriegs* (1991).

**SANDER L. GILMAN** is the Goldwin Smith Professor of Humane Studies at Cornell University and Professor of the History of Psychiatry at Cornell Medical College. A member of the Cornell faculty since 1969, he is a cultural and literary historian and the author or editor of over thirty books, the most recent being *Freud, Race, and Gender* (1994) and *The Case of Sigmund Freud* (1993). He is the author of the basic study of the visual stereotyping of the mentally ill, *Seeing the Insane* (1982), as well as the standard study of *Jewish Self-Hatred* (1986). He has been

Visiting Historical Scholar at the National Library of Medicine, Bethesda, MD; the Northrop Frye Visiting Professor of Literary Theory at the University of Toronto; the Old Dominion Fellow in the Department of English at Princeton University; the Visiting B. G. Rudolph Professor of Jewish Studies at Syracuse University, and a visiting professor at Colgate University, Tulane University, the University of Paderborn, and the Free University of Berlin. His honors and awards include a Guggenheim Fellowship. He is the president of the Modern Language Association.

**JOST HERMAND** was born in Kassel, Germany. Since 1958 he has been Professor of German Literature at the University of Wisconsin, Madison, and he has held the Vilas Res Professorship of German. His areas of specialization include nineteenth- and twentieth-century German literature, literary criticism and method, and German culture. Among his many publications are *Der deutsche Vormärz* (1967), *Synthetisches Interpretieren* (1968), *Blacks and German Culture* (1968), *Faschismus und Avantgarde* (1980), *Geschichten aus dem Ghetto* (1987), *Der alte Traum vom neuen Reich* (1988), *From the Greeks to the Greens* (1989), *Arnold Zweig* (1990), *1914/1939: German Reflections of the Two World Wars* (1992).

**NEIL G. JACOBS** is Associate Professor for Yiddish language and linguistics in the Department of Near Eastern, Judaic, and Hellenic Languages and Literatures at Ohio State University. His primary areas of research and publication are Yiddish historical linguistics, Yiddish phonology, and Yiddish linguistic geography. He is the author of *Economy in Yiddish Vocalism: A Study in the Interplay of Hebrew and Non-Hebrew Components* (1990).

**IRENE KACANDES** is Assistant Professor of Germanic Languages and Comparative Literature at the University of Texas at Austin. She received her Ph.D. in Comparative Literature at Harvard University and has also studied at the Free University of Berlin, and Aristotle University, Thessaloniki, Greece. She has published articles on narrative theory, German and Greek literature in *Text and Performance Quarterly*, *Seminar*, and the *Journal of Modern Greek Studies* and is currently completing a book on oral strategies in contemporary fiction.

**SIMA KAPPELER** was born in postwar Germany into a close circle of Holocaust survivors. She grew up in a Yiddish/Polish-speaking home. In Switzerland she studied French and English literature at the University of Zurich. She continued her studies at Harvard University in the Department of Comparative Literature where she received her doctorate in nineteenth-century French and German literature. She currently teaches in the Department of French and German at Ohio State University.

**ALAN LEVENSON** received his Ph.D. in History from Ohio State University in 1990. In 1991 he taught at the College of William and Mary and is now Assistant Professor at the College of Jewish Studies in Cleveland, Ohio. The focus of his research and publication is European Jewish History with an emphasis on Germany.

**DAGMAR C. G. LORENZ** is the author of *Ilse Aichinger* (1981), *Franz Grillparzer. Dichter des sozialen Konflikts* (1986), and *Verfolgung bis zum Massenmord. Holocaust-Diskurse aus der Sicht der Verfolgten* (1992). She was born in the

Federal Republic of Germany, studied in Göttingen and Cincinnati, and is Professor of German at Ohio State University. She is a member of the Executive Board of the Melton Center for Jewish Studies, Ohio State University.

**SUSANN MOELLER** was born in West Germany. She studied Comparative Literature at the University of Georgia and German literature at Ohio State University, where she received her Ph.D. in 1990. She taught at Columbus State Community College and Ohio Dominican College, and was Director of the Worthington Arts Council. Her research and publication interests include contemporary German Jewish literature, popular culture, and women's art and literature. She is the author of the poetry anthology *I Dance in Your Light That Is Also My Own*. Her book on the reception of the works of Edgar Hilsenrath is in press.

**MARGARITA PAZI**, author of numerous publications on Jewish authors of German language, particularly the "Prague Circle," was born in Bohemia, Czechoslovakia. Via Mauritius she immigrated to Israel in 1945 and teaches as a Professor of German language and literature at Tel Aviv University. Her most recent book is *Ernst Weiss: Schicksal und Werk eines jüdischen mitteleuropäischen Autors in der ersten Hälfte des 20. Jahrhunderts* (1993).

**ROSLYN ABT SCHINDLER** received her Ph.D. from the University of Pennsylvania in 1972. She is Associate Professor of Humanities in the College of Lifelong Learning at Wayne State University, Detroit, and Director of the Interdisciplinary Studies Program, a baccalaureate program for adults. She also serves as Associate Dean for Degree Programs at CLL. In addition to Holocaust studies, her main areas of research, presentations, and publications include interdisciplinary studies in adult education.

**EGON SCHWARZ** was born in Vienna. After the Nazi invasion of Austria he left his native country for America. He studied German and Romance literatures. He is the Rosa May Distinguished University Professor in the Humanities at Washington University, St. Louis, Missouri. He published *Hofmannsthal und Calderon* (1962), *Das verschluckte Schluchzen. Poesie und Politik by R. M. Rilke* (1972), *Joseph von Eichendorff* (1972), *Keine Zeit für Eichendorff* (1979).

**LUKE SPRINGMAN** received his Ph.D. in German Literature from Ohio State University. He was an instructor at OSU and an Assistant Professor at Minot State University, North Dakota. He teaches German and Russian as an Assistant Professor at Bloomsburg University, Pennsylvania. He is the author of *Comrades, Friends and Companions: Utopian Projections and Social Action in German Literature for Young People* (1989).

**ASTRID STARCK** is Professor of German and Yiddish at the Université de Haute Alsace in Mulhouse, France. She introduced the study of Alsatian Yiddish to the German Department at UHA, founded the Society for the Study of Alsatian and West Yiddish (CREDYO), and organized the first Congress on Alsatian and West Yiddish in France in 1989. She is the author of *Ingeborg Bachmann, Malina (1971): Lecture plurielle du roman d'Ingeborg Bachmann* (1987) and articles in the field of German and Yiddish literature and language.

**GUY STERN** is Distinguished Professor of Germanic and Slavic Languages and Literatures at Wayne State University in Detroit. He is the author of, among other works, *War, Weimar and Literature: The Story of the "Neue Merkur," 1918–1925* (1971), *Alfred Neumann* (1979), and *Literature im Exil* (1989). A Festschrift, *Exile and Enlightenment*, was dedicated to him in 1987. He was decorated with the Goethe Medal of the Goethe Institute in 1988. He served as guest professor at the University of Frankfurt in 1993 and introduced to German universities a course on "Jewish authors in Germany today."

**GABRIELE WEINBERGER** received her Ph.D. from Ohio State University in 1988. She is Associate Professor of German at Lenoir Rhyne College. She specializes in nineteenth- and twentieth-century Holocaust studies, women's literature, and film studies. She is the author of *Nazi Germany and its Aftermath in Women Directors' Autobiographical Films of the Late 1970s* (1992).

**PETER WERRES** studied in Heidelberg and Washington. He joined the faculty of George Washington University in 1969 where he teaches German literature. He is the director of the George Washington University Summer programs in Germany, and has held several visiting professorships at other institutions. His areas of research and publication include the Brecht reception in postwar Germany, political poetry and songs, Biermann, Degenhardt, contemporary writers of Jewish descent in German-speaking countries, as well as aspects of the works of Kafka, Frisch, Handke, and Walser.

**JACK ZIPES** is Professor of German at the University of Minnesota. Aside from his many publications on fairy tales such as *Breaking the Magic Spell* (1979), *Fairy Tales and the Art of Subversion* (1983), and *The Brothers Grimm: From Enchanted Forests to the Modern World* (1991), he has also written extensively on Germans and Jews in *Germans and Jews since the Holocaust* (1987) and *The Operated Jew* (1991). He has also written on contemporary German theater and literature. He is a co-editor of *New German Critique*, and serves on the editorial board of *The Germanic Review*. His numerous awards include a Guggenheim Fellowship.

# Insiders and Outsiders

# Introduction

## Dagmar C. G. Lorenz

Until the end of the eighteenth century Jewish authors did not use the German language to write about Jewish topics. They had lived side by side with the Christian majority for centuries, albeit in a separate sphere.[1] This *status quo* changed during the Age of Enlightenment when a Jewish–Gentile dialogue began, for example the friendship between Mendelssohn and Lessing. The Napoleonic occupation accelerated the emancipation process. Laws improving the status of German Jews were passed under the protest of large segments of the Gentile population who feared for their own privileges.

During the nineteenth century German became the major language of European Jewry. The German Jewish literary tradition is often cited as evidence of a successful symbiosis. Sol Liptzin described Germans and Jews as "two souls in one bosom" as late as 1944.[2] However, numerous Jewish authors viewed German–Jewish relations with skepticism and thematized the discord between German Jews and Gentiles. Toward the end of the Weimar Republic Theodor Lessing observed that in the hostile German environment assimilated Jews tended to identify with their adversaries, a proclivity he termed "Self-Hatred."[3] In a recent study, Sander Gilman reassessed Lessing's thesis and showed that the texts and the language of Christianity, on which all secular Western discourses are based, are the source of Gentile and Jewish anti-Semitism.

Aside from more general topics, members of the first generation of emancipated Jews wrote about their life overshadowed by anti-Jewish prejudice. They established a discourse of their own against the centuries-old resentment. Historically, politics and economics had determined whether this resentment remained limited to discrimination and oppression or whether it led to pogroms and massacres. The medieval hate-rhetoric persisted during the Reformation and was secularized in the eighteenth century. The nineteenth century witnessed the beginning of three major emancipation movements: of Jews, women, and the working classes. Concurrently nationalist and racist anti-Semitism replaced religiously motivated Jew-hatred. In the last decades of the nineteenth century, racist pamphlets flooded Europe and created an atmosphere of ethnic fanaticism. Only a few decades after the first wholesale genocide of the twentieth century, committed by Turkish nationalists against the Armenians, Nazi Germany passed 'racial' laws that segregated Jews and

Gentiles—even after assimilation Jews were still considered aliens. *Kristallnacht* (1938) marks the beginning of the Nazis' war against the Jews. Jewish men and women were stripped of their citizenship and deported to labor and death camps.

Critics and historians have hesitated to discuss anti-Semitism and the Holocaust as an integral part of German and European civilization.[4] However, Gotthold Ephraim Lessing's tolerance as expressed in *Nathan the Wise* has remained the exception, while moderate and even 'humanist' intellectuals held anti-Jewish prejudices. Not only Lenz, von Arnim, Raabe, and Freytag, but also Stifter, Grillparzer, and Fontane based their Jewish characters on the traditional stereotypes. Herder's, Fichte's, and Wagner's anti-Jewish diatribes have to be mentioned here as well. In the light of these invectives, the Nazi ideology can hardly be considered a *novum*.

In opposition to bourgeois theory, Walter Benjamin identified oppression, even mass murder, as phenomena inherent in Western civilization. He maintains that most historians do not acknowledge this fact because of their dependency on the ruling classes.[5] The resentment against Jews and women, the two groups who have been traditionally cast in the role of the 'other,' are at the basis of European superstition and occultism: Christian folklore attributes satanic traits to both. As late as the twentieth century Jews were accused of ritual slaughter, women of witchcraft. Reproducing anti-Jewish clichés, Gentile authors created a self-referential hate discourse. Religious and pseudo-spiritual anti-Jewish and misogynist discourses overlap thematically and in terms of argumentation. It is no coincidence that numerous high-ranking Nazis, members of a vociferous male supremacist movement, were affiliated with occult societies.[6] Even their methods of persecution call to mind medieval witch hunts and the Inquisition: surveillance, dress codes, ghettoization, restriction of births and marriages, detention, and the use of terror.[7]

The toleration of the Jewish minority has always been subject to sudden recall. The awareness of a constant threat to life and livelihood resulted in a fundamental existential insecurity on the part of the minority. The eighteenth-century emancipation debates were conducted without the participation of those under discussion. Most 'enlightened' treatises such as Christian von Dohm's *Über die bürgerliche Verbesserung der Juden* (1783) propose the absorption of the minority into the mainstream—Dohm considered emancipation as synonymous with the end of Judaism. He could not fathom that Jews would not abandon their heritage for the sake of social acceptance into Gentile society. Dohm's goal, a homogeneous German state with the enlightened Christian male as its norm, was shared by most of his contemporaries. Understandably, orthodox rabbis reacted to documents such as the *Edict of Tolerance* (1782), issued by Austria's Joseph II, with misgivings. They realized that it undermined the Jewish communities and left assimilation as the only viable alternative.

It was precisely these developments that set the stage for the mass exodus from the ghetto. During the Age of Romanticism some Jewish intellectuals and professionals had entered German public life. Dorothea Veit Schlegel, Rahel Levin Varnhagen, Heinrich Heine, and Fanny Lewald, as well as members of the Mendelssohn and Arnstein families, had tried to escape the stigma of their Jewishness by conversion and intermarriage. However, as the numbers of apostates rose, German bureaucracy made it increasingly difficult to exchange Jewish-sounding names for 'neutral' ones. Gradually an invisible ghetto was created on the basis of surnames.[8]

Jewish men and women were stereotyped differently. In the works of Gentile men Jewish women figures suggest a sexuality outside bourgeois norms. Much like the women of color in colonial literature, they were attributed the allure of exoticism. In addition, their alleged erotic appeal contained a warning to Gentile "blue stockings," for example in Gutzkow's *Wally die Zweiflerin*. Jewish males, on the other hand, were depicted in negative terms and never as potential lovers or as husbands of Gentile women except, of course, in the works of Jewish authors. Early industrial mass culture caused widespread fear of social and economic instability. Enemy images such as the Jewish banker and industrialist suggested simple answers to complex problems.

The ambivalence of Rahel Varnhagen, Marx, Heine, Börne, and Lewald toward their Jewish and German identity is symptomatic of the dilemma caused by life in a hostile environment. These intellectuals learned that assimilation and baptism did not guarantee integration, while conversion, even as a matter of form, separated the apostates from their community of origin. Moses Hess came to regard anti-Semitism as a German character trait and concluded that the 'Jewish Question' could only be solved by establishing an autonomous Jewish state.[9] Felix Theilhaber and Ignaz Zollschan explained the rift between Jews and Germans on the basis of racial concepts. Most Jewish critics, however, underestimated the destructive potential of German nationalism, although they were its main target.

Jewish authors challenged the ethnocentric German discourse from a variety of perspectives. The novelist Fanny Lewald opposed it as a feminist and an advocate of emancipation; Stefan Zweig, Claire Goll, and Karl Kraus as pacifists. Others questioned the mainstream from a social, religious, or political point of view. Texts such as Heine's novel fragment *Der Rabbi von Bacharach* and his *Hebräische Melodien*; the works of Franz Kafka, Arthur Schnitzler, Jakob Wassermann, Else Lasker–Schüler, Claire Goll, Nelly Sachs, Gertrud Kolmar, and, after 1945, those of Arnold Zweig, Ilse Aichinger, Veza and Elias Canetti, Erich Fried, Edgar Hilsenrath, and Ruth Beckermann belong to this oppositional tradition. The reception of dissident literature was traditionally affected by its authors' ethnic and religious background, their gender or sexual orientation.[10] Alternative discourses repeatedly lost their basis for production and reception. Repressed by the establishment and its historiography, the names and achievements of the advocates of emancipatory movements were easily forgotten and rarely rediscovered.

In the aftermath of the anti-Jewish riots of 1819, the *Verein für Kultur und Wissenschaft der Juden* was founded with the objective of informing the public about Jewish culture and religion. Heinrich Heine, one of its members, wrote *Der Rabbi von Bacharach* (1824/25) with this mission in mind. His integration of Jewish and German themes remained exemplary. To this day his fragment is a core text of German Jewish literature. Its diction and motifs influenced contemporary writers such as Fleischmann and Biermann. Heine's topic, survival at any cost, foreshadows not only Elias Canetti's thesis that death is man's only enemy, but also the staunch decision of many Holocaust authors to survive, come what may. Heine's concepts are diametrically opposed to Germanic heroism as reflected in the medieval epics hailed by nineteenth-century scholars. His views reflect the experience of a persecuted group that could never take survival for granted. At the same time *Der Rabbi von Bacharach* is a profoundly 'German' text as its protagonist's love for Germany shows. In the language of Romanticism, Heine describes Germany as the fatherland of Jews and Gentiles appropriating German national symbols such as the Rhine River to show that Jews love their country just as much as the Gentiles, despite anti-Semitic notions to the contrary. *Der Rabbi von Bacharach* stood at the beginning of the German Jewish literary discourse. Perhaps it remained a fragment because the conventions of the dominant literary discourse and the educational novel were unable to accommodate a Jewish hero. The German Jewish epic tradition began with Phillippson's *Die Marannen* (1837) and Riespart's *Die Juden und die Kreuzfahrer* (1841).

*Der Rabbi von Bacharach* addresses the misfortunes caused by the hatred of Christians in a seemingly light-hearted but critical manner. Authors of the following generations such as Franz Kafka, Bertha Pappenheim, Jakob Wassermann, and Lion Feuchtwanger continued to oppose anti-Jewish propaganda with literary and ideological tools, but the propaganda was insidious and eroded the morale of its victims, for example Otto Weininger. The achievements of German-Jewish artists, writers, editors, and journalists, their contributions to papers such as *Berliner Tageblatt, Vossische Zeitung*, and *Frankfurter Zeitung* show that Jewish intellectuals occupied a central position in German and Austrian letters that proves the partial success of assimilation.[11] The works of authors such as Theodor Herzl and Jakob Wassermann reveal the reason for its ultimate failure: the intolerance of the Germans and Austrians.

Belonging to a marginalized group and desiring to be German caused a 'tragic dualism' for most Jews. The 'Jewish Question' was a political dilemma and an identity problem.[12] Even if those who assimilated did so to escape their Jewish identity, as, for example, Hugo von Hofmannsthal and

Ludwig Wittgenstein, who were not Jewish by religion and only in part by origin, their background set them apart from the mainstream.[13] Intellectuals of Jewish background were resented for their roots in the bourgeoisie as well as for their often progressive views. Their successes gave rise to the myth of a Jewish world conspiracy.[14] On the basis of Darwin's and Mendel's theories on evolution and heredity, hatred of Jews became acceptable as the pseudoscience of anti-Semitism, which operated with easy-to-grasp radical concepts.[15] Gobineau's *Essai sur l'inégalité des races humaines* [Essay on the Inequality of Human Races] (1853–55) set the paradigm for early racist anti-Semitism's pronouncing the Jewish 'race' the most destructive of human 'races.' Most later anti-Semitic literature is based on Gobineau, for example Nilus's *Protocols of the Elders of Zion* and Chamberlain's *Grundlagen des 19.Jahrhunderts* [The Foundations of the Nineteenth Century], a tool of racist propaganda as early as in World War I. Literary authors who are still respected today disseminated anti-Semitic stereotypes, for example Gustav Freytag, Wilhelm Raabe, Thomas Mann, and the cartoonist Wilhelm Busch, not to speak of the now obscure anti-Semitic fiction and journalism by Arthur Dinter and Julius Streicher.

Progress toward emancipation usually aroused defensive or aggressive reactions among conservatives and nationalists. When in 1848 Jews were granted the right to choose their place of residence, when they achieved partial emancipation in 1867, and when their citizenship rights were confirmed by the Imperial constitution in 1871, protests and riots followed. Disoriented by the changes brought on by the Industrial Revolution, the nationalist lower nobility and the middle classes feared the Jewish competition. Wilhelm Marr, the founder of the first anti-Semitic association (1879), blamed a Jewish conspiracy for the economic collapse of 1873 in *Der Sieg des Judenthums über das Germanenthum* [The Victory of the Jews over the Germans].

Anti-Semitism was supported by the academic establishment and became a social and political tool. In the 1870s fraternities replaced the anti-Jewish clauses with 'Aryan clauses' to keep students with a Jewish background from joining. The Catholic and the Protestant clergy alike joined forces with the anti-Semites. Metropolitan areas such as Vienna, Munich, and Berlin became centers of anti-Semitic activities. Otto von Bismarck used anti-Semitism to discredit liberal politics. Karl Lueger was elected Mayor of Vienna on the basis of his anti-Semitic platform. In Linz Karl Schönerer called for the removal of Jews from public life. Adolf Hitler spent his formative years in Linz and Vienna and was thoroughly imbued with Austrian anti-Semitism.

The reception of authors such as Arthur Schnitzler shows how tenuous assimilation actually was. Schnitzler was boycotted, censored, and insulted at a time when the Viennese Jewish culture formed, which authors like Elfriede Jelinek and Ruth Beckermann today claim as their intellectual roots (Mayer, p. 438).[16] Also Zionism has to be understood in part as a reaction to anti-

Semitism. By 1932 it had become the dominant force in Jewish Vienna while the *Centralverein deutscher Staatsbürger jüdischen Glaubens* (CV), which sympathized with the Social Democrats, was the strongest Jewish association in Berlin. In *Der Judenstaat* Theodor Herzl urges emigration to Palestine because he sees no future in assimilation.[17] The immigration of Eastern European refugees at the turn of the century, Socialists and orthodox Jews, added to the complexity of the situation of Jews in Austria and Germany.

Bertha Pappenheim, Arnold Zweig, Alfred Döblin, and Martin Buber studied and wrote about Eastern European Jews. Joseph Roth's prose works constitute a bridge between the German and Yiddish literary tradition. There are parallels in form and content between Roth's *Hiob* (1930), Döblin's *Berlin Alexanderplatz* (1929), Israel Joshua Singer's *The Family Carnovsky* (1943), and Feuchtwanger's *Geschwister Oppenheim* (1933). All these social critical texts are written from the dual perspective of an outsider who actually is an insider. This tension is also characteristic of works that do not directly address Jewish topics, for example Roth's *Die Geschichte der 1002. Nacht* (1937).[18]

Authors who envisioned a Jewish renewal were in the minority. Most Jews did not believe that they belonged to a separate race and had no emotional ties with Palestine. Karl Kraus and Karl Kautsky considered intermarriage and apostasy the solution to the 'Jewish Question.' The cosmopolitans Stefan Zweig, Arthur Schnitzler, Sigmund Freud, and the most Viennese of Viennese, Peter Altenberg, distanced themselves from East European culture and Zionism. Bertha Pappenheim, the founder of the Jewish Women's Association, worked for better living conditions for Jewish women in Germany. Most assimilated Jews avoided any association with East European immigrants and the Yiddish language because they feared that they might jeopardize their hard-earned privileges or because they considered East European Jews as members of a foreign culture.[19] Frequently the children of these Jewish immigrants entered the upper middle class as lawyers, doctors, bankers, journalists, and actors—a natural development, since the cultural and professional spheres were the only social spaces open to talented Jews (Pomeranz, p. 20).

As tensions increased, anti-Semitism and nationalism contributed to a Jewish *renouveau*. Between 1890 and 1910 twenty-four organizations representing Jewish interests were founded.[20] After World War I anti-Semitism spread among the former nobility, officers, entrepreneurs, and professionals as a result of the economic and political instability. The myth that the Jews were responsible for the defeat and the loss of the standing army following the treaty of Versailles brought national frustration and resentment to a boiling point (Bunzl, Marin, p. 41).[21] These issues are reflected in literature as well. The narrative strategies of Jewish authors suggest how difficult it was to express criticism from a Jewish point of view. For example, the inner monologue in Schnitzler's *Leutnant Gustl* exposes bigotry without putting the author on the spot. In *Jud Süß* Feuchtwanger embarks on a latently anti-Semitic discourse to ensure his readers' receptiveness to the later criticism of Gentile society. Several authors of Jewish descent, such as the satirist Kurt Tucholsky and the Viennese cabarettist and socialist worker, Jura Soyfer, identified right-wing radicalism as the foremost danger to their societies. Fearing an alliance between the National Socialists, industry, and the masses, in other words, a Fascist revolution, they turned to Marxism.[22]

The works of Jewish authors, regardless of which school of thought, indicate that 1933 (in Austria, 1938) did not mark the end of a symbiosis. Their lives were affected by violence—destruction and self-destruction—for example Peter Altenberg's mental problems; the murders of Rosa Luxemburg, Gustav Landauer, Walther Rathenau, and Theodor Lessing; the suicides of Otto Weininger, Egon Friedell, Stefan Zweig, and Walter Benjamin; as well as the assault on Karl Kraus in 1936, which preceded the author's death. Else Lasker–Schüler was beaten up, but escaped to Switzerland. Joseph Roth died of alcoholism in Paris. Gertrud Kolmar and Alma Johanna König were killed in death camps. Even the suicides of Paul Celan, Jean Améry, Bruno Bettelheim, and Jerzy Kozinski (in 1970, 1978, 1990, and 1991, respectively) must be considered delayed reactions to the Holocaust experience.

The discourse of German superiority was complemented by that of the inferiority of all other nations. It had already been used to justify the colonization of Eastern Europe and, after 1870, Africa. Anti-Semitic hate rhetoric effected a psychological desensitization so that the program of the NSDAP, Hitler's *Mein Kampf*, and Nazi publications such as *Der Stürmer*, *Völkischer Beobachter*, and *Der Angriff* met with little protest. Hitler's promises were probably welcomed by many who felt safe from the implied violence. The Nazi rhetoric addressed an audience familiar with anti-Jewish invectives from Luther to Streicher. Against this background it is not surprising that National Socialism succeeded in changing the political atmosphere within a few years.

The ideological cornerstone of the NSDAP, founded in 1920, was anti-Semitism. Those who knew Hitler's *Mein Kampf* (1925) or the Nazi press were informed about the goals of the Nazis: imperialist wars, world domination, persecution of 'non-Aryans,' particularly Jews, and the control of women and reproduction. In Austria the burning of the Palace of Justice (1927) initiated the shift toward the right. In Germany the emancipation movements, started in the nineteenth century, ended on January 31, 1933. Soon thereafter the first concentration camps opened and businesses owned and operated by Jews were boycotted. Jewish professionals were dismissed from office. The book burnings of 1933 and censorship stopped the expression of liberal opinions and the publication of German Jewish literature except in designated 'Jewish' publishing houses.

Already then, a number of authors were certain that the end of German–Jewish coexistence had come. Feuchtwanger's *Die Geschwister Oppenheim*, Arnold Zweig's *Bilanz der deutschen Judenheit*, as well as diaries and letters attest to the crisis in Germany and internationally that threatened Jews in Europe and in the Middle East. The Nazi regime eliminated their Leftist opponents first. The Nuremberg Laws of 1935 legalized the segregation of Jews and persons classified as Jewish. Harassment and persecution were stepped up while most countries, including the United States, hesitated to accept Jewish refugees. On 9 November 1938, the SA, SS, and civilians destroyed synagogues, shops, homes, and apartments owned by Jews; 26,000 persons were arrested during the rampage. Five days later Jewish students were dismissed from public schools. During the invasion of Poland, Germany began to pursue her genocide program. The propaganda machine proclaimed the final battle between "Aryans" and Jews, but the deportations and orders for mass murder were concealed. Even after the decisive defeat at Stalingrad, Germany proceeded with the genocide. In 1944 the first concentration camps were liberated and, when Germany capitulated on 8 May 1945, the first trials against Nazi criminals had already begun.

Anti-Semitism survived not only in Central Europe, but internationally. Attacks on Jewish communities and hate crimes continue to occur worldwide. In Germany and Austria support groups formed to protect former Nazis, SS veterans, and those who had taken possession of property stolen from Jewish owners. Some neo-Fascist organizations used the idea of European and German unity as a cover for their programs. Mediterranean workers and immigrants from Third-World countries have become the target of racism propagated with stereotypes similar to those used to vilify the Jews. But also anti-Semitism, even without a Jewish presence, is still widespread. Sander Gilman maintains that the Holocaust is the center of modern Jewish identity. In contrast to other critics he believes that the German language continues to be a legitimate medium to express the Jewish experience.[23]

Most of the Jewish authors who became prominent in postwar Germany and Austria did not address the Holocaust directly. Some, like the GDR writer Bruno Apitz in his bestselling novel *Nackt unter Wölfen*, focused on the Communist resistance. Holocaust literature written from a Jewish perspective surfaced in the 1960s, inspired by the Eichmann trial (1960–62), the Auschwitz trials (1962–64), and the student movement (1968), which had sparked a public debate on the Holocaust.

However, it took the American television mini series *Holocaust* to inspire a broad-based public debate in West Germany in 1979. Its representation of individual experiences made the Holocaust emotionally accessible to more than 300,000 viewers,[24] but authors such as Lea Fleischmann criticized the vagueness of the term "Holocaust" as ineffective to describe the mass murder. The visit of U.S. President Reagan to the Bitburg military and SS cemetery and the election of a former Nazi as President of Austria *after* his past had been internationally exposed resulted in an international wave of anti-Semitism in 1989.[25] Since the euphoria of the German unification in 1989/90, anti-Semites, racists, and chauvinists have gained credibility and popular acceptance more than ever before—history seems to be on their side. At the same time the immigration of Jews from the former East block countries has reached an all-time peak.

In Germany and Austria the majority and the minority continue to speak a different language and write a different historiography. German literature written from a distinctly Jewish perspective meets with resistance, whereas the established anti-Semitic discourses are perpetuated by mainstream authors. Many works that ostensibly convey anti-Fascist, liberal, and democratic points of view do not transcend cultural, religious, and racial biases. What seems to be changing is the fact that more and more German-speaking Jews break the silence and, instead of denying their heritage and background, actively work at shaping a new Jewish identity.

## NOTES

1. Hans Otto Horch, *Auf der Suche nach der jüdischen Erzählliteratur. Die Literatur der 'Allgemeinen Zeitung des Judentums' (1837–1922)* (Frankfurt: Lang, 1985), p. 13.

2. Sol Liptzin, *Germany's Stepchildren* (Philadelphia: The Jewish Society of America, 1944), pp. 1ff.

3. Theodor Lessing, *Der jüdische Selbsthaß* (Berlin: Jüdischer Verlag, 1930).

4. Cf. Zygmunt Baumann, *Modernity and the Holocaust* (Cambridge: Polity Press, 1989), p. 7.

5. Walter Benjamin, "Über den Begriff der Geschichte," *Gesammelte Schriften,* ed. Tiedemann and Schwepphäuser, I/II (Frankfurt: Suhrkamp, 1974), p. 696.

6. Jean Michel Angebert, *The Occult and the Third Reich* (New York: Macmillan, 1974), pp. 163ff.; Charles Schüddekopf, *Der alltägliche Faschismus* (Bonn and Berlin: Dietz, 1981), p. 148.

7. Cf. Vamberto Morais, *A Short History of Anti-Semitism* (New York: Norton, 1976).

8. Dietz Bering, *Der Name als Stigma. Antisemitismus im deutschen Alltag 1812–1933* (Stuttgart: Klett–Cotta, 1987).

9. Moses Hess, *Rom und Jerusalem. Briefe* (Tel Aviv: Ivrith, 1935; first published in 1862).

10. Cf. Hans Mayer, *Außenseiter* (Frankfurt: Suhrkamp, 1975).

11. Nahum Goldmann, *Mein Leben als deutscher Jude* (Frankfurt, Berlin, and Vienna: Ullstein, 1983), p. 458.

12. Jacob Katz, *Out of the Ghetto. Social Background of Jewish Emancipation 1770–1870* (Cambridge, MA: Harvard University Press, 1973), p. 1.

13. Steven Beller, "Class Culture and the Jews of Vienna, 1900," in *Jews, Antisemitism and Culture in Vienna*, Oxaal, Pollak, and Botz, eds. (London: Routledge, 1987), p. 42; Robert S. Wistrich, "Social Democracy, Antisemitism and the Jews of Vienna," ibid., pp. 111–120.

14. John Bunzl and Bernd Marin, *Antisemitismus in Österreich* (Innsbruck: Inn Verlag, 1983), p. 24.

15. Richard Wagner, "Das Judenthum in der Musik," *Gesammelte Schriften und Dichtungen* V (Leipzig: Frisch, 1899), pp. 66–85; Jacob Katz, *From Prejudice to Destruction. Anti-Semitism 1700–1933* (Cambridge, MA: Harvard University Press, 1980), p. 2.

16. Helmut Kreuzer, *Die Bohème* (Stuttgart: Metzler, 1968), p. 208.

17. Klara Pomeranz Carmely, *Das Identitätsproblem jüdischer Autoren im deutschen Sprachraum. Von der Jahrhundertwende bis zu Hitler* (Königstein: Scriptor, 1981), p. 19.

18. Egon Schwarz, "Arthur Schnitzler und das Judentum," *Im Zeichen Hiobs*, p. 67; Bernd Hüppauf, "Joseph Roth: *Hiob*. Der Mythos des Skeptikers," ibid., pp. 309–325.

19. Elias Canetti, *Die gerettete Zunge* (Frankfurt: Fischer, 1979), p. 94.

20. E.g. Verein zur Abwehr des Antisemitismus (1892), Centralverein (1893), Zionistische Verbindung für Deutschland (1897), Jüdischer Frauenbund (1904). Cf. Peter Melcher, *Weissensee. Ein Friedhof als Spiegelbild jüdischer Geschichte in Berlin* (Berlin: Hauge und Spener, 1986), pp. 57–62.

21. Elias Canetti, *Masse und Macht* (Frankfurt: Fischer, 1980), p. 197.

22. Jura Soyfer, *Das Gesamtwerk*, Horst Jarka, ed. (Vienna, Munich, and Zurich: Europa, 1980), p. 68.

23. Sander Gilman, *Jewish Self-Hatred. Anti-Semitism and the Hidden Language of the Jews* (Baltimore and London: The Johns Hopkins Press, 1986), p. 319.

24. Peter Diem, *'Holocaust.' Anatomie eines Massenereignisses*, ed. Generalintendanz des Österreichischen Rundfunks. Bericht zu Medienforschung (1979), p. 41.

25. Josef Haslinger, *Die Politik der Gefühle* (Darmstadt: Luchterhand, 1987), p. 19.

# Historical Perspectives: Emancipation and Assimilation

# *Chicken Soup*,
# or the Penalties for Sounding Too Jewish[1]

## Sander L. Gilman

Can the study of the relationship between German Jews and East European Jews provide a model for the image and the response of different marginal groups in different historical circumstances? To begin to answer this I want to turn to the work of one of the foremost sociologists of the American Jewish experience, Jackie Mason. The career of Jackie Mason, the last of the "Borscht Belt" comics, had an extraordinary rebirth during 1987. An act designed for the Catskills that had brought Mason to fame during the 1960s (including a much publicized spat with the TV power Ed Sullivan) led to bankruptcy in 1983. Suddenly this same act became the vehicle that brought him stardom (again) in the late 1980s. Mason understood what had happened: "The Jewish people took me for granted, the young people saw me as an anachronism, when I went to Broadway where I never ever thought I'd succeed." And the reason for his invisibility was his language; "People said I was too Jewish and I even suffered from anti-Jewish prejudice from Jews themselves. There was a profound rejection problem: the reverse discrimination of Jews against other Jews who talk like me in show business. I think they were ashamed and embarrassed about my accent, that I was somehow symbolic of the whole fear that Jews would be discriminated against again."[2] For Jackie Mason, the move to Broadway provided a neutral space in which sounding Jewish, which in our contemporary American context means speaking with a Yiddish accent, was no longer associated with a "Jewish" environment; that is, the audience (Jewish or not) no longer identified with the comic as a representative of the self.

During the fall of 1989 Jackie Mason starred an ill-fated "sit-com" entitled *Chicken Soup* on ABC. It was canceled on 8 November 1989, even though it was the thirteenth highest rated network television show. *USA Today*, a good barometer of middle-class opinion, thought "Mason's ethnic shtick wouldn't play to the masses."[3] The use of the Yiddishism in this very phrase placed the discourse of this Jew who sounds too Jewish beyond the pale of political language, the language of middle-class comedy. We have seen in the past decades, as Henry L. Gates, Jr. has recently noted, that the representation of the African American on American television has moved from that of Amos and Andy to Dr. Clifford Huxtable, from the representation of the African American sounding too "black" to one possessing the dominant discourse of American culture.[4] For Jews, the seeming lack of movement from the Jackie Mason of the 1960s to the Jackie Mason of the 1980s was offensive. The Jewish Defense League picketed the ABC studio in New York and "Dan Bloom, a Jewish children's book author from Alaska, tried organizing a grass-roots campaign against the show. . . . He didn't like the Jewish stereotypes portrayed." Bloom observed: "I . . . got the feeling he offended many Jews in America. They've heard this type of humor in their homes, but in the public living rooms of America for everybody to hear it seemed embarrassing."[5] Henry Gates quotes W. E. Du Bois from 1921 that "the more highly trained we become, the less we can laugh at Negro comedy." The Jew who sounds too Jewish, for some American Jews, represents the hidden Jew within, the corrupt Jew of the Gospel, the mark of difference that offends even after the Jew is integrated into the mainstream of American culture.

The question of Mason's discourse was not limited to the reception of his television program. Mason's role as a Jew who sounds too Jewish, a Jew visibly marked by his discourse, had become a source of comment during September and October of 1989. In the campaign for mayor in New York City, Mason backed the Republican candidate Rudolf Giuliani, who had made a special effort to attract the traditionally Democratic Jewish voters to support him rather than the African-American Democratic candidate, David N. Dinkins. Giuliani's desire for Jewish support in this contest was articulated by Mason in September 1989 when he stated in an interview in *The Village Voice* that "there is a sick Jewish problem of voting for a Black man no matter how unfit he is for the job. All you have to be is black and don't curse the Jews directly and the Jew will vote for black in a second. Jews are sick with complexes."[6] Mason's comment about the nature of African/American/Jewish relations led to a firestorm of accusations about Mason's 'racism' and forced Mason to withdraw from his public role in Giuliani's campaign. What was most interesting was the subsequent revelation that Mason had earlier called Dinkins "a fancy *shvartze* with a mustache" during a late August meeting with four reporters from *Newsweek*.[7] It is this Yiddishism which generated a further debate about the visibility of the hidden language of the Jews.

Let us now turn to a world that seems completely apart: Vienna at the turn of the century. The playwright–physician Arthur Schnitzler in 1907 recorded his first Edison cylinder and notes in his diary how he is struck, upon first hearing his own voice in a recording, by its particularly 'Jewish' high-pitched quality.[8] It is the hearing of oneself as a Jew that evokes a specific type of Jewish voice, the high pitch, disagreeable nasality of the Yiddish speaker attempting to speak German. Maybe we are not that far away from the American experience at the close of another century. Sigmund Freud evokes this image of the Jew talking with a marked Yiddish accent in a letter to his friend Emil Fluss on the return trip from Freiburg in Moravia to Vienna in 1872:

> Now this Jew talked the same way as I heard thousands of others talk before, even in Freiburg. His face seemed familiar—he was typical. So was the boy with whom he discussed religion. He was cut from the cloth from which fate makes swindlers when the time is ripe: cunning, mendacious, kept by his adoring relatives in the belief that he is a great talent, but unprincipled and without character. I have enough of this rabble.[9]

The 'misreading' of the text is a repression of the discourse of the male Eastern Jew—the parvenu marked by his language and discourse as different and feminized, a point to which we shall return. The feminization of the Eastern Jew (read: Jewish male) by Western Jews is a theme that haunts the pseudo-scientific literature written against the Jews during the nineteenth century, the literature that was given the 'scientific' label of 'anti-Semitism' during that period. By the beginning of the twentieth century the pseudo-scientific literature of Jewish race hatred had become a genre in and of itself. Its most representative work, Otto Weininger's *Sex and Character*, is a pseudo-scientific study by a self-hating Jew that attempts to reveal the inner, destructive nature of both Jews and women.[10] Published after the author's suicide in 1903, *Sex and Character* was seen by thinkers as diverse as Freud and his American contemporary, the feminist theoretician Charlotte Perkins Gilman, as a major scientific contribution to the discussion of human psychology.[11] Weininger sought to create parallel categories of difference, showing that all Jews are 'merely' women. This was exemplified for Weininger by the Jew's discourse as a marker for difference, since Jews, like women, express their nature in their language. Women flirt or chatter, rather than talk (p. 195). Weininger hears the male Jew's discourse reveal his inner being: "Just as the acuteness of Jews has nothing to do with true power of differentiating, so his shyness about singing or even about speaking in clear positive tones has nothing to do with real reserve. It is a kind of inverted pride; having no true sense of his own worth, he fears being made ridiculous by his singing or his speech" (Perkins Gilman, p. 414). It is not Weininger's pseudo-scientific discourse of the assimilated philosopher, but rather the marked discourse of the Eastern Jew that surfaces here. The image of the Eastern Jew as the feminized male, the circumcised and therefore castrated male, reappears in the discourse of a Western, acculturated Jew. The Jew sounds different; the Jew is different—and the Jew who is the definition of difference for the acculturated Jew is the Eastern Jew.

This difference is not always a negative one. By the turn of the century, Yiddish had come to have a specific locus in the consciousness of Germans as the primitive pidgin spoken by the Eastern Jew, as it was depicted in the writings of the German Jewish language reformer Eduard Engels; or it could be understood as the true roots of a primitive, nonrational discourse, as German Jews such as Martin Buber perceived it. In either case it was exotic, distanced from the daily world of the German-speaking Jew. *Mauscheln*, the use of a Yiddish accent, intonation, or vocabulary items, was the mark of Eastern Jews who wished to acquire the cultural status of German speakers but, by attempting to achieve this status, revealed themselves as outsiders. These Jews posed a threat to the integration of German-speaking Jews in the West by accentuating their 'hidden' difference. The Eastern Jew was distanced by the German Jew into the world of the comic or the fictions of storytelling. They were thus placed in the past or at the fringes of Western 'culture.'

Though the creation of images of difference is ubiquitous, their representation differs markedly from culture to culture, from age to age, from thought-collective to thought-collective. Even when they become pathological, their basic structure is essential to the universal need to define ourselves as separate and yet part of the world, to control the inchoate nature of our experience and environment.[12] German Jews needed to define their own safe space and the difference of the Eastern Jew, especially the perceived difference of language and culture, was the model for the definition of that space. Is Jackie Mason right? Do we as acculturated American Jews undertake much the same exercise? What is our means of creating a safe space? What is the image of the Jew that haunts our society; is it the Jew as victim, as warrior, and is it projected onto other groups of Jews?

The vocabulary of difference depends on the culture, either broadly or narrowly defined, in which it is rooted. However, there may be overt differences or hidden similarities in the representation of marginal (as well as reference) groups. The adaptation or repression of the representation of difference enables these groups to function as self-defined thought-collectives, defined by their own discourse of difference. The basic forces of psychic organization are articulated (and therefore structured) within the rhetoric of a time, an age, a gender, a class (or all of these). We thus bear the weight of our place in history and this weight helps shape who we believe ourselves to be and we act upon this. The development of such a vocabulary of difference within the history of Western thought has led to a very specific image of the Eastern Jew among acculturated, self-defined Western Jews; a response, I will argue, as true of the American Jewish discourse about Eastern Jews as it was (and is) of the German Jewish discourse about the Eastern Jews. We can see an example of this process of individuation and differentiation—the structure of the image of the Jew who sounds too Jewish—in the attempt to create an absolute boundary even as this boundary historically shifts and slides. Jewish authors have felt compelled to respond to this image of difference, and to pose a counterimage of the talking Jew, for within their creation of texts, Jewish authors are talking Jews.

What is the talking Jew? I have argued in my study *Jewish Self-Hatred* that there is a long tradition of representing the 'hidden' language of the Jew as a signifier of specific difference.[13] And that the difference represented is always an attempt to present the qualities of the Jew (usually negative, but sometimes indeed positive) as separate from the referent group. The image of the Jew who sounds too Jewish is a stereotype within the Christian world that represents the Jew as possessing all languages or no language of his or her own; of having a hidden language that mirrors the perverse or peculiar nature of the Jew; of being unable to truly command the national language of the world in which he/she lives, or, indeed, even of possessing a language of true revelation, such as Hebrew.

The stereotype of the Jews' language is rooted in the earliest history of the rise of Christianity (or rather in the separation of the early Church from Judaism) and is mirrored in a static manner in a series of texts—the Gospels, or, as the early Christians referred to them, the *New Testament*—which were generated dynamically over time.[14] As early as Eusebius and Athanasius (in the fourth century ACE) these texts become the central canon of Christianity as the so-called "pseudo-Gospels" (such as the Gospel of Nicodemus) are removed. In the Gospels, Christians are given a representation of the Jew who sounds too Jewish and a direct message about the inherent difference of the Jew. It is in the *continuity* of the Gospels at the center of Christianity—not in the theology or indeed in the practice of the Church—that the representation of the Jew who sounds too Jewish is preserved. And it is to this central stereotype that Western (that is, Christian or secularized) society turns when it needs to provide itself with a vocabulary of difference for the Jew. Thus it is quite unimportant whether the Gospels (or the "Q" document) were first drafted in Aramaic or Greek. What is central is that in the reception of the Gospels there is a contrast between the language of the Gospel narrative (whether Greek, Latin, English, or German) and Jesus's *ipsissima verba*.

The creation of the image of the Jew who sounds too Jewish in the reception of the Gospels can be understood by examining/comparing analogous passages. Let us turn to the Gospels in their canonical (i.e. received) order and read one passage, the last words of Christ, in all of them. Focusing on the presentation, we see that in the first set of passages Jesus Christ speaks in Aramaic. Matthew, the first gospeler, represents Christ whose last words are as follows: "And about the ninth hour Jesus cried with a loud voice, saying, 'Eli, Eli, Lama Sabachtani?' that is to say, My God, My God, why has thou forsaken me?" (27:46) Mark has Christ "at the ninth hour ... [crying] with a loud voice, saying 'Eloi, Eloi, Lama Sabachthani?' which is, being interpreted, My God, My God, why hast thou forsaken me?" (15:34) The significance of this lies in the presentation of Christ as speaking the language of the

Jews: his words need to be translated into Greek, Latin, German, or English for the self-labeled Christian reader to understand. The reader is thus made aware of the foreignness of Christ's language—he speaks the language of difference; he is a Jew who sounds Jewish. Placed in the mouth of Christ, the 'hidden' language of the Jews is the magical language of difference. It generates a positive image of difference. But it still labels him as a Jew.

But in the second ("later") set of passages, Christ speaks directly to the reader. If we take the parallel passage from Luke we can trace the same course with very different results. Christ is taken to Calvary and there he is crucified. "And when Jesus had cried with a loud voice, he said, Father into thy hands I commend my spirit: and having said thus, he gave up the ghost" (23:46). In John, the last of the Gospels that related the life of Jesus, Christ is taken to Golgotha and there "he said, It is finished: and he bowed his head, and gave up the ghost" (19:30). His language needs no translation; it is transparent, familiar not foreign. The later Gospels provide a verbal sign of difference between the image of the Jews and that of the early Christians represented in the text—Jews who were at the time becoming Christians in a world in which the valorized language was Greek. As Christian readers who read through the Gospels in their canonical order, we thus abandon that which sounds like ourselves (whether we speak Greek, Latin, German, or English). He becomes a Christian. Thus the existence of a 'hidden' language that would mark Christ as a 'real' Jew, i.e. as a non-Greek-speaking Jew and therefore of lower status, was impossible.

In Luke and John there is no need for translation or interpretation. The language of this passage is completely transparent to the Christian reader of the Gospels. The reader of the passage understands that Christ speaks the same language as the reader. This "lucanization," according to Morton Scott Enslin, "reflects a marked sameness of tone, their smoothness and freedom from the little idiosyncrasies which stamp the man himself. . . ."[15] This movement in the Gospels from the image of Christ as a Jew who sounds too Jewish to that of the Christian, whose discourse is separate and distinct from that of the Jew, becomes clearest in the writings that codified the view of the early Church. In *Acts*, Peter's first speech to his fellow Jews in Jerusalem is recounted in a manner that differentiates between Greek, the language of his readers (now feeling themselves as 'Christians'), and the representation of the Jews' discourse. He writes, for example, "And it was known unto all the dwellers at Jerusalem; insomuch as that field is called in their proper tongue, Aceldama, that is to say, The field of blood" (1:19). But the utterances of Jesus in *Acts* never need this type of translation. His language is consistently accessible. His language is not the language of the Jews.

The rhetoric of European anti-Semitism can be found within the continuity of Christianity's image of the discourse of the Jew, and this is the model of the 'different' language and essence ascribed to the Eastern Jew. It is Christianity that provides all the vocabularies of difference in Western Europe and North Africa, whether it is in the most 'religious' language or in the secularized language of modern science. For it is not that merely the Jew is the obvious Other for the European. Anti-Semitism is central to Western culture because the rhetoric of European culture is Christianized, even in its most secular form. This made the negative image of difference of the Jew found in the Gospel into the central referent for all definitions of difference in the West. And this is the image that is internalized and projected by self-defined, acculturated Jews onto their darkest nightmare, the Eastern Jew.

The image of the Jew who sounds too Jewish is the counterimage of the hidden language of the Jew. The language used by the Jew reveals or masks the Jew's corrupt nature. But the informed listener hears the Jew hidden within no matter whether this difference is overt or disguised. The image of the 'hidden' language and corrupt (and corrupting) discourse of the Jews is reflected within the tradition of Jews dealing with their internalized sense of difference. Thus the memory of language is never neutral for Jews, especially German Jews. The ancient Western tradition labels the language of the Jew as corrupt and corrupting, as the sign of the inherent difference of the Jew. This tradition sees the Jew as inherently unable to have command of any 'Western,' that is, cultural language. The Jew is not only "not of our blood," as Msgr. Joseph Frings of Cologne expressed it in 1942, but also "does not speak our language."[16] The Jews' language reflects only the corruption of the Jews and their discourse, a corruption that is made manifest in the essential Jew's language from the eighteenth century to the present, Yiddish. It is against this view that Jewish writers—Jewish because they internalize the label of "Jew"—must establish dominance over the language and discourse of their culture. The image of the language of the Jews and the idea of a "Jewish" language and discourse is central to any self-definition of the Jew in the Christian West.

We can take a specific example from the 1940s, the most recent period when the Jews were simply labeled unable to command the language of their "host" nations. The stigma of being Jewish was central to the definitions of all German "Jews," no matter what their prior religious, ethnic, or cultural self-definition. Theodor Adorno, writing in 1945, juxtaposes in two aphorisms his view that "Anti-Semitism is the rumor about the Jews" and "Foreign words are the Jews of language."[17] Jews are the product of language and language becomes like the anti-Semite's image of the wandering or cosmopolitan Jew. The language of the anti-Semite here defines the nature of the Jew and his/her discourse. Thus, the Jew becomes the agent who uses corrupt language, while the corrupt discourse becomes the embodiment of the nature of the Jews in Germany; but he also sees the nature of language (within the historic German demand for a 'pure' language) as creating a category of exclusion and stigma. The interchangeability of these two categories reflects the interchangeability of the image of the Jew as possessing a unique, corrupting and corrupt discourse embodied in the Jew's language—whether in the Jews' use of the language of culture or that special language of the Jews, Yiddish. For language purists of the 1920s and 1930s the most corrupt version of German was *Mauscheln*, the language ascribed to the Eastern Jew who attempted to speak German.

Let me return to an example I evoked earlier in my essay: the relationship between language and essence of the Eastern Jew evoked in the letter Sigmund Freud wrote to his friend Emil Fluss. Freud was always most unclear about his relation to the Eastern Jews with whom he felt himself most closely related. His early letters are full of the stereotypes of the language and thought of the Eastern Jew. These images reappear in slightly altered guise when he turns to the creation of ideas of gender, especially ideas that link concepts of gender with psychopathology. Let us turn for our example to the case of Dora from 1904, perhaps the most intensively interpreted of Freud's case studies. Dora is a "case of hysteria" and, for Freud, it is the discourse of the hysteric, which is her prime signifier. It is the ordered narrative of the patient about her illness that is disrupted in the hysteric. In other words, the hysteric lies—"the patients' inability to give an ordered history of their life in so far as it coincides with the history of their illness is not merely characteristic of the neurosis. It also possesses great theoretical significance."[18] The relationship between the sexual etiology of the hysteric and the hysteric's discourse represents the underlying shift from an image of race to one of gender (for the corrupt discourse of the Jew is a primary marker of difference). The counterexample is brought in Freud's notes, a case study of a patient who "had been for years . . . treated without success for hysteria (pains and defective gait)." She narrates her "story . . . perfectly clearly and connectedly in spite of the remarkable events it dealt with. . . ." Freud concludes this "could not be . . . [a case] of hysteria," and immediately instituted a careful physical examination.

It is with the differential diagnosis between syphilis (also understood as a Jewish disease) and hysteria that Freud locates his image of the Eastern Jew. The association of the syphilitic infection of the father and the neurosis of the daughter is linked by Freud in his analysis of the physical symptom of leucorrhoea or genital catarrh, an increased "disgust[ing] . . . secretion of the mucous membrane of the vagina. . . ." Dora associates this with her lesbian "disgust" toward Herr K.'s attempted heterosexual seduction (in Freud's reading) and the feeling of his "erect member against her body." Freud's conclusion is that for Ida Bauer "all men were like her father. But she thought her father suffered from venereal disease for had he not handed it on to her and to her mother? She might therefore have imagined to herself that all men suffered from venereal disease, and naturally her conception of venereal disease was modelled upon her one experience of it—a personal one at that. To suffer from venereal disease, therefore meant for her to be afflicted with a disgusting discharge." Freud thus interprets one of the two dreams narrated to him by Dora in terms of the connection between the "disgusting catarrh," the wetness of bedwetting and masturbation, and her mother's compulsive cleanliness. "The two groups of ideas met in this one thought: 'Mother got both things from her father: the sexual wetness and the dirtying discharge.'" In the recurrent dream the connection (right word) is made through the symbolic representation of the "drops," the jewels her mother wishes to rescue from the fire that threatens the family. Freud interprets the "drops," the jewelry (*Schmuck*), as a "switch word" while "jewelry" (*Schmuck*) was taken as an equivalent to "clean" and thus as a rather forced contrary of "dirtied." Freud stresses that the "jewels" become a "jewelcase" in the dream and that his term (*Schmuckkasten*) is "a term commonly used to describe female genitals that are immaculate and intact."

One can add another layer of misreading.

There is a subtext in the hidden language of the Jews. In Viennese urban dialect, borrowed from Yiddish, *Schmock* has another meaning. Even in German ideolect *Schmock* had come to be the standard slang term for the male genitals.[19] The "hidden" meaning of the language of the Jews is identical to the lying of the hysteric, the central symptom of hysteria according to Freud. This transference can be seen in Freud's early description of the discourse of two Eastern male Jews in a letter to his friend Emil Fluss. The "misreading" of the text is a repression of the discourse of the male Eastern Jew—the parvenu marked by his language and discourse as different and diseased. Hidden within the female genitalia (the *Schmuckkasten*) is the image of the male Jew as represented by his genitalia (the *Schmock*). The replacement of the "Jewish" penis—identifiable as circumcised and diseased, but the "German" vagina stands at the center of Freud's revision of the identity of Ida Bauer. It also represents the substitution of the language of German culture for the hidden and repressed language of the Eastern Jew that haunted Freud's image of difference. It is cast in the very language that he uses and which he evokes.

But the myth of the "hidden" language of the Jew is not a "German" or a "German Jewish" problem. The image of the Eastern Jew as the Jew who sounds too Jewish—the post-Shoah manifestation of the internalization of the image of the hidden language of the Jew—can and does materialize in contemporary Jewish culture throughout the Galut. Its roots lie in a Jewish internalization of the Christian image of the innate difference of the Jew. One can turn to the intense competition for acceptance between the German Jewish and East European Jewish communities in the United States for one salient example. In 1939 Karl A. Menninger recounted his own midwestern Christian discomfort at hearing the editor of the *New York Times*, Arthur Sulzberger, tell "a story involving the imitation of the Jewish accent of Dr. [A. A.] Brill [the pioneer East European Jewish psychoanalyst], which I thought was in very bad taste. As a matter of fact, it was the second time he had told it in my presence, and he admitted that he had told it in his office when he made a speech to the employees a few days ago. He is such a cultivated, dignified fellow that it is amazing to hear him come out with this ridicule of the accent of other Jews...."[20] Menninger supplies his own reading of Sulzberger's reason for distinguishing between his discourse and that of someone whom Menninger sees as a "fellow Jew." Menninger comments that Sulzberger was "timid about being known to be a Jewish newspaper owner" (p. 284). That is, he was anxious about his discourse, the discourse of the journalist being identified as a hidden Jewish discourse. The charge that the media was in the hands of the Jews had first been lodged in Germany in the mid-nineteenth century. The force of this charge had been exacerbated by the public response of the American media to the rise of the Nazis. Sulzberger's fear of the Jew within was articulated by him in his identification of the discourse of the Eastern Jew as aberrant, at a time in 1939 when, in Germany as well as in the United States, the anxiety of all Jews, even extremely acculturated ones such as Sulzberger, about their status as members of the dominant culture was high.

The extent of the power of the hidden language of the Jews in the 1980s may well reveal itself in a piece that appeared this past summer in *Esquire*—not the natural locus for texts dealing with this question. The novelist Daphne Merkin, an associate publisher at Harcourt Brace Jovanovich, comments on her inner life as a child of a survivor of the Shoah:

> Floating always among us was an awareness of the importance of avoiding if one could help it, "too Jewish" an appearance, the dread stigma of "too Jewish" a voice. My sisters, accordingly, emerged with carefully modulated accents that sounded vaguely foreign, a mix of German and British. I, by some cruel twist of fate, developed an accent that sounded unmistakably, harshly "New Yawk." My mother and sisters wanted to know why I talked as if I came from Brooklyn, but somehow I must have wanted to shed all vestiges of the dominant culture and get back to the lusty Jewish core.... Can racial self-hatred be passed along, like a bad gene?[21]

Merkin comments on the fantasy of self-hatred, on the rejection of the Jewish core, of "the prominent nose, darker coloring, or intensity of gaze I associated with being Jewish." For Merkin, the return to the "lusty Jewish core" is the act of talking with a "Jewish" accent here, the accent of the urban environment, of New York. This is not an accidental association. It is not merely that more Jews live in New York than in Jerusalem, but there is a traditional association between the idea of the American city and that of the Jew. For the nineteenth- and early twentieth-century mind, cities are places of disease and the Jews are quintessential city dwellers.[22] For the turn-of-the-century Viennese psychiatrist Richard Krafft–Ebing, the Jew is the ultimate "city person" whose sensibilities are dulled.[23] And for Henry James, returning to the haunts of his childhood in 1907, this city of Jews—New York—is the deathbed of the English language, the "East side cafés" have become the "torture room of the living idioms."[24] After the Shoah, the "hidden" language of the Jews in New York continues to be represented in the language of the immigrant-survivor (the mixed dialects of Merkin's sister as well as literary figures such as the protagonist of Saul Bellow's *Mr. Sammler's Planet*). Merkin attempts to set herself apart from this tradition by merging her language with the general culture, but the discourse of her attempt at acculturation, the language of "New Yawk" is also marked as a language of Jews, but of American Jews, not the European survivor.

The image of the city of Jews haunts Adolf Hitler's image of Vienna, the city in which he first learned to "see" the Jew, and, therefore, became aware of the "hidden" difference in his language of the Jew even when he or she is speaking 'good' German. Merkin attempts to make the acculturation of her Jewish discourse into a positive marker; one can, however, note that the "Jewish American Princess" speaks a similar 'jargon.' Debbie Lukatsky and Sandy Barnett Toback in their *Jewish American Princess Handbook* (1982) append a glossary of "Jewish Jargon" to the volume.[25] "Jewish" terms such as *chuppa* ("Marriage canopy. More decorative than symbolic") and *shagits* ("Blond-haired, blue-eyed forbidden fruit who ends up marrying a shiksa") compete with terms such as *guilt* ("Jewish hereditary disease. Symptoms including a churning stomach and feelings of deep-seated anxiety. Highly contagious, especially when the Princess spends too much time in the company of her mother") and *money* ("the ultimate aphrodisiac [Credit cards acceptable]"). Such lists were standard in all of the anti-Semitic literature of the late nineteenth and early twentieth centuries, when West European Jews were no longer marked by a "special" accent as they came to speak German, French, or English. The lists pointed to the inherent hidden language of the Jew, his or her cultural difference, and corruption. This legend of the Eastern Jew as the Jew who sounds too Jewish now takes on new meaning for the Jews in the 1980s. Merkin brings her piece to a close with the realization that

> there is no sign that the world has grown more fond of the Jews, so there is no sign I will ever be free of a certain fascination with the darker impulses at work in myself and others.... There is some kind of relief in being able to recognize the aggressor, even identify with him for a while, and then walk on. Like tipping one's hat at one's enemy, it may not be a grandstanding gesture, but it's definitely a civilized one. (p. 85)

The true civilized gesture in Merkin's piece, however, lies not in its message, but in its medium. Her essay on the seduction of the Other who is one's self was written in a completely acculturated style and appeared in *Esquire*, a popular "men's" magazine with intellectual pretensions. Merkin's act of writing frees her from her sense of self-hatred in proving that she really is a member of the cultural elite of "New Yawk."

Phillip Lopate presented the counterargument to Merkin by simply reversing the meaning of a specifically Jewish (read: Eastern Jewish) quality to Jewish identity in the United States.[26] In a long piece on "Resistance to the Holocaust" in *Tikkun*, he criticized the "kitsch" aspects of the Shoah, seeing it as an event in world history, and bemoaned the special, indeed central, status given to it by many contemporary Jews in the United States and Israel. He notes that his first exposure to this "Shoah-ization" (my word—not his) of the discourse of modern Jewry came in a "large communal Seder in Houston, about 1982":

> ...the introduction of references to the Holocaust in every second or third prayer seemed to have a different function. For many of the people at the Seder in Texas, the Shoah *was* the heart of their faith; it was what touched them most deeply about being Jewish. The religion itself—the prayers, the commentaries, the rituals, the centuries of accumulated wisdom and tradition—had shriveled to a sort of marginally necessary preamble for this negative miracle.

This is the negative, corrupt discourse of the Jew—the replacement of a "true" language of difference (in the prayers, commentaries, etc.) with a false center—the metaphor of the Shoah. But what is the "real" reason for this substitution, indeed, what is the "real" hidden language that marks the "true Jew" according to Lopate?

> The importance of the Shoah for such assimilated Jews must be considered within the broader framework of the erosion of Jewish group memory in the modern period. By group or "collective" memory, I mean simply all the customs, rituals, ceremonies, folkways, *Yiddishkeit*, cuisine, historical events, and so on that used to be the common inheritance of every Jew.

This is an extraordinary leap, one that must be contrasted with that of Merkin.

The real Jew is the East European Jew whose *Yiddishkeit* (and Lopate stresses the authenticity of this experience by employing the "real" language of the Jews, Yiddish) is the mark of the "hidden" language of the Jew. This is the "New Yawk" of Merkin, the goal she as the child of Shoah survivors seeks—the authenticity of a never-never world of the *shtetl* transported into Sholem Aleichem's "New Yawk." It is an intact world, a world with shared experiences that excludes the "acculturated" survivors of the Shoah. For here Lopate reveals his hidden agenda. These Jews gathered around the Seder table in Houston may be many things, but they are not assimilated—they have not disappeared into the mass culture of the American experience. They may well be acculturated, like many of the West and some of the East European Jews who died in the Shoah, but their participation in a Seder indicates their self-identification as part of a cultural subgroup. Lopate's definition of the Jew postulates a "good" talking Jew (himself) and a "bad" talking Jew (the object of their investigation). Their act of writing in English without sounding "too Jewish" "proves" to the reader their command of the "good" discourse of the Jew.

Lurking in our post-Shoah debates about the definition of Jewish identity is the ghost of the conflict between German Jew and Eastern Jew. The romanticized fantasy of the Eastern Jew of a Martin Buber or an Arnold Zweig is matched by the rejection of the discourse of the Eastern Jew by a Sigmund Freud or a Karl Kraus. Parallel manifestations exist in the United States today: sounding too Jewish marks you as different, marks you as exotic. It is a struggle that can have no winners, but which reflects the constant problem of Jewish self-definition within the Galut.

The context for this struggle remains the Christian model of the inherent difference of the Jew as manifested in the representation of the discourse of the Jew. The image of Christ in the Gospels serves as the paradigm for the difference between someone who sounds "too Jewish" and one whose Jewishness vanishes once his language becomes acculturated (at least in the text). Certainly the 'real' sociological 'facts' of Jewish acculturation—the polylingual abilities of Jews, which grew out of their persecutions—played a role in shaping this image of the Jew as using all languages and possessing only his/her own hidden discourse. But it cannot explain the powerful continuity of the image of someone who sounds "too Jewish" among those Jews who have not lived in a cultural transition. What we see is how Jews internalize the image of being too Jewish in a culture in which being Jewish in any manner is a sign of inherent difference, and how they shape their internalization of this charge of their own incompetence as members of the culture in which they live. This is a tension that forms the sensibilities of Jewish writers and thinkers in the Christian West.

## NOTES

1. This essay served as the keynote address at a conference on the relationship between German Jews and East European Jews held in the spring of 1990 by the German Department at Columbia University.

2. Glenn Collins, "Jackie Mason, Top Banana at Last," *New York Times* (24 July 1988), section 2, pp. 1, 14.

3. "Highly Touted 'Soup' Goes Down the Drain," *USA Today* (8 November 1989), pp. 1D–2D.

4. Henry L. Gates, Jr., "TV's Black World Turns—But Stays Unreal," *New York Times* (12 November 1989), section 2, pp. 1, 40.

5. *USA Today*, ibid.
6. Cited in the *New York Times* (28 September 1989), B1.
7. Cited in the *New York Times* (2 October 1989), B1.
8. In the unpublished manuscript of the diaries (entry for 4 April 1907) in the University Library at Cambridge University.
9. Sigmund Freud, "Some Early Unpublished Letters," translated by Ilse Scheier, *International Journal of Psychoanalysis* 50 (1969), p. 420.
10. All citations are from the English translation of Otto Weininger, *Sex and Character* (London: William Heinemann, 1906). On the relationship between Freud and Weininger, see the exemplary essay by Peter Heller, "A Quarrel over Bisexuality," in Gerald Chapple and Hans H. Schulte, eds., *The Turn of the Century: German Literature and Art, 1890–1915* (Bonn: Bouvier, 1981), pp. 87–116.
11. Charlotte Perkins Gilman, "Review of Dr. Weininger's *Sex and Character*," *The Critic* 12 (1906), p. 414.
12. Klaus Theweleit, *Male Phantasies*, translated by Stephan Conway, 2 volumes (Minneapolis: University of Minnesota Press, 1987; originally published in 1977–78). Compare George L. Mosse, *Nationalism and Sexuality: Respectability and Abnormal Sexuality in Modern Europe* (Madison: University of Wisconsin Paperback, 1988).
13. Sander L. Gilman, *Jewish Self-Hatred: Anti-Semitism and the Hidden Language of the Jews* (Baltimore: The Johns Hopkins University Press, 1986).
14. See Rosemary Reuther, *Faith and Fratricide: The Theology Roots of Antisemitism* (New York: Seabury Press, 1974).
15. Morton Scott Enslin, *Christian Beginnings* (New York: Harper Bros., 1938), p. 421.
16. Cited by Saul Friedländer, *Kurt Gerstein: The Ambiguity of Good*, translated by Charles Fullman (New York: Alfred A. Knopf, 1969), pp. 148–149.
17. Theodor Adorno, *Minima moralia: Reflexionen aus dem beschädigten Leben* (Berlin: Suhrkamp, 1951), p. 200.
18. All references to this are to Sigmund Freud, *Standard Edition of the Complete Psychological Works of Sigmund Freud*, edited and translated by J. Strachey, A. Freud, A. Strachey, and A. Tyson, 24 volumes (London: Hogarth, 1955–1974); here, volume 7, pp. 16–17. The discussion of this case is documented in Charles Bernheimer and Claire Kahane, eds., *In Dora's Case: Freud–Hysteria–Feminism* (New York: Columbia University Press, 1985). See also Dianne Hunter, "Hysteria, Psychoanalysis, and Feminism: The Case of Anna O," *Feminist Studies* 9 (1983), pp. 465–488; Maria Ramas, "Freud's Dora, Dora's Hysteria: The Negation of a Woman's Rebellion," *Feminist Studies* 6 (1980), pp. 472–510; Arnold A. Rogow, "A Further Footnote to Freud's Fragment of Analysis of a Case of Hysteria," *Journal of the American Psychoanalytical Association* 26 (1978), pp. 330–356.
19. It is clear that these two words have very different etymologies. In the German use of the words there is an immediate, if false, association between them.
20. Howard J. Faulkner and Virigina D. Pruitt, eds., *The Selected Correspondence of Karl A. Menninger, 1919–1945* (New Haven: Yale University Press, 1988), p. 282.
21. Daphne Merkin, "Dreaming of Hitler," *Esquire* (August 1989), pp. 75–83.
22. Richard Krafft–Ebing, *Psychopathologia Sexualis: A Medico-Forensic Study*, revised translation by Harry E. Wedeck (New York: Putnam, 1965), p. 24.
23. Compare Otto Binswanger, *Hysterie* (Vienna: Deuticke, 1904), p. 82.

24. Henry James, *The American Scene* (London: Chapman & Hall, 1907), pp. 129–131.

25. Debbie Lukatsky and Sandy Barnett Toback, *Jewish American Princess Handbook* (Arlington Heights, IL: Turnbull and Willoughby, 1982), pp. 142–143.

26. Philip Lopate, "Resistance to the Holocaust," *Tikkun* (May–June, 1989), pp. 55–65. The debate with Bauer is included.

# Residues of Otherness:
# On Jewish Emancipation during the
# Age of German Enlightenment

## Barbara Fischer

With the establishment of a German nation in 1871, about one hundred years after the publication of Gotthold Ephraim Lessing's *Nathan der Weise* [Nathan the Wise] and Christian Wilhelm von Dohm's *Über die bürgerliche Verbesserung der Juden* [On the Improvement of the Civil Status of Jews], it became clear that the Enlightenment notion of tolerance had not succeeded in transforming the attitudes of the German general public toward Jews. The Enlightenment project for the emancipation of Jews in Germany had indeed become a legal *fait accompli* by 1871, yet the everyday conflicts between the two groups had not disappeared with the introduction of the tolerance ideal into German political discourse. As the history of emancipation shows, German Jews who had, as Shulamith Volkov points out, "gone a long way in the direction of acculturation and *Verbürgerlichung* . . . were clearly not losing their character."[1] The continued collective consciousness of German Jews triggered, in turn, a series of reactions among nationalist groups in Germany. Anti-Jewish sentiment actually grew, developing what Reinhard Rürup calls the "post-emancipatory phenomenon" of anti-Semitism.[2] A reassessment of the eighteenth-century notion of tolerance must therefore be undertaken with the acknowledgment that its culmination in "post-emancipatory" anti-Semitism represents not so much a rupture as a historical and discursive consequence.

    Humanist intellectuals of the late eighteenth and early nineteenth century had articulated—either in good or not so good faith—a project of tolerance and assimilation that developed dialectically into something other than what they might have originally foreseen. It is not my intention to argue that Jewish integration into German society was accomplished by coercion. The process of Jewish assimilation should be understood as part and parcel of the establishment of the German bourgeoisie. The road toward German Jewish assimilation was, in effect, paved by Jewish *and* non-Jewish Enlightenment thinkers. They both recognized in the complex new social structures an incipient mode of existence that promised Jews a way out of the ghetto. In the following analysis, I shall attempt to determine how the space between majority and minority—which tolerance should supposedly bridge—is constructed in both literary and political discourses professing the ideals of Enlightenment.

The English philosopher John Locke argues in his *Epistola de Tolerantia* [A Letter Concerning Toleration], written in Amsterdam in 1685 and published in 1689, that the religious beliefs of everyone who subjects himself to the sovereignty of the laws of the state must be tolerated. Locke points out at the beginning of his text that intolerance contradicts the Christian precepts of charity and brotherly love; nonetheless, he envisions in the separation between church and state the only real possibility for religious tolerance. Thus, he would grant the Jews equal rights as citizens, since their faith would not necessarily make them worse citizens:

> No private person has any right in any matter to prejudice another person in his civil enjoyments because he is of another church or religion. All the rights and franchises that belong to him as a man, or as a denizen, are inviolably to be preserved to him. These are not the business of religion.[3]

In Locke's articulation of tolerance, religious domination is subordinated to citizenship. Consequently, a citizen who obeys the laws of the state and who is socially integrated has the right to expect the state's protection against religious intolerance. Religion becomes therefore a private matter, a matter of personal belief, whose practice is ensured as the citizen's inalienable right.

It is significant in this context that, in his *Letter Concerning Toleration*, Locke anticipates by almost a hundred years Lessing's hierarchization of the Jewish and the Christian religion in *Die Erziehung des Menschengeschlechts* [The Education of Mankind] and places Christianity at a higher level of spiritual development than Judaism.[4] In Locke's view, this hierarchization was justified by the fact that only the Christian religion could permit a separation between church and state. In contrast, Judaism represented an absolute theocracy that had never and could never allow for such a separation (Locke, *Letter*, p. 73). This account of Judaism would seem to lead to the inescapable conclusion that only by renouncing his own religion could a traditional Jew subject himself to the laws of a non-Jewish state.

Locke's treatment of tolerance was to find an echo in the textual production of German intellectuals in the half-century following the publication of his *Letter*. A 1725 speech by Johann Christoph Gottsched—a prominent figure in early German Enlightenment—discloses an apparent parallel with the Lockian discussion of tolerance. Gottsched argues in his academic speech *Von dem verderblichen Religionseifer und der heilsamen Duldung aller christlichen Religionen* [On the Dangers of Religious Zeal and the Beneficial

Toleration of all Christian Religions] that "religious zeal is highly pernicious, whereas toleration of members of different denominations would be useful and sensible."[5] In the issue of *Der Biedermann* of 20 September 1728, he refers specifically to the Jewish question. The "harshest punishment" of twelve Jews during the Portuguese Inquisition provides Gottsched with the occasion for the following reflection:

> It is perhaps in the interest of the welfare of the Portuguese nation not to put up with this riffraff; if so, it would behoove the Portuguese to rid themselves of it. Were this not so, however, the sentencing of these people could not be seen as rightful. Who has summoned us, human beings, to become the judges of our fellow-beings' consciences? Each of us will one day be made accountable for his actions: May he then live and believe according to his own conscience.[6]

As does Locke, Gottsched differentiates between nation and religion. The expulsion and persecution of Jews are thus legitimated only as "a matter of national security." As for the religious judgment, the deciding factor should be moral reason, not one's appurtenance to a particular creed.

The tolerance ideas come to be realized at the private level in the exemplary and enduring friendship between the influential Jewish Enlightenment philosopher Moses Mendelssohn and the most prominent literary figure of the German Enlightenment, Gotthold Ephraim Lessing. This metonymic concord between Judaism and Christianity seemed to ensure the possibility of a public practice of religious tolerance. As the most prominent eighteenth-century Jewish intellectual, Mendelssohn was an influential promulgator of Jewish emancipation. Lessing, on the other hand, as author of perhaps the best-known literary endorsement of tolerance, *Nathan der Weise*, emerged as a strong non-Jewish advocate for social acceptance of Jews. Mendelssohn's and Lessing's projects could therefore be subsumed to an inside/outside dialectic of theoretical articulations of emancipation, Mendelssohn on the 'inside' of the Jewish community, Lessing on the 'outside,' which required only political and social praxis for their realization.[7]

It was the statesman and historian Christian von Dohm who took up the definition of the parameters of Jewish integration into bourgeois society in his treatise *Über die bürgerliche Verbesserung der Juden*, published in two parts in 1781 and 1783. Dohm urged that in the interest of universal human rights and of the State, Jews should be converted into 'useful' citizens. Like Lessing in "Über das Lustspiel *Die Juden*" [On the Comedy *The Jews*] (1754) and Wilhelm von Humboldt in *Über den Entwurf zu einer neuen Konstitution der Juden* [On the Proposal of a New Constitution of the Jews] (1809), Dohm ascribed the purported wretched living conditions of Jews to the legal marginalization that had been consistently forced upon them. Their social 'inferiority,' in other terms, was a direct result of their status as *non*-citizens.

> All the Jews are reproached for is caused by the political conditions in which they now live; and any other race, under the same circumstances, would be guilty of the same offenses.[8]

Along with the political emancipation of Jews, Dohm contended, must come a process of "education" or assimilation into the dominant culture and society. In return for this process of social improvement or transformation, full citizenship and legal equality will be granted. The political emancipation of the Jewish minority is thus articulated in terms of a mercantile exchange. The transference of tolerance onto the legislative sphere does not appear to take the form of acceptance and respect for cultural and religious difference, but rather becomes a commodity to be 'purchased' with service rendered to the state.

In the first part of his work, Dohm seems to profess a more traditionally humanistic concern for the plight of the Jews. Yet, in the second part, written as a response to the critiques leveled at his earlier piece, he unmistakably subsumes any consideration for the specific problems of Jews to the general interest of the state. Dohm specifies that his primary intent was not to deal with the oppressive conditions of Jews, but to address matters of the state:

> I did not desire to inspire pity for them, nor did I want to ask for a better treatment for them, but to show that sound reason and common human feeling, as well as the interests of the bourgeois society, call for this improved treatment. ... I was astonished that my work was sometimes called a deliverance or apology of the Jews, and that I could be taken to be their advocate.[9]

Dohm acknowledges, in fact, that the religious attachment of Jews would weaken progressively with their social and political integration. To those hypothetical critics who would point out that this mode of civic improvement actually requires the dissolution of the entire fabric of Judaism ("But then the Jews will cease to be actual Jews?"), Dohm replies offhandedly: "What if they do! Why should the state, which demands nothing else of [the Jews] but that they become good citizens, concern itself with that?"[10] Dohm is not so much contradicting the notion of tolerance here as taking its emancipatory project to its logical conclusion. What already seems implicit in Locke's discussion of the separation between church and state is made explicit: in order for tolerance to bridge the gulf between Judaism and Christianity, between minority and majority, in a secular social space where both Christian and Jew would enjoy full equality under the law, the minority culture would apparently have to alter itself substantially.

The effect Dohm's writings were to have on the political debates and subsequent reform policies concerning the status of Jews should not be underestimated. At the same time, as he himself concedes, Dohm is not interested in Jews as an oppressed minority nor in the legal and unconditional protection of their cultural and religious identity, but in the assimilated bourgeois subjects into whom they must be transformed in the interest of the state. He speaks derogatorily of the necessity to cleanse Jews of their cultural "depravity" (*Verderbtheit*) (I, p. 109), characterizing Judaism as "a false way, which they believed to be the right one," and a nation, "whose members had just begun to attain civilized status."[11] He asserts that "the Jews are, like the rest of us, human beings *too*" (my emphasis).[12] The residue signified by the modifier *too (auch)*, appended to Jewish humanity, is Judaism itself. In order to become human beings *tout court* the Jews must ascend to the status of 'useful' state citizens. This social ascension, it seems, can take place only through an erasure of the 'remnants' of Jewish tradition, which would appear to make the Jew's humanity only a qualified one.

In a critique of the first part of Dohm's work, Johann David Michaelis, a Göttingen professor of Oriental Studies, who was not only a paradigm of the eighteenth-century Orientalist scholar but also, in my opinion, a profound anti-Semite, qualifies as an 'exception' the rare Jew, who, in contrast to the general Jewish population, had a virtuous and civilized "character."[13] Michaelis calls into question the feasibility of a legal emancipation of Jews, asserting that the Mosaic Laws forbade assimilation into a secular society. For Michaelis, then, Jewish emancipation was impracticable. He does, however, consider the question of their 'usefulness' to the state, suggesting that Jews could become "even more useful" as settlers of hypothetical

> sugar plantation colonies that have succeeded in draining the European metropolis of people, and offset the wealth they possess with an unhealthy climate. Perhaps such a people can become useful to us in agriculture and manufactures, if one goes about it the right way.[14]

Perhaps unbeknownst to him, Michaelis's proposal had already been enacted approximately three centuries earlier by King John II of Portugal, who in 1493 had sent to the African island of Sao Tomé the recently baptized children of Jewish refugees from Castille–Aragon to 'protect' them from the influence of the Mosaic Law.[15]

This projected deportation would, in fact, become an effective way of countervailing what Michaelis feared could be the establishment of a "most contemptible Jewish State" (*verächtlichster Judenstaat*) if, as Dohm suggested, Jewish citizens were legally exempted from military conscription and the Prussians were to suffer the same heavy casualties that they did in the Seven Years War.[16] Although Michaelis's statements seems to have nothing in common with tolerance, the logic of his intolerance does not contradict that of Dohm's emancipatory discourse. The conclusions to which they come are diametrically opposed. Dohm postulates the social desirability of Jewish emancipation; Michaelis argues that it would be both unlikely and socially pernicious. But their premises are the same: bourgeois citizenship and a continued adherence to the tenets of Judaism seem to be incompatible.

As will be recalled, Michaelis's dread of the rise of a "Jewish State" within the bourgeois state anticipates the rhetoric of post-emancipatory anti-Semitism mentioned in the beginning of this paper. Hence, about a hundred years after the publication of Michaelis's critique of Dohm, the nationalist scholar Richard Mayr resurrects the former's objections to Jewish emancipation:

> Why then was the wall dividing the ghetto from the city torn down, if not to do away with the ghetto? Instead, not a few Jews are now busy transplanting the ghetto into the center of cultivated and privileged society.[17]

According to Mayr, the success of the policy of emancipation must be measured against the extent to which the cultural and political center absorbs or "does away" with the marginalized culture. As long as a residue of 'Jewishness' subsists after the process of social integration has been achieved, the majority—absorbent—culture runs the risk of being 'tainted.'

The last articulation of tolerance I will discuss is that of the liberal humanist Wilhelm von Humboldt. Humboldt expresses a similar lack of concern for the disappearance of the minority culture. In *Über den Entwurf zu einer neuen Konstitution für die Juden*, which was written in July 1809 during his appointment as Director of Culture and Education for the Prussian Ministry of the Interior, Humboldt recommends an immediate conferral of civil rights upon Jewish subjects. In his view, a gradual process of social reform would tend to exacerbate Christian prejudices against Jews, since a partial legal emancipation could only reinforce prejudicial public opinion about Jews. An immediate legal emancipation of the Jewish population, Humboldt argues, "would promote more schisms and the Jewish hierarchy would collapse by itself."

> One would not introduce a new Orthodoxy among the Jews, but rather, by means of a genuine and just tolerance, would promote more schisms [among them] and the Jewish hierarchy would collapse by itself. Individual Jews will become aware of the fact that they actually had no religion but only a ceremonial law, and driven by the inherent human need for a higher faith, they will turn of their own accord to the Christian one.[18]

Similarly to Lessing and Locke, Humboldt places Christianity at the summit of the religious hierarchy. The legal enactment of tolerance, in other words, is to be enforced from the top, and aims at the progressive inclusion and dissolution of the minority culture into an unquestionable higher social order.[19]

As Moses Mendelssohn once observed: "It is our luck that one cannot press for human rights without, at the same time, remonstrating against our own."[20] Yet, in order to participate in an imminent order of civilization, to become a citizen of the future bourgeois state, 'the Jew' was expected, in effect, to gradually shed his Jewishness. Only by renouncing the cultural identity and religious practices that marked him as an "other"—in short, only by ceasing to be traditionally Jewish—could the Jew be tolerated by the German bourgeois subject.

Thus, the logic of tolerance appears to lead to an inescapable double-bind. On the one hand, emancipation leads to the gradual *erasure* of Jewish cultural difference. On the other hand, since the realization of this ideal is always projected into the future, the erasure remains a partial, incomplete one. It is, therefore, not entirely paradoxical that when the ideal of the bourgeois state undergoes a radically nationalist redefinition it will be possible to clamor for the eradication of these "residues of otherness."

## NOTES

1. Shulamith Volkov, "Jews in 19th-Century Germany: Notes on Becoming a Minority." Paper presented at the Conference on Jewish Identity in the German World: "Emancipation, Assimilation, and Thereafter." University of California at Berkeley, Department of German 1990, p. 131.

2 Cf. *Emancipation and Anti-Semitism* (Frankfurt am Main: Fischer Taschenbuch, 1987), p. 114. Reinhard Rürup argues that modern anti-Semitism is both historically and practically a post-emancipatory phenomenon: "Bei der durch den Antisemitismus geschaffenen 'Judenfrage' der siebziger Jahre handelte es sich nicht um eine Wiederaufnahme der älteren, emanzipatorischen 'Judenfrage,' sondern um einen qualitativ neuen Sachverhalt. Der moderne Antisemitismus ist nicht nur *chronologisch*, sondern auch sachlich ein postemanzipatorisches Phänomen. Er findet die rechtliche Gleichstellung als ein Faktum vor und wendet sich gegen das emanzipierte Judentum. Seine 'Judenfrage' ist nicht mehr die Frage nach der Emanzipation der Juden, sondern—wie es in vielen Wendungen heißt—die Forderung der 'Emanzipation von den Juden.' "

3. John Locke, *A Letter Concerning Toleration*, edited and translated by Mario Montuori (The Hague: Martinus Nijhoff, 1963), pp. 31f.

4. In *Die Erziehung des Menschengeschlechts* (1780), Gotthold Ephraim Lessing describes the Old Testament (Judaism) as morally inferior to the New Testament (Christianity), which he considers as the forerunner of enlightenment, universalism, and humanism.

5. "[D]er Religionseifer eine höchst verderbliche, die Duldung fremder Glaubensgenossen hingegen eine höchst nützliche und vernünftige Sache sey." Johann Christoph Gottsched, *Gesammelte Reden*, IX/2. In *Ausgewählte Werke*, ed. Rosemary Scholl (Berlin and New York: Walter de Gruyter, 1976), p. 463. The translations are those of the editors.

6. Johann Christoph Gottsched, *Der Biedermann. Faksimiledruck der Originalausgabe Leipzig 1717–9*, ed. Wolfgang Martens (Stuttgart: Metzler, 1975).

7. A comparison between Mendelssohn's and Dohm's use of the term *Mensch* points to a crucial distinction between the former's articulation of tolerance and Dohm's. Christian Konrad Wilhelm von Dohm, *Über die bürgerliche Verbesserung der Juden* II (Hildesheim, Olms, 1973), p. 20.

8. Dohm, *Verbesserung* I, p. 35. "Alles, was man den Juden vorwirft, ist durch die politische Verfassung, in der sie itzt leben, bewirkt, und jede andere Menschengattung, in dieselben Umstände versetzt, würde sich sicher eben derselben Vergehungen schuldig machen." Gotthold Ephraim Lessing, "Über das Lustspiel Die Juden," *Politische Denkschriften* IX. In *Gesammelte Schriften*, ed. Bruno Gebhardt (Berlin: B. Behr's, 1903).

9. Dohm, *Verbesserung* II, p. 17: "Ich wollte nicht Mitleiden für Jene erregen, nicht von diesen eine bessere Behandlung derselben erbitten, sondern zeigen, daß gesunde Vernunft und allgemeine Menschlichkeit, so wie das Interesse der bürgerlichen Gesellschaft, diese bessere Behandlung fordern.... Es mußte mich daher allerdings sehr befremden, wenn man zuweilen meine Schrift eine Rettung, Apologie der Juden nennen, und mich bloß für ihren Vertheidiger nehmen könne."

10. Dohm, *Verbesserung* II, p. 174: "Aber dann werden die Juden aufhören eigentliche Juden zu seyn?... Mögen sie doch! Was kümmert dieses den Staat, der nichts weiter von ihnen verlangt, als daß sie gute Bürger werden."

11. Dohm, *Verbesserung*, p. 122: "Einen Weg, den sie zwar irrig den richtigen glaubten"; p. 18, "[eine Nation], die nur erst anfängt, sich zu einer gesitteten zu bilden."

12. Dohm, *Verbesserung* II, p. 20: "Daß die Juden, Menschen, wie wir übrigen *auch* sind."

13. In a critique of Lessing's play *Die Juden* (published in 1754) Michaelis had asserted that Lessing's virtuous Jew defies verisimilitude since "such a virtuous soul" could never be produced by "a people of such morals, lifestyle and upbringing." Gotthold Ephraim Lessing, "Über das Lustspiel *Die Juden*," p. 290.

14. Johann David Michaelis, "Hr. Ritter Michaelis Beurtheilung," *Über die bürgerliche Verbesserung* II, p. 4:. "Ein solches Volk kann uns vielleicht durch Ackerbau und Manufacturen nützlich werden, wenn man es auf die rechte Weise anfängt, noch nützlicher wenn wir Zuckerinseln hätten, die bisweilen die Entvölkerung des europäischen Vaterlandes werden, und bey dem Reichthum den sie bringen ein ungesundes Clima haben."

15. For this reference, I thank Louis Madureira.

16. In order to underscore the startling parallel between Michaelis's and late nineteenth-century anti-Semitic rhetoric, I shall give the full quote in German: "Dazu kommt noch, daß bei schweren Kriegen, wie der von 1756–1763 für die preußischen Staaten war, die Söhne des Bauern und Bürgers Soldaten werden müssen; in einem solchen Kriege würde der mit Kriegsdiensten verschonte Jude sich sehr ausbreiten, und fast lauter jüdische Handwerker würde man am Ende des Krieges sehen. Stände gar den Juden frey, Acker, oder adeliche Güter an sich zu kaufen, und reiche Juden, die in andern Ländern nicht dergleichen Rechte hätten, wünschten ihr Geld anzulegen, so würden sie unsere Deutschen auskaufen, und dann hätten wir den wehrlosesten verächtlichsten Judenstaat." Michaelis, op. cit., p. 46.

17. Richard Mayr, *Beiträge zur Beurtheilung G. E. Lessing's* (Vienna: Alfred Hölder, 1880), pp. 141–142. Mayr's book constitutes one of a variety of late nineteenth-century anti-Semitic interpretations of Lessing's works.

18. Humboldt, "Entwurf," p. 105: "Man... führe nicht eine eigne Orthodoxie unter den Juden ein, sondern befördere durch natürliche und billige Toleranz vielmehr Schismen, und die jüdische Hierarchie wird von selbst zerfallen. Die Individuen werden gewahr werden, daß sie nur ein Cärimonial—Gesetz und eigentlich keine Religion hatten, und werden, getrieben von dem angeborenen Bedürfnis nach einem höhern Glauben, sich von selbst zu der christlichen wenden."

19. Humboldt's lack of concern for the Jewish people finds an even more forceful expression in his private correspondence. In a letter dated 30 April 1816 to his wife Karoline, Humboldt states: "Ich liebe aber eigentlich auch nur die Juden *en masse, en détail* gehe ich ihnen sehr aus dem Wege" [But I actually only love the Jews *en masse, en détail* I very much try to avoid them]. *Juden und Judentum in deutschen Briefen aus drei Jahrhunderten*, ed. Franz Kobler (Königstein, CZ: Athenäum, 1984), p. 208.

20. "Es ist ein Glück für uns, wenn man auf die Rechte der Menschheit nicht dringen kann, ohne zugleich die unsrigen zu reklamieren." Quoted after Hannah Arendt, *Rahel Varnhagen. Lebensgeschichte einer deutschen Jüdin aus der Romantik* (Munich: Piper, 1959), p. 19.

# The Wandering Jew's Rhine Journey:
# Heine's *Lorelei*

## Jost Hermand

Hardly any other work of German literature has been so highly praised and at the same time subjected to such attacks as Heine's *Book of Songs* (*Buch der Lieder*).[1] On the one hand, there are those who have identified totally with his poems as the expression of a deeply felt inconsolable lover's grief, thereby securing this work a place in world literature as Heine's most successful book. On the other hand, from bourgeois realists like Friedrich Theodor Vischer to critics and fetishists of language like Karl Kraus and Theodor W. Adorno, there are those who have dismissed the heartaches expressed in the *Book of Songs* as artificial, as journalistic, as empty rhyming, and even as deceitful virtuosity. Accordingly, such readers as these design to accept only Heine's *Romancero* and his last poems from the mattress–grave as expressions of truly poetic creative genius.[2]

It is only in recent decades that earlier, now somewhat antiquated alternatives between "genuine and artificial, true and false, poetic and unpoetic" seem to be giving way to the realization that these two sides of the *Book of Songs* are complementary facets that should not be separated arbitrarily. And so today the rich contrasts of the juxtaposition of emotionality and irony that give this collection of poems its unmistakable stamp are interpreted more frequently in a way Heine himself already tried to encompass with compound terms such as "lyrical-malicious" or "sentimental-malicious."[3]

With regard to this point, however, many Heine scholars are often content merely to represent the contrast expressed here between "poetry and life" as indicative of inner strife, of ruptures, or at least of ambivalence, which somehow point toward the future. By doing this, they set up Heine in an extremely vague way as a precursor of a "modernism" that is just as vaguely defined, thus leaving no place at all for any kind of ideological objectives. This approach, to be sure, may contribute to dismantling some of the earlier biases against these poems, but it does not connect their controversial reception to their intention in a meaningful way.

Looked at somewhat more closely, Heine was of course concerned in the *Book of Songs* with the existential, ahistorical aspects that are always present in a relationship between a man and a woman. However, he also wanted to portray in these poems his own concrete social situation, which is overlooked only too easily by structuralist or psychological approaches. With respect to the social roots of the poems in this collection, at least two such concrete situations can be distinguished: an exoteric one, which can be circumscribed as "bourgeois," and a more esoteric one, which is connected with Heine's role as a Jewish outsider within the framework of love relationships in the society he is portraying.

In the realm of bourgeois love in Heine's time, the only thing that was tolerated was chaste yearning—in short: the wish for a "union of hearts." In such a milieu, less attractive candidates for marriage were constantly subjected to humiliation. They had to watch in hopelessly resigned bitterness in the parlors of well-to-do families while the prettified daughters of the house were snatched away from under their noses by young men with the necessary cash or with promising career prospects. Faced with these conditions, there was often nothing for outsiders—like Heine—to do but to cover up their anguish at least partially with compensatory irony. Symptomatic of this is Heine's "Amalie experience," to which earlier scholarship devoted a great deal of attention. However, after William Rose's relatively recent research,[5] it is generally no longer assigned the overwhelming significance that it was given in the more positivistic or biographical scholarship of the late nineteenth century. At that time—and especially from a German Jewish perspective—scholars often attempted to rank Heine alongside Goethe as a genuine love poet whose writing always stemmed from a particular experience.

So much for the exoteric elements, which play a role in almost all the one hundred and forty poems of the *Book of Songs* having to do with "unhappy," "unrequited," or "hopeless" love.[5] By contrast, the esoteric meaning of the unhappy love portrayed here is much more difficult to uncover. After all, Heine was not just any middle-class young man of little means. Although highly gifted, he was Jewish, which—according to the ideas of the time— meant that he had not been baptized. It was only inevitable, then, that all the German Christian young women would view him as alien to them at the time, around 1820. That is, such a man did not even come into question as a lover or husband for a young Gentile woman. These women and girls could tease him with their smiles on the dance floor of bourgeois society, but they could not really love him.

Consequently, after reading the *Book of Songs*, an anti-Semite like Count August von Platen–Hallermünde mockingly called him a "Petrarch of the Feast of the Tabernacles" because of his endlessly languishing love poetry. In his literary satire *Der romantische Ödipus* [The Romantic Oedipus, 1829], Platen portrayed Heine as a man whose kisses stank so strongly of "garlic" that every well-mannered Christian woman would surely reject him with a gesture of disgust.[6] And Platen even went so far then as to circulate a poem with the title "An den Dichterling Heine" [To the Poetaster Heine], in which he made fun of the "mutilating" circumcision of this "Hebraic joker." [7]

We know how strongly Heine reacted to these attacks later in his travel sketch *Die Bäder von Lucca* [The Baths of Lucca].[8] By contrast, in his *Book of Songs*, which appeared before this scandalous affair, he kept his Judaism mostly to himself. Although this is the esoteric main theme of many early poems, he still characterized his lover's grief in rather general terms at this time in order not to expose himself as a "Jew." For this would have spoiled all his chances to gain a foothold—at least professionally—in German Christian society, even if it was impossible for him to be accepted on human terms. Thus, in these poems love appears almost entirely as the pain of rejection—or as a fleeting erotic pleasure with young women from classes below the level of bourgeois society. But since Heine immediately encountered resistance from the *Biedermeier* critics of the early 1820s against his book of "erotic" poems, he eliminated them again when the *Book of Songs* was printed in 1827, retaining only those poems that expressed a very general longing for love, and a feeling of heartache was just as general. And this was duly honored by his critics.[9]

For these reasons, the Jewish component is expressed only in a very hidden way as a theme in this volume. Only in one place—as if Heine wanted to take revenge on all the bourgeois German Christian young women who despised him as a Jew—does the unloved persona of this volume suddenly give full vent to his irritation. This happens in the poem *Donna Clara*, where a Spanish knight totally "infatuates" the beautiful but anti-Semitic daughter of an *alcalde* with his irresistible charms. Only after she reawakens in his arms does he admit to her gloatingly that he is the "Son of the distinguished/ Eminent and learned Rabbi/Israel of Saragossa" (I: 158).[10]

In the *Book of Songs*, Jewishness appears positively (although very indirectly) only where India suddenly appears as a possible *locus amoenus*, because at this time Heine viewed India as the original homeland of the Jews. These are the passages where he dreams of love's fulfillment under "palms" or alongside "lotus blossoms" (I: 78), or where he mentions the "pine," "in the North on a bare plateau," which is dreaming of a "palm tree/ Far away in the Eastern land" (I: 88).

But with the exception of these passages, almost all the poems are about the unloved man who casts his longing glances at the German Christian girls and women, lamenting his sorrows (I: 37). They, however, treat him with the greatest suspicion and with no understanding, laugh at him mockingly, look at him without returning his love (I: 37), "hurt" him (I: 83), reject him and repulse him coldly, make him "wretched" (I: 123), "break his heart" (I: 83), "poison" him with their tears (I: 115), and "destroy" him (I: 137), to mention some of the ways of expressing unrequited love found here. And this is not all. Over and over again, this unloved man must witness how the young women to whom he would like to give his heart go ahead and "marry" someone else—even if the rival is the "stupidest of stupid young men" (I: 86). So wherever "Hans and Greta" become a couple, the "poor Peter" of this volume is always left out in the cold (I: 45).

The only thing that remains for Heine's lyric "I" in such a situation is "suffering" (I: 38), "shrill and ringing laughter" (I: 68), and the poetic effort to make "little songs" out of "great pain" (I: 89). But the poems he puts on paper in his frustration are almost all "filled with poison," as he says (I: 96). Because of the prevailing social conditions—that is, the deep abyss that separates him as a Jew from the eligible German Christian women—even the attempt to bridge this chasm with the supposedly "divine power" of love is condemned to failure from the outset. In this situation, no emotional ties can develop or even begin. And so the love being professed here is located almost entirely in a world of mere appearances. Yet indeed, it is precisely here, where these poems put into question most radically the genuineness of the feelings being expressed, that they come closest to social and psychological truth. All expressions of love or even unhappy love in such a world shaped by religious or other traditional prejudices necessarily verge on being hypocritical, mendacious, frustrated, or desperate. Therefore, as Heine himself noted, only a "malicious-sentimental" tone is appropriate here.

Accordingly, Heine's girls and women are not at all the "exalted ladies" of Petrarchism[11] who encourage men to strive toward renunciation and thus toward a better, nobler life. Rather, he portrays them for the most part as mocking, hypocritical, derisive, heartless creatures, and even as snakes and sphinxes (I: 83). But because of the general falseness of existing conditions, where there are no feelings that can bridge the abysses between religious or racial differences, even his own persona, his so-called lyric "I," can appear only as a flattering liar or a deceiving deceiver. "Hollow vows I feigned to swear, / Lying love talk false as those," it says in one place with all desirable openness. And what follows is just as revealing, namely, that his adored one has turned away from him—"with good reason" (I: 135).

In many of these poems, then, the deeply longed-for union with the beloved takes place only in a dream, in the grave, or in death. And in such verses, where Heine passes from the concrete situation to the symbolic or allegorical, it becomes even clearer that the adored woman does not stand only for some bourgeois young lady with the proper dowry, some Gretchen with violet-blue eyes, or some seductive beauty with "blonde" hair (I: 49). Rather, all of these girls and women are also manifestations of that "Germania" whom Heine had courted especially during the time he spent in the *Burschenschaften* [fraternities]. This phase in his life coincided for the most part with the period when he was writing the cycle of poetry called "Youthful Sorrows" in the *Book of Songs*. It lasted until 1820, when he was expelled from the *Burschenschaft* in

Göttingen because of being a Jew,[12] which he felt to be one of the greatest traumas of his life.

Therefore, it is certainly true that the *Book of Songs* is the "urn with the ashes of my love" (I: 149), as Heine himself declared, but love must be taken here in the broadest sense of the word: as the love of German society where Heine was rejected as a Jew not only by the members of the *Burschenschaften*, but also by the most beautiful and charming creatures there, the young women. Accordingly, the book is both an erotic *Passion* (whose unheroic hero finds himself thrown back on poetic compensation because of the impossibility of fulfilling his awakened hopes for love), as well as a social and political *Passion*. And none of the poems in this volume expresses this better in both hidden and open form than the most famous one, Heine's *Lorelei*.[13]

There is already a poem in the *Youthful Sorrows* in which the Rhine, where his "boat is sailing gaily," appears as the quintessence of the dangers threatening him. "Luring promise beckons gleaming," we read here, yet "In its heart hide death and night." And then it continues: "Stream, you ape my darling's splendor," that is, "Outward joy and inward guile" (I: 41). But while the metaphors in this poem remain unreflected and lead to no real development, they suggest deadly consequences in the second poem of the cycle *The Homecoming*, which is generally called *The Lorelei* although it has no title. The "sadness" has become even greater in the meantime (I: 107), but its cause is not divulged to the readers. And they are also not told what "old tale" "will not depart from" the mind of the poem's author. Both of these things—the sadness and the tale—point to a trauma that is being expressed in a veiled, reserved way. And the "fairest maid" who is sitting high above the cliff, combing her "golden hair," is not any kind of concretely bourgeois, German Christian figure. Rather, she remains a figure from a tale, whose "magical melody" attracts the "boatman in his little boat" so violently and unleashes such "wild-aching passions" in him that he "sees not reef or shoal" but rather only "the maiden before him." And so the poem concludes:

> I think, at last the wave swallows
> The boat and the boatman's cry;
> And this is the fate that follows
> The song of the Lorelei.

Keeping the foregoing considerations in mind, when we read these intimate, eerie verses that so skillfully imitate the tone of a folksong, we cannot help but ask who this boatman and this Lorelei really are. If there has ever been such a thing as a poem with a hidden cast of characters, then this is certainly one of the best examples. Of course, the "boatman in his boat," who embarks on the dangers of life's journey, is an ancient figure from sagas and tales. However, at this particular time, the figure has a very specific meaning for Heine, who was just introducing the figure of the Flying Dutchman into German literature in his "North Sea III" (II: 223). This boatman, this Flying Dutchman, this Wandering Jew, or whatever he may be called, is for Heine the man who is restless, whose moorings are unsecured, who is floating on a treacherous surface, who is threatened by the winds and the reefs. And yet in spite of all these dangers, he does not focus his attention solely on mastering his journey through life, as his reason commands him. Rather, he lets himself be seduced again and again into dangerous escapades by Siren-like figures of women with long "golden hair," thus becoming swept up in the most threatening whirlpools and rapids. Beyond all "rational control," this boatman is fixated in his yearning for love in what is really a "masochistic" way on an unattainable and therefore, in the final analysis, "negative" love object,[14] which can be called "Lorelei," but also "Germania." The boatman hopes for final redemption and thus emancipation if he finds acceptance, and perhaps even love from her. But she is constantly fluttering around him with fleeting temptations and enticements, or she simply spurns him, subjecting him all the time to new humiliations and frustrations. And so the only thing left for him is pain that cannot be assuaged or healed. Only the so-called fast girls, the ones who can be bought, open their doors and their bodies to him, while all the so-called better girls and women turn away from him. As a Jew, he could not "win" them even by promising to marry them.

If the "political" can be expressed in the "personal," then the *Book of Songs*, which seems so unpolitical at first glance, is actually one of the most political books in German literature. To be sure, there is no solution offered in this volume to the problems that it raises. Because of the extreme nature of his position as an outsider, the lyric "I" of this book sees himself surrounded in Germany by female figures who can do nothing but refuse him as married women under patriarchal control or as girls put on display as candidates for marriage. Consequently, before his inner eye, irritated by frustration, they take on the forms of slippery snakes or sphinx-like Sirens. To put it concisely: Germany is the rock upon which the Lorelei is sitting, and she does not care in the least whether the infatuated boatman sinks or not. However, the poem veils this esoteric reference very carefully, and it imitates the tone of a folksong of patriotic German men's singing societies as set to music by Friedrich Silcher. It could even be included in National Socialist poetry anthologies under the heading "author unknown."

As we know, it was only in the early 1830s that Heine was able to free himself from this masochistic fixation on the most beautiful and the most threatening image Germany offered him. It was in Paris, in the emancipatory teachings of Saint-Simonism, that he found that new "rock"—as it is called in the poem *Seraphine* from the cycle *Sundry Women*—upon which he hoped to build the "church of the third Testament." Here there would be no more "stupid torment of the flesh," and thus no more "suffering" (IV: 325). But after the suppression of the hopes awakened by the July Revolution, even this endeavor proved to be an illusion. And so, in the early 1840s, Heine boarded a "new boat" on "foreign waters," and embarked with "new comrades" to new shores (IV: 420). But on this boat, too, his heart became "heavy" when he thought of his fatherland, his "home," to which he remained fixed in close attachment in Paris until his death. But this is already another, larger story, which would have to encompass all these motifs in Heine's entire relationship to Germany.[15]

*Translated by Carol Poore*

## NOTES

1. Cf. Jost Hermand, *Streitobjekt Heine. Ein Forschungbericht 1945–1975* (Frankfurt: Athenäum, 1975), pp. 86–103.

2. Cf. Gerhard Höhn, *Heine Handbuch* (Stuttgart: Metzler, 1987), pp. 64–67.

3. Cf. Heine's letter to Moses Moser, 19 December 1825.

4. William Rose, *The Early Love Poetry of Heinrich Heine* (Oxford: Oxford University Press, 1962).

5. Cf. Höhn, op. cit., pp. 52ff., and my "Vom *Buch der Lieder* zu den 'Verschiedenen.' Heines zweimalige Partnerverfehlung," in Gerhard Höhn, ed., *Heinrich Heine. Ästhetisch-politische Profile* (Frankfurt: Suhrkamp, 1991), pp. 214–220.

6. August von Platen–Hallermünde, *Die verhängisvolle Gabel. Der romantische Ödipus*, Horst Denkler, ed. (Stuttgart; Reclam, 1979), pp. 176ff.

7. On this point, see my article "Heine contra Platen. Zur Anatomie eines Skandals," Rolf Hosfeld, ed., *Heinrich Heine und das neunzehnte Jahrhundert* (Berlin: Argument, 1986), p. 108.

8. Cf. my *Der frühe Heine. Ein Kommentar zu seinen "Reisebildern"* (Munich: Winckler, 1976), pp. 150–167.

9. Cf. my article "Vom *Buch der Lieder*," p. 221.

10. Quotations are taken from Heinrich Heine, *Sämtliche Schriften*, Klaus Breigleb, ed. (Munich: Hanser, 1968–). Translations are taken from Hal Draper, translator, *The Complete Poems of Heinrich Heine* (Boston: Suhrkamp, 1982).

11. On Heine's alleged Petrarchism see Manfred Windfuhr, "Heine und der Petrarchismus," Helmut Koopmann, ed., *Heinrich Heine* (Darmstadt: Wissenschaftliche Buchgesellschaft, 1975), pp. 207–231.

12. Cf. Eberhard Galley, "Heine und die Burschenschaft," *Heine Jahrbuch* 11 (1972), pp. 66ff.; and also my article, "Eine Jugend in Deutschland. Heine und die Burschenschaften," Walter Grab, ed., *Gegenseitige Einflüsse deutscher und jüdischer Kultur* (Tel Aviv: Institut für deutsche Geschichte, 1982), pp. 111–132.

13. On the following, see also the commentaries on the *Lorelei* in both the historical critical editions of Heine's works: Pierre Grappin, ed., *Düsseldorfer Heine-Ausgabe* I/2 (Hamburg: Hoffmann und Campe, 1975), pp. 879–887; Heinrich Heine, *Säkularausgabe* I, K2, Hans Böhm, ed. (Berlin: Akademieverlag; Paris: Editions du CNRS, 1982), pp. 298ff.

14. Cf. Höhn, op. cit., p. 53.

15. On this point, see Walter Hinck, *Die Wunde Deutschland. Heinrich Heines Dichtung im Widerstreit von Nationalidee, Judentum und Antisemitismus* (Frankfurt: Insel, 1990); and my article "Der 'deutsche' Jude H. Heine," Helmut Scheuer, ed., *Die Dichter und die Nation* (Frankfurt: Suhrkamp, 1992).

# Jews and Anti-Semitism in Fin-de-Siècle Vienna

## Egon Schwarz

What we have to deal with is not, as one might assume, the history of one city, but the tale of two cities. One is a city whose wonders have been celebrated in song and operetta, in poems and on canvas, in novels, plays, and films. The splendor of the Habsburg court, the sponsorship of the arts by ambitious wealthy families, the motley crowds of a multi-ethnic culture, the ceaseless arrival of foreign artists, lured to Vienna by the rumor of a light-hearted, sybaritic life—all of these factors contributed to a historic fame, the last reflections of which are still visible today.[1]

But there is another side to this city. Underneath the gilded surface are disruptions caused by a rapidly industrializing economy, the incursions of capitalism into an essentially still agricultural society, the fever of financial speculation, and the long-lasting repercussions of a stock market crash in which countless persons lost their life's savings. All this took place in a society divided along strict hierarchical lines where a double system of justice existed, one administered by the courts, the other by an honor code that led to incessant duels. The latter were illegal, but no one was willing to enforce the ban. The ideology according to which one must wash off a presumed blot on one's honor with blood was of course deeply anachronistic, but instead of weakening, it revived toward the end of the nineteenth century, causing historians to speak of a 'refeudalization' of Austrian society. At the same time there was economic hardship and poverty, inadequate housing and hygienic conditions, political tension and ethnic strife that led to violent clashes in parliament. Mark Twain described such clashes in his well-known humorous vein. But these clashes were funny only to an outsider. The widespread oppression of linguistic minorities led many to describe the vaunted multinational Empire as a multinational prison.[2] One hears mostly of the first Vienna, the glistening culture of an imperial capital. It will be my task to reveal Vienna number two, or, to be exact, one aspect of this darker underside, the virulent racial anti-Semitism rampant in the Austrian realm.

First, however, let me try to define anti-Semitism.[3] It would probably be even more appropriate to describe what 'the Jews' are, but that is so complex a problem that nobody has yet succeeded in solving it. Perhaps they are a people like others in the distant recesses of history. But when the Romans overran their country and destroyed the spiritual center of their life, the Great Temple in Jerusalem, at the beginning of our calendar, they were dispersed all over the earth and lost their unity once and for all. Soon they were found in every corner of the far-flung Roman Empire, in North Africa, in India and China, in Spain, the Balkans, and in Northern Europe. Recently, a tribe of black Jews turned up in Ethiopia and no one is sure how they wound up there. In the early Middle Ages the Khasar nation adjacent to the Black Sea converted to Judaism and soon disappeared—no one is certain where to. Some believe that they formed the ethnic substratum of the Yiddish-speaking millions in Eastern Europe. Nevertheless, all these disparate splinter populations retained a semblance of common ground in their religion, their traditions, and collective memories. But the separation of the various Jewish groups, the inevitable adaptation to their surrounding societies, the adoption of diverse languages, and a myriad of other distinguishing details made it increasingly impossible to say what they all had in common.

As so-called modernity swept across Europe during the Renaissance; as the ideas of the Enlightenment spread, beginning with the seventeenth century; and as the French Revolution initiated capitalism, democratization, and industrialization everywhere; as irresistible thrusts of secularization weakened the absolute hold religion had over the masses, none of the customary traits that characterized other ethnic and national groups sufficed to define the Jews. As the walls of their ghettos were falling, they began to live among their neighbors; as they wore the same clothes and participated in the same cultural endeavors, it became harder to recognize them as a separate entity; as the knowledge of Hebrew receded into the background and became the possession of scholars and priestly specialists; as they spoke the Spanish of the Spaniards, the French of the Frenchmen, the German of the various German-speaking territories; as large numbers abandoned the ancient rituals, converted to one of the existing Christian churches, and intermarried even with the aristocracies; as they acquired the political rights of citizenship, they became more and more indistinguishable from the nations of Europe.

The Nazis, scorners of religion and fervent adherents to the pseudo-science of racism that had developed in the nineteenth century, would have loved to prove that the Jews were a race. But the Nazis failed in their attempt. While publicly clinging to racial theory, the so-called Nuremberg Laws (1935), which spelled life or death for millions, relied on religion as the sole criterion to distinguish between Jews and non-Jews. According to the Nuremberg Laws, an Aryan or non-Jew was a person who had four *Christian* grandparents—note: Christian, not Aryan, although the Nazis allegedly despised religion as a category to determine ethnicity. Considering the many families who had undergone baptism or had intermarried with Christians, this meant that there were countless individuals in Germany and Austria in whose veins the blood was flowing that, according to the Nazis, was poisoning the nation. Incidentally the Nazis knowingly excused high-ranking collaborators whom they needed, such as General Milch and SS leader Heydrich, from the blame of Jewishness.

It is true that because of the persecution in Eastern Europe toward the end of the nineteenth century and the anti-Semitism that was growing more virulent in the West, many Jews revived the age-old idea of returning to the ancestral Jewish homeland in Palestine. The Zionists proclaimed the Jews to be a nation that had degenerated in their diaspora or dispersal but could be restored to its ancient unity. Yet such declarations really did not solve the problem. While a Jewish state was established and Hebrew successfully adopted as its official language, even today the vast majority of Jews live outside of Israel, and Israel itself is a divided and endangered state. What has happened can be described in the following way: The Jews who live scattered in all parts of the world have remained as fragmented as ever, while those living in Israel have ceased being Jewish and have become Israelis. Such is the case today. At the time with which we are dealing here, the turn of the nineteenth century, the idea of emigration into a distant barren land attracted mainly the impoverished and oppressed Jewish masses living in ghetto-like towns in Eastern Europe, but was rejected by most of the well-accommodated Jews in the West. As things stand now the Jews are a divided 'something'; they are not a race; they are not a nation; they have no unity in religion, culture, or language; at the most they share a common fate in the way they have been treated in history. Under these circumstances it is no wonder that the great French existentialist philosopher, Jean-Paul Sartre, who wrote a shrewd psychological study about the 'Jewish question,' defined a Jew as someone who thinks of himself or herself as a Jew or is regarded as a Jew by others.

Whether we accept this definition as satisfactory or not, with the reference to 'the others' we have drifted from a glance at the Jews to a consideration of anti-Semitism. I believe that more than any other force the hostility against the Jews and the restrictions imposed upon them ensured their cohesion and guaranteed their unique survival through the ages. In persecutions they clung to their faith and to one another, developing the traits that are supposed to be innately Jewish. Since they were not allowed to own land, it is not surprising that there were few farmers among them. Since they could not exercise any trades other than those related to the management of money, it is no miracle that many became financial experts. Since pressure was put on them from without, they developed a solidarity from within. Since they were constantly under suspicion, it is understandable that they should exhibit signs of nervous insecurity. Since they were periodically robbed, forcibly baptized, or burned at the stake, it is not surprising that the survivors were always on the alert and ready to change their residence. Having been expelled from Spain, from England, from France, and from many other places where they made their temporary homes, it stands to reason that they developed the mentality of fugitives, that they cherished mobile possessions, that they became timid wanderers between the nations and adopted the philosophy of *ubi bene ibi patria* [my fatherland is where I am doing well]. Paradoxically, or perhaps not so paradoxically, as soon as the Jews acquired civil rights like the majority, they became the fiercest patriots of their country of residence.

In the social sciences these phenomena are known as 'self-fulfilling prophecies': a strong assumption such as an irrational prejudice produces as a reaction in its victims the very traits they are supposed to have had in the first place. Modern historians agree that the hatred of Jews in Western societies, now ramified into every sphere of life, is basically of religious origin and largely due to persecution of the Jews by the Christian Churches and the Christian populace, from the Crusades to the eighteenth century. The Jews were accused of having murdered Christ, of the ritual slaughter of Christian children, of the willful desecration of the Host, of poisoning wells and causing the Black Plague as well as a number of other crimes, and in general of hating Christianity and plotting the takeover of the Christian world.

In its claim to both secular power and a monopoly on salvation, the Catholic Church manipulated the ignorant masses, instigating plundering and mass murder. It staged burnings at the stake, forced baptism, and mass expulsions, passed special laws and humiliating dress codes, and ordered the exclusion of Jews from respectable occupations and their incarceration in ghettos. These punitive measures could succeed because of the economic interests involved and because they were directed against a defenseless minority, a convenient scapegoat for the punishment, which was a welcome diversion from real problems.

The Reformation brought no relief. For a while Luther seemed more favorably inclined toward the Jews, hoping to convert them to his brand of Christianity. But when they proved obdurate he turned against them with a vengeance.[4] Henceforth, the Protestant Churches did not treat the Jews any better than their Catholic predecessor. Emperors and princes, estates and towns regarded the Jews, who had paid them large sums for their so-called protection, as merchandise, which they pawned, sold, or traded away at will. The financial claims of the Jews were often canceled by decree or wiped out by looting and massacres. Papal bulls, anti-Jewish sermons, polemic treatises, inflammatory pamphlets, literary and pictorial caricatures poured out of the poison of hatred and derision into the masses, laying the foundations for a bias that made possible the pogroms of the nineteenth and the mass exterminations of the twentieth century. Since we are dealing here with modern anti-Semitism I cannot dwell on pre-modern practices, but I considered it necessary at least to touch upon the medieval roots of Judeophobia.

The period in which modern anti-Semitism gained sweeping momentum was the second half of the nineteenth century. Legal and social emancipation brought about the gradual integration of the Jews into all European societies, reducing their recognizability on the basis of residence, etc. Thus, new methods of exclusion had to be devised if the role of the Jews as lightning rods and scapegoats was not to be lost. This is the moment in history that saw the birth of racial anti-Semitism. Its function was to recast ancient Christian prejudices against the Jews in a new mold and to make the stigma of being Jewish ineradicable by baptism or any other means. In addition to mingling traditional religious and economic accusations with new sociobiological ones, modern anti-Semitism is distinguished by three more features: it creates an interlocking system of beliefs that encompasses all of history; it serves mass movements as their central ideology; and it helps those threatened by industrialization to wrest power from the privileged and successful.

It has also great psychological advantages in that it strengthens the self-esteem of weak characters, giving them the feeling of belonging to a *Gemeinschaft*, a natural community, and channels diffuse anxieties in one single direction. The spectacular successes of the natural sciences and technology, the transfer of Darwin's concept of the 'survival of the fittest' from the realm of nature to the realm of society, and the rise of all kinds of racial and biologistic theories had prepared the ground.

This story has been told often enough. A flood of incendiary anti-Semitic writings inundated the world, political groups whose sole aim was the incrimination of Jews were formed, and anti-Semites were elected to parliaments. While at first they did not have much practical political impact, little by little their doctrines were incorporated into the ideological baggage of large political parties, thus acquiring 'respectability.' To show that we are not dealing with isolated aberrations but a madness with a method, let me glance at a widely-read book, one of many like-minded ones, by the French anti-Semite Alphonse Toussenel, *Les juifs, rois de l'époque* [The Jews, Kings of the Epoch].[5] This work had a demonstrable impact on an even more popular work, Edouard Drumont's *La France Juive* [Jewish France]. It can be maintained that Drumont unleashed the anti-Semitism that precipitated the infamous Dreyfus Affair and divided the country. The very first paragraph of Toussenel's frequently republished book starts with the following revealing statement:

> I use the despised term 'Jew' to designate not only Jews themselves, but any petty dealer, any unproductive parasite who lives on the substance and labor of his fellow man. Jew, usurer, money changer are synonyms for me.[6]

Toussenel acknowledges having been reproached for invoking the name of an actually existing people in order to denounce despicable behavior and repulsive activities in general. His answer was that he had to do this because he could not find in his language a word other than Jew to express the abuses he wished to lambast. He ends his diatribe with the following astonishing words: "Not all Jews I attack are from Judäa" (Toussenel, p. XI), making it patent that Judaism is a mere symbol, Judeophobia nothing but a manipulative psychological expedient. Such a black-and-white system of thought is generally referred to as Manichaeism. It operates with a bipolar logic that divides all phenomena into good ones and bad ones, focusing the world's woes on a single target for the purpose of ridding the universe of evil once and for all. By excluding the Jews, society will be cured of all its defects. Such gross simplifications give rise to a strange circular thinking characteristic of the racial anti-Semites: All Jews are evil, all evil is Jewish. In this manner it becomes possible to blame the Jews for contradictory phenomena, for example, pacifism and war mongering, communism and capitalism, at the same time. Such incompatibilities are not recognized as flaws of logic but are blamed on the Jews themselves who are supposed to create all these 'isms' in order to attain their overriding goal of enslaving the Christians and ruling the world.

This sleight-of-hand mechanism is repeated in practically all countries with a Christian background. There is no language in which no anti-Semitic pamphlets have been published. Some go so far in dehumanizing the Jews as to relegate them to the status of insects. "One must have the courage," says the nineteenth-century German anti-Semite Paul de Lagarde, a respected scholar of Oriental languages, "to trample the Jews, this proliferating vermin, to death. You don't negotiate with trichinae and bacteria, nor can trichinae and bacteria be educated; they must be annihilated as quickly and thoroughly as possible."[7] These are barely disguised incitations to genocide. The Nazis did not have to invent anything. They merely had to put into practice what had long been elaborated in theory. It is no accident that this anti-Semitic ideology soon found its way into works of fiction as well, carrying it into broad segments of society through popular novels that are published and republished to this day.

Even though there is no instrument to measure such elusive emotions, it is difficult to resist the impression that anti-Semitism in Austria reached an even more virulent intensity than in the German *Reich*. Historical reasons can be adduced to reinforce this assertion. One was the acquisition by the Habsburg monarchy of Eastern provinces where large numbers of Jews were settled in little towns and villages. Driven by economic pressure and lured by the promises of an expanding capitalism, they began migrating to the West, with Vienna as a favorite destination.[8] The Jews already present and well established in the capital saw with disfavor the arrival of great masses of Eastern Jews who were immediately recognizable as strangers by their dress and hairdos, their religious customs, and their Yiddish language. Due to this influx the Jewish element in the city reached 10 percent by the turn of the century. But this number must be supplemented by those Jews who did not belong to the *Kultusgemeinde*, the organization officially recognized as the representation of the Jews of Vienna. Many of those who were completely assimilated and estranged from the religion of their forebears did not care to be members of this organization and therefore did not show up as Jews in any census, nor did the many who actually converted to one of the Christian denominations, be it for reasons of conviction or convenience. The same applies to their offspring. The rate of intermarriage between Jews and non-Jews was high. When the Nazis occupied Austria, introducing the Nuremberg laws, all of a sudden the number of Jews and descendants of Jews shot up much beyond the official 10 percent.

The artisans and small shopkeepers of Vienna, as well as other strata of the population who felt put at a disadvantage by the new industrialization and speculative capitalism, could easily unload all manner of resentment upon the conspicuous newcomers, but of course they lumped them together with the rest of their co-religionists. This was true of other societies, notably Germany and France, but not to this numerical and qualitative extent.

Another Austrian peculiarity was the multi-ethnic composition of the Empire where innumerable nationalities and linguistic groups lived together in various degrees of tension. "Irredentism," that nineteenth-century word for national liberation, produced additional fuel for anti-Semitism. Since the Jews were the only minority distributed all over the Austro-Hungarian territories and the one most loyal to the monarchy—the reason why they were dubbed the *Staatsvolk*, the state people—all the dissatisfied ethnic minorities could hold them responsible for their real and imagined grievances. If they adapted themselves to one nationality, they alienated others. When the Jews of Hungary, for instance, shed their stigmatized German orientation and became Hungarian super patriots, they did not endear themselves to the nationalities the Hungarians were oppressing, such as the Slovaks and the Croatians. A symbolic date to remember is the crash of the stock market in 1873, which reverberated through the entire Empire. It was blamed on the Jews and unleashed a fury of anti-Semitism that was never to abate entirely.

In this explosive situation two particularly aggressive movements have to be singled out, those of Georg von Schönerer and Karl Lueger. Since they have been analyzed in depth numerous times by scholars such as Peter Pulzer and Carl Schorske, I will merely point out in this essay that the two movements differed mainly in their attitude toward the dynasty.[9] Schönerer and his adherents were Pan-Germans, enemies of the Habsburgs, advocating the incorporation of the German-speaking Austrians into the *Reich*. This *Anschluss* [annexation] was finally engineered in 1938 when Hitler annexed Austria. In contrast to Schönerer, Karl Lueger remained loyal to the dynasty, relying on the support of the Catholic Church as well as the Catholic masses. But Schönerer and Lueger had a central concern in common, anti-Semitism, the putty that held their fragmented constituencies together, the fuel that inflamed their passions.

Of the two, Lueger, a populist, was by far the more adroit politician. The Christian Socialist party he founded was destined to have lasting successes; it was the party of Austro-Fascism between the wars, and today's ÖVP, the Austrian People's Party, is its direct offspring. Resorting to anti-Semitic rabble rousing, Lueger was elected to public office several times and, after initially resisting, the Emperor had to consent to his being installed as Mayor of Vienna in 1897. The *Osservatore Romano*, the official mouthpiece of the Vatican, followed up with a campaign of vilification of Jews and Liberalism, regarded as twin phenomena. Thus it was really the first time that a declared anti-Semite became the head of an important European metropolis, occupying a position of prestige and power.

Let me make clear that Lueger also used anti-Semitism with cynical demagogy to capture votes. He was often accused by purists of privately consorting with Jews while abusing them in public. His answer became famous: *Wer a Jud is bestimm i* [I decide who is a Jew]. Even more explicit is the opportunistic analysis of the uses of anti-Semitism in the following statement:

> Since anti-Semitism has contributed substantially to the development, expansion and power of the Christian Socialist Party, we shall continue to make use of this reactionary principle in future political actions until it ceases to be a source of strength.[10]

Such naive admissions clearly show that it is not the leaders alone who manipulate the innocent and gullible masses. On the contrary, they could count on a widespread and deep-seated prejudice that had been fanned by centuries of religious indoctrination.

As one can read in *Mein Kampf*, anti-Semitism in fin-de-siècle Vienna influenced Adolf Hitler profoundly when he lived in the city as a young man. The figure and the political maneuvers of Lueger became models he admired and emulated. It should not be forgotten that Hitler was born in the Austrian town of Braunau and that he is the typical product of the turn-of-the-century anti-Semitic subculture of Austria. Nor do I attribute it to statistical accident that so many of the extermination and concentration camp henchmen were Austrians. The events surrounding the Waldheim election in 1986 demonstrate how slowly old prejudices die. There is a phenomenon observable in present-day Austria—but not only in Austria, there are other instances, for example Japan—that can be called anti-Semitism without Jews.

Political anti-Semitism would have been bad enough. But there existed an even more pervasive social anti-Semitism that impregnated the atmosphere in which the Jews had to live their daily lives. An indication of its increasing strength is the attitude of the students. They were organized in so-called *schlagende Burschenschaften*, fencing fraternities, whose ritualistic duels dominated university life. The duel, a medieval relic given up as an anachronism in other societies, served to maintain social divisions. There were those whose *honor* had to be defended with the sword at the slightest provocation and those lower social echelons who were excluded from the ritual. A *Gymnasium* education was the dividing criterion. Jews had been accepted into these feudalistic fencing societies. Theodor Herzl, the founder of Zionism, was a member. He left only after an anti-Semitic plank was inserted into the statutes. Fraternity anti-Semitism reached such dimensions that a big rally was held outside Vienna in 1882, and a resolution adopted the wording the Viennese playwright and novelist Arthur Schnitzler recorded in his autobiography *Jugend in Wien* [Youth in Vienna]:

> Every son of a Jewish mother, every person with Jewish blood in his veins is without honor by virtue of his birth and lacks all finer impulses. He is ethically inferior. Therefore, association with a Jew discredits. All dealings with Jews are to be avoided. A Jew cannot be insulted, hence a Jew cannot demand satisfaction for any insults addressed to him.[11]

No one can miss the characteristic ring of aristocratic pseudo-poetry mixed with the modern tone of racial anti-Semitism in this rhetoric. Of course, being excluded from the dueling honor code meant relegation to a second-class social status.

Let me give another example of the social anti-Semitism that poisoned fin-de-siècle Austria. The protagonists are two Austrian poets of great stature, both natives of Prague, Rainer Maria Rilke, already a celebrity at the time, and young Franz Werfel, who was just then breaking into the public sphere with his expressionist poetry. This is what Rilke had to say about their first encounter in a letter to his aristocratic friend and sponsor, Princess Marie von Thurn und Taxis:

> I saw a great deal of Werfel.... It was sad, "a Jew-boy" said Sidie Nadherny, taken aback, and she wasn't wrong. I had been about to open my arms to this youth, but instead of doing so I folded them behind my back like some indifferent person taking a walk. Ten times a day I repeated to myself that this was the poet who had wrought all these wonders. In his absence I was still able to feel enthusiasm for him, but when he was around I felt so embarrassed that I couldn't look him in the face. Not that he was unpleasant, on the contrary he was extremely intelligent, perhaps too much so for the good of his poetry, which suffered when you thought of it as contrived, cleverly calculated by a Jewish sense of merchandise.... For the first time I felt the mendacity of the Jewish mind, which is separated from everything that binds us together and yet manages to talk about it, nourished by an almost negative mode of experiencing. It is a mentality that infiltrates all things without possessing them, like a poison that penetrates everything, taking revenge for not belonging to an organic whole.[12]

The elaborate syntax and select vocabulary in this passage serve to couch the crude clichés of the prevalent anti-Semitism in terms acceptable to members of the more refined high society. Deprived of its disguise the message conveys that there is something physically disgusting about a Jew. Innocently one approaches him, and though nothing repulsive in the ordinary sense adheres to him, one recoils, nauseated by the aura that surrounds him. The Jew is bright, this much is conceded, but his very brightness prevents true poetry from welling up from within his unconscious. For the Jew is first and foremost a rationalist. When poetry and Jewishness coincide, the result is artificiality, fabrication. The Jew pretends to be an inspired poet, wresting his creation from the intuitive depths, but this is pure pretense for commercial reasons. For the Jew regards poems—like everything else—from the point of view of business. It is an example of the falseness and rootless negativity of the Jewish spirit, which does not know deep attachments to anything and yet is capable of discussing everything. The Jew is a parasite who revenges himself for his exclusion from the communal organism by spraying his poison everywhere. Put in these terms, the message is the same as that in countless anti-Jewish pamphlets.

Franz Werfel, the centenary of whose birth was recently celebrated in Vienna, would have been saddened had he been aware of this letter and deeply shocked if he had known that Rilke penned it. For us it characterizes the anti-Semitic atmosphere that enveloped this society from its nether regions to the highest cultural sphere.

It is therefore all the more remarkable that so many Jews reached renown and prominence in the spheres of Austrian culture and indeed represented that culture before the world. Looking around, one is astonished to discover that a large number of the fin-de-siècle luminaries were Jews or of Jewish extraction. Let us cast a glance at some areas of cultural activity to confirm this view.

I can of course mention only the most prominent names such as Edmund Husserl, the founder of phenomenology, and Ludwig Wittgenstein, the son of a very wealthy Jewish family, two of the most important philosophers of the twentieth century. And if we construe the notion of fin-de-siècle very broadly, we can add the names of Martin Buber and those Jewish members of the Vienna Circle of philosophy who had a lasting impact on the development of philosophy in the United States.

The founder of psychoanalysis, a movement that conquered and transformed the world, was Sigmund Freud; he remained conscious of his Judaism as a positive force despite his atheism. Most of the other psychoanalysts of this school were also Jewish. So was his most famous dissident, Alfred Adler. Otto Weininger who committed suicide at the age of twenty-three acquired posthumous fame, or more accurately, notoriety, with his *Geschlecht und Charakter* [Sex and Character]—I will return to him at a later point.

In music we have to refer to the composer Gustav Mahler who was also the conductor of the world-famous Vienna Opera, and Arnold Schönberg, the inventor of the twelve-tone system of composition, sometimes mislabeled 'atonal music.' In literature there were Arthur Schnitzler, Karl Kraus, Peter Altenberg, Richard Beer–Hofmann, Alfred Polgar, Felix Salten, Joseph Roth, Hermann Broch, and many others. Hugo von Hofmannsthal, best known in the United States as the librettist of many operas by Richard Strauß, the most famous of which is no doubt *Der Rosenkavalier* [The Cavalier of the Roses], was only in part Jewish, but he owed his social standing to the prestige and wealth of his great-grandfather who had been nobilitated by the Emperor, hence the *von* in his name.

Moritz Szeps and Moritz Benedikt, the editors of influential newspapers, were Jews, and so were many of the journalists[13] and authors of the famous feuilletons such as Egon Erwin Kisch, Theodor Herzl, Max Nordau, and Theodor Hertzka. Also Jewish were the linguist Fritz Mauthner, the philosopher of law Hans Kelsen, the anatomist Julius Tandler, the theater director Max Reinhard, the sociologists Max Adler and Josef Redlich, whose disciple Paul Lazarsfeld came to the United States and introduced empirical, statistically-oriented sociology into American universities. Of great historical significance were the founders and leaders of the Social Democratic Party, the so-called Austro-Marxists, Viktor Adler and Otto Bauer, whose intellectual offspring Bruno Kreisky shaped the political destiny of the Second Austrian Republic.

Add to all of these the Jewish *salons* such as that of the Wertheimsteins, where the city's intelligentsia assembled, and the many rich Jewish families who supported the arts in other ways. Add the theaters, including the famous *Burgtheater*, with their succession of widely acclaimed Jewish actors, the Jewish song, waltz, and operetta composers (even the famous Strausses were of Jewish descent), the opera and operetta singers, and last but not least the enthusiastic Jewish audiences who kept this enormous edifice intact. One must come to the conclusion that the Jews, as the anti-Semites vociferously lamented, actually played a preponderant role in the cultural life of fin-de-siècle Vienna.

In view of this reality the question has often been raised, what caused the conditions that favored the Jewish prominence in Austria. The anti-Semites attributed it to demonic qualities in the Jews, their uncanny shrewdness, their unscrupulous business practices, their insatiable thirst for money and power. A more dispassionate analysis would probably explore the phenomenon along the lines of drive and opportunity. First, one has to recognize that certainly not all Jews were successful. The majority lived in the districts of Leopoldstadt and Brigittenau, and led lackluster existences in dearth and mediocrity. If indeed possible, it takes two, three, or more generations for a cohesive group of immigrants to move up. Take for example the rise of the Eastern

Jews from the squalor of Hester Street and the sweatshops of the Lower East Side in New York to the relative affluence of their grandchildren.

This leads to the consideration of opportunity. For centuries the Jews had lived in abject poverty in the Eastern parts of Europe, in the regions that are now Russia, Poland, Latvia, Lithuania, Hungary, Romania, without the slightest hope for economic prosperity or artistic prominence. This fact alone suffices, in my opinion, to deflate theories advanced by some to the effect that Jews possess natural abilities that will somehow prevail everywhere in spite of all historical afflictions. Guilt and atonement, election and trial, enslavement and redemption—all these vague and mythic conceptions are derived from the one underlying idea of the Jews as the Chosen People. The need to explain the disproportionate success of a minority that was either half-heartedly tolerated or brutally persecuted has evoked eccentric hypotheses of all sorts.

A sociohistorical orientation leads to different methods of analysis. Such an approach emphasizes the fact that Jews were limited by society to certain manual trades and commercial occupations. This meant that they had an urban middle-class status imposed upon them in times that were still half feudal. In the East, too, Jews were town dwellers who were engaged in active dealing with a rural peasant population. The superiority of the clever, eloquent, agile, and literate traders over the villagers, close to the soil and schooled only in the rhythms of nature, is a phenomenon known even in antiquity and by no means limited to Jews. Phoenicians and Armenians in the Mediterranean region, Chinese in some Asian countries, and Indians in Africa have experienced a similar fate under comparable conditions. Literally bursting out of their Galician *shtetl* as a result of changing conditions, those lower-middle-class traders and craftsmen entered a dynamic and volatile world. Accustomed to privation, alienation, and hostility, expecting neither sympathy nor assistance, held back for centuries in poverty and humble circumstances, they suddenly found new horizons of expectation. Arriving in Vienna, they found themselves cast into a seething cauldron filled with a variety of ethnic groups and nationalities and exposed to a situation of expansion that demanded of them to develop all their talents.

Their typical progression was repeated so often that one can almost see it as an unavoidable paradigm: departure from the Eastern ghetto; entrance into a branch of trade, business, or industry; the rise to relative affluence; marriage to the daughter of an already assimilated family. Better educated than her husband, she filled her children with the love for German culture and German literature in particular. When the offspring of these unions grew up, they sometimes devoted themselves to the improvement of their father's businesses, but just as often they turned to a profession such as medicine or law. Their children in turn became intellectuals, artists, writers, musicians. Of course this sequence was accompanied by a mental development, as its end product already indicated: the loss of orthodoxy, indeed of almost the entire

Jewish cultural heritage, sometimes even the adoption of the Christian religion, renunciation of Yiddish in everyday speech and of Hebrew as the sacred language, adaptation of Western manners, assimilation.

We can now survey the chain of causality that explains at least in general terms why so many Jews were found in the intellectual spheres of Vienna at the turn of the century and beyond, before their fate took a tragic turn in 1938. Thomas Mann described this process in his famous novel *Buddenbrooks* for which he received the Nobel Prize. It must be noted, however, that his protagonists are not Jewish, they are Christian burghers of the North German town of Lübeck with Mann's own family as the main models. This points to the fact that the development of the Jews in Austria–Hungary is not all that unique. For the European bourgeoisie, education and culture were tools in the struggle against the aristocracy. The Jews, largely bourgeois and urban, merely represent a subclass in a more general process. In their case the prejudice they encountered made their struggle more difficult, but it also spurred them on to great achievements. Many Jews told themselves that they had to be twice as good as the others to succeed.

To move from the realm of abstraction to concrete examples, I should like to quote from an anthology entitled *Jüdische Portraits* [Jewish Portraits] in which an enterprising German journalist, Herlinde Koelbl, interviewed a number of Central European Jews, asking them in essence the same question we have been posing: Why did the Jews play such an extraordinary role in the cultural life of many countries? One of her interviewees was the Viennese writer Georg Stefan Troller who became famous for his film *Whereto and Back* in which he documented the exodus and subsequent fate of Viennese and other Jews. His answer to the question was:

> It would be necessary to investigate to what extent this is really true. The assertion that the Jews occupied too many leading positions was abused for propaganda purposes. Still the thing was quite simple: the Jews did not want to be locked up in the ghetto. But to gain the same rights, they had to make an effort. And because they couldn't be farmers or generals, they advanced themselves as doctors, lawyers, movie and theater directors, writers and journalists.

Let me also quote the answer given to the same question by the famous Viennese conductor Erich Leinsdorf, now living in New York: "I think," he said, "the Jews did what they were allowed to do with ambition and diligence."

> And because their entire existence was at stake, they became especially capable in these fields, be it as bankers or violin virtuosos. It's all the same. And since you can't forbid people from thinking, a considerable number of great thinkers came from Jewry. As far as the great musical talents are concerned, I believe a lot depends on the mother. (Koelbl, pp. 161f.)

It is clear that these personal views, their simplicity notwithstanding, parallel the more complex analysis we have attempted. We have painted a picture with islands of successes and achievement arising out of a churning sea of prejudice, discrimination, and hatred. How did the Jews react to this situation? They were certainly not passive, but devised a plethora of psychological schemes of adjustment, pathological escape mechanisms, and programs of social action. Through their organizations they protested against false accusations and injustice in the courts, bureaucracies, or the private sphere. Cries for greater assimilation and against the influx of Eastern Jews could be heard. Some owners of overly tender souls even committed suicide. Intermarriage and conversion to the Christian religion were on the increase. It is strange to find out that at one point in his career Theodor Herzl, who would later become the prime mover of the Zionist idea, advocated the mass conversion of the Jews as an antidote to their plight. He daydreamed of a long procession of Jewish converts-to-be streaming into St. Stephen's Cathedral, with himself as the leader and instigator of this act of self-effacement. And Zionism itself must be counted among the strongest remedies to the diseased state in which Jews were living. The hope of some day returning to Jerusalem had never died out among religious Jews; it was part of their ritual, and now and then messiah-like figures would arise who pretended to lead the Jews back to their ancient homeland, of course without succeeding. But now at the turn of the century, as a result of a new, organized, and politicized anti-Semitism, a *renouveau juif* was taking place, a renewal and reinvigoration of Jewish culture. Many young Jews rebelled against their parents' fruitless attempts to assimilate themselves to an unwilling majority, to hide or minimize their Jewish identity. Sensing that all attempts at coexistence had failed and that their continued presence was threatened with danger to life and limb, many Jews reaffirmed their Jewishness by cultivating the Jewish heritage and advocating an exodus to Palestine.

In his novel *Der Weg ins Freie* [The Road to Freedom] Arthur Schnitzler presented his readers with a gallery of Jewish types, each exemplifying a different aspect of the multiple attitudes available to them at that moment in history.[14] There is the successful businessman who clings to his Judaism in the face of his family's embarrassment. There is his son who flirts with an aristocratic lifestyle and conversion. There is the Jew who joins the Social Democrats, hoping that social revolution will eliminate class warfare and anti-Semitism, and there is the upright Jew without illusions who is willing to defend his spot in the world without budging and without cringing before his enemies. But in the end it all boils down to a clash of ideas between those who would emigrate in order to establish a Jewish national home in Palestine and those who would stay where they are, namely in their beloved Vienna, and make the best of their condition. I shall paraphrase significant passages from a discussion in which a Zionist defends his position vis-à-vis a writer, Heinrich Bermann, a replica of Schnitzler himself, who holds opposite views:

> It is not a question of the few Jewish government officials who are not promoted, the few Jewish army volunteers who are not given professorships or only with great delay—these are inconveniences of a low order so to speak; we are concerned with entirely different people whom you don't know well enough or not at all, about whom you haven't thought sufficiently even though you had an obligation to do so: old men, not at all uneducated, on the contrary, learned wise men who were crying because they were afraid of never reaching the land of their ancestors, afraid that even if the boldest Zionist plans became a reality their children and grandchildren might not be able to settle there.[15]

Bermann defends his position with equal eloquence. He regards

> Zionism as the worst affliction ever besetting the Jews. . . . Nationalism and religion, these words, in their frivolous and insidious superficiality, had always enraged him. The idea of a fatherland was pure fiction, a concept of politics, vague, changeable, not to be pinned down. Only the concept of home was real, . . . and so was the feeling of home, the right to a home. [And it was Vienna where he was born that he regarded as his home.] As far as *he* was concerned he felt no ties of community with anyone, absolutely no one on earth. Not with the crying Jews who attended the Zionist Congress in Basel, not with the boisterous Pan-Germans in the Austrian parliament; neither with Jewish usurers nor with robber barons from the high aristocracy; with a Zionist innkeeper as little as with a Christian-Socialist grocer. Never would he feel bound to people who were alien to him just because he knew that he and they shared the experience of persecution and of a hatred that burdened them both. He was willing to accept Zionism as a moral principle and as a welfare measure if the Zionists honestly stuck to such goals; but the idea of erecting a Jewish state on a religious and national basis seemed to him to be a senseless rebellion against the spirit of historical evolution. (Schnitzler 1978, p. 93)

The following are the thoughts of the Gentile aristocrat who is witness to this debate between two fundamental Jewish viewpoints:

> An understanding of this people's mysterious fate dawned upon him, a fate that found expression in each and every one of its members, in those who endeavored to escape from their origin as if it were a disgrace, a pain, or a fairy tale without relevance as well as in those who pointed to it as a fate, an honor or an irreversible fact of history. (Schnitzler 1978, p. 94)

Arthur Schnitzler himself was one of those upright Jews to whom I have alluded. Unflinchingly he acknowledged the sociopsychological fact of anti-Semitism, but he insisted on living out his life as a Jew in Vienna, the city he regarded as his emotional home.

There is one Jewish reaction to anti-Semitism we have not dealt with yet, Jewish self-hatred. Of all the many forms and shadings that anti-Semitism is capable of assuming, this is certainly the strangest one. And yet it was widespread. Let me cite the example of Karl Kraus, a prolific writer, a gifted thinker, a great figure of literature who had countless readers and is still an important subject of scholarship. He was born of wealthy Jewish parents in Bohemia, but raised in Vienna from childhood on. In 1911 he was baptized a Catholic, remaining in the Church until 1923. In his journal *Die Fackel* [The Torch], he attacked in skillful satires the venality, the corruption, and hypocrisy of contemporary society. Himself a master stylist, his yardstick was language, the purity of which he endowed with magical attributes. With symbolic intent he once sued a printer for having misplaced a comma in one of his writings. He was convinced that, no matter how hard it tried to disguise itself, a dishonest mind would be revealed in its linguistic acts. Kraus identified the linguistic and moral corruption around him with capitalism and with the resulting decline of the Habsburg Empire. But fundamentally he was a conservative. "Politically," he said, "I have not even progressed as far as the French Revolution." Thus his anti-capitalism must be classified "as coming from the right" (Schnitzler 1968, p. 94). Kraus was one of the few writers who rejected World War I from the very beginning. One of his literary achievements is *Die letzten Tage der Menschheit* [The Last Days of Mankind] in which he denounces this war.[16] It is probably the greatest pacifist play of all times. Obviously I cannot do justice to the work in this article. Suffice it to say that the scenery is half of Europe, the war front, the *Hinterland*, private homes, the squares and streets of Vienna; and that every possible crime, every hypocrisy, every lie and folly perpetrated in that war are castigated with Kraus's implacable incisiveness and sharpness of wit.

But one peculiar trait of this play must be emphasized in the interest of our topic. While no one in its pages is left unscathed, it is the Jewish merchants, newspaper men and women, as well as war profiteers that Kraus, himself a Jew, denounces the most unsparingly. Such Jewish self-hatred was a consequence of the general anti-Semitism endemic in Viennese society. How can we explain this self-destructive trait? One of the most malignant side-effects of a ubiquitously practiced discrimination is the poisoning of the victims themselves. Subject to all currents in their environment, they absorb with the air, so to speak, the very venom concocted by their enemies. Psychologists call this mechanism internalization. Karl Kraus was by no means alone in hating himself as a Jew; he merely exemplifies a widespread phenomenon. Jewish self-hatred could take on many forms, such as subservience to the Gentile majority, neurotic timidity and self-effacement, frantic assimilation, baptism, and, as I have indicated, even suicide, all instances of what Jean-Paul Sartre describes as "inauthentic behavior" in his treatise on the 'Jewish Question.'[17]

Let me return to the case of Otto Weininger, active in the same period. An unbalanced and morbid genius, much admired by Karl Kraus and his circle, Weininger illustrates every conceivable negative reaction to the Jewish condition: anti-Semitic self-castigation, conversion (in his case to Protestantism), and finally suicide. I have already mentioned his major work, a 600-page treatise entitled *Geschlecht und Charakter* [Sex and Character].[18] The study went through dozens of editions and was translated into a host of languages. It is a merciless invective against women and Jews, based on biological metaphysics, disguised as science, which was typical of the time. Misogyny, be it said *en passant*, was another contemporary affliction. The Nazis loved Weininger's work and were fond of citing it against those of the author's own religious background. Today, almost a century later, his ideas seem absurd. But at the time and long after the author's death they found many adherents. Dietrich Eckart, Hitler's mentor and the editor of the official Nazi newspaper *Der völkische Beobachter*, was one of Weininger's admirers. Otto Weininger, he declared, was the only decent Jew he knew of.

Weininger's world is a strictly dualistic one, divided into the feminine and masculine principles. Even the individual cell, indeed protoplasm itself, is feminine or masculine. In the human being neither of the two entities ever appears in its pure form, but all the good qualities are supposedly masculine while every vice and every baseness in the world is reserved for the feminine principle. Man is creative, logical, intellectual, ethical, and capable of genius, whereas woman embodies the exact opposites of all these virtues. Weininger distinguishes between two basic types of women: the prostitute and the mother. As prostitute she represents the essence of lasciviousness as opposed to love, as mother she is a possessive hyena.

But there is an anti-Semitic twist as well: Jews are the most feminine men of all. They are afflicted with the same physical and mental failings as women. Like women they lack an ego, which Weininger considers the seat of self-esteem, hence they are lascivious and amoral; they are pimps. By a curious flash of insight Weininger cites Jewish self-hatred as proof of their innate inferiority. To him Jews are shameless materialists, their rationalist tendencies supposedly corrode idealism, they lean toward Communism, empiricism, and atheism—all of which Weininger deplored. Indeed, he stated that Jews were worse than women, who at least find moral support in looking up to and believing in men. Weininger considered Zionism a paradox. Since Jews hated themselves, they would be incapable of living in a state where all inhabitants were Jews. Added to all their other weaknesses he perceived the inability of Jews to grasp the idea of the state. Weininger admired naked power and ruthless efficiency. Jewish passivity he equated with feminine weakness. Only as a strong individual, he claimed, could a Jew overcome his Jewishness. He drew the bitter consequences of his theories. In 1903 he rented a room in the house where Beethoven had died and put a bullet through his heart.

These examples of different variations of anti-Semitism, Jewish or otherwise, have to suffice to make my point. Cultural life in fin-de-siècle Vienna has been compared to a veritable explosion, akin to a nova in the starry universe. The metaphor is well chosen since it alludes both to the blinding beauty and the unbridled ferocity of the phenomenon. For reasons we have tried to elucidate, Jews played an eminent, indeed, a crucial role in the creation of this culture. In my opinion they would not have reached such heights without anti-Semitism. But I am convinced that, conversely, without anti-Semitism this same culture would not have met with such an ignominious demise.

NOTES

1. That Vienna to which the exhibition at the Künstlerhaus, "Traum und Wirklichkeit" [Dream and Reality] in 1985 was dedicated.
2. Cf. Steven Beller, *Vienna and the Jews. 1867–1938* (New York: Cambridge University Press, 1980); idem, "Class Culture and the Jews of Vienna, 1900," *Jews, Antisemitism and Culture in Vienna*, Oxaal, Pollak, and Botz, eds. (London: Routledge, 1987).
3. Cf. Vamberto Morais, *A Short History of Anti-Semitism* (New York: Norton, 1976).
4. Martin Luther, "Von den Juden und ihren Lügen," *Luthers Sämmtliche Schriften*, Reformationsschriften, vol. XX, Walsh, ed. (St. Louis: Lutherischer Concordia-Verlag, 1890), 1860–2029.
5. Alphonse Toussenel, *Les juifs, rois de l'époque* (Paris: E. Denty, 1888), p. IX. Translations from other languages are my own.
6. Ibid., p. XI.
7. Paul de Lagarde, "Judentum," *Ausgewählte Schriften* (Munich: Lehmann 1924).
8. Joseph Roth, "Juden auf Wanderschaft," *Werke in drei Bänden* (Cologne: Kiepenheuer & Witsch, 1956), pp. 625–690. Here: "Wien," pp. 657ff.
9. Peter Pulzer, *The Rise of Political Anti-Semitism in Germany and Austria* (Cambridge, MA: Harvard University Press, 1988); Carl E. Scorske, *Fin-de-Siècle Vienna: Politics and Culture* (New York: Knopf, 1979).
10. From the newspaper *Die Reichspost* (10 October 1936). Quoted in *Antisemitismus in Österreich*, John Bunzl and Bernd Marin, eds. (Innsbruck: Inn, 1983), p. 30.
11. Arthur Schnitzler, *Jugend in Wien. Eine Autobiographie* (Vienna, Munich, Zurich: Molden, 1968), p. 156. Written 1915–1920.
12. Rainer Maria Rilke and Marie Thurn und Taxis, *Briefwechsel*, vol. I, Ernst Zinn, ed. (Zurich: Niehaus & Rokitansky, 1951), pp. 323–324. Written in Paris, 21 October 1913.
13. Herlinde Koelbl, *Jüdische Portraits* (Frankfurt am Main: Fischer, 1989), pp. 245–250.
14. Arthur Schnitzler, "Der Weg ins Freie," *Gesammelte Werke. Die erzählenden Schriften* I (Frankfurt am Main: Fischer, 1961), pp. 720–722. Also Arthur Schnitzler, *Das erzählerische Werk* IV (Frankfurt am Main: Fischer, 1978).
15. Some passages in this essay are English renderings from my article "Schmelztiegel oder Hexenkessel? Juden und Antisemiten im Wien der Jahrhundertwende," in *Dichtung, Kritik, Geschichte. Essays zur Literatur 1900–1933*, Egon Schwarz, ed. (Göttingen: Vandenhoeck & Ruprecht, 1983). Schnitzler, *Das erzählerische Werk* IV, p. 92.
16. Karl Kraus, *Die letzten Tage der Menschheit* (Frankfurt: Suhrkamp, 1986).

Theodor Lessing referred to Kraus as a "leuchtendes Beispiel" of self-hatred in *Jüdischer Selbsthaß* (Berlin: Jüdischer Verlag, 1930), p. 43.

17. Jean-Paul Sartre, *Anti-Semite and Jew* (New York: Schocken, 1974), pp. 90ff.

18. Otto Weininger, *Geschlecht und Charakter* (Munich: Matthes und Seitz, 1980). Cf. Theodor Lessing, *Jüdischer Selbsthaß*, pp 80ff.

# Historical Visions:
# Anna Seghers on the Revolution in Haiti

## Sima Kappeler

The successful rebellion of the Black slaves of Haiti, which led to the foundation of a Black republic in 1804, has inspired a number of German writers. The most famous literary document was produced by Heinrich von Kleist and published in 1811. The creation of *Die Verlobung in St. Domingo* [The Betrothal on Santo Domingo] can be connected with the writer's imprisonment at the Fort de Joux, France, in 1807, where Haiti's greatest Black general was imprisoned and died. Kleist's novella inspired Anna Seghers, who wrote *Die Hochzeit von Haiti* [The Wedding on Haiti] in 1948. Hans Christoph Buch, a more recent German writer, published in 1976 a historical overview entitled *Die Scheidung von San Domingo* [The Divorce on Santo Domingo]. Buch returned to the topic of the Black rebellion and focused on it in his novel *Die Hochzeit von Port-au-Prince* [The Wedding in Port-au-Prince] (1984).[1]

Anna Seghers became interested in the topic in connection with her flight from the Nazis in 1940, which led her to Haiti on her way to Mexico. She became further inspired when reading Toussaint's biography. The title of her text *Die Hochzeit von Haiti*, which is included in the collection *Karibische Geschichten* [Caribbean Stories], recalls Kleist's *Verlobung*. Both texts, however, use the same historical moment for quite different purposes.

Seghers's narrative focuses on a family of Jewish jewelry dealers. This choice of a group of White outsiders, which is used in order to stage an encounter with the Black population, recalls Kleist's choice of a Swiss family. Seghers's focus on that specific minority, which is in general not associated with Black slaves, might have some biographical reason, since Anna Seghers (whose actual name was Netty Reiling), was the daughter of a Jewish antique dealer. We can even detect some resemblance between her own biography and the story of her protagonist, since both embrace the revolutionary cause, which eventually becomes more important than their Jewish background.

*Die Hochzeit von Haiti* is far more concerned with the details of the political situation on the island at that time than Kleist's novella. The story begins with the depiction of a group of recently immigrated Jews, whose interest in politics is limited. The jewelry dealers Nathan and Mendez left France and were attracted to the island because of its prosperity. The wealth of that French colony is represented by Nathan's most noble client, Count Evremont. The title of the story actually refers to the wedding of the Count's daughter, which has to be deferred because of the revolution.

The story's focus on political questions can be seen in relation to Seghers's Marxist concerns. The rise and fall of the White and Mulatto planters is contrasted to the long-term, more stable situation of the Jews. The introduction of the Jew as a third party makes both the Blacks and the Whites appear in a different light since they are, thanks to that plot line, less directly opposed to each other. This deflection of opposition sets the specific historical moment within a larger perspective, evading that tragic climax which characterizes Kleist's novella. While Kleist already strives for a clash through the generic choice of the novella, Seghers avoids any further heightening of the drama in order to insert her narrative within a larger ongoing revolutionary process.

Racial issues between Whites and Blacks are set against the far older drama of the Jewish situation, even if that specific story remains untold. The larger question of economic stability is dealt with in the difference between the vulnerable plantation business, which depends on slavery, and the more independent and therefore less vulnerable jewel trade. Seghers depicts the vulnerability of the individual in relation to the instability of property and value. The question of race and slavery is presented in the context of the changing economic situation. "Everyone found work, everyone was needed, offers were made regardless of skin color or origin."[2]

The Jew, who is frequently used to represent the victim, emerges here rather as he who survives despite reversals. Seghers is careful not to pass any harsh judgment either on the White planter or on the Jewish dealer but to show the instability of the system. The Jew's dependence on the planter's prosperity is not pointed out since there is some interest in an optimistic outlook with the prospect of gradual progress. The story thus avoids binary oppositions and distributes social, intellectual, and ethical differences regardless of the color line.

It is consistent with this outlook that the exotic landscape is not being romanticized. Its beauty is shown in relation to prosperity. There is therefore nothing paradisical about the island and it is not perceived independently of its people but rather as a backdrop for the historical drama that is about to be staged. The father–son relationship that is unfolded in the Jewish family through the structure of the three generations can be viewed as a microcosmic reflection of the relation between the colony and the mother country. Both plot lines depict the emancipation of the son. This dissolution of ties, however, has to be paid for at a high price. But the brief moment of triumph is being celebrated despite the fact that the son figures have to die as a consequence of their separation from the father. "It [the island] was impoverished, exploited, economically dependent on the rich nations of the world. However, it remained a Negro state" (p. 59). The emancipation of the Black slaves from the White planters is viewed within the larger context of emancipation. However, the supremacy of White culture, to which the text itself belongs, is not problematized. The acknowledgement of this supremacy is put into the mouth of Toussaint, the Black leader. "White culture appeared to him like a radiant, limitless castle" (p. 35). White culture emerges thus, despite the dire circumstances, in an idealized form. The intellectual difference between Blacks and Whites is emphasized by Michael who otherwise identifies with the Blacks, but who has a less optimistic view than his counterpart Toussaint when it comes to the question of a successful rebellion against the mother country. "At the same time he understood that for these people the gap separating that which is attainable on earth and the limitlessness of ideas, which Toussaint had just now pondered himself, was considerably smaller than for him" (p. 54).

The colony itself with its White and Mulatto planters is described as a place where a certain drama, which is no longer tolerated in the mother country, can still be staged. The colony can thus be viewed as removed in time and space and endowed with laws and rules that are no longer applicable on the main scene, and slavery is only one of these old sets of rules. "In keeping with the peculiar colonial dealings common in these parts, but improper at home, most of the remaining old estates were converted into plantations" (p. 8). That stain of ambiguity is being passed on from the Whites, whose morality is criticized by the mainland, to the Mulattoes, who are seen in a dubious light by the White planters, so that the morality of the former seems to be reflected in their dubious color.

"Mulattos of undeniable, albeit dubious, wealth were waiting, eager to do business, or out of sheer curiosity" (p. 11). The island is interested in forgetting its past, the exploitation of the Black slave as well as the importation of criminals and prostitutes from the mother country. There seems to be a general interest in a discontinuity of memory and an effort to be oblivious to ancestry and moral issues. In contrast to this general trend, the group that has been moved center stage is inseparable from memory and almost defined by it insofar as it constitutes its identity. The important issue of ancestry and continuity, which is at stake in that colonial society, thus reappears as symbolized by the three generations of the Jews.

The White race in the colony strives for an erasure of memory, thus negating both its less noble origin when compared to the aristocracy of the mother country and its mingling with the Blacks. The Blacks, however, as in Kleist, have to remember in order to evade punishment (p. 29).[3] Memory for the Blacks signifies memory of torture and punishment, which is being passed on to the next generation in order to promote either obedience and humility or else bring about rebellion and change.

There are, however, various strategies in the text to negate the possibility of disobedience and rebellion. One of them is to posit an effaced or angelic Black slave. "The Black servants stood behind the chairs, as if each one of the guests had brought his watchful shadow" (p. 16). This image, which compares the Black servant to a shadow, seems to claim some natural connection between Black and White in which the White person represents the "real" object and the Black person the mere reflection of it. The image of the angelic slave also points to the desire to negate the actual power relation between the two races. "During the trip into the mountains the two Black men remained visible from the vehicle. They were enshrouded in an iridescent cloud of dust, barely touching the ground like two Black angels" (p. 15). This perception, which compares humans to angels, can equally be found among the Blacks who seem to idealize their White masters despite their cruelty. "They had remained surprisingly White-skinned under the raging sun. . . . The house slave . . . was afraid to make mistakes or to spill something. A minor oversight meant having to work in the fields, if not being beaten half to death. At the same time she admired the inexplicable White of the Whites. It was hard to imagine that its purpose was to bring forth more little angels like these" (p. 8). This passage thus reveals a strange split in the slave's consciousness. Her gaze seems to be hypnotized by the master's Whiteness, which she associates with the angelic. What is suppressed are crucial aspects of reality such as exploitation and procreation.

This emphasis on aesthetics, which occurs throughout the text under various guises, could be interpreted as a negation of the impending conflict that will subvert the clear distinction between Black and White as well as between beauty and ugliness. It might, however, also be viewed as a reference to the relativity of appearance and color that puts a class system built on such distinctions on slippery ground. It might be interesting to look in this connection at a close-up of Count Evremont's daughter, whose wedding has to be deferred because of the revolution. "Evremont adorned his daughter with the jewelry he had ordered in Paris a long time ago. The pleasing but insignificant beauty of his child whose height and gestures were still those of an adolescent suddenly sparkled as if illuminated by a new, more perfect light" (p. 16).[4] This passage, which somehow shows the father as the creator of his daughter, demystifies beauty, depicting it rather as something that depends on perception as well as on hierarchy and development. Imperfection can appear beautiful under a perfect light. The theme of the deceptive nature of appearance occurs as well in Kleist, but while appearance in Kleist is related to the question of skin color, it is here concerned with the difference between beauty and ugliness.[5] The beauty of Margot, the Black slave, is shown in its dependence on the economic situation. Margot first appears in a dehumanized way as an object of exchange. She is not exchanged for money but for a precious piece of furniture. This detail gives a picture of the complex economic relations between the members of the White aristocracy. "Because this ship . . . was supposed to bring a little house slave, a surprisingly adept fabric cutter for her age. A first cousin of the countess of Evremont had finally agreed to exchange her for a valuable heirloom, an inlaid musical clock" (p. 11). This piece of information makes us further grasp how much has to be severed and destroyed in order to bring about the liberation of the Black slaves. The way in which the slave's place within that system of inheritance and exchange is depicted reflects the conviction on the part of the Whites, that this is a perfectly natural order in which everything falls into place. The theme of exchange, which becomes more significant if we think of Seghers's Marxist orientation, faintly recalls that other African economic order which had to be both destroyed and negated in order to establish that particular colonial system. During the rebellion that "natural order" is destroyed, which is illustrated in a scene where a former White superintendent is treated like an object and thus likewise dehumanized before being killed. "He was discovered in his tree. He was shaken down like a coconut. He was cracked. A negro dug his teeth into him and sucked him dry" (p. 27).

Margot's first appearance in the text evokes the cliché of the beautiful Black slave who inevitably arouses sexual desire. This short moment, which might be read as a reference to that specific historical reality, is, however, revised and emerges as an instance of misreading. "At this point a short Black woman brazenly pushed herself through the door frame underneath his arm. Because of the dampness, her youthful, healthy scent was so strong that not even Michael could escape from it, although he normally avoided temptations of this sort" (p. 29). This encounter between a White outsider and a Black slave girl is related in a way that recalls animals signaling to each other through the sense of smell, thus evoking the stereotype of Black animal sexuality. But the woman assumes here the role of the seducer and not that of the rape victim. The slave's beauty is further viewed in the context of her particular social situation. "Now that he noticed her small breasts under the wet cotton dress, he realized that his first impression had been correct. The girl was extraordinarily beautiful. Looking at her, he could appreciate the rage and jealousy of White women. They were more creative than men and punished their female slaves at the slightest wrongdoing with the utmost cruelty" (p. 29).

Both the protagonist and the reader are disappointed in their expectation of an illicit love scene between a White man and a Black girl. While Kleist includes such a scene of interracial seduction, Seghers defers it for the sake of a more urgent cause—namely that of the revolution. The couple Michael and Margot reappear later as a conventional family with a strong focus on their child.

The discussion of beauty and ugliness can be further related to that of appearance and perception and to the question of injustice and rebellion. We find a somewhat similar concern in Kleist's text, but there the question of appearance and perception is closely linked to that of shades of color, which are presented as a decisive factor in a question of life and death. Seghers pursues a different plot line. The Black and White couple Michael and Margot seem to be situated in a sort of no-man's land. They lead a secluded life removed from patriarchal figures. We can notice a similar setup of seclusion in Kleist but the absent patriarchal figure, who happens to be Black, overshadows the scene because of his impending return. In Seghers's story both father and grandfather are safely removed to the other side of the Atlantic.

While Michael is depicted as the revolutionary who has already been prepared for his role by the *Society of the Friends of the Black*[6] in France and will be a crucial help to Toussaint, he is equally depicted as the obedient son whose "dark" past as a revolutionary seems to be almost nonexistent once he returns to England and marries the woman his father has chosen for him. Michael's double life, the fact that he first has a Black and then a White family, resembles the family structure of White planters, but there is some significant difference since the two families do not exist simultaneously. The Black family dies and is replaced by the White Jewish family. There is thus something secret and repressed about Michael's revolutionary self since a confrontation with the patriarchal figure does not take place.

While Michael seems to identify more and more with the revolutionary cause and the fate of the island, which is mirrored in his personal losses,[7] the final passage attempts to go beyond private boundaries and to point to some realm where political and racial differences are surpassed and where common origins are emphasized instead. "These two dead men [Michael and Toussaint] remind one of the trees which were planted alongside the military highways across Europe. They become diseased and rotten at the same time. Their simultaneous death in two different parts of the world, appears less enigmatic, if one knows that they sprang from the same seed" (p. 60). This final passage strives for a universal and conciliatory vision of human fate through an erasure of racial difference. The imagery seems, however, to undermine this thrust by using precisely that vocabulary which is associated with the racial concerns of the Third Reich, whose presence must inevitably haunt any literary document that was produced so shortly after its collapse.

## Notes

1. Heinrich von Kleist, *Die Verlobung in St. Domingo*, Roland Reuß and Peter Staengle, eds. (Basel: Stroemfeld/Roter Stern, 1988). Translations follow: *The Betrothal on Santo Domingo*, translated by Ronald Taylor in *Six Germanic Romantic Tales* (London: Angel Books, 1985), pp. 71–102.

2. Anna Seghers, *Karibische Geschichten* (Berlin: Aufbau-Verlag, 1962), p. 47. Translations by the editors.

3. "I shall never forget the oath he had the impudence to swear in my presence. I

developed a gall-bladder complaint as a consequence, and shortly afterwards Monsieur Villeneuve also ordered me to be given sixty lashes, as a result of which I have suffered from consumption to this day" (Taylor, p. 79).

4. Cf. also Hans Christoph Buch, *Die Hochzeit von Port-au-Prince* (Frankfurt am Main: Suhrkamp, 1984).

5. Cf. Sander Gilman, "The Aesthetics of Blackness in Heinrich von Kleist's 'Die Verlobung in St. Domingo,'" *MLN* 90 (1975), pp. 661–665.

6. "Gesellschaft der Freunde der Schwarzen."

7. "His inside had been singed, now it had turned to smoke and ashes like Le Cap" (p. 59).

# Jean Améry and Austria

## Ruth Beckermann

I cannot recall how I discovered Jean Améry in the late 1960s—in which way and through which text he came to me. Somehow he came into our would-be existentialist high-school student group via the books of Sartre and Camus. Being existentialist meant something like wearing white lipstick and a black turtleneck sweater and carrying at all times a few books by French authors under one's arm. In the beginning, of course, we considered Améry a Frenchman.

Améry's book—in all likelihood it was *Jenseits von Schuld und Sühne* [Beyond Crime and Punishment]—belonged to the secret book treasures we read under our desks during physics and chemistry classes. We selected them at random, but with a sure instinct: Schnitzler's *Reigen* [La Ronde], D. H. Lawrence's *Lady Chatterley's Lover*, Camus's *La Peste* [The Plague], and Kafka's *Der Prozeß* [The Trial]. We needed these books as an antidote against the atmosphere in Austria.

The children of Jewish parents who had ended up in Vienna, uprooted and shaken up, were looking for allies in this country, which was all too similar to the martial prewar country described by Améry. To be sure, there was one big difference. Before, it was possible to identify with this country, one could say WE, perhaps even in a very special way, like Hanns Mayer, a child of this country, who noticed relatively late that he was not a part of the national community. *Afterwards*, such an identification was (perhaps luckily) no longer possible. We lived in Vienna, but we socialized almost exclusively with Jews. We celebrated our birthdays and festivals, and spent our Sundays and holidays with other Jews. Many of them spoke Hungarian, Romanian, or Polish. It was as if they transmitted to us postwar children a bygone and distant Austria that figured in the literature of the world of yesterday. In the present time, Austria was a place with which one did not become involved. Only in school did we notice the break between the world inside, family and friends, and the world outside. From now on we followed the unwritten law to disclose nothing we discussed at home to the outside. Even the word "Jew" was taboo.

We encountered Améry at a relatively late date. His topics were not exactly suited for children. First came Schnitzler and Zweig. Also they were secret allies against the daily infamy of the old and young, against the crucifix on the classroom wall and the rod in the bag. No matter how different our chosen writers were, they named the stale atmosphere we felt without being able to express it. Schnitzler discussed everything that mattered to us in his drama *Professor Bernhardi* and particularly in his novel *Der Weg ins Freie*. However, his was a different time.

Then came Sartre. His essay about the Jewish question was new—and he spoke to us. To us as Jews. It may be unimaginable from today's point of view, but we were in a way incredibly proud to be Jews. Our pride was based on the Biblical heroes and the modern heroes of the State of Israel. We felt strong as the descendants of the Hebrews and superior to the Austrians. At the same time we were ashamed to be the children of people who only a few years ago had been considered vermin and even in the present time did not want to be obvious. Secretly we were afraid that there was some truth in the Nazis' denunciations. We read texts such as Sartre's essay on the Jewish question secretly in order to avoid our fellow students' suggestive questions. If they discovered us anyway, we blushed as if we had been caught with a porn magazine.

No matter how heated the debates about Sartre's essay, what counted (as Claude Lanzmann pointed out in retrospect) was that the text of this most prominent European philosopher, which had appeared in *Temps Modernes* as early as December of 1945, confronted the final solution of the Jewish question with something other than embarrassed silence. Sartre told the survivors, yes, you exist with your history and the opportunity to determine your fate. Améry may have felt something similar when he referred to Sartre, the politician and moralist, his master, his great teacher. After the experience of the concentration camps he considered Existentialism the philosophy that saved his life.

One knows nothing at the age of sixteen. One knows everything.

We did not understand the sentences of Sartre, Améry and Camus, but we did understand that their texts had something to do with our feeling of being thrown into an existence without an emotional safety net. We understood Améry when he equated the loss of his home country with the loss of certainty, when he spoke about the anonymity of exile and how torture in the concentration camp had destroyed his trust in the world. We understood that Améry articulated all that about which our parents remained silent. He had never been one of the famous writers who—even in exile—were well known and expected here and there. He was one of those people who crowded the consulates to obtain a visa, who depended on the charity of Jewish organizations, who were suddenly jerked out of this civilization into a train, onto a ramp, into a barrack. We read about the indignity and were even more ashamed.

Améry belonged to a counterworld that questioned not only the dullness of the others, but also our parents' attempts to adjust to the world of appearances. In retrospect their desire to live, forget, make up for lost time, dance, and drink to the fullest is an understandable reaction. At that time we considered their willingness to compromise as highly immoral. Améry, on the other hand, embodied purity, rigor, and irreconcilability. Améry was no teacher and role model, but one of those much more important figures who provide a framework for one's own life and thoughts. He was a pillar detached from all others, and yet connected with them by a person who chooses them and places them side by side in order to walk among them and look for herself. To this day, the name of Jean Améry remains a secret maxim.

I would be happy to be able to say about him what he himself wrote about Elias Canetti in 1973: "What was a secret maxim ten years ago is now a part of the contemporary intellectual inventory." To a limited extent Améry, particularly his works about aging and suicide, is known only in the western part of Germany. To this day, only two of his books have appeared (in 1992) in his beloved France. His most important work, *Beyond Crime and Punishment*, has not been translated yet. Surprisingly enough. Strangely enough.

It is hardly surprising that Améry has not been integrated in his home country's intellectual inventory, such as it is. The Second Republic of Austria, from the time of its creation a corrupt and crooked nation through and through, has had no use for the great moralist. Austria's relationship with Améry reflects the country's character. It takes only a few words to describe it. His affiliation with this land—his home country, its landscape, language, dialect—on the other hand, is very ambivalent and permeates his entire work. This will be discussed later.

What did postwar Austria, the Second Republic, offer Hanns Mayer, whom it had thrown out in 1938? In the spring of 1945 it returned to him his passport at the consulate in Brussels—one should not even have to mention something so obvious. This simple act is only worth mentioning if one knows how many exiles were strung along and exposed to bureaucratic subterfuges in Austrian consulates all over the world. In the fall of the same year, Leopold Langhammer, with whom he had worked at the VHS or Volkshochschule in the Zirkusgasse, hinted that he might have the opportunity to get involved in the reconstruction of the public education system. I assume that Améry could only shake his head at this suggestion. After all, the most successful of all popular educators, Adolf Hitler—that great Austrian—had just recently abdicated, applauded by his own people until the very end, and once again some eternal optimists seemed to think that one could reform the masses with courses on Marx, Reich, and Esperanto.

In January 1967, twenty-two years later, the president of the Österreichische Gesellschaft für Literatur [Austrian Society for Literature], Wolfgang Kraus, invited Améry for a lecture. However, this took place five years later, on 11 April 1972. Améry spoke about the Left and tolerance. One year later another lecture sponsored by Kraus followed—"Vom Nutzen und Nachteil der Ideologie für das Leben" [About the Advantage and Disadvantage of Ideology for Life]. Both events were accompanied by a television appearance in the series *Jour fixe*. Aside from Améry's participation in the Salzburg *Humanismusge-*

*spräche*, the press also reported his keynote address at the book exhibit in 1974. However, only the title of the speech is mentioned, "Über die Möglichkeiten geistiger Repräsentanz" [About the Possibilities of Intellectual Representation], while the address of the Minister of Education is discussed in great detail.

As far as I know, no Austrian paper or publishing house, neither radio nor television, invited him to work for them. It is true, however, that in 1972 Améry was offered the title of Honorary Professor, which he rejected, of course. He likewise declined to be decorated with a medal two years later. In 1976 he accepted an honorary membership in the Austrian PEN Club and one year later the City of Vienna elected him as one of its prizewinners. However, rather than being honored for his literary accomplishments, he was recognized as a journalist—another one of the Viennese tricks that make it possible to insult someone who wishes and deserves to be acknowledged as a writer while praising him.

Their intentions were good. As good as the unavoidable honorary tomb or *Ehrengrab* at the Central Cemetery in Vienna. The title, the medal, and the honorary tomb—all that sounds good and costs nothing. The title, the medal, and the honorary tomb are accessories in a game with the petty vanity and the great nostalgia that takes hold of the émigrés after a certain age. They make it possible to quickly co-opt the people to whom the Austrians returned their former property only unwillingly (if at all), and who were granted minimal budget pensions. Perhaps there was even the afterthought that these people living in New York or London might be useful in one way or another.

How was Austria to handle Améry's exacting and rigorous intellect? Qualities such as exactness, rigor, and relentlessness are considered unappealing. At the very least, someone like Améry is scary to those who want above all to be appealing. Beware of him, don't let him look into the grubby rooms where one hand washes the other. Where everyone, particularly every Jew, has to be good for something; useful to the leftists or the right-wingers, the Church or the Labor Union; at least, however, useful to the image of Austria overseas, in hostile territories, i.e. America.

Améry's thinking accommodated neither the socialist nor the Christian camp. *Au contraire*. The left and the right had reached an agreement in post-1945 Austria. The consensus of both major parties rests on the claim that Austria was the first victim of German aggression. In the political scheme of the Second Republic, the Jews were not needed. Austria accorded the political resistance the representative role symbolic of a well-functioning democracy that the Jews played in the Federal Republic of Germany. The resistance was glorified to fit the basic myth of the Second Republic, despite the fact that it had not been any more significant than in the so-called *Altreich* (Germany before 1938). After 1945 Jews were once again allowed to live in Austria, provided they were nice and quiet, or (as was emphasized by the first Federal

Chancellor Julius Figl) they were allowed to live there as Austrians, not as Jews. As if nothing had happened, in other words. After the fact they were deprived of their separate experience during the Nazi regime.[1]

In 1955 this Austrian policy proved ultimately successful; it led to the constitution and to unrestricted autonomy. At that time Austria proved to itself, once again, the effectiveness of opportunism, provided it goes hand in hand with the necessary charm. The Austrian population considered the lies about their role during the Third Reich, which, in effect, they were, as the necessary adjustment to the conditions of the time and as the necessary means to dodge the consequences of the defeat of 1945 so-called foreign rule. Popular consciousness and word choice termed 1938 the year of liberation and 1945 that of the occupation. Supposedly 1938 was the liberation from a much-hated Catholic Fascist regime that had defeated and outlawed the mighty workers' movement and whose dictatorial rule had already lasted for four years. On the other hand, 1945 was the occupation by the Allies, after the dream of a Greater German Empire had shattered. It had been the dream of all Austrian parties since the decline of the Habsburg monarchy.

The new image of Austria was actually created from the perspective of the perpetrators, but it was presented as the victims' point of view. Now it was considered advantageous to distance oneself from Germany. By doing so, Austria achieved preferential treatment compared to Germany. It was neither separated nor stigmatized, it experienced no mass expulsions, and it paid relatively little in reparations. All foreign soldiers were recalled and the country became independent. Everyone rejoiced in a new patriotism. In hindsight, it became apparent that the struggle for a free Austria had been the objective all along, even during the Nazi years.

The patriotic consensus existed until the mid-1980s and broke down only as a result of the international disapproval of Waldheim's lies. Lack of dissimulation was considered the mark of a spoilsport, for example Günter Anders, George Clare, and Jean Améry, who wrote:

> I was present when in 1938 Hitler's men and the disgusting fellow himself were received with an enthusiasm that climaxed in unrestrained festivity lasting for days, even weeks. I was not present during the invasion of the Russians who, quite by accident, elevated Karl Renner to the position of Head of State, despite the fact that he had been a yes-man. I was not present when Austria cast itself as the small, insignificant, miserable, and pitiable victim of Hitler's territorial conquests. I was again present, accidentally, when the State Contract was signed, and to my own surprise witnessed that every single Austrian was of the opinion that he was personally responsible for the equilibrium between the two countries (which coincidentally had become superpowers), guaranteeing Austria a certain security and independence.[2]

Améry considered Austrian national consciousness as profoundly incredible, as something not resulting from historical processes, but superimposed by a world event from which it suffered at first and which it later declared its claim to fame.

Supposedly there was nothing left of this subversion of the spirit, which could still be felt during the interwar period. At that time, Améry claimed, the intellect "separated from social interplay, began to ferment and constituted itself as the negation of power as twelve-tone music, philosophical neopositivism, psychoanalysis, and individual psychology" (*Aspekte*, p. 15). Nothing of that is left. Power and intellect, historiography and literature ignored most recent Austrian history. Only in Ingeborg Bachmann did Améry sense suffering about the past. According to him, Handke's or Frischmuth's texts were void of it. They were alien to him. He finds it again only in Thomas Bernhard, whose prose he loved and with whom he had more in common than it seems.[3]

Initially the Austrians invoked their great past. Then they discovered the usefulness of the dead Jews of the turn of the century, while gladly leaving the legacy of the Nazi times and the great Austrians by the names of Adolf Hitler, Adolf Eichmann, Odilo Globocnik, Seyss–Inquart, and Alois Brunner to the Germans. Like all information about the persecution of the Jews, be it books or films, Améry's works were imported. The literature dealing with the Holocaust in historical, sociological, and psychological terms was written by Germans. The translations of international works appeared on the German book market. Until 1980 not even a handful of books was published about the specifically Austrian situation. Explanations that cite the limited possibilities of Austrian publishers collapse after a glance at the monumental production of apologetic literature in Austria.

Even if we know about the guilt of the Austrians and do not fall for their self-chosen victim role, it is difficult to get a clear picture of the situation more than forty years later. During this time the image of the Nazis as Germans has been firmly lodged in our consciousness as the result of TV documentaries, novels, cartoons, and especially feature films. Hitler himself is considered an Austrian as little as Eichmann during his trial in Jerusalem.

Eberhard Fechner's admirable discussion of Nazism in the past and present in his television documentary "Der Prozeß" [The Trial] shows some Austrians as defendants in the Majdanek trial, which took place in the Federal Republic. The Austrian public barely paid attention to it. Judges and lawyers were Germans. Despite the fact that the film was shown on Austrian television, the geographic distance and the accent of those involved allowed for complete detachment on the part of the Austrian viewers. The reaction to these Austrian concentration camp henchmen resembled that of mercenaries in foreign armies or the reaction to Austrian foreign workers on the German job market. Although the number of party members per capita was nowhere as high as in the Ostmark (Austria under Nazi rule), and although Austrians could and did achieve all ranks in the Nazi hierarchy, Nazism (as well as its postwar debate) is treated as an imported item that has nothing to do with Austrian reality.

What was Améry to this country?

Title, medal, honorary tomb. Only the street name is still missing. There is an Améry-Weg in Stuttgart. Therefore an untiring Wolfgang Kraus wrote letters to the mayor of Vienna to petition for such a street name. In vain. Street names may not cost anything, but the people might disapprove. "What is a Frenchman to us?" the people of Vienna might ask. And that would be by far the best reaction a Jew could expect.

A double expulsion shaped Améry's relationship to Austria. At first he was expelled from his home country in the narrower sense of the word. Upper Austria slowly transformed itself into a land of enemies. From there he went to Vienna from where he escaped eight years later. Améry was a man of the province. His father was a native of Hohenems. He grew up in Ischl. His mother was an inn-keeper. He attended the Gmunden *Gymnasium*. Thus his memories are a rare document of a Jew from the Austrian province.

By no means was he a Jewish child aware of being a stranger among the country folk where he had ended up. He did not want to adapt and assimilate. He was not even aware of being different. Every day he wore his white knee socks and leather and *Loden* costume (local costume). Schnitzler and Freud would only wear those for country excursions. He read—without questioning it—stuffy, conservative authors like Agnes Miegel, Karl Heinrich Waggerl, and Börries von Münchhausen.

Like everyone else he lifted his hat upon seeing the summer guests, mainly Jews, who continued to travel to Bad Ischl on their summer vacation even after the Emperor's death, as if they wanted to invoke the good spirit of imperial tolerance. Like everyone else he was happy when the resort turned back into a village during the winter months and rustic dances took place instead of five o'clock teas. He wrote:

> The atmosphere was happy and rustic. No one felt that he had to act like the entourage of the ladies and gentlemen from the capital. Everyone talked, trampled, spat as they liked. The young people danced to the tunes of the accordion—although it was not called that at the time—playing country waltzes that were transformed into dionysian music. One in particular delighted the happy crowd, which sang along in booming and squeaking voices while the couples, not without native grace, skipped and stomped: "Join your heads and the asses." Those were the lyrics that evoked roaring delight and promised pleasure. The words were accompanied by strong mimics. Behinds and skulls collided to the tune of unadulterated native belting and squealing. In the early morning hours when outside only now and then the horse-drawn sled jingled through ice and snow, things could get rough in the smoke-filled rooms. Hatred, jealousy, and envy as well as anger kept under control during the day made the floors tremble. Perhaps someone had spat into so-and-so's beer?[4]

This is how they sat at the inn during Améry's childhood, this is how they drank and danced through the Nazi times and were reunited in Hans Lebert's tavern. Hatred, jealousy, and envy unite them on an even more profound level since they talk about each other's respective deeds. There they sit around the tables of the tavern, the old man, who beat Jews to death, the old man who raped a Polish woman, the old woman who had been a concentration camp guard at the nearby KZ. They sit and are no longer silent.

Looking back, Améry described himself as a "dull reactionary" who was ignorant of twelve-tone music, psychoanalysis, and socialism, someone who was as "provincial and hopelessly idyllic in the sense such a village is idyllic" as was the countryside "resounding with the echoes of comfortable grumbling."[5]

> During that time one lived in isolation from modern life. Those who had the opportunity were out there in the German Reich, in its feverish capital Berlin, and whoever tried to achieve a measure of modernity in Vienna got a sore head from beating his head against the granite Alpine skull. (*Wanderjahre*, p. 11)

In his world, the one acquired by reading and the one he experienced himself, landscape, or more precisely "that which I called landscape," was most predominant.

> The forest, the mountain and valley, the path through the fields, the hollow path, the path made of wood, the rocks, the heather, the black-toothed line of the hills on the horizon, the sickle of the moon and the evening star, the night disembarking serenely into the land, Stifter's forest trail, the forest eyes of Peter Hille shimmering greenish-golden, the iron nights of Thomas Glahn, the mill in the green valley which one saw only rarely in those days—they were a thing of the past— the tunes of the bugle hovering over it—in 1930 the bugle of the mail carriage existed only on the postcards of the Austrian Federal Postal service, the Nordic birch forest of Jens Peter Jacobsen, where a shot was fired in the fog. The black and silent forest, through which the anemic, nervous weaklings of Hermann Bang hiked, the darkness of the forest, the solitude of the forest—the magic of the eternal cipher Forest. (*Wanderjahre*, p. 10)

Améry enumerates, he quotes, he serializes. His *Unmeisterliche Wanderjahre* do not contain a description of his childhood; he does not even refer to the locations by their names. "The country was called Austria. It was an Alpine country" (*Wanderjahre*, p. 10). That is all he says—after all he does not want to describe but to reflect. Only in his *Örtlichkeiten* does he find the ironic distance to which we also owe the sketch of life in Ischl. Even there, however, he encounters the man hiking through the forests, the ten-year-old village boy as if he were a stranger; he does not find himself again.

He is unable to save his earliest and most important experiences across the many divides; he cannot nurture and shape them. Nothing at all lasted. After the expulsion from his country, torture, and the concentration camp, it would have taken an enormous poetic power to create a narrative work based on the forest universe. Telling stories about his life, which, after all, was his major theme and the material from which he created, was not his metier. While evoking an image, he already destroys it by interpreting it. No matter how lovingly he deals with the works of others (I consider his book reviews to be among his most beautiful texts), he judges himself harshly, erasing good and bad memories with such sentences as: "One's home country is the country of one's childhood and youth. Those who have lost it, remain lost" (*Wanderjahre*, p. 10). If detailed memory is inadmissable, not only the country of one's childhood and youth, but also one's own person is reflected exclusively in negative terms.

There was no anti-world for Hanns Mayer like the one some Jewish Austrian authors were able to save in spite of everything that happened, which they carried along in their luggage, so to speak, and loved to evoke in their popular memoirs. Neither was there a grandfather who told Hasidic stories nor sweet tea and a large family circle. In the memoirs of many survivors a WE manifests itself from the start. It is juxtaposed to the experiences of the others, the anti-Semites who not only attacked one's own person, but also one's entire milieu. The attacks directed against oneself were directed at the same time against the so-called Jewish spirit, against everything of which this subversion supposedly consisted, which manifested itself until 1938 in the coffee houses and the press, theaters and galleries. Améry could not fall back on any familiar Jewish, nor a liberal or socialist collective. His WE was not defined in social terms. It was an all-encompassing, rural, a very vague and German WE. He had felt fine surrounded by dialect, literature, the landscape of the province. Everything he valued and considered important was now taken over by the enemy. The folk songs, the lake, the forest. He was ousted from his home country, which he, while falling, saw in a new and destructive light. Suddenly everything he carried within him was unbearably false. He had to destroy his home country within.

Nothing is permanent. In the concentration camp he meets a Jew from Vilnius who asks him where he is from. He hesitates. What are Hohenems, Ischl, Gmunden to the Polish Jew, he asks himself. His landmarks are not located on any Jewish migration route of modern times. Nothing could be saved. About the mother we only hear that she owns a tavern in Ischl–Eglmoos and insists on proper speech and proper table manners about which her son couldn't care less. His grandfather appears as a serious-minded Jewish gentleman who concerns himself occasionally with his grandson's education. Three, four sentences about his mother and his grandfather, not one word about friends, classmates, and first loves. Not one single character in this Upper Austrian province of the 1920s seems to deserve to be isolated from the sinister picture as an exception. Not even Améry himself. He writes:

> The real nostalgia is not self pity, but rather self destruction. It consisted of the deconstruction of our past bit by bit. This was impossible without contempt and hatred of the lost self. The hostile home country was destroyed by us. At the same time we erased the part of our own lives connected with it. (*Schuld*, p. 88)

As is often the case, Améry is talking of a diffuse community of fate, a WE, while in reality he generalizes his subjective experiences. *He* had to erase his hostile home country as well as that part of his life which was entangled with it. The explanation that everything lost its meaning after Auschwitz and that as a result the loss of one's trust in the world overpowered the entire person, including his past, is too facile. Not even the most drastic experience can shape a human being entirely. Other causes for Jean Améry's self-destruction can be found in the *morbus austriacus*, as he calls it with reference to Thomas Bernhard, a sickness unto death that is found even more so in his early life with which he does not deal. He reflects on and interprets his life anew repeatedly, while revealing little of his personal history.

Améry effects the destruction of his child-self in the first chapter of the *Unmeisterliche Wanderjahre* and that of his youth in the second chapter. In it he proceeds to deconstruct the internalized home country he had believed to have found in Vienna at the age of eighteen. He was evicted from the forest and went to Vienna, into the coffee house. "The slow transformation of the home country into enemy territory was noticeable. Therefore quite a few people with genealogical problems were searching for an intellectual home" (*Wanderjahre*, p. 33). At the same time we hear about his simultaneous enthusiasm for Wittgenstein, Schlick, and Neurath, and exile literature, Thomas Mann and Josef Roth. Complaints about having neither read the right books such as Lenin, nor having actively resisted emerge time and again. "You were not only inauthentic as a refugee from action, but also as a coward before the word" (*Wanderjahre*, p. 51).

We hear nothing about his friend Ernst Mayer, with whom he edited the literary journal *Die Brücke* nor his first literary attempts, nothing about Hermann Hakel and Friedrich Bergammer, nothing about the *Jahrbuch 1935*, nor about his activities in the VHS (*Volkshochschule*) Zirkusgasse, his meeting with Hermann Broch, his marriage, and his first novel.

His first novel. Améry wrote a four-hundred-page manuscript in 1935 entitled *Die Schiffbrüchigen* [The Shipwrecked], which, by the way, outlasted the Nazi era in an apartment in the Berggasse in Vienna. The novel was not published. I am only familiar with a plot summary that Améry wrote later. As early as 1935 this first novel shows us a human being whose basic existential outlook is that of a deportee, a person who has failed. The unemployed intellectual Eugen Althager is left by his wife; his political illusions vanish in the February days of the year 1934. Althager drifts to the periphery of society. He becomes a gambler and the companion of a prostitute. Améry writes:

> The ideas of suicide that overshadow Eugen Althager's development demand prompt attention. But Eugen, who never had illusions about his strength, knows that he is not strong enough to face the situation. Once again, he lets chance take over and uses a trivial street fight as a means to commit suicide indirectly.

He has a confrontation with a nationalistic fraternity student, accepts his challenge for a duel, falsely claiming to be an "Aryan." With the melancholy, resigned support of his friend and second, Heinrich Hessl, he, who never held a weapon in his hand, enters sword fights and is killed as expected. At this point we reach the end of the first year after the beginning of the book. A meaningless life is terminated by an altogether caricaturesque, meaningless death.[6]

Améry wrote these sentences at the age of twenty-three. One ought not to interpret them hastily, but one ought not to forget them either. Above all they show that the eighteen-year-old Améry, who in 1930 left his home country in the narrower sense of the word and went to Vienna, had already experienced the decisive rupture, the ejection from his inner home, from the WE.

In 1938 he lost the past irretrievably during the chaos and enthusiasm of the Viennese population during the annexation. "All of a sudden the past was submerged, and one did not know one's identity any longer" (*Schuld*, p. 77). The content of his consciousness was erased, the history of his country and the images of the landscape whose memory he repressed:

> They were intolerable to me since the morning of March 1938 when even the windows of remote farms flew the blood-red cloth with the black spider on a white background. I was a human being who no longer could say "we" and therefore resorted to saying "I" by force of habit, but without the feeling of being fully in possession of his own self. (*Schuld*, p. 78)

Even the persecution is discussed exclusively with regard to himself. We do not find out what happened to his family and friends. Everything was submerged. Nothing could be saved. "The experience of persecution," he wrote, "was ultimately that of an extreme loneliness. What for me is at stake is the salvation from this ever-present feeling of being abandoned in the past."[7]

Someone who had identified so strongly with all of humanity and was rejected by it might have ventured to establish a tentative *WE* in a revolutionary act, the individualistic conquest of National Socialism from within. Such a person ought to have been showered with money and above all love by those who built their new Austria—this at least is our wish. What an illusion, what nonsense, the kind one finds in Christian schoolbooks. For twelve years the Jews had been tumors, rats, vermin. Why should the Austrians love them now? And how much love could possibly have been left in the Austrian people?

It is no coincidence that Roberto Rosselini's film *Deutschland, Stunde Null* [Germany, Point Zero] has no distributor in Germany and Austria and is never shown. In this film we see how during the "years of hunger" (a relative term in view of famines elsewhere in the world)[8] after the collapse of Germany a ten-year-old German boy administers poison to his sick father, as if it were the most normal matter in the world to eliminate useless eaters. Today these ten-year-olds are only fifty-five years of age. They are efficient and proud of their country, which is better developed than ever before. They have little love left. A proud people with stone faces—no matter whether people are deported, whether emaciated concentration camp prisoners are being released, whether asylum-seekers are beaten up. Asylum-seekers. Also the few authors who even bother to write articles against the hunt for people call them asylum-seekers and foreigners instead of writing about people with faces, names, and places. Germany or Austria were one and the same for the survivor Jean Améry. Their behavior was the same, but now, for opportunistic reasons, they insist that there was a basic difference. Hence Améry states that he considers the German language his homeland, but Germany a foreign country.

For twenty years he refused to have anything to do with this country and with Austria. He settled in Brussels and wrote articles for a Swiss agency. He sat on his observation stand and watched the intellectual development of France and Germany. Only in 1968 did he enter the German scene with *Aufzeichnungen eines Überwältigten*. From then on he visited there frequently, made appearances on radio shows, and undertook reading tours. But he remained in Brussels and read German and French books. This was how he could live—to be sure, under the condition to remain marginal without getting involved in the formation of the literary scene and taking a position only on rare occasions, to have only a faint voice occasionally at meetings of the Berlin Academy of Arts (*Akademie der Künste*), to be left alone, even there. To be the only one to raise his voice in favor of Israel during the Yom Kippur War of 1973. He heard only an embarrassed murmur on the part of his colleagues who are always willing to sanctimoniously lament the dead Jews, but would not lift a finger to help Jews who are alive.

Améry undertook excursions to Germany in small dosages, but they were still too many. Well-meaning faces, stone faces, and always the question why he was still concerned with the past. Every contact with the familiar language, particularly the vacations in the landscape of his childhood where he intuits every nuance, made it painfully clear that he did not belong here any longer. His travels took him nowhere. Therefore he also went to the *Salzkammergut*, the only place he possibly could have called home once upon a time. He went there to terminate his life at a time chosen by him. He deliberately staged his death in a Salzburg hotel, named *Österreichischer Hof*. His act brought the man who had once hiked through the forests and who had been driven from his inner home country, full circle. "He who has lost the country of his childhood and youth remains forever lost" (*Schuld*, p. 84).

Perhaps the tensions between the alien home country and the strange country that was becoming ever more familiar had become increasingly unbearable, the more Améry had, once again, become involved with Germany. He wanted the impossible, he wanted to be loved, and instead earned only respect because of his experiences. He was pigeonholed as a "survivor," his suffering filled minutes on the air and the programs of publishing houses. He saw through it. Neither his pedagogical illusions nor his personal vanity could water down his analysis: "What dehumanized me has become merchandise that I sell" (*Schuld*, p. 128).

Paradoxically, the country of the perpetrators is the market for the books and films of the survivors and their children who unfortunately are not cynical enough to differentiate between business and emotion. They still imagine that the Germans and Austrians listen to them. And the people enthusiastically applaud when the foreigners burn. Into which hideout has the "other" Germany, which supposedly does exist, crept since Hoyerswerda and Rostock? Despite all the explanations in Eastern and Western Germany, the simple question remains: What kind of people are those?

In today's context, the black and white, the good and evil of Améry's perspective on Germany and Austria has regained its validity after the stark opposites were fading into shades of grey. This is why I would like to conclude with a quote from Améry about Germany during the 1960s:

> Fateful country, where some are positioned into eternal light and the others into eternal obscurity. I traveled through this country back and forth on the evacuation trains, which took us from Auschwitz to the west under the pressure of the last Soviet offensive and then from Buchenwald to the North, to Bergen-Belsen. When the railroad tracks took us through the snow across a corner of Bohemian territory, the farm women came running to the death train carrying bread and apples. The guards had to drive them away by firing warning shots. In the Reich, however, there were faces of stone. A proud people. A proud people, still. I admit that their pride has put on weight. It no longer protrudes from their grinding jaws, but shines in the complacency of a good conscience and the understandable joy about having made it once again. This pride is no longer based on heroic acts of war, but on a productivity unparalleled worldwide. But it is the same pride as before, the same impotence as before. Woe betide the conquered. (*Schuld*, p. 128)

*Translated by Dagmar C. G. Lorenz*

## NOTES

1. Cf. Ruth Beckermann, *Unzugehörig. Österreicher und Juden nach 1945* (Vienna: Löcker, 1989).
2. Jean Améry, "Aspekte des Österreichischen," *Im Brennpunkt. Ein Österreich* (Vienna: Europa, 1976). Translations by the editor.
3. Cf. Jean Améry, "Morbus Austriacus" and "Atemnot," in *Der integrale Humanismus* (Stuttgart: Klett–Cotta, 1977), pp. 228–267.
4. Jean Améry, *Örtlichkeiten* (Stuttgart: Klett–Cotta, 1977), p. 12.
5. Jean Améry, *Unmeisterliche Wanderjahre* (Stuttgart: Klett–Cotta, 1971), p. 14.

6. *Marbacher Magazin* 24 (1982), p. 43.
7. Jean Améry, *Jenseits von Schuld und Sühne. Bewältigungsversuche eines Überwältigten* (Stuttgart: Klett–Cotta, 1977), p. 114.
8. This is an illusion to the film *Hungerjahre in einem reichen Land* by Jutta Brückner.

# Jewish Languages and Discourses

# Structure, Standardization, and Diglossia: The Case of Courland Yiddish

## Neil G. Jacobs

The Yiddish dialect of Courland (in present-day Latvia) is of interest to both the Yiddish linguist and the general linguist. For the Yiddish linguist, Courl(and) Y(iddish) is seen as a conservative dialect, one that preserves a number of features which provide information valuable for the historical reconstruction of E(astern) Y(iddish) dialects.[1] More generally, CourlY is frequently referred to as heavily "Germanized" owing to the influence of the coterritorial Baltic German of Courland. Culturally and socially the Jews of Courland are described as being very assimilated to German patterns.[2] Many Courland Jews were declared to speak the Courl G(erman) of their non-Jewish coterritorialists (see below). Thus, for the general linguist and sociolinguist, the investigation of CourlY would seem to offer a potential wealth of information about the CourlY speech community in a diglossic situation with a structurally similar—and supposedly culturally dominant—(Courl) German.[3]

In the present paper it will be suggested, however, that consideration of the data reveals another picture. Common assumptions about dominant language, diglossia, etc. are shown to be insufficient—or simply wrong—as regards the case of CourlY.

CourlY does indeed show a heavy German influence.[4] However, it turns out that this influence is almost entirely limited to lexical items—loan words. In terms of structure, the influence of CourlG upon CourlY is insignificant. Rather, as will be shown in the present paper, the contact-induced changes of structural import in CourlY are the result of CourlY being an integrated member of the greater EY dialect network. Thus, CourlY—as with other EY dialects—was subject to the regional, pan-regional, and supraregional pressures of the Yiddish speech community in its broadest sense.

Unfortunately, very little work has been done on CourlY. Linguistic data in the present paper are taken from the two—to my knowledge—only scholarly linguistic works devoted to CourlY. In 1923 Max Weinreich devoted an entire chapter of his four-chapter dissertation to CourlY. Three years later Kalmanovitsh provided an article-length response to Weinreich.[5] In addition, data were obtained through (my) listening to CourlY informant tapes of the *Language and Culture Atlas of Ashkenazic Jewry* (*LCAAJ*) at Columbia University, New York.[6]

The name *Courland* (German *Kurland*, Latvian *Kurzeme*, Yiddish *kurland*) refers to the area corresponding approximately to the Courland province of interwar-independent Latvia. Population groups found in this area during the periods relevant to the present study include Latvians, Germans, and Jews, as well as others. Its physical geography—i.e., its Baltic location—has left its mark on the human geography of Courland. The Baltic region has long been an area of intense interaction—economic, military, cultural, and linguistic. An investigation of any individual language or dialect in the Baltic region must be open to questions of pan-Balticisms, if not a Baltic *Sprachbund*.

Kalmanovitsh dates the Jewish settlement in Courland to the mid-seventeenth century; Ariste gives a sixteenth-century date.[7] In *Shtaplen* Max Weinreich emphasizes linguistic parallels between forms found in CourlY and forms found in older W(estern) Y(iddish) documents. This fits into Weinreich's overall picture (cf. *History of the Yiddish Language*) of Yiddish originating in (western) German lands, with subsequent migration of Yiddish speakers eastward.[8] Whereas Weinreich was not unaware of a Slavic component in CourlY, it was Kalmanovitsh who emphasized the importance of the Slavic component to the investigation of CourlY (164). Kalmanovitsh pointed out that CourlY was for 250–300 years not coterritorial with Slavic. Since CourlG lacks a parallel or similar Slavic component, the many words of Slavic origin in CourlY thus testify that CourlY was not "born" in Courland, but rather at a time and in a geographic area where there was intimate contact with Slavic.

It is relevant to the present discussion to classify CourlY in the context of Yiddish dialects generally. A common representation of the major branches of the Yiddish dialect tree may be given as follows:[9]

```
         /              \
Western Yiddish    Proto-Eastern Yiddish
                       /
              Proto-Southern         Proto-Northeastern
               /      \                /        \
          Central  Southeastern   Courland   Northeastern
```

Linguistically, CourlY is viewed as a subregion of Northeastern Yiddish (NEY), sharing a common P(roto-)NEY stage (see Herzog, p. 163). Because CourlY has been quite conservative in its retention of features otherwise lost in NEY (most notably in its retention of a number of distinctions in vowel quantity and quality) it is especially valuable in the historical reconstruction of PNEY, and of PEY.

Geographically—in terms of the internal dynamics of Jewish geography—

Courland Jews saw the broader Ashkenazic world divided into Courland Jews (*kurlender*) versus Samogitian Jews (*zameter*). Generally, Zamet/Samogitia is the province to the immediate southeast of Courland. For Courland Jews, however, the term *zameter* was used to refer generally to any non-Courland Jew (Weinreich, *Shtaplen*, p. 195).

The German presence in Courland must, for the most part, be traced back to two distinct migrations. The first, dating to the thirteenth century, consisted of speakers of Low German. A second migration, dating to approximately the sixteenth century, consisted of High German speakers. High German supplanted Low German in Courland (by approximately the end of the eighteenth century), though not without some Low German survivals in High German speech, as well as systematic relexification. For example, speakers could have a dialect-conscious rule of the sort: replace (Low German) *u:* with (High German) *au*, e.g., Low German *hu:s* →High German *haus*. Speakers (of Low German?) would then systematically apply this "rule" to any long *u:* they encountered (on Swedish-origin *ru:t* yielding CourlY *raut*, see below).

Jews and Germans came to Courland in separate migrations, from different geographic regions, and during different periods. The fact remains, however, that Yiddish and German were coterritorial and most likely in intimate contact in Courland for approximately 300 years. Thus it would be reasonable to seek an explanation for the oft-referred-to Germanization of CourlY in terms of language contact in Courland.

German was long the dominant language of commerce and city life in the Baltic region. Furthermore, it indeed seems to be the case that many Courland Jews in the early twentieth century were speakers of CourlG (for example, Max Weinreich). Thus it would be easy to posit the following scenario: CourlY speakers were in contact with speakers of CourlG for approximately 300 years. Since CourlG was dominant not only for Jews, but also for local Latvians and others in the economically and socially powerful Baltic German cities, it might then be suggested that a diglossic situation had arisen between CourlY and the structurally similar CourlG. At first, according to this scenario, Courland Jews would use CourlY among themselves (in L(ow) functions), but would use CourlG in typical H(igh) functions. Through time, it would then be assumed, Courland Jews would increasingly use German in all inter- and intra- group situations, in both H and L functions.

The German influence that one actually finds in CourlY is mostly or entirely lexical. Weinreich in *Shtaplen* and Kalmanovitsh in *Der yidisher dialekt in kurland* are able to provide hundreds of examples of Germanisms that are found in CourlY, but not in other Yiddish dialects. Weinreich and Kalmanovitsh classify the Germanisms as deriving from either a New High German (NHG) or Low German (LG) source.

Compare the following examples of NHG loans in CourlY with the Modern Standard Yiddish (StY) and Standard German (StG) items:

| CourlY | (Cite)[11] | StY | StG | gloss |
|---|---|---|---|---|
| u(:)r | MW, p. 209 | zejgɐr | Uhr | 'clock, watch' |
| farpasn | ZK, p. 181 | farzamɐn | verpassen | 'to miss' |
| taugɐništ | MW, p. 219 | gorništ | Taugenichts | 'good-for-nothing' |

The above examples appear to be rather straightforward NHG loans into CourlY. There is moderate adaptation to Yiddish phonology/morphology, e.g., German prefix *ver* = Yiddish *far*, German *nichts* 'nothing' = Yiddish *ništ*. In fact, there is a systematic adaptation to the phonology/phonotactics of (Courl) Yiddish. For example, consider the regular pan-Yiddish development of source Middle High German (MHG) *pf* is to *f* word-initially, and *p* after a vowel; cf. StY *ferd*, *kop*, StG *Pferd*, *Kopf* 'horse,' 'head.' This Yiddish constraint against affricate /pf/ is reflected again in the later CourlY loans from NHG (examples from MW, p. 205):

| CourlY | NHG | gloss |
|---|---|---|
| fingstn | Pfingsten | 'Pentecost' |
| šnupn | Schnupfen | 'sniffles' |
| štump- | stumpf- | 'dull' |

The problem of LG loan words in CourlY raises some intriguing questions that merit further study. The Jewish presence in Courland is dated after the time that High German (HG) is assumed to have supplanted LG in Courland. Determining the source of LG loans in CourlY could shed valuable light on the language situation in Courland generally. That is, did CourlY obtain the low-Germanisms from a HG source (where they would have been remnants/survivals from earlier LG Courland speech), or did CourlY obtain them directly from contact with LG speakers in Courland? In the latter instance, this would say something about maintenance of LG in Courland. Some examples of low-Germanisms in CourlY are:

(1) *ditkɐ* 'a three-kopek coin' (ZK, p. 175). This term is used to denote the smallest unit coin available; cf. CourlY *nit vert kejn ditkɐ* 'not worth anything, the smallest amount' with StY *nit vert kejn grošn*. Kalmanovitsh cites Berlin German usage of this etymon for the five-Pfennig coin, and traces it back to *Deut* 'a small Dutch coin.'

(2) *jeneral* 'general' (ZK, p. 177). This shows the LG spirantization of *g* > *j*. Kalmanovitsh cites this form in a CourlY expression taken from German. The Latvian calque of the same expression shows the *j*-form as well.

(3) *mang* 'among' (ZK, p. 178). Yiddish generally uses a variant of *cvišn*; cf. StG *zwischen*.

Some purported low-Germanisms in CourlY may in fact reflect pan-Balticisms from Hanseatic times or even earlier. For example, Weinreich (*Shtaplen*, p. 235) gives CourlY *raut* 'window pane.' He states that this etymon is used in CourlG as well, and traces it back to MHG *rûte*, but concludes that the lending source into MHG is unknown. I suggest that this word represents a Skandinavism in CourlY and CourlG; cf. modern Swedish *ruta* 'quadrangle; window pane.' The appearance of this etymon on the southeastern shores of the Baltic would thus be traced back to a time of Swedish presence in the area. Further strengthening this claim is the borrowing of this etymon into Estonian: *ruut* (Lehiste, personal communication).[12] Another possible Skandinavism in CourlY is *šnikɛrn* 'to cut without purpose; to cut into small pieces.' Weinreich (*Shtaplen*, p. 239) states that this word also occurs in CourlG, and relates it to *šnajdn* 'to cut.' If so, however, the *k* would be difficult to explain (cf. the German consonantism in the related words *schneiden*, *Schnitt*, *Schnitzel*, etc.). On the other hand, a possible source is suggested through comparison with modern Swedish *snickare* 'carpenter,' i.e., someone who cuts wood.

Kalmanovitsh ("Der yidisher dialekt," p. 164) correctly emphasizes the importance of the existence of a structurally integrated Slavic component in CourlY. The absence of Slavic-origin parallels in CourlG provides evidence that CourlY was indeed "born" elsewhere. Both historically and linguistically that elsewhere is to be found in a common PNEY origin outside of Courland, i.e., on Slavic speech territory.

It does not imply, however, that Slavisms found in PNEY (or in PEY) could not undergo subsequent independent developments within CourlY. Consider the following examples:

(4) CourlY *jagdɛ* 'strawberry' (MW, p. 220) has undergone semantic narrowing in CourlY; in StY *jagd* means 'berry' in the general sense; cf. Polish *jagoda* 'berry.'

(5) CourlY *vunc-n* 'moustache' (MW, p. 218), StY *voncɛ-s*; cf. Polish *wąsy*. Generally in Yiddish, noun-final schwa triggers the *s* plural. The CourlY form shows adoption of a "German" model plural, and subsequent reanalysis of the base form *voncɛ* (+ suffix) to *vonc* (+ suffix), after syncope of schwa before the nasal. However, this series of events is not limited to CourlY; compare EY regional *fragɛ – fragn* 'questions' vs. StY *fragɛ-s*.

(6) CourlY *cepɛ–* 'badger; touch; bother' (MW, p. 203). This form of the Yiddish Slavism reflects the well-known NEY hushing/hissing confusion (see below); cf. StY *čepɛ-*.

CourlY clearly is to be classified as part of the NEY dialect area, deriving from a common PNEY stage. The German influences, for the most part, are limited to the linguistic surface: loan words. There are, however, a few points of potential structural import that must be mentioned here briefly. For example, CourlY /a:/ is found exclusively in loan words, primarily from CourlG; e.g., *kra:n* 'crane,' *ja:* 'yes.' Long *a:* in the German loans thus conveniently filled a preexisting gap in the long-vowel system in CourlY (see Herzog, p. 164; Jacobs, 1984, pp. 88ff.). Additionally, CourlY shows a number of surface phonetic features that could be ascribed to CourlG (or general Baltic areal) influence, including: the realization of diphthong /ej/ phonetically as [æj], long /e:/ as [ɛ:], the "light" [l], and the lingual [r]. Such features do suggest areal contact, but have not had an impact on the structure of CourlY.

Overwhelmingly, however, the CourlY data reveal it to be a subregion of NEY. This is seen, for example, in consideration of: hushing/hissing confusion; in the gender system; in the issue of vowel length. As a point of departure, a rather clear example is seen in the comparison of (a part of) the phonemic vowel system of CourlY with general NEY, MHG, and NHG. This is illustrated in the following table taken from Weinreich (1923, p. 201):

*in present-day Literary German*

| | Haus | Auge | Brot | breit |
|---|---|---|---|---|
| | (MHG *û*) | (MHG *ou*) | (MHG *o*) | (MHG *ei*) |

*in Lithuanian Yiddish ( = NEY)*

| | *oj (ou, ui)* | *ej* | | *ej* |
|---|---|---|---|---|

*in Courland Yiddish*

| | *au* | *öi* | | *äi* |
|---|---|---|---|---|

Using MHG as the common point of departure, it is seen that modern literary German and modern Yiddish have had a separate linguistic evolution. MHG /u:/ (û) and /ou/ have merged in modern German, but not in Yiddish, and conversely, MHG-origin /ou/ and /o:/ have merged in (Eastern) Yiddish, but not in German. Furthermore, CourlY preserves three of the four historical phonemic distinctions, while NEY generally has undergone further merger to two distinctions.[13] In many such features, CourlY systematically reflects a conservative NEY subregion.

In common with NEY generally, CourlY has a two-gender system (masc.–fem.) vs. the historical three-gender system (masc.–fem.–neut.) found elsewhere in Yiddish, as well as in (Courl) German. CourlY shows Uriel Weinreich's intermediate gender: *di land—afn land* 'the country—on/in the country.'[14] Furthermore, in this NEY gender system, diminutives take the gender of the base noun (as opposed to the morphologically-assigned neut. in three-gender varieties of Yiddish and German). Thus, CourlY has fem. gender in *(di) entl* '(the) duck,' although this is a recent loan (cf. StY *kažkɞ* 'duck'< Slavic) from German, where it would presumably have neut. gender.[15]

The hushing/hissing problem, commonly referred to as *sabɛsdikɛr losn* (cf. StY *šabɛsdikɛr lošn*),[16] traces back (at least) to a general PNEY phenomenon. Examples from CourlY include:

| CourlY | StY | gloss | |
|---|---|---|---|
| cepɛ- | čepɛ- | 'badger, touch' | ( Slavic) |
| blondzɛn | blondžɛn | 'to stray' | ( Slavic) |
| šukɛ | sukɛ | 'booth for Sukkoth' | ( Semitic) |
| šæjxl | sejxl | 'logic; sense' | ( Semitic) |

Max Weinreich (1923, p. 202) states that the hushing/hissing confusion in CourlY (*š–s*; *č–c*) is found only in non-German-component words, but not in German-component words. So here, the German model does seem important. For example, Yiddish regularly distinguishes between German <-ss-> from shifted *t*, and from *ss:* StG *Wasser* (< *t* ) 'water,' *küssen* ( *ss* [earlier *sn*]) 'to kiss,' StY *vasɛr, kušn*, but CourlY *vasɛr, kusn*. Where the German model has [š], CourlY does as well; e.g. StG *schreiben*, CourlY *šrajbn* 'to write.'

In twentieth century NEY—including CourlY—the hushing/hissing confusion has been unstable and in retreat. Restoration of historical hushing/hissing distinctions in NEY may be attributed to pan-EY standardizing trends (U. Weinreich 1952). Examples of standardizing tendencies are also found in CourlY. For example, M. Weinreich (1923, p. 203) writes that CourlY (like CourlG) traditionally avoided the phoneme /ž/. The German loan *Kirschner* 'furrier' > (general) Yiddish *kiržnɛr* (the voicing of *š* > *ž* was an internal Yiddish development). Older CourlY avoided /ž/ with the doublet: *kirznɛr* ~ *kiršnɛr*, i.e., through adoption of one of two strategies: hush > hiss, or devoice *ž* > *š* on the German model. Significantly, Weinreich (1923, p. 203) writes that /ž/ has been (re)introduced into CourlY in the most recent times (i.e., up to ca. 1923) "through literary influences." Those influences are clearly Yiddish, not German.

The maintenance of vocalic length distinctions is seen as the primary feature distinguishing CourlY from general NEY (Weinreich 1923, pp. 199ff.); e.g., CourlY *bi:n* 'bee' vs. *bin* '(I) am' (cf. NEY *bin* 'bee; (I) am'). From my listening to *LCAAJ* tapes of three Courland locations it was evident that CourlY had preserved historical vowel length, but that the system was in collapse.[17] For example, alongside expected length in *gɛru:fn* 'called' (Najri), *ri:ga* 'Riga' (Libave/Liepaj), *vɛ:g* 'road' (Rejte Dine), one finds unexpected length or instability in *cɛri:sn* 'ripped' (Najri), *bru:nɛms* ~ *brunɛmɛr* 'fountains,' *šif* ~ *ši:f* 'ship' (Rejte Dine), and unexpected short vowels in *štOt* 'city' (Rejte Dine), *šOxn* 'neighbor' (Libave/Liepaj). Instability in long/short vowel distinctions would not result from CourlG influence, where such distinctions were intact. Just such a situation could obtain, however, from contact with lengthless general NEY, as well as from ongoing nineteenth- and twentieth-century standardizing tendencies.[18]

In overly simplistic traditional paradigms, changes in a minority language are attributed to influences from a dominant metropolitan variant. Thus, CourlY was presumed—as a matter of course—to be especially open to influences of the German *Kultursprache* (in its CourlG form).[19] Many of the recent (nineteenth and twentieth century) changes in CourlY suggest a situation of diglossia. In the present paper I have tried to show that it was not with the German *Kultursprache* that "Germanized" CourlY was diglossing. Rather, the recent changes of structural import in CourlY were viewed as resulting from influences from NEY and pan-EY standardizing trends.

Traditional notions of "dominance" live on, however. As mentioned above, Jews and Germans arrived in Courland via historically and geographically distinct migrations. Yet in his description of Riga German, Guido Eckardt sees Riga Jewish speech as an imprecise, unclear form of German.[20] He illustrates this with a (questionable) anecdote in which the "German" speech of the Jews displays clearly a number of Yiddish phonological and morphological features. Not naming the Jews by name, Eckardt refers to "a fraction of our population" who usually speak German, but do not especially place much weight on the "purity of the pronunciation or the sentence construction," as this does "not lie in the nature of this social class" ("liegt nicht in der Eigenart dieser Gesellschaftsklasse"). It is significant that Eckardt regards Courland Jews as constituting a part of his German speech community, while no such view is put forth concerning the speech of coterritorial Latvians. The considerable similarities between Yiddish and German of course play a role in Eckardt's perceptions. Eckardt's perceptions, however, are not borne out by the data discussed in the present paper.

The following anecdotal information suggests that twentieth-century CourlY speakers were sensitive to pan-EY dialectal and supralectal pressures. In 1989 I encountered a woman, born in the United States in approximately 1915. Her immigrant parents spoke CourlY to her, but she spoke English exclusively from her school years on. By 1989, her retention of Yiddish was only partial: mainly words, and some phrases. When asked to produce the Yiddish for 'to buy' she produced *kɔ̂yfn*. She then spontaneously added: "I know it's really *kejfn*, but I guess I'm supposed to say *kojfn*" (cf. NEY *kejfn*, StY *kojfn*). The woman had spent nearly all her life in Lancaster, Ohio, cut off from any Yiddish speech community. Her self-"corrections" likely reflected her parents' sensitivity to the sociolinguistic situation of Courland Jews in the early twentieth century.

Finally, the probable Skandinavisms *raut* and *šnikɐrn* suggest the appropriateness of further research into CourlY in the context of Baltic areal-linguistic phenomena. The influence of Hanseatic German on medieval Swedish is well known.[21] Linguistic influences in the other direction should be investigated as well. It would be interesting to ascertain which features common to many or most languages in the Baltic region may be considered of Swedish origin. The Swedish historical presence in the southern Baltic region was considerable. Interestingly, the inland Jews of the Latgalia province called coastal Baltic Jews *švejdn* 'Swedes' or *švejdlɛx* 'little Swedes,' a fact Lazerson connects to a Swedish incorporation of Livonia (Livland) and the Baltic coasts from 1660.[22]

An investigation of the language of Courland Jews must consider the multiple sociolinguistic environments in which Courland Jewry found itself. To speak simply of a Germanization of CourlY is insufficient. CourlY speakers were exposed to a number of areal influences—among them CourlG, Latvian, as well as common Balticisms. However, the main sources of ongoing changes in CourlY of the late nineteenth and early twentieth century are to be found in the interaction of CourlY speakers with NEY and the broader EY speech community.

## Notes

1. Marvin I. Herzog, *The Yiddish Language in Northern Poland: Its Geography and History* (The Hague: Mouton, 1965), pp. 151ff. (Also Part III of the *International Journal of Linguistics* 31/2.)

2. Borekh Rivkin (ps. Borekh Avrom Vaynrib), "Di kurlender litvakes," in Mendl Sudarski et al., *Lite* I (New York: Kultur-gezelshaft fun litvishe yidn, 1951), pp. 407–516.

3. I would like to thank the Melton Center for Jewish Studies at Ohio State University for funding a research trip to New York City to use the facilities at the YIVO Institute for Jewish Research, and of the *Language and Culture Atlas of Ashkenazic Jewry* (*LCAAJ*) in my research on CourlY. I thank Professor Mikhl Herzog, director of the *LCAAJ* for access to the Courland (and other) tapes, as well as for personal discussion about CourlY. I would also like to express my appreciation to Zachary Baker and Dina Abramowicz of the YIVO library for assisting me in a literature search for relevant linguistic and non-linguistic materials on Jewish Courland. I also thank Professor Mark Louden, University of Texas/Austin, for providing me with material on Riga German. Finally, it is my pleasant duty to thank Professor Ilse Lehiste, Ohio State University, for patient and valuable discussion of a number of issues concerning Baltic German. Any mistakes or shortcomings in the present article are the sole responsibility of the author.

4. This should be held distinct from the more general phenomenon of Germanization in Yiddish called *daytshmerish* and defined by Mordkhe Schaecter as "the tendency to appeal to standard German (*daytsh* 'German') as a model of 'correctness' for the Yiddish Language." "The 'Hidden Standard': A Study of Competing Influences in Standardization," in Marvin I. Herzog, Wita Ravid, and Uriel Weinreich, eds., *The Field of Yiddish* 3 (The Hague: Mouton, 1969), p. 284.

5. The comments and discussion by Alfred Landau make mention of the

CourlY material: "Miluem tsu M. Vaynraykhs 'shtaplen,'" *Yidishe filologye* 1 (1924), pp. 55–61 of Max Weinreich, *Shtaplen. Fir etyudn tsu der yidisher shprakh-visnshaft un literatur-geshikhte* (Berlin: Farlag Vostok, 1923). However, Landau focuses on parallels between Germanisms in CourlY and Galician Yiddish. This is of only indirect relevance to the current discussion, and will thus not be dealt with further here.

6. *LCAAJ. Tapes of the Language and Culture Atlas of Ashkenazic Jewry*. On file, Columbia University, New York.

7. Zelig Kalmanovitsh, "Der yidisher dialekt in kurland," *Filologische shriftn fun Yivo* 1 (Vilne 1926), p. 166; Paul Ariste, "Tsu der haspoe fun yidish oyf nit-yidishe shprakhn," *Yivo bleter* XI/1–2 (1937), pp. 83–85.

8. For a claim that Yiddish originated in the east, on bilingual German–Slavic territory, see Paul Wexler, "Yiddish—The Fifteenth Slavic Language," focus article, *International Journal of the Sociology of Language* V (1991), pp. 9–150.

9. Herzog, *The Yiddish Language*, views Proto-EY (PEY) = Proto-Northeastern Yiddish (PNEY). The inclusion of a PEY stage distinct from PNEY represents a modification based on arguments found in Neil Jacobs, *Economy in Yiddish Vocalism: The Case of Central Yiddish*, dissertation, Columbia University, 1984 (Ann Arbor: University Microfilms). A revised version appeared as *Yiddish Vocalism: A Study in the Interplay of Hebrew and Non-Hebrew Components* (Wiesbaden: Harrassowitz, 1990).

10. In terms of Jewish geography, the (cultural and linguistic) boundaries of Courland extend beyond the political provincial boundaries.

11. Author and page number are given as MW = Max Weinreich, *Shtaplen*, ZK = Zelig Kalmanovitsch, "Der yidisher dialekt in kurland."

12. A Low German form of the word (cf. Dutch *ruit*) might be a possible source (L. Inghels, personal communication). However, the presence of a stem -*u* in non-nominative forms of the word in Estonian suggests a source in an oblique form in older Swedish weak nouns (nominative: -*a*; accusative/dative/genitive: -*u*); likewise, Finnish regularly borrowed the oblique form in such Swedish loans.

13. Kalmanovitsh (p. 167) claims that Weinreich's *öi* diphthong actually had a fully-rounded glide, thus: [ɸy]. In my listening to the *LCAAJ* CourlY tapes, I heard [ɸy] as well. On the issue of rounded glides in Yiddish, see Neil Jacobs, "Glide Substitution in Northeastern Yiddish," unpublished paper read at the Linguistic Society of America Annual Meeting, January 4, 1991, Chicago.

14. Uriel Weinreich, "The Seven Genders of Yiddish," unpublished paper read at the Linguistic Society of America Annual Meeting, December 29, 1961, Chicago; Neil Jacobs, "Northeastern Yiddish Gender-Switch: Abstracting Dialect Features Regionally," *Diachronica* VII/1 (1990), pp. 59–100.

15. The presence of an -*l* (as opposed to a *t*- or *k*-based) diminutive marker is a Yiddish feature.

16. See Uriel Weinreich, "Sábesdiker losn in Yiddish: A problem of linguistic affinity," *Word* VIII (1952), pp. 360–377.

17. The locations were selected from across Courland: Rejte Dine, Loc. # 56247; Najri, Loc. # 56254; Liepaj/Libave, Loc. # 56214.

18. For recent discussion of processes of standardization in EY, see Kerstin Hoge, *From 'Anti-Daytshmerish' to the 'Hidden Standard': The Dynamics of the Yiddish Standardization Process*. Master's thesis, Ohio State University.

19. On Yiddish influences upon Baltic German, see Valentin Kiparsky, *Fremdes im Baltendeutsch. Mémoires de la Société Néophilologique de Helsingfors* XI (1936) and review of Kiparsky in Ariste, "Tsu der hashpoe fun yidish."

20. Guido Eckardt, *Wie man in Riga spricht*. [ = Separat-Abdruck aus der "Baltischen Monatsschrift" (1904), 7] (Riga: Komissionsverlag von Jonck & Poliewsky, 1911).

21. Elias Wessén, *Om det tyska inflytandet på svenskt språk under medeltiden*. Skrifter utgivna av nämnden för svensk språkvård, XII (1967) (Stockholm).

22. M. Lazerson, (1942). "A bisl baltish-yidishe geografye," *Yidishe shprakh* 2/3 (1942), pp. 84–87.

# Alsatian Yiddish Theater at the Turn of the Century

## Astrid Starck

Alsatian Yiddish Theater was set in a country when so-called folk literature was flourishing throughout Europe—a literature based mostly on regional languages and in which satire, criticism, and humor are the primary aspects.[1] European folk literature was also based on an interest in village and country life, which was doomed to disappear because of rural depopulation. This theater combined philosophical tendencies derived from German Humanism with ideas expressed by Herder as well as in Romanticism and Naturalism. The influence of Wilhelm von Humboldt is noticeable in its overall folkloristic approach. The language through which a culture is expressed acquires primary importance as its privileged vehicle. Had not Goethe, during his stay in Strasbourg and under Herder's influence, collected folk songs and recorded customs and traditions? This process, regional and yet far from confining itself to a restricted geographic space, acquired a universal value owing to the very fact of its pan-European emergence. Nineteenth-century dialect literature was strongly influenced by the ideas of the Age of Enlightenment: Through everyone's specificity and the diversity of cultures, the right to difference could be claimed, which made it possible to reach universality.

Alsatian Yiddish theater is no exception. It cannot be studied separately, not only because it arose in a region that possessed five languages: two languages regarded as cultural languages—French and German—and three vernacular languages—Alsatian German, Alsatian Yiddish, and Yenish, which has often been mistaken for Alsatian Yiddish.[2] Alsatian Yiddish theater has never been the subject of a specialized study, for it has not produced any well-known writers. Alsatian Jewish writers, though quadrilingual, usually chose to write in French, since French was their language of Emancipation. Such was the case with Daniel Stauben/Auguste Vidal (translator of Leopold Kompert's 'ghetto stories') and for Léon Cahun. However, some writers opted for both German and French (Alexandre Weill) and some for Alsatian German or Yiddish (Léon Bollag Kahn), while others still opted for Alsatian Yiddish (Mayer Woog, Alexandre Weill, Simon Wormser). Only one writer produced in three languages, Weill, who started writing in German, then in French, and finally in Alsatian Yiddish.

All these writers had one thing in common: much like the Eastern Yiddish writers, they staged the life of their region as filtered through the medium of several languages. They portrayed Alsatian Jewish culture both in critical and idyllic terms. But it is Alsatian Yiddish that best reflected and expressed country life, being the mother tongue of Alsatian Jews. For example Stauben, an Alsatian Jewish writer who, incidentally, wrote in French, depicting a country wedding in one of his stories, refers to the fact that Yiddish-speaking Alsatians expressed themselves better than their German neighbors who had been invited to the wedding and were doing their best to speak 'correct German.'[3] Attention must be drawn to the fact that the people speaking the local dialects came into contact with one another, the Alsatian Christians were interested in Yiddish or used it in their theater, not merely for comical purposes but for a better reciprocal understanding.[4]

The Alsatian Yiddish theater, which had its own tradition of *purim spil* and performances of the story of Queen Esther, made especially great strides at the end of the nineteenth century, but one must not forget that Yiddish literature in the West had never ceased to be productive. The trouble is that Yiddish literature, by attempting to provide a chronicle and testimony to the past (collections of tales, proverbs, and expressions) failed to be productive in terms of the future. Moreover, well-known writers felt that writing in Yiddish stood in the way of assimilation and modernity. Yet neither the ideals of the Enlightenment on and against the so-called 'jargon,' nor those of the French Revolution, which aimed to eliminate 'foreign languages' in Alsace, were able to rid Alsace of its local language, at least during the nineteenth century.[5] However, there can be no doubt that these concepts proved to be obstacles to literary development that have not been overcome to this day.

As for Alsatian Yiddish, it now exists only as a spoken language. Claude Vigée, a contemporary poet whose literary production includes the four existing languages—French, Alsatian German, Alsatian Yiddish, and German—is the most noteworthy representative of the acute linguistic problem particular to Alsace.[6] Alsatian Yiddish is still considered an insignificant language. Despite the fact that it is perceived to be at the very root of Alsatian Jewishness, it is no longer used as its particular mode of expression. This situation is well worth taking note of and studying, because it is not restricted to Vigée: it was the result of the negative attitude toward Yiddish in general inherited from the Jewish "Enlightenment" and its scholarly traditions. Most German-speaking Jewish intellectuals considered Yiddish a ghetto language, some did not even think that it was a language in its own right, but a bastardized form of German.

Let me point out that discourses on Alsatian Yiddish were never held in this language but always in German (before 1914) or in French (after 1918). We must also note that the particular ambivalence toward Western Yiddish and Alsatian Yiddish arose from the distinction between the written and oral modes, between a literary and a vernacular language. To take an example: in his compilation of Yiddish proverbs and expressions, Abraham Tendlau, who based his work on the oral language, writes in his introductory chapter that he is quite pleased with the immanent disappearance of this barbaric jargon, testimony to life in the ghetto.[7] His compilation is an account of a bygone age. Max Grünbaum's attitude is quite different in his anthology of Yiddish texts, translations, paraphrases, or his adaptions of Biblical or Talmudic texts, because he dealt with a literary language that had never been discredited.[8] The same approach is to be found in Alsace, with one difference: the interest in the dramatic production, based on the oral language, remained geographically restricted. Up to this day, Alsatian Yiddish has not been perceived even by its own speakers as an independent entity, that is, as a Jewish language within a larger body, but rather as a heterogeneous mixture of languages void of logic and grammar. It is still regarded as a hybrid of distorted German and Hebrew, an idea that is not supported by modern linguistic scholarship. Yet it prevented Alsatian Yiddish from existing and developing in its own right, whether in the written or oral mode.

The theater was the ideal milieu in which to set a living oral language. It provided an escape from the confinement to which this language had been subjected at the end of the century, by being petrified in glossaries and lexicons. By its very existence it disproved the allegation that Alsatian Yiddish had disappeared since it represented on stage everyday life in many Alsatian places. There are numerous Alsatian Yiddish playwrights; unfortunately only about thirty of their plays were ever published. Until recently all kinds of plays written in Alsatian, Lorrainian, and Swiss Yiddish were performed. It would be interesting to study the role, impact, and frequency of this theater as well as the response to it. Except for Weill the writers were and remain little known. As a young man he frequented the literary circles in Paris and was a friend of Heinrich Heine and Victor Hugo.

Little is known concerning these authors' lives. They came from the country and belonged to the folk theater. Mayer Woog's production was the largest: he wrote about twenty plays between 1874 and 1894. He is followed by Weill with three plays (1885–1889), Bollag with one play (1902), and Wormser with one play (date unknown). All of these plays were written in verse; a few of them included folk songs. It was an optimistic, humorous theater designed to rid people of their shortcomings and educate them. The authors wrote comedies of manners and burlesque farces in which they indulged to their heart's content in situational comedy and *quid pro quo*s. They had no interest in serious dramatic development.

Like in all folk theater, weddings are among the major themes: they provide an excellent background against which the opposition between tradition and modernity is shown. All the characters representative of the Jewish world are brought together under this theme: the *schnorrer* or beggar asked to dinner on Sabbath evening; the *schadchen* or matchmaker (Woog's work figures *Schadchen Johle*, the hero of a folk song); the *saufer* or scribe who comes and checks the *mesusoths*; the *gaasejopper* or goat dealer, broke, old-fashioned, and unable to find someone willing to marry him; the barber who acts as a dentist and a healer; the village idiot; the gossips who gather at the market, often in the evenings.[9] Not only are young girls no longer willing to have their fiancé chosen by their fathers, but what is more, women, especially widows, are reluctant to marry: the suitor does not suit them either physically, because he has a goiter (a pretext also for criticizing doctors who are depicted as quacks; cf. *Doktor Fauscht*), or socially because he is a *schlemiel*, a good-for-nothing, or morally because he is no example to follow. Love as a basis for marriage is more important than the dowry or social conventions. Love as a sickness escapes the shrewd look of quack doctors. Of course, the plays have happy endings, for eventually fathers always yield to reason.

Another important theme is the relation between Jewish and Christian communities. It is illustrated in one example by an extraterrestrial correspondence between a Christian, an inveterate boozer, and his friend Wolf, who remains on earth.[10] The first becomes a go-between relating earthly events after they happen, a burial for instance. This reminds us of a later short story written by Sholem Aleichem, "The Letters Stolen at the Post-Office," or more recently of Max Frisch's *Manhattan Transfer* in which the hero, still alive, attends his own burial. These extraterrestrial missives make life in the hereafter seem ordinary by making it similar to life on earth. At the same time they emphasize the continuity from one life to another.

Comedies combine traditional religious life and secular life: during the golden wedding of a couple, some of the guests indulge in tales that are humorous paraphrases in the Biblical style ("Creation of the World") or Talmudic style ("The Kugel's Prayer"), i.e. illustrating a precept. These tales are followed by an examination at the *Kheder*, the Jewish school where, in the presence of both leading secular and religious citizens, the pupils display their ignorance as well as 'diabolic' behavior in the eyes of the inspector who goes on the warpath against those French teachers with modern irreligious ideas.[11] He advocates the traditional method of beating pupils in order to hammer into them what he calls knowledge, which is to say, in fact, ignorance (cf. *The Polish Lad* by Linetzki and *The Bajazzo* by Karl Emil Franzos). This reminds us of the campaign against Yiddish speaking teachers, often of Polish origin, who were regarded as old fashioned and uneducated speakers of jargon. These are opposed to the new French-speaking and Francophile teachers whose task it is to do away with Alsatian Yiddish (ibid.).

In the working classes, French was regarded as an aristocratic language that made quite an impression. Weill shows this in his play written in Alsatian Yiddish, *Der Gershing Narr*, in which his hero thinks that a proposal written in French is more likely to be accepted.[12] But will it be understood? In a short story by the same author, two sisters tell one another their secrets and one of them confesses, shamefully, that the biggest fault for which her fiancé reproaches her is her ignorance of French. "You are French, are you not?" says he, "and yet you cannot speak a single word of French!"[13] Similarly humorous (or tragic) situations recur in Alsatian German literature where dialect speakers are not spared. It is worth noticing that nineteenth-century writers, even when they write only in French, stand up for Yiddish and show a great understanding for the linguistic situation in which they themselves grew up. In fact, they act as intermediaries: they give people who cannot speak Yiddish an access to the Alsatian Yiddish culture and they give Yiddish-speaking people who cannot speak French an access to French through their own traditions and habits linked with everyday life. These authors should have done the opposite in Alsatian Yiddish so as to invest it with a literary value as well as the status of a cultural language, as was the case for Eastern Yiddish, which developed not only a literature of its own but undertook to translate the literature of the rest of the world.[14]

The ancient, close bond with Polish teachers followed by the massive arrival of immigrants from Central and Eastern Europe, as well as the arrival of Zionist Jewish students at the University of Strasbourg, favored an exchange with the Eastern Yiddish speakers and their literary production. Indeed, we can see that the development of the Alsatian Yiddish theater went hand in hand with the development of the Eastern Yiddish theater. And their thematic material and their aims were closely related, if not identical: to educate and enlighten people, to give them a moral conscience while giving them a good time. One cannot help but think of Shloyme Ettinger (*Serkele*), Abraham Ber Gottlober (*Der Dektuch*), Eisik Meir Dick, Abraham Goldfaden and his play *Shmendrik*. The hero of this play became the namesake of a silly character and corresponds to the *Narr*—jester or fool—of the Alsatian Yiddish theater. The comedy 'heroes' of this theater are both typical characters of the Jewish community, but at the same time marginal people. As such, their place within the Jewish tradition is, in my opinion, uncertain, as the author has already opted for modernity and acts as a spokesman for it.

I would particularly like to refer to the most prolific author of the Alsatian Yiddish theater, Mayer Woog. He died at the beginning of the twentieth century, a poor and abandoned man, in the Jewish poorhouse of Mulhouse (Alsace) as Dr. Elias informs us in an article published in the *Jewish Almanach* dated 1903–1904.[15] Elias lays stress not on Woog's literary works— for he considers him a poor writer—but on his linguistic, sociological, and folkloric testimony. But in doing this, Elias shows that he shares the concern prevalent at the beginning of the century: collecting customs, traditions, folklore, and its means of expression, language, in this case Alsatian Yiddish.[16] Elias shares the Zionist point of view and has a global vision: he sees in Woog the writer of the 'Alsatian ghetto' who cannot be regarded separately but rather as a link in the chain of the diaspora. On both sides of Europe, traditions and customs echo one another: such was the subject, at the end of the nineteenth century, of the collection of short stories written by Leopold von Sacher–Masoch, *Jüdisches Leben* [Jewish Life]. According to Elias, Woog is content with a snapshot vision limited to the present, which he describes and where he finds his characters among his own contemporaries.

Little is known about Woog's life. He was born in Hegenheim, one of the largest communities in the Sundgau, during the second half of the nineteenth century. He attended school for a while in Basel, Switzerland, and later had to give up his trade as a draper when he became blind (*Blind-Maier*, blind Maier). He then settled down in Allschwil, near Basel. To earn a living, says Arthur Zivy in his collection *Alsatian Yiddish*, Woog became a playwright. As a hawker selling books, he went, accompanied by a child, to Basel, Mulhouse, and La Chaux-de-Fonds to sell his booklets. Zivy also insists on the poor literary value of Woog's writings but emphasizes the fact that they constitute a linguistic goldmine.

A few words about the environment in which Woog grew up will have to suffice here. The nineteenth century witnessed the development and the decline of the community of Hegenheim: in 1861 there were 644 persons belonging to the Jewish community, whereas there were only one hundred in 1905. For fifty years, until 1884, this community was under the care of Rabbi Moses Nordmann, who had liberal leanings and had carried on Talmudic studies. He had also been educated in French and at German universities (Nancy, Würzburg and Heidelberg). The relationship between Hegenheim and Basel had been very close: one must remember that in 1848, the Jewish community of Hegenheim had endured a riot by the village inhabitants, some of whom found shelter in Switzerland later. The proximity of the frontier and neighboring dialects can be felt in Woog's vocabulary where Alemannic words from the Sundgau (*konnt, Haieri*), Swiss words (*Anke, Fotzelschnitte*), as well as French words pronounced in the Alsatian manner (*absoluma, La Schodfo, bugher, deschpediere*, etc.) are to be found.

Woog left Hegenheim to settle down in Allschwil, near Basel. The two places are very close, but Woog moved from country to town without forgetting or forsaking his mother tongue, which he shared with several other languages. The presence of different but coterritorial languages is characteristic of the Alsatian German and Alsatian Yiddish theater.

One more point should be made—a fundamental remark that runs counter to the usual discussion of Alsatian Yiddish—namely, that Alsatian Yiddish itself is never called into question in the different plays: different protagonists address each other in their own language and everyone seems to understand each other. For example, in front of a speaker of German, the Yiddish speaker does not abandon his language, trying to imitate the German speaker. This is a characteristic feature that ought to be studied. True, from time to time, we are told that, unfortunately, one would like to understand everything but that it is impossible.

Most of the protagonists' remarks relate to letters from Germany and are written in a deliberately inflated style. For example, the village teacher is called in to translate them (we are in Alsace at the time when it had been annexed by Germany). The characters are assigned characteristic names to represent speakers of different languages. The linguistic parts are quite varied: characters are not confined to one certain language in relation to their social hierarchy. Nevertheless, young girls seem to feel a strong attraction toward German suitors—either officers or manufacturers—who do not speak Yiddish any longer. This attraction can run counter to the parents' wishes. In this case, the wedding can take place only because the young girl leaves home and forces this marriage upon her parents. The range of language, the standard of language, and the choice of a language in a given situation intrinsically contain their own commentary. They constitute a direct interpretative view that the audience can hear.

Doubtless, one must also look for an explanation of the renewal of the Alsatian Yiddish theater in the language itself. First of all, let us point out the fact that it developed after the annexation of Alsace–Lorraine (1871) as a characteristic expression that hinders assimilation. However, it abandons the old Hebraic way of writing Yiddish to switch to Gothic lettering. We are faced with a question: why did this change occur at a time when the Hebrew alphabet was still in common use in correspondence, newspapers, and also in religious literature? The ascendancy of Germany, it is true, had a strong influence on the intellectual, cultural, and linguistic life of the Yiddish-speaking world of the time. Even the style of Eastern Yiddish, the Hebraic spelling, was Germanized in those days. Though Yiddish itself was regarded as a 'corrupt' branch of German, it was regarded as a branch of German all the same.

Alsatian Yiddish meant to set itself up as a literary language, a position it was to share with the other languages present in the area. It coexisted geographically next to the others and enabled everyone to read Yiddish: Hebraisms were very numerous in Alsatian German and a lot of the Christians understood Yiddish. Therefore, one can imagine that readers and audiences were large in numbers. Western Yiddish and Alsatian Yiddish were accused of abandoning their way of writing and having thus brought about their untimely end. I do not think that the playwrights intended to do such a thing.

Woog's attitude was probably influenced by the fact that both Alsatian and Swiss German were in the process of becoming literary languages at the end of the nineteenth century. The Alsatian Yiddish theater set down in writing an oral language that conveyed an oral mode in writing to which the writers added a 'literary scope.' Woog was indeed never aware of doing pioneer work. To him, Alsatian Yiddish was just another language, with its speakers firmly set in everyday life. In this respect he differed from the respected writers who wrote Yiddish only to make fun of it.

The Alsatian Yiddish theater was an important aspect of Jewish culture in Alsace. It was situated at the crossroads of tradition and modernity, but it was not able to set itself up as the founder of a future theater, probably because it had, in terms of its characters, a view of its own existence that was either too derisive or too humorous. I would like to point out the fact that, except for the interest shown by Zionists for whom this theater took on a very special importance (it appeared at Zionist Congress in Basel), it was not able either to attract followers or to win well-known writers to its cause—for the numerous reasons mentioned here. The acknowledgment of its existence is, however, of capital importance, as it provides an environment in which Alsatian Yiddish can continue to come alive.

## NOTES

1. I can quote among other examples Ludwig Thoma (Bavaria), Ferdinand Raimund and Johannes Neopmuk Nestroy (Austro-Hungarian Monarchy), and Jeremias Gotthelf (Switzerland).

2. Cf. Louis Wilhelm, *Catalogue de la Section Alsacienne et Lorraine*, III (Strasbourg: Bibliothèque universitaire régionale, 1926–1929), pp. 345–346.

3. Daniel Stauben, *Scènes de la vie juive en Alsace* (Paris: Lévy frères, 1860), p. 75.

4. Stauben relates an acutal experience that took place in Wintzenheim, where a large Jewish community flourished. A Christian blacksmith named Rodolphe used to tour from village to village to perform his puppet show. Every other day he would enact a play in Yiddish, especially the story of Joseph and Esther. Stauben, *Scènes de la vie juive*, p. 68. Mayer Woog portrayed a Yiddish-speaking Christian. Mayer Woog, *Brief vom Schnappsackhaieri an der Wolf* (Basel: published privately, 1874).

5. Cf. Zosa Szajkowski, "Der kamf kegn yidish in frankraich (XVII.–XIX. 5.5. Iorhundrt)," *Yivo-Bleter* 14 (New York 1939), pp. 46–77.

6. I cite these writings in *Alsatian Yiddish*. Claude Vogée (Strauß), "A Pessach Brief," *Du bec à l'oreille* (Strasbourg: Editions de la Nuée-Bleu, 1977), pp. 88–93.

7. Abraham Tendlau, *Sprichwörter und Redensarten deutsch-jüdischer Vorzeit. Als Beitrag zur Volks-, Sprach- und Sprichwörter-Kunde. Aufgezeichnet aus dem Mund des Volkes* (Frankfurt am Main: Keller, 1860), p. IV.

8. Max Grünbaum, *Jüdischdeutsche Chrestomathe* (Leipzig: Brockhaus, 1882).

9. The tradition of the *Frauenbusengesprach* of gossiping. Cf. Shakespeare's *Merry Wives of Windsor*, or *Dorfweiber-Schmües* in Alsatian Yiddish.

10. Mayer Woog, *Der Brief vom Schnappsackhaieri an der Wolf* (Basel 1874).

11. Mayer Woog, *Der Chasenetag im Greisenalter!* (Hegenheim: published privately, 1891).

12. Alexandre Weill, *Der Gershing Narr* (Straßburg: no date), p. 9.

13. Alexandre Weill, *Couronne, histoire juive* (Paris: Poulet–Malassis et De Broise, 1887).

14. Cf. the publication *Schweizer Volkskunde* [Swiss Folklore] of 1917, which

works toward the same end. E. Hoffman–Krayker asks the owners of texts to publish them and Immanuel Olsvanger publishes proverbs and expressions in Alsatian Yiddish.

15. Dr. Elias, "Ein elsässischer Jargondichter," *Jüdischer Volkskalender für das Jahr 5664* (Buch- und Kunstverlag Brünn 1903/1904).

16. Arthur Zivy, *Elsässwr Jiddish. Jüdisch-deutsche Sprichwörter und Redensarten* (Basel: Victor Goldschmidt, 1966), p. 5.

# The Debate about Hebrew, in German: The *Kulturfrage* in the Zionist Congresses, 1897–1914

## Michael Berkowitz

The German language played an important role in the pre-state Zionist Movement in Europe.[1] In the wake of the Holocaust, however, it is understandable that many commentators find it difficult to reflect on the centrality of German in early Zionism. Furthermore, the place of German is obscured because the Zionists were very successful in creating the myth that the Hebrew language was a most effective cohesive force in the movement. Nevertheless, from 1897 to 1914, the idea that Hebrew should and could be a vital rallying point for a regenerated Jewish nation was never an unchallenged goal in Zionism.

German was, in fact, the main language of discourse of the Zionist Organization: it was the language of the annual and biennial Zionist congresses and the Zionist's central organ, *Die Welt*. German was crucial as well because it provided a cultural tie to the largely Yiddish-speaking Jewish masses and the Eastern Jews who had recently migrated westward.[2] Furthermore, for assimilated Jews in Central Europe, German promoted the perception that Zionism occupied "high" cultural ground.[3] And last, as the focus of my remarks, the use of German helped to tone down the divisive Zionist *Kulturdebatte* especially in the context of its preeminent institution, the Congress. In light of the movement's goals, it seems that no other language could have been as constructive as German. It was the only language in which such disparate Zionist constituencies could speak to each other—both literally and figuratively.

From 1897 to 1902, the *Kulturdebatte* in the Zionist congresses was essentially a dispute between two distinct factions in the movement: the first were referred to as "cultural Zionists" or *Kulturisten*; they maintained that Zionism should take a prominent role in developing and propagating a secular national culture, featuring the revival of the Hebrew language. To varying degrees, they were admirers of Ahad Ha-Am, the outstanding Hebrew essayist of his day, for whom the paramount goal of Zionism was the gradual establishment of a Jewish cultural center in Palestine. The most outspoken adversaries of the *Kulturisten* were the small phalanx of orthodox Jews who had joined Zionism; they would later form *Mizrachi*, the initial orthodox-Zionist party. The orthodox feared that the *Kulturisten* wanted to replace traditional Judaism with a modern, secularized Jewish ideology and way of life, in which former religious elites would have little say.[4]

For the most part, such views were not groundless. With roots in the tradition of the *Haskalah*, or Jewish Enlightenment, many *Kulturisten* did articulate a decided anti-clerical stance. They aspired, at least, to "trim" what they saw as the "excesses" of rabbinic Judaism.[5] The spiritual objections of orthodoxy, that Zionism represented a false or premature messianism, are well known. The material grounds for their rejection of Zionism, and specifically Zionist Hebraism, are less apparent or admitted.[6] The orthodox perceived that with its potential of establishing Zionist-oriented *chadarim*, *yeshivot*, and communal organizations, the movement "might oust them from their main source of livelihood—teaching."[7] Quite possibly Theodor Herzl, the movement's leader, was aware that "material as well as religious motivations were intertwined in fearing that the orthodox would virtually declare war on Zionism."[8] The highly assimilated Herzl firmly maintained that the movement must be as inclusive as possible in order to succeed. He deftly managed to sidestep this conflict by keeping Zionism's official position on culture as vague as possible.[9] Herzl wished not to offend or alienate the few orthodox who had declared themselves in favor of the movement, and he sought to prevent the erection of barricades that might keep the masses of East European orthodox—who generally opposed Zionism—from rallying to the movement in the future.[10]

The *Weltanschauungen* of the secular Hebraists and orthodox Zionists were in contentious opposition during the prewar years, and similar tensions are still being exercised in the modern state of Israel. Yet had the congress discussions been in Hebrew, most of the rabbis would have considered it politically inopportune to enjoin the debate. However much the *Kulturdebatte* afforded some of the more raucous scenes in the Zionist congresses, a few of the orthodox might not have been present at all had German not been the Zionists' public language. Their attendance was crucial in order for Zionism to assume the appearance of an assembly representing all of Jewry, in nurturing a party system in the Zionist organization, and in concretizing the Zionists' professed bond to traditional Judaism.

In effect, then, it was by default that German was significant in this regard because it largely precluded the official use of Hebrew in the movement's first decade. There is little doubt that greater stress on Hebrew would have made Zionism into an even narrower sect. In addition, though, German is important because it allowed Zionism to distance itself from Yiddish.[11] "German, of necessity, would likely be the official language," Herzl proposed in *Der Judenstaat*, even though he held "nothing against French or English." Obviously, to him, German would be the most easily assimilated "language of culture" for the Yiddish-speaking Jewish masses. Herzl ruled out Hebrew on the grounds of practicality: "We can no longer speak to each other in Hebrew," an indisputable fact around the turn of the century.[12] Most Jews might have been able to sound out Hebrew characters and repeat prayers, but they had little mastery of Hebrew as an everyday spoken language. On the other hand, it was not that difficult for Yiddish speakers to understand the gist of a speech in German—or vice versa.

Replacing Yiddish, however, was far from Herzl's greatest priority, and certainly the advancement of Hebrew never rose above a peripheral concern. Herzl saw the goals of the *Kulturisten* as premature, rather than fundamentally undesirable.[13] He may have sensed that Hebrew culture was not the best means for nationalizing the Jews, that Hebraization was too esoteric a concept for a plurality of the Jews. Herzl had, after all, come of age in the multilingual Habsburg Dual Monarchy, and he might have anticipated the volatility and emotion embedded in Yiddish, the tongue of the masses. Herzl was not alone in this; even some prominent Hebraists drew similar conclusions about the unlikelihood of Hebraism to attract an enthusiastic following.[14]

The relationship of Zionism to Yiddish was a focal point for several major speeches and debates at the congresses. At the inaugural Zionist Congress of 1897, Nathan Birnbaum (who later became an ardent Yiddishist and after that a founder of the orthodox *Agudat Israel* party) asserted that "the great wave of Yiddish culture" was too wedded to its European environment to comprise a unique Jewish culture. Birnbaum used the dichotomy of *Kultur* versus *civilization*, current in Germany, to distinguish his preferred variety of Jewish national expression.[15] Only the Hebraists, the speaker suggested, were capable of developing an authentic Jewish national ethic, since their goal was a complete, new national life for Jews on an equal footing with that of other nations—as opposed to cultural autonomy in the Pale of Settlement (SP V, pp. 30–31). To assimilated Western Jews, Birnbaum's disparaging remarks about Yiddish struck a familiar chord. In some respects, he had characterized middle-class Jewry's attitude toward the rapidly vanishing language of their parents and grandparents, or what they themselves had spoken in their childhood.

Within the congress setting, the first orthodox rebuttals to the *Kulturisten* acknowledged their fear of the supplanting of Judaism, exemplified by Martin Buber's appeal in 1898 for all Zionists to contribute toward the *Kulturist* agenda.[16] The next year it was argued that the so-called cultural program served little purpose for the Jews with whom Zionism was supposedly most concerned—the poor of the Pale of Settlement. Although the leading *Kulturisten* professed to champion "democracy" in Zionism, the orthodox rabbi asked what their relation actually was to the masses of impoverished, religious Jews (SP V, pp. 30–31).

An extensive attack on Hebraism as an aristocratic crusade ensued at the Congress of 1907, in which the speaker, Daniel Pasmanik, claimed that Hebrew was diverting energy from the social struggle in which Zionism ought to be engaged. His charge that the *Kulturisten* were exclusive and elitist was the first such condemnation in a Zionist congress from a secular standpoint (SP VIII, pp. 305–306). This line of opposition to cultural Zionism would grow and develop in response to ever more urgent demands for Hebraization. "Without national culture, Zionism has no purpose, and no connection with history; it would become superficial, cowardly, and quickly die out in a time of distress," according to an official statement of 1909. "In Zionism, as a living progenitor of the Hebrew language, one finds the seeds and essence of all national, moral, intellectual, and spiritual development for the Jews."[17] Although they claimed to appreciate Yiddish, the *Kulturisten* nonetheless asserted that it "is entirely different and signifies something completely opposed to Hebrew. Hebrew is the ancient spirit; Yiddish, the reality; Hebrew, the language of Zion; Yiddish, the language of exile, the *Galut*."[18]

At the Thirteenth Zionist Congress, a speaker on behalf of the Labor Zionist [*Poale-Zion*] party, Leon Chsamowitsch, argued that the stress on Hebrew was an "archaic tendency" that "did not represent the thought and interests of the organizations of Zionist workers, and especially not the masses. The language question was not yet closed," he warned (SP X, p. 209). Such criticisms played out some of the tension between the diaspora nationalism of the *Bund* versus Zionism, albeit in the confines of the Zionist camp. At a later Congress, "Ahad Ha-Am-ism" would be specifically reproached as narrow-minded, chauvinistic, and pernicious.[19]

"We work in the spirit that a complete Jew must master Hebrew culture and language, and in fact, revere Hebrew," the *Poale-Zion* speaker reported. "But it is not the language of the people. We cannot accept the extreme standpoint that the language of the people is excluded. That requires the most profound contempt for the people, and a distaste for the masses." He charged that "Hebrew cannot unite the lower classes. . . . The masses are repulsed by this national movement." What then, the speaker asked, should be Hebrew's principal role? "In *Erez Israel* [the Land of Israel] it is an entirely different question: there it can be the colloquial speech."[20]

Indeed, it was in the *Yishuv*, the Jewish settlement in Palestine, where a direct affront on German occurred. A dispute known as the "Language War" broke out over what language should be used in the technical college in Haifa.[21] A wave of enthusiasm for Hebrew erupted in Palestine, which prompted impressive demonstrations in Europe. By 1913, the myth of the regenerative power of Hebrew had developed tremendously (cf. Friedman). But along with its religious and political problems, the Hebrew language was still at an embryonic stage, which severely limited its practical use in the movement.

Overall, before the outbreak of World War I, polemics directed specifically against the German language were sparse.[22] As we have seen in the

*Kulturdebatte* over the place of Yiddish and the working classes, German was again instrumental as a singular means of communication. Undoubtedly, many of the most important Zionists would never have welcomed a highly visible forum such as the Zionist congress, if Yiddish were the main medium of discourse. German, in effect, supplied an acceptable, respectable common ground and provided a critical distance from both Hebrew and Yiddish. In the prewar years, for Jews in search of a unique synthesis of memory, history, culture, meaning, and politics, Yiddish and Hebrew stirred their deepest passions. These same considerations would help account for the tragic fate of German, in Zionist eyes, in the years to come. German would be vilified as a unique purveyor of radical evil through the Nazi perpetration of the Holocaust, and this legacy would doggedly persist. It would nearly be forgotten that it was the German language that had expressed the Jews' greatest hopes for national liberation even within the fold of Zionism.

## NOTES

1. When German is specifically mentioned in the history of Zionism, it is usually in the context of the so-called "Language War" in 1913. This was a dispute that erupted in the Jewish settlement in Palestine, or *Yishuv*, over the issue of whether German or Hebrew should be the language of tuition in the new technical school in Haifa. Historians have recognized that the implementation of Hebrew was no simple task. Palestine's Jewish immigrants, speaking a number of languages, faced great difficulties in adopting a new daily language, and Hebrew was certainly important in providing a basis of sociability, especially for youth. Still, the leaders of the German Jewish organization that had sponsored technical education in Palestine, the *Hilfsverein der deutschen Juden*, thought that German ought to be the language of tuition for scientific education—for primarily pragmatic considerations. A revolt of sorts broke out, especially among the teachers in the *Yishuv*, supported by numerous demonstrations in the diaspora, in which they demanded that Hebrew be used across the board in the Jewish schools. The Language War was certainly a prodigious force in linking language to a national consciousness for the Jews of Palestine. But the story of the relationship of German to early Zionism runs much deeper and is far more complex. See Isaiah Friedman, "The *Hilfsverein der deutschen Juden*, the German Foreign Ministry and the Controversy with the Zionists," *Leo Baeck Institute Yearbook* 24 (1979), pp. 291–319; Michael Berkowitz, *Zionist Culture and West European Jewry before the First World War* (Cambridge: Cambridge University Press, 1993), pp. 11–76

2. *Stenographisches Protokoll der Verhandlungen des IV. Zionisten Kongresses in London* (Vienna: "Erez Israel," 1900), pp. 110–111.

3. Even some committed Hebraists shared the notion that Hebrew was not developed enough to be a useful means of discourse on modern subjects; see the *Jewish Chronicle* 19 (September 1913), pp. 18–19; 12 (September 1913), pp. 28–29.

4. Alex Bein, *Theodor Herzl*, translated by Maurice Samuel (Philadelphia: Jewish Publication Society of America, 1940); Stanley Nash, *In Search of Hebraism: Shai Hurwitz and His Polemics in the Hebrew Press* (Leiden: E. J. Brill, 1980), p. 203.

5. Maurice Friedman, *Martin Buber's Life and Work. The Early Years: 1878–1923* (New York: Dutton, 1981), p. 53; Chaim Weizmann to Catherine Dorfmann (12 September 1901), nos. 128 and 27, (August 1902), no. 300, in *The Letters and Papers of Chaim Weizmann. Series A: Letters*, vol. I, ed. Leonard Stein (London: Oxford University Press, 1968), pp. 180, 384; Leon Simon, *Ahad Ha-Am* (Philadelphia: Jewish Publication Society of America, 1960), pp. 83, 112.

6. Moses Gaster to Richard Gottheil (30 October 1898), A203/113, p. 39, Central Zionist Archives, Jerusalem (hereafter cited as CZA).

7. See Gaster to Gottheil (30 October 1989), A203/113, pp. 39, 30, CZA; Haim Avni and Gideon Shimoni (eds.), *Zionism and its Jewish Opponents* [in Hebrew] (Jerusalem: Hassifriya Hazionit, 1990), especially Yosef Salmon, "The Response of East European Orthodoxy to Political Zionism," pp. 51–74; and Salmon, *Religion and Zionism: First Encounters* [in Hebrew] (Jerusalem: Hassifriya Hazionit, 1990).

8. Joseph Goldstein, "The Zionist Movement in Russia" (Ph.D. dissertation, Hebrew University of Jerusalem, 1982); quoting Almog, p. 175. The most recent (and most judicious) treatment of this issue to date is that of Ehud Luz, *Parallels Meet: Religion and Nationalism in the Early Zionist Movement, 1882–1904* (Philadelphia: Jewish Publication Society, 1988), esp. pp. 135ff.

9. *Stenographisches Protokoll der Verhandlungen des IV. Zionisten Kongresses in London* (Vienna: "Erez Israel," 1900), pp. 110–111.

10. *Stenographisches Protokoll der Verhandlungen des III. Zionisten Kongresses gehalten zu Basel vom 15. bis 18. August 1899* (Vienna: "Erez Israel," 1899), pp. 206–207. Hereafter cited as *SP III*.

11. *Jewish Chronicle* 12 (September 1913), pp. 28–29.

12. Theodor Herzl, *Der Judenstaat: Versuch einer modernen Lösung der Judenfrage* (Leipzig and Vienna: M. Breitenstein's Verlag-Buchhandlung, 1896), p. 75.

13. Joseph Wenkert, "Herzl and Sokolow," in Raphael Patai (ed.), *Herzl Yearbook II* (New York: Herzl Press, 1959), p. 189.

14. Shai Hurwitz, quoted in Stanley Nash, op. cit., p. 154; Hugo Hermann, "Erziehung im Judentum," *Vom Judentum: ein Sammelbuch herausgegeben vom Verein jüdischer Hochschüler Bar Kochba in Prag* (Leipzig and London: T. Fischer Unwin, 1911), p. 143. Still, the Zionist movement had been deeply ambivalent about Yiddish. A Yiddish edition of *Die Welt* had existed for several years; a number of Yiddish stories were published in the featured product of the Jüdischer Verlag, the *Jüdische Almanach*, and several of that press's books which were promoted as Jewish cultural treasures, such as *Jung Harfen*, were originally Yiddish.

15. See Norbert Elias, *The Civilizing Process: The Development of Manners*, translated by Edmund Jephcott (New York: Urizen Books, 1978), pp. 3–40.

16. *Stenographisches Protokoll der Verhandlungen des V. Zionisten Kongresses in Basel vom 2. 27. 28. 29. und 30. Dezember 1901* (Vienna: "Erez Israel," 1901), pp. 393–394. Hereafter cited as *SP V*.

17. "Bericht des Aktionskomitees, Allgemeine Übersicht der zionistischen Bewegung (1907–1909) (Kulturell-Politischer Teil)," *Stenographisches Protokoll der Verhandlungen des IX. Zionisten Kongresses in Hamburg vom 26. bis inklusive 30. Dezember 1901* (Cologne: Jüdischer Verlag, 1909), p. 360.

18. Idem, p. 376; "Die Bedeutung der Palästinaarbeit," *Festschrift des zionistischen Vereines "Jeshrun," 1901–1911* (Troppau, Moravia).

19. "Bericht des Aktionskomitees. Allgemeine Übersicht der zionistischen Bewe-

gung (1907–1909), (Kulturell-Politischer Teil)," in *Stenographisches Protokll der Verhandlungen des IX. Zionisten-Kongresses in Hamburg vom 2. bis 9. September 1913* (Berlin and Leipzig: Jüdischer Verlag, 1913), pp. 74ff.

20. *Stenographisches Protokoll der Verhandlungen des IV. Zionisten Kongresses in London,* pp. 215–216. See *Vom Judentum: Ein Sammelbuch herausgegeben vom Verein jüdischer Hochschüler Bar Kochba in Prag* (Leipzig: Kurt Wolff, 1913), passim; see *SP VIII,* pp. 109–110, 282, 285, 289–290; *SP IX,* pp. 53, 212ff., 218, 267ff., 277–278; *SP XII,* p. 75. See also pp. 85ff.

21. For the anti-Zionist argument see Paul Nathan, *Palaestina und palaestinensischer Zionismus* (Berlin: H. S. Hermann, 1914).

22. The main exceptions are in the controversy following the publication of Theodor Herzl's utopian novel, *Altneuland,* and in Ahad Ha-Am's essay criticizing the First Zionist Congress.

# Babylon or Jerusalem:
# Berlin as Center of Jewish Modernism in the 1920s

## Delphine Bechtel

In 1922, the Warsaw-based Yiddish poet Melekh Rawicz [Ravitsh] was raging. In an article entitled "The Deserters of the Yiddish Truth,"[1] published in the Warsaw journal *Di vog* [The Scale], he fulminated:

> Somewhere in Berlin, in the smoky atmosphere of the *Romanisches Café*, a large number of our best creators of the Yiddish word are sitting, pretending to create Yiddish culture.... But somebody who is sitting in the *Romanisches Café* and is looking at us from afar, dragging the carriage of our culture, is a *deserter*. (pp. 40–41)

The historical occasion of this anger is the massive exile of an entire generation of East European Jewish writers to Berlin, a West European capital that had always been synonymous with assimilation in the Yiddish literary tradition. A *daytsh* [German Jew], a *berlintshik* [Berliner]—these words with clear derogatory connotations had been used to apply to adherents of the German Jewish *Haskalah* [Enlightenment], who, with Moses Mendelssohn at their head, had decried Yiddish language and East European Jewish culture as "corrupt" or even "semi-animal."

Nonetheless, during a few years between 1920 and 1928, Berlin became a major Yiddish literary center, with more than twenty journals[2] and a plethora of publishing houses. The most talented individuals of the Soviet Yiddish literary circle known as the *Kiev group*, with Dovid Bergelson, Der Nister, Dovid Hofshteyn, Leyb Kvitko, as well as the Lithuanian-born Moyshe Kulbak, resettled in Berlin. All were fleeing the civil war and the famine raging in post-revolutionary Russia, as well as the horrendous wave of hundreds of pogroms perpetrated by the counterrevolutionary armies in the Ukraine, which caused about 100,000 Jewish deaths. The Soviet Yiddish writers were joined by a close group of researchers, historians (Simon Dubnow, Elias Tsherikover), and linguists (Max Weinreich, Nokhem Shtif), who turned Berlin into the cradle of the scholarly study of the Yiddish language, literature, and history.

The same wave of emigration had also drawn famous Russian writers to

Berlin, such as Nabokov, Biely, Gorki, Ehrenburg, Lunz, Tsvetaieva, and avant-garde artists such as Marc Chagall, El Lissitzki, Joseph Tchaikov, Nathan Altmann, and Issachar Ber Rybak. Their presence provided a stimulus for the creation of interdisciplinary magazines for art and literature.

The first and foremost of the Berlin Yiddish journals, *Milgroym* [The Pomegranate], presented itself as an interdisciplinary and international, pan-Jewish journal for arts and letters. The illustrations on the cover and the flyleaf of the first issue, representing a pomegranate painted in the style of popular art and a woodcut of Jerusalem, indicate a strong dedication to Jewish folklore and tradition. The journal included pieces of Yiddish, German Jewish, and non-Jewish arts and letters. Stories by Der Nister or Bergelson jostled with translations of Arthur Schnitzler and Arno Holz, articles on Georg Brandes, Cézanne, Hermann Struck, Max Liebermann, or synagogue frescoes, Jewish glass-painting, even essays on Buddha and Lao-Tse. The internationalist platform turned into an eclectic dispersion.

The editors of *Milgroym* clearly were torn between their desire to create international bridges between Yiddish, European, and German Jewish cultures, and, on the other hand, the centrality of what was happening in Eastern Europe, where the masses of the Jewish people were living—and dying. This double orientation can quite clearly be attributed to the division between the literary editors, the Soviet émigré writers Bergelson and Der Nister, and the artistic editor, the art historian Rachel Wischnitzer–Bernstein.[4]

This division brought about a fundamental divergence regarding the relation between the writer and tradition. In the first issue of *Milgroym*, Dovid Bergelson had emphasized how uprooted the whole generation had become after the "great, ineluctable destruction" of World War I and the pogroms. According to him, "there is no more law, no more space and order . . . a chaotic life lies in me . . . there is no unified meaning in my life."[5]

Similarly, other Yiddish writers mostly expressed a sense of *fragmentation*, paired with a sense of disorientation, alienation, and loss of transcendence and totality. The following poem of Dovid Hofshteyn provides another example:

> And I, what should I do
>> When in front of my eyes
>>> Continuously stand
>>>> Phosphorous questions-lightnings
>>>>> "Where?"
>>>>> "Where to?"
>
> I am tired already
> Of hovering
> Of dizzying
> Of soaking in foreign waters.[6]

In contrast, in the very same first issue of *Milgroym*, in an article devoted to modern Jewish painters, Rachel Wischnitzer–Bernstein praises the new artists' "feeling of national unity," their "feeling part of the national organism."[7] She claims for the new Jewish artists (Chagall, Rybak) who look for their inspiration in Hasidic tales and old synagogue murals the name "ecstatics," and hopes that a "new religious art" will grow, "with mythic characters, folk legend and Holy stories" (Wishnitzer–Bernstein, p. 5). For her, the "religious pathos" of these ecstatic or expressionist artists comes precisely from the "apocalyptic atmosphere of world-destruction" (ibid., p. 7).

The contradictions between Der Nister and Bergelson on the one hand, and Mark and Rachel Wischnitzer–Bernstein on the other hand, led to a split that has gone unnoticed by Yiddish literary scholars up to now. On the editorial page of the second issue of *Milgroym*, the names of Der Nister and Bergelson have been removed, not only from the editorial board, but even from the list of contributors, which still contained other famous Yiddish writers (Hofshteyn, Kulbak, Opatoshu). Starting with the third issue of *Milgroym*, a new literary editor, Moyshe Kleinmann had been hired.

The reasons why Der Nister and Bergelson may have left the journal are still hypothetical. But there is a good chance that they have to do with the reaction their presence and occupations in Berlin had triggered back home, in Poland and Russia. In Warsaw, Rawicz, the editor of *Di vog*, was raging against the writers who pretended to build Yiddish literature "on the twig of Berlin, which sprouted yesterday and is blooming only today." He lamented that some of the best elements of Yiddish culture were "cut off from us," and he warned that "physical severance entails intellectual severance" (p. 39). Those who distanced themselves physically and intellectually from a struggle for Yiddish, which Rawicz worded in terms of war to defend a culture and its territory, could then be regarded as traitors to the cause and deserters.

In another modernist Warsaw journal, *Albatross*, Perets Markish vociferated in a similar way against the exile of the elite of Yiddish letters to Berlin, but he framed his anger in a precise historical, cultural, and national context:

> When one dips his feather not in ink, but in blood, and when one does not write on paper, but on the skin of human bodies, and the feathers are not made of steel, but of sharpened elbows, and the Jewish people is disappearing, and Yiddish culture is dying in the midst of devastated streets and destroyed cities, when the last wall of the Temple is in flames. . . .
> Then, what are the High Priests doing?
> They are going to Berlin, to market a new Jewish people, a new Yiddish culture, to leaven and let harden a new territory for the Jewish spirit.
> And when they go to Berlin and feel obliged to set up the tabernacles and the luggage they brought out from the Russian Egypt, of course, Berlin must become, in the twinkling of an eye, the only center of Yiddish culture, of Yiddish spirit, of Yiddish in general. . . .
> And Berlin becomes Jerusalem!
> They build the third temple—the *Kultur-lige*.[8]

Markish described the situation of the Jewish people and of Yiddish culture on the eve of destruction in visionary, apocalyptic, and expressionistic terms. For him, Yiddish culture was likened to a holy place in danger of annihilation, like the Temple of Jerusalem in flames. The Berlin émigrés could then be likened to "Great Priests" engaged in a reverse exodus that had led them from the "Russian Egypt" (which should be the center of Yiddish culture, but which was now seen as the place of exile and periphery) to Berlin, an illegitimate new center of Jewish life, which was supposed to become, in the eyes of the émigré writers, a new "Jerusalem," and to the sacrilegious rebuilding of a third temple there. Moreover, Markish's main claim against them was that they went there for financial reasons, that they "market a new Jewish people and a new Yiddish culture" there, that they "sell" the pogroms, while being safely preserved from living through them and fighting for their lives and culture on the battlefield.

Being under such attack, the Yiddish writers in Berlin kept a low profile, making almost no mention of their presence in Berlin in their writings of the time, or playing it down later on in their memoirs. When in 1924, in the sixth issue of *Milgroym*, Dr. M. Bienenstock enumerated the main Yiddish literary centers—America, Ukraine, and Poland—and the minor ones in Galicia and Vienna, he did not include Berlin on his list, although he was writing for *Milgroym*, the main Yiddish literary journal in Berlin. Others wrote nostalgically about the Revolution they had forsaken, or else the world of the *shtetl*, such as Einhorn who declared in the poem "My Home," "my soul belongs to my *shtetl*." I have not been able to locate anything the writers wrote then and there about Berlin, a city referred to in *Milgroym* as "By the rivers of Babylon." [9]

Moyshe Kulbak is perhaps the only writer of the group who wrote extensively about his stay in Berlin. After his return to the Soviet Union, he published in 1933 a cycle of over sixty short poems, entitled *Disner Tshayld Harold* [Childe Harold of Disno], a poetic mock-epic about his *Lern- und Wanderjahre* in Berlin, much in the style and tone of Heine's *Deutschland, ein Wintermärchen*. In the opening stanzas, which describe the train journey from Russia to Berlin, he already differentiates his main character, the peaceful *lyulkeman* [man with a pipe] from the others, defining his motivations as follows: "He goes to study in Europe. To each one his own: a bird sings, a bolshevik makes revolutions, a man with a pipe could do nothing else but study."

The man with the pipe is also distinguished by the author from three other categories of Soviet citizens: first, the bourgeois who are crowding the trains to Berlin, fleeing the revolution; second, the Moscow businessmen who are swamping the Kurfürstendamm with "millionaires, checkbooks, and gold"; and, finally, the Bolsheviks who are watching the train depart but are staying in Russia because their task is the Revolution. By openly admitting that the

Revolution was not his primary goal, Kulbak defines himself, through his persona *lyulkeman*, as an outsider in relation to both bourgeois and Communist society. His independence of thought later cost him his life. He was one of the very first Yiddish writers arrested under Stalin in the 1938 purge, and he died soon thereafter in a camp.

In *Disner Tshayld Harold*, gentle irony applied to the criticism of the German petty bourgeois mentality alternates with an affected enthusiasm for nightlife and modernity, to form a mock-hymn to the city of Berlin:

> O Country, where electricity runs
> In wires, and champagne in people's veins
> Where each worker is a Marxist
> And each grocer a Kantian.

The references to Kant and later to Goethe, or to German culture in general, appear more and more ambiguous as Goethe is revealed as a repository of nationalistic feelings deeply buried in the German collective unconscious: "he brings to the surface what is buried deep below." Concomitantly, the German culture *lyulkeman* came to discover appears as a threatening mix of "sweet terror, Spengler, Keyserling, and Lasker–Schüler."[10] The vibrant cultural and nightlife, which was at first the object of the young immigrant's enthusiasm, appears later on rather as a society sliding toward decadence and death, "the agony of a distant effervescence," of which the European literary and artistic avant-garde is just another obscene symptom:

> Expressionism screams with red feet
> Dada with pants fallen down.

Kulbak himself, who had come to Berlin "to study," seems to emerge somewhat confused out of the weird mix of cultures created by his self-imposed autodidactic education: "A little Blok, a little Schopenhauer, Kabbalah, Peretz and Spinoza." The result was "alienation, and sadness, sadness, sadness."

The end of the Berlin cycle ends with the depiction of "the other Germany," that of the worker's movement, the street fights opposing the Communists and the Nazis, and the prophecy of the revolution looming over German society. For Kulbak, Berlin was doomed by historical necessity, just as Sodom was because of its corruption:

> Europe . . . you sin, old Sodom
> Down with Beethoven and Goethe
> and with the Cathedral of Cologne.

The fate of Yiddish literature in Berlin was also determined by its reception and translation by the German Jews. Certain segments of German Jewry had already been introduced to East European Jewish culture and literature through Martin Buber's rediscovery of Hasidic tales and philosophy, as well as through their war experiences on the Eastern Front during the occupation of Poland. German Jewish intellectuals in particular became fascinated by Yiddish culture and discovered its literature. They were introduced to it by some excellent highbrow journals such as Fritz Mordechai Kaufmann's *Freistatt*, Buber's *Der Jude, Ost und West*, and *Neue Jüdische Monatsschriften*, as well as by the efforts of Buber's *Jüdischer Verlag*.

At the same time, a plethora of unprofessional and very approximate translations of Yiddish literature started to flood the market. The choice of the works translated is revealing. It is mainly the work of the older generation, of the classics, such as Mendele, Sholem Aleichem, Perets, Scholem Asch, or of vaudeville theater such as Lateiner. With the exception of one novel by Bergelson, the younger generation of writers living right there on their doorstep in Berlin remained widely ignored by the translators, the German Jewish cultural leaders, and the public. Why?

A part of the answer is provided by Gerhard [Gershom] Scholem's article "Zum Problem der Übersetzung aus dem Jiddischen" in which he reviews three volumes translated by one of the most prolific but most problematic translators, Alexander Eliasberg. Scholem charges him in particular with creating a "sentimental atmosphere" that is entirely absent from the Yiddish originals, of writing an *Übertragung* [recasting] that sometimes "leaves out things too Jewish" and sometimes throws in arbitrary additions. Scholem eventually makes out a list of the "gems" to be found in Eliasberg's translations, stigmatizing the "lack of connection of the translator to his object."

Eliasberg, as many other translators of Yiddish up to this day, had in fact committed the crime of a misreading, a misprision of the text, dictated to him by prejudices about Yiddish literature that were widespread among most German Jews. They looked back to the world of Yiddish literature and culture as to a place of origin tinged with sentimentalism and nostalgia, because they needed to romanticize it in order to define their own identity. They did not want to make the effort of really understanding its modernist, avant-garde aspects. No wonder, then, that they ignored the uprooted, modernist Yiddish writers who lived among them. While Else Lasker–Schüler dedicated the "coat of arms of the city of Thebes" to the journal *Albatross*, which had moved to Berlin in 1923, and while Max Brod and Stephan Zweig inscribed their names on the editorial board of *Milgroym*, they never contributed anything else to those journals.

Moreover, most German Jews who were assimilated or even "deutschnational" were rather embarrassed by this rediscovery of East European Jews. They looked on Yiddish literature with extreme suspicion. One of the most typical examples of this attitude is the German Jewish critic Ludwig Geiger, son of Abraham Geiger (the founder of the German Jewish reform movement) and clearly an assimilationist. He welcomed each new translation from the Yiddish in the *Allgemeine Zeitung des Judentums*, but his reviews are quite revealing.

On the occasion of the publication of Perets's drama *Die goldene Kette* [The Golden Chain], he complained about the editor's spelling out the two first names of the author (Jizchok Leib) in full, because they sound too Jewish. "Jizchok Leib really does not sound gratifying." After giving a few examples of Jewish writers who used only the first initial of their too-Jewish sounding names, he concluded that "J. L. Perez is truly preferable to us than Jizchok Leib." [12]

Reviewing the German translation of Mendele Mocher Sforim's novel *Fishke der Krumer* [Fishke the Lame], which takes place in the underworld of Jewish beggars and thieves, Geiger expressed strong doubts "whether it is opportune to present the public at large with such atrocities," [13] lest the readers should conclude that "those Jews are a filthy, dangerous kind of the worst criminals, the true scum of humanity." Although he ascribed those thoughts to the anti-Semites, the ferocity of his tone indicates that these prejudices were not really foreign to him, perhaps even that he was afraid of finding them in himself, as a form of Jewish self-hatred quite prevalent in German Jewish society of that time. Again, in another review of selected stories by Sholem Aleichem, Ludwig Geiger protested violently against the title the editor gave the anthology, *Aus dem nahen Osten* [From the Near East], "for this title ... really contradicts our feelings; this East may be geographically close to us, but in spirit, it is awfully far."

The encounter between the East European Jewish émigré writers in Berlin and their German Jewish brethren seems, then, mainly the story of a mutual misunderstanding. The Yiddish writers who had sought the collaboration of German Jewish writers soon became disillusioned about the latter's lack of real understanding of their culture. They came to consider them assimilated *Yekkes*, the embodiment of traits they did not want to emulate. Besides, National Socialism was on the rise. The Soviet Union claimed to offer state support for Yiddish culture. In 1926, Dovid Bergelson proclaimed himself a Soviet writer. Almost all the members of the Berlin group returned to the Soviet Union. They were later all executed on the same day, 12 August 1952.

## Notes

1. "Di dezertern funem yidishn emes," *Di vog* 2 (September 1922), pp. 35–43.
2. Leo and Renate Fuks ("Yiddish Publishing Activites in the Weimar Republic, 1920–1933," *Leo Baeck Institute Yearbook* XXXIII [1988]) list seventeen periodicals; Arthur Tilo Alt ("A Survey of Literary Contributions to Post-World War I Yiddish

Journals in Berlin," *Yiddish* 7/1 (1987)) lists nineteen, but even a preliminary survey of the material available at YIVO yields more. Among them, the literary journals are *Milgroym, Dos bukh, Kunst-ring almanakh, Der onheyb*, and *Dos fraye vort*.

3. The publishing houses include Wostok [East], Yidisher literarisher Farlag, Klal-farlag, Shveln, Yidisher Kultur-Farlag, Funken, and more.

4. Rachel Bernstein (born 1892) was married to Mark Wischnitzer, a historian and enthnographer who founded the Rimon publishing house in London. Rachel Wischnitzer, a historian of Jewish art and editor of the artistic part of the first two journals devoted to Jewish art (*Milgroym* and its Hebrew counterpart, *Rimon*) later became director of the Jewish Museum in Berlin (1934–1938).

5. Dovid Bergelson, "Der gesheener oyfbrokh" [The Break that just Happened], *Milgroym* 1 (1922), p. 43.

6. "Di lid fun mayn glaykhgilt" [The Song of My Indifference], *Milgroym* 1 (1922), p. 44.

7. R. Wischnitzer–Bernstein, "Die naye kunst un mir" [The New Art and We], *Milgroym* 1 (1922), p. 4.

8. *Biznes: Moskve–Berlin* [Business: Moscow–Berlin], *Khalyastre* 1 (1922), p. 62. The *Kultur-lige* [League for Yiddish Culture] was founded in Kiev in 1917 and gathered more than 100 Yiddish cultural organizations—among them the major publishing house in the Ukraine that was transferred to Berlin and Warsaw after its partial liquidation in 1921.

9. V. Latski Bartoldi, "Khsides un antisemitizm" [Hassidism and Anti-Semitism], *Milgroym* 1 (1922).

10. Eduard von Keyserling (1855–1918), German prose writer depicting the boredom and resigned aestheticism of the milieu of the Baltic and East Prussian aristocracy.

11. In *Jüdische Rundschau*, 12 January 1917.

12. *Allgemeine Zeitung des Judentums* (Berlin, 16 March 1917).

13. Ibid. (Berlin, 4 July 1919).

# Authors of German Language in Israel

## Margarita Pazi

In Israel authors writing in German were and are in a difficult situation: they are not merely authors who write in a language different from the language of the country.[1] The language in which they create their prose and poetry may no longer be taboo, but it is without question associated with images of inhuman cruelty, piles of defenselessly slaughtered people, and the symbol of horror: Auschwitz. Hence to the German-speaking immigrants the language problem—the most difficult problem one faces when getting acclimated to a country—was threefold: it was a practical, cultural, and emotional problem.[2]

In the small piece of land that had been declared the home country of the Jews in the 1917 Balfour Declaration, Ivrith, as modern Hebrew is called, had prevailed over Yiddish after many years of dispute and reflection. The objections on the part of orthodox Jews against profaning the holy language were met with effective counterarguments, above all by pointing out that the Bible was the emotional home sphere of the Middle-Eastern immigrants. The language of the Bible and prayers thus became the language of pioneers. Words and terms that throughout the millennia had expressed religious concepts now communicated everyday situations.

Those immigrants from Eastern Europe familiar with Hebrew from the traditional curriculum of religious schools had no actual language problem. The situation of the immigrants from Central and Western Europe, on the other hand, was different. Their existential difficulties rarely allowed for intensive studies of the Hebrew language, whose syntax and letters differed so substantially from their own. Attempts to learn it were met with support, and occasional lapses into the language of origin were considered leniently as a transitional phenomenon. However, this was not the case with German. Since 1933 German was taboo and remained so for decades to come. Frequently this attitude of rejection was shared by those most affected by the German immigrants for whom this language was associated with oppressive memories.

Not knowing Hebrew contributed also to the intellectual and cultural isolation of those new immigrants for whom German was only the foreign language in which they were most fluent. In order to at least accommodate their need for information, a weekly paper was established in 1933 and appeared until 1985 (since then in irregular intervals) under the title *M. B. Wochenzei-*

*tung des Irgun Olej Merkas Europa* [Association of the Immigrants from Central Europe]. In 1935 a German-language daily newspaper was founded, which appears to this day.[3] In the early 1940s a number of publications and journals circulated. Most of them ceased to appear after a very short time for lack of readership, but also because in some instances they gave rise to some rather aggressive protest due to the language in which they were written— German. This situation, for example, caused irregularities in the case of the German daily newspaper and forced the Haifa journal *Orient* out of circulation.[4] *Orient* published clearly defined political authors such as Louis Fürnberg or sympathizers such as Arnold Zweig, but also confirmed Zionists such as Max Brod and politically disinterested writers such as Else Lasker–Schüler. Because of its political direction and its connection with Arnold Zweig, the Haifa journal was credited in recent years with a greatly inflated significance.

In the cities, small "culture circles" formed that offered private lectures and performances. Within the framework of the "Kraal," which she had founded, seventy-seven-year-old Else Lasker–Schüler was able to attract an interested and grateful audience in Jerusalem. Her last volume of poetry, *Mein blaues Klavier* [My Blue Piano], appeared in Jerusalem in 1943. Another circle formed around Max Brod, which continued to exist after his death; in Tel-Aviv a *Kreis für fortschrittliche Kultur* [Circle for Progressive Culture] was established that organized evening programs of readings and lectures. That an extensive program for all of these presentations was met with great public interest is obvious from the invitations for these events.

After 1945, as concentration camp survivors, who in the course of the persecutions had acquired as a common language (a mixture of Slavic Yiddish and Gestapo German), came to the country, a counterdevelopment evolved: the German language became a necessary means of communication. At the same time, however, the awareness of the full extent of the Nazi crimes increased the animosity against all things German.

The foundation of the state of Israel in 1948, the war of liberation, and the economic problems of admitting and integrating more than half a million Jews who had been expelled from neighboring Arabic countries—at a time when the Jewish population amounted to barely a million—changed the situation. As problems were confronted and mastered, a feeling of security and self-reliance increased and gradually changed the attitude toward the German language. While the associations connected with it could and can never be completely overcome, they no longer dominated the entire conception.

It would be futile to search for an explanation or justification for the continuing ties with the German language after 1933 and the Shoah. However, one further aspect shall be elucidated in this context: for European Jews it cannot be assumed that the place of birth and mother tongue coincide. Not only in Eastern Europe, but to a large extent also within the borders of the former Austro-Hungarian monarchy, the question of the mother tongue cannot be answered unequivocally. Whatever the case may be, the German language was the language of culture that, in large parts of Central Europe, stood for acculturation and integration. However, while bilingualism and trilingualism in the Crown Lands of the *k. und k.* [Imperial and Royal] monarchy and Eastern Europe were not uncommon because of the multilingual character of these areas, in Germany the German language had absolute precedence.

The first immigration wave from Germany beginning in 1933 consisted mainly of Zionists who, emotionally and ideologically prepared for life in the country, were also protected from the psychological trauma of being no longer considered worthy of belonging to the Germans. However, the language of their thoughts and memories was now also the language in which their racial inferiority and, much worse, in which accusations against them had been expressed. Authors were the ones most affected by this syndrome, as well as those who until this point had only felt the urge and the desire to record their thoughts and emotions in a written form.[5]

Until 1974, when the association of writers of German language was established under the umbrella of the general writer's association in Israel, there had been no central institution that protected or promoted the interests of authors writing in German, or even recorded them statistically. From biographical compilations it is evident that in the years prior to the war a considerable number of people entered the country who later became known as writers. But there also arrived already famous authors. In 1933 Arnold Zweig arrived. In recent years this militant fighter for the Zionist ideal has frequently been the object of studies that selectively stress the circumstances which forced him to return to East Berlin in 1948. Many of these studies are symptomatic of the ideological tendencies of their authors. Else Lasker–Schüler immigrated in 1938. She certainly was not happy in Jerusalem—however, old and sick as she was, where would she have been happy at that time? 1935 was the year when Josef Kastein immigrated. He mastered the language, overcoming the problems more skillfully than many others. However, he was plagued by personal and health problems until his early death in 1946.[6] Max Brod was on the last train that passed the Polish border before the invasion of the German troops into Czechoslovakia. Since that time he considered his life a "gift" and he readily accepted the existential difficulties in the country. Lola Landau–Wegner also arrived in 1936 and began her "third life" with the same intensity and flexibility that had already impressed the critics of her first volume of poetry in 1916. In addition, a number of German-speaking Jews, among them some who aspired to be writers, found a safe haven, as mentioned earlier. In the course of the next decades they recorded their thoughts and feelings in the "forbidden" language. They did not dare hope that their manuscripts would ever be published. However, some of them persevered and made a breakthrough. It is not possible to mention all of these authors here.

Their stories and poems can be explored with the help of anthologies and recently published studies. At this point I can only attempt to examine the special character of the literature they created, as well as its goals and potential effects.

A look at the countries of origin of Israeli authors writing in German provides an ethnographic impression of the vanished "German culture and language islands" in Eastern Central Europe. The considerable differences in their concepts of homeland, landscape, and perceptions of environments are the results of these regional differences, which also affect these authors' language. An example of this is their at times surprising choice of adjectives. The same is true for their use of verbs and terminology, which causes some of the works of multilingual authors to exhibit subtle distinctions as far as their conceptualization and literary representation are concerned. Generational factors, too, play a role in their usage of the German language. The careful pondering and weighing of expressions in the works of Fritz Nashitz and Werner Kraft, only to mention two older authors, has given way to a much freer, bolder choice of words in Jenny Aloni, Netti Boleslav, Alice Schwarz, just to name a few. Metaphors and puns created in the author's subconscious mind transcend the language boundaries—in almost all of these authors the influence of the local language, Ivrith, cannot be overlooked. This language of their children and environment at large is reflected in the syntax, which often is adopted from Ivrith. Even subconscious use of Ivrith vocabulary occurs in their texts. The effects of the fundamentally different mentality of Ivrith is noticeable in the style and syntax characteristic of Israeli literature written in German. To be sure, there are a few exceptions—Werner Kraft is the most notable one. The ongoing linguistic and intellectual tension results in an expanded identity on the author's part, enlarging and enriching his identity.

Israeli literature written in German can be considered as a part of German literature. However, this does not mean that it is "German" literature, for reasons that go beyond the linguistic aspects addressed above. The Shoah determines this literature beyond the differences of age and origin more strongly than any philosophical discussion. This is not only apparent in the phenomenological representations of the twelve years of the "Thousand-Year Empire." It motivates the choice of topics and the literary approach—the linkage of motifs and the portrayal of characters. Memory is the source of literary impulses in more than one sense: memories of that which existed before the horror, of childhood, school and friends, of life in a stable, seemingly well-intentioned environment, as well as memories of what occurred later and was experienced, suffered, and survived or, in more merciful cases, what came to light in stories and reports. Many of the authors evoke recollections repeatedly due to their compulsion to record the memory of the millions of murdered people. In the work of some authors this is expressed as a syndrome of traumatic visions of fear and vulnerability, as in the case of Benno Fruchtmann. Others such as Frida Hebel manifest it by emphasizing religious elements. Another example of this is the immanent disposition of hope typical of Ester Rabin's books for young people. At times the various levels of consciousness and memory in the works of younger authors amount to a latent, protest-like recollection of events and situations. In Jenni Aloni's prose these events and situations are intensely amalgamated while, in contrast, in Rusia Lampl's work they are suggested by the multitude of possible ways of communication between different groups of immigrants in spite of their disparate mentalities and lifestyles. The adherence to the German language can be interpreted as a form of protest: Manfred Steuermann and Werner Kraft insisted on the German language as their individual property independent of historical events; Shalom Ben-Chorin participated actively in Jewish–Christian discussions and wrote an extensive work on this subject, while Max Zweig authored numerous dramas with religious and historical themes.

The endeavor to balance the emotional chaos evident in the associative narratives by emphasizing formative narrative elements to develop moral patterns (often by means of a change in consciousness) is aided by an openness to establish contact and adapt oneself. Such patterns become apparent in the depiction of processes and contrasting patterns in historical studies. Examples of this are Heinz Weissenberg's Moses trilogy and Alexander Czerski's partly biographical novels and stories, which derive their impact from the conflict-laden tension between the traditional worldview acquired in the process of education and later insights, as well as the influence of fundamentally different ways to think and respond as a result of the experience of persecution, emigration, and life in a Jewish society.

The affirmation of life (which is never entirely absent, even in the presence of the most sinister motifs) and the rejection of any kind of poetic escapism into an ideal never-never-land characterize this literature in general. The Israeli–Arab conflict, the wars, and, as their closely associated opposite, the building of the country dominate literary representation. The choice of narrative themes and their configuration are based on social historical reality and personal experience. However, in the characterization of the protagonists and the emphasis on psychological instances, the personal exposure and the effects of experience and memory on the part of the author are also reflected. Texts that aim at instruction and communication do not always steer clear of a simplification of problems that borders on the naive. The latter evolves from the author's wishful thinking and hopes, rather than his or her lack of factual information. One would be mistaken to assume a distance from current events or a lack of involvement with Israel. All the texts are enriched by associations and visions. They show absolute confidence in the young generation of Israelis. An important trait is the avoidance of self-indulgent glorification as well as the air of victory and conquest. However, the prose and lyric poetry reveal an uncompromising resolution to never again become victims without protection and defense.

It serves the further elucidation of the position of literature written in German in Israel to point out its affinity with works by the older generation of Israeli authors of Hebrew language. Characteristic of the authors writing in German is the tendency to show solutions of contemporary political problems and social circumstances as individual decisions. The differences between Hebrew and German lyric poetry, however, are far more distinct. The primary reason is the difference in language. Hebrew lyric poetry is marked by the unlimited poetic possibilities, which on the levels of language, imagery, and historical events evolve in the perpetual fluctuation between past and present. Hebrew poets can evoke associations and meanings in their readers who studied the Bible from early youth as a source of history, geography, and natural history as well as religion.[7] These call for elaboration and explanation in the German language, which interfere with the rhythm and linguistic fluency. And yet, the lyric poetry created by these authors has a concrete evocative power and intensity. Landscape descriptions are most common. In the case of Jenny Aloni they communicate glowing colors of fruits and the shimmering pallor of the sand with an almost painful intensity.[8] The fauna and flora that are so different from those of the countries of their birth, the seemingly endless nuances of red and purple, the grayish-blue of the Judean desert that changes to reddish at sunset evoke in the different authors associations, memories, and visions of the future. For the most part we owe this poetry to women authors.

Another focus of some of the poems by Netti Boleslav, who died at an early age, and Jenni Aloni is the syndrome of the survivors' guilt expressed in unrelenting questions about the justification for this life while so many were killed. Under these auspices the complete dedication to the beloved new country appears almost as the betrayal to the people who were murdered. Alice Schwarz's poetry contains bits of memory that turn the most mundane objects into memorial plates. Lillith Pavel explores in her reflections whether it is right to remember the past—the forests and meadows—and to make German verses. Hanna Blitzer expresses confidence and hope in the present and in the future.

And again and again Jerusalem. In no other instance is the autonomy of Israeli poetry as incontestable as in the shift of the image and term "Jerusalem" from being a symbol and the center of religions to turning it into the backbone and heart of the country where these poets found their true home. Jerusalem is a part of their identity and the intersection of their difficult reality—their life under constant existential threat. In their poems Jerusalem becomes the epitome of permanence. It is the holy city as well as a part of their own experience of reality in the new state.

Israeli literature written in German is neither able nor expected to mediate between the author's country of origin—his or her birthplace—and Israel. Every memory is steeped in too much pain. The notion "homecountry," country of birth, is difficult to pin down. Landscapes, colors, smells, and acoustical impressions may evoke a fleeting notion of home without culminating in an emotionally charged feeling of a homeland. This is only possible in conjunction with a feeling of belonging, which long ago ceased to exist. One also has to use the concept "home in language" carefully since authors in particular have to establish their "home in language" over and over again. In 1935, in his much-quoted letter to Tucholsky who at this time was already dead, Arnold Zweig rejected the "ridiculous untruth" that Jews are a nomad people. He instead made the apodictic statement, "The Jews feel their roots and are at home where the graves of their ancestors are." Little could he know that only a few years later this definition of a homeland was to assume a tragic significance for his Jewish contemporaries and their children through the words of another Jew, one of this century's greatest lyric poets of the German language: in Paul Celan's gruesome verses about a "grave in the clouds" in his poem "Todesfuge" [Death Fugue].

Israeli authors of the German language—for reasons of language alone—cannot indulge in illusions of influencing the young people of Israel. The vast majority of their publications are intended for a non-Israeli, non-Jewish reading public, a fact that may also explain the goal and meaning of the essays, and the literary and poetic texts. They do not reach the children of the victims, but it is much more important to remind the children of those who carry the guilt and responsibility for the Shoah, lest they forget. Alfred Kittner's association, conceived on a descending plane as he sees the city lights of Tel-Aviv, expresses it in an exemplary way in his poem: "And every light is a *Yahrzeit* candle." Perhaps every text written by an Israeli poet in German is a *Yahrzeit* candle.[9]

*Translated by Dagmar C. G. Lorenz*

## NOTES

1. The following anthologies and essays on literature written in German in Israel illuminate the situation of Israeli German literature.

**Anthologies:** *Stimmen aus Israel, Anthologie der deutschsprachigen Literatur in Israel*, ed. Meir M. Faerber (Gerlingen: Bleicher, 1979). Dov Amir, *Leben und Werk der deutschsprachigen Schriftsteller in Israel. Eine Bio-Bibliographie* (Munich: K. Saur, 1980). *Nachrichten aus Israel, Deutschsprachige Literatur in Israel*, ed. Margarita Pazi (Hildesheim: Olms, 1981). *Heimat ist anderswo, deutsche Schriftsteller in Israel*, ed. Alice Schwarz–Gardos (Vienna, Freiburg: Herder, 1983). *Hügel des Frühlings. Deutschsprachige Autoren in Israel erzählen*, ed. Alice

Schwarz–Gardos (Vienna and Freiburg: Herder, 1984). *Auf dem Weg. eine Anthologie deutschsprachiger Literatur in Israel*, ed. Meir M. Faerber (Gerlingen: Bleicher, 1989). *Karmel Impressum. Die deutsche Sprache, deutschsprachige Literatur und Presse in Israel. Eine Anthologie*, ed. Paul Tischler (Munich 1990). *Mnemosyne Israel, Zeitschrift für Geisteswissenschaft*, ed. Armin A. Wallas (Klagenfurth 1990).

**Essays:** Margarita Pazi, "Deutsche Literatur in Palästina/Israel," *Akten des 7. Internationalen Germanisten Kongresses* 5 (Göttingen: Vandenhoeck, 1986); "Staub und Sterne deutschschreibende Autorinnen in Erez-Israel und Israel," *Deutsche Literatur von Frauen*, vol. 2, 19th and 20th Century (Munich, n.p., 1988); "Deutschsprachige Literatur in Israel," *Deutsch-jüdische Exil- und Emigrationsliteratur im 20. Jahrhundert* (forthcoming); "Drei israelische deutschschreibende Autorinnen," *Doch die Sprache bleibt. Eine Prosa-Anthologie des PEN Zentrums deutschsprachiger Autoren im Ausland*, ed. Ilse R. Wolff (Gerlingen: Bleicher, 1990).

Introductions to some of the above-mentioned anthologies and collections contain information about some of the following authors: Jenni Aloni, Netti Boleslav, Frida Hebel, Lola Landau, David Neumann, and Max Zweig. In addition Alice Schwarz–Gardos, Meir M. Faerber, Shalom Ben Chorin, and Jürgen Nierad have published on the topic.

2. Decades before this emotional complication, the foundation of the Technion in Haifa occasioned the question of whether the language of instruction at this first college in the country could be Ivrith or whether for scientific reasons it had to be German. The Hebrew language prevailed, the instructors, not the students, had to learn a language new to them and create new expressions and terms.

3. Editorship and title of the paper changed. Since 1 January 1974 it appears under the title "Israel Nachrichten" [Israel News].

4. *Orient* appeared for a year, April 1942 to April 1943; the printing shop that produced the paper was destroyed on 2 February 1943 by arson. The black market buying and selling of paper was mentioned as one reason for the attack. At any rate, the weekly caused violent objection in some circles. *M.B.* also published articles protesting against the anti-Zionist tendency of *Orient*.

5. In the early 1930s a number of German Zionists arrived who took an active part in the intellectual and social development of the country and occupied important positions also after the foundation of the state.

6. In 1942 his last work published during his lifetime appeared, "Eine palästinensische Novelle" [A Palestinian Novella], which was privately published. It was very badly reviewed in *Orient*.

7. It is quite common in a Hebrew literary text, for example, to shift into the language of the prophets. Also the language of the earlier and later Middle Ages is interpolated, next to entirely modern, almost slanglike ways of expression.

8. This is in contrast to modern Israeli painters who concentrate with their color schemes mainly on the mixed shades of the landscape.

9. On the day of the passing away of a relative a memorial candle that burns for twenty-four hours is lighted.

# Nationalism, Symbiosis, and Anti-Semitism

# Thomas Mann's *Wälsungenblut* in the Context of the Intermarriage Debate and the "Jewish Question"

## Alan Levenson

Thomas Mann's novella *Wälsungenblut* (1905) revolves around the intense and ultimately incestuous relationships of Siegmund and Sieglinde, two scions of a self-made Jewish businessman. In his characterization of the languid, spoiled Aarenhold children, and in his intertwining of the climax of Wagner's *Die Walküre* with the less-than-Valhallan sexual pull of this brother and sister pair, Mann is typically elegant. But if *Wälsungenblut* is elegant it is also nasty. Wendelin, a "little slav," serves the rich Jews submissively. Herr Aarenhold, a Hermann Kafka at the dining table, elicits embarrassed disdain in his more cultured children. Frau Aarenhold personifies the parvenu Jewess, elder brother Kunz presents the reader with a stiff Hussar, more Prussian than the Prussians. Collectively, the twins' description includes the basic physical stereotypes of Jews (drooping nose, intense black eyes, full lips, heavy beard). Most importantly, the siblings' cuckolding of von Beckerath, Sieglinde's hapless fiancé, smacks of conspiracy, disdain of the Gentile, self-service, and vice. In short, *Wälsungenblut* presents a veritable litany of anti-Semitic stereotypes.[1]

This point was not lost on Mann's Jewish father-in-law, the mathematician Alfred Pringsheim, who demanded that Mann withdraw the story from publication and remove the telltale Yiddishism that the "goy" was *beganeft*, "robbed," a verdict pronounced by Siegmund after the sibling's illicit liaison. Pringsheim's objections prevailed and Mann withdrew *Wälsungenblut* from publication. As Hans Vaget noted, even today this tale rarely receives due recognition as a "jewel of decadence literature."[2] Those who have bothered to deal with the anti-Semitic content of this tale have referred to Mann's irony as a mitigating factor, apparently assuming that his marriage to Katja Pringsheim obviates the possibility that Mann took anti-Jewish rhetoric seriously.[3] But this reads Mann's courageous anti-Nazism back into a less clearcut period, when even Jews were mesmerized by the language of race. Sander Gilman, an astute analyst of racial discourse, places this story in the recurring triad of urban life—decadence—Jewish sexual exclusivity.[4] In this essay, I would like to place Mann's *Wälsungenblut* in a more specific context and I hope a more illuminating one—the debate over intermarriage and its relationship to the 'Jewish Question.'[5]

The 'Jewish Question' sparked many literary ruminations about German–Jewish intermarriage, which neatly represented the erasure of the final borderline dividing German from Jew. Felix Dahn's *Ein Kampf um Rom*, in which Miriam, a Jewish woman, despises the unctuous Jew, Joachim, and throws in her lot with the Goth Totila, typifies the treatments of this theme. This "good Jew" versus "bad Jew" dichotomy operates most memorably in Gustav Freytag's best-selling novel *Soll und Haben* [Credit and Debit]. Bernhard Ehrenthal represents the good Jew, whose principal desire is to be as different from his coreligionists as possible; the flight from Judaism receives the novelist's unambivalent praise.[6] The literature on intermarriage from the Jewish side is richer in quantity, if not quality. Fanny Lewald's semi-autobiographical *Jenny* offers a protest against social convention, and supports the concept of romantic love. Lewald remained true to her fictional character, concluding a real-life marriage with the author Adolf Stahr.[7] In the "ghetto novels" and in German Jewish historical fiction of the 1850s–1880s the theme of intermarriage sometimes realized, sometimes frustrated received frequent treatment.[8] These tales served a variety of apologetic purposes: Jews were displayed as tolerant, legitimately torn between love and religious obligation, and able to reform anti-Semites through their sterling behavior.

The centrality of the intermarriage issue to Jewish perceptions of the 'Jewish Question' can be best illustrated by the many dramatizations appearing in the Jewish press. To take but two examples, in the conservative *Israelitische Wochenschrift (IWS)* a feuilletonist imagined a Jewish man named Joseph Portbach who married a Gentile woman. The Gentile wife, with the help of Portbach's ubiquitous (and evil) mother-in-law, wins the youngest (male) child over to Christianity in violation of their prenuptial agreement. More representative, however, is the following serial romance from the *Allgemeine Zeitung des Judentums*, the most widely-read Jewish periodical. A young, cultured Jewish woman falls in love with a dashing Austrian army officer. Finally, after four weeks worth of tribulation, she convinces herself that their different backgrounds and career aspirations make the match impossible. Thus the possibility of true love between Jew and Gentile is affirmed, without affirming the social feasibility of intermarriage. Jewish writings on intermarriage often display this dual objective: to laud German–Jewish compatibility while defending the Jewish preference for endogamous marriages. Rejecting intermarriage, Jewish spokespersons perceived, could readily be interpreted as contempt for Christians, the unmistakable thrust of the original concluding sentence of Mann's *Wälsungenblut* (Vaget, p. 374).

Ultimately, however, the literary precedents to Mann's tale seem less important than the political and the "scientific" debates over exogamy versus endogamy and its relationship to the 'Jewish Question.' One could cite a bevy of nineteenth-century predecessors to the sort of *völkisch* anti-Semitism that ultimately found expression in the NSDAP's 1935 *Law for the Protection of German Blood & German Honor* (Nuremberg Laws), which made intermarriage illegal.[9] But no individual did more to popularize the notion of race warfare in Germany than the expatriated Englishman, Houston Stewart Chamberlain, whose *Foundations of the Nineteenth Century* (1899) won many enthusiastic admirers, including Kaiser Wilhelm II.[10] Chamberlain claimed that the Jews' strategy of allowing their daughters to marry Gentiles, but prohibiting their sons from doing the same, effectively preserved their own racial purity, while poisoning the "host" race. This Jewish conspiracy would lead to a time when the Jews constituted the last pure race in Europe, while the indigenous Europeans had become, "a herd of pseudo-mestizos, a people beyond all doubt degenerate physically, mentally, and morally."[11] The real Judaism, for Chamberlain, was the Jewish race, and intermarriage a pivotal part of its racial strategy. *Völkisch* anti-Semites, however, were not alone in placing a high premium on the issue of intermarriage, the mixing of Jewish and German blood.

In one of the clarion calls of the anti-Semitic movement, Heinrich Treitschke pronounced that,

> the emancipation has been carried out so fully as to preclude every ground for further Jewish demands. Nevertheless, the Jews foreswear the blood-mixing, which has always been the most effective means toward an equalizing of tribal differences.[12]

Thus, as opposed to *völkisch* anti-Semitism, mainstream anti-Semites argued that the Jews' refusal to intermarry posed the greatest threat to German–Jewish amity because it signaled a refusal of Jews to fully embrace their *Deutschtum*. Eventually, the issue of intermarriage provoked rancorous debates within the anti-Semitic ranks but more moderate Germans also focused their attention on Jewish exogamy.

While historians continue to debate whether German political liberalism tended more to chauvinistic nationalism—and consequently less to an acceptance of cultural diversity than its western counterparts—German cultural liberalism certainly did not incline toward an acceptance of cultural diversity, especially when it came to the issue of a continued Jewish presence. Theodor Mommsen, the noted historian of classical antiquity, defended the Jews against Treitschke's attacks. Yet Mommsen's correspondence makes it clear that he, too, saw little chance for complete acceptance as long as the Jews preserved their distinctiveness. And, *mirabile dictu*, it was the issue of familial distinctiveness that Mommsen seized upon as emblematic of the Jews' unwillingness to mix with Germans. Mommsen assigned value to the Jews principally because they were an "element of ferment"; the ambiguity of this phrase may be gauged by the speed with which it was seized upon by opponents of Jewish equality. Perhaps Pringsheim had this well-known example in mind when he stormed over to his son-in-law's flat. Despite the decline of anti-Semitic parties in the 1890s, social anti-Semitism grew in intensity,[13] the debate on the 'Jewish Question' and on Jewish–Christian intermarriage actually peaked in the first decade and a half of the twentieth century. A generation after the Mommsen–Treitschke debate, a spate of works by Jewish authors predicted the demise of German Jewry. In response, two collections of articles entitled *Diskussion: Kultur-Parlament* and *Judentaufen* brought the issue of Jewish intermarriage to the general German intelligentsia.[14]

Dr. Max Marcuse, one of the first sexologists, argued that Jewish assimilation was both desirable and possible. Marcuse saw no biological hindrances to intermarriage, the philosopher Eduard von Hartmann's well-known claims of racial antipathy notwithstanding.[15] For "state and society," Marcuse considered assimilation highly desirable and also possible: Chinese Jews had assimilated to disappearance and, closer to home, the Jews of Italy stood on the brink of complete absorption. Only in this way could the 'Jewish Question' be solved. Conceding the disproportionately high number of "degenerate" Jews, Marcuse countered that the Jews' positive attributes more than compensated for these failings—Germany did not have to worry about getting the short end of the stick in the intermarriage trade-off.[16]

While other members of the German intelligentsia joined Marcuse's "praise" of Jewish qualities, this represented philo-Semitism with a twist. For none of the non-Jews represented in *Judentaufen* regarded Jews as fully part of the German people. Moreover, none seemed to think that Jewry possessed any intrinsic value apart from its ability to mix with Germans. Richard Nordhausen considered that a drop of foreign blood would freshen and invigorate the otherwise sleepy Germans (*Diskussion*, p. 41). Typical of this underlying consensus, Herbert Eulenberg considered the complete assimilation of German Jews desirable, but felt that the burden now lay entirely with the Jews. Their devotion to particularism—and Eulenberg meant endogamy—belonged to the last century, not to the twentieth.[17]

Richard Dehmel, the best-selling poet and novelist, argued that a single, stable race would be produced by the German–Jewish mixture. He stressed the equivalence of Germanic and Jewish family values, as well as the economic and intellectual abilities of the Jews. Dehmel surely numbers among the few non-religious philo-Semites in the *Kaiserreich*. Dehmel spoke highly of intermarriage and with unusual personal experience—he had twice married Jewish women.[18] But if Dehmel willingly met Jews on non-Christian turf, what Jacob Katz once called a "neutral society," it was also a society devoid of religious particularism. For Dehmel, his wives and children had all declared themselves *konfessionslos* [without denomination]. Like many Marxists, Dehmel envisioned the solution of the 'Jewish Question' only against the background of a wholly secularized society.[19] The voice of ethnic diversity, truly alone in the wilderness, belonged to Heinrich Mann. Mann shrank back in horror from the notion that the Jews would aspire to be no more than lieutenants in the officer reserve corps. Would it really be desirable, Mann asked, to remove the ethical influences of Jews from public life and the spiritual influences of the Jewish woman from love? Judging from these two thick volumes, the majority of Mann's non-Jewish contemporaries seem to have thought so (*Judentaufen*, p. 69).

The Jewish respondents in these volumes reflected the fact that in addition to anti-Semitism, exogamy, apostasy, and infertility now loomed as a threat to continued Jewish existence. Many objected to the three questions posed by Arthur Landsberger, author of the introduction to *Judentaufen*, which were as follows:

(1) Can the Jews achieve total assimilation through intermarriage and baptism?

(2) Is the Zionist ideal of a Jewish state either desirable or realizable?

(3) Will the anti-Semitic movement gain in strength if neither (1) nor (2) occurs?

Professor Siegmund Maybaum, a leading figure within German Jewry, objected to posing the problem in this manner since it could so easily be used as grist for the anti-Semitic mill. Maybaum, however, had to admit that Jewish spiritual, ethical, and economic solidarity with the German nation did not seem to suffice as a proof of assimilation. Ludwig Geiger contended that to consider intermarriage and baptism the only means of completing the process of assimilation—which was how he read the non-Jewish respondents—was to proffer a gross insult to one hundred years of German Jewry. What did the Germans demand, asked Geiger, that they crossbreed in order to produce more blond-haired, straight-nosed offspring? As a *sine qua non* of assimilation, Maybaum and Geiger firmly denied the necessity of baptism and intermarriage. The terms of the emancipation bargain, already unfavorable from the Jewish side, permitted no further concession (*Judentaufen*, pp. 44–48)

Notably, two of the most prominent Jewish academics debated the reality and significance of Jewish race purity and intermarriage. Ignaz Zollschan, an Austrian physician, began his treatise *Das Rassenproblem* with an emphatic agreement to Chamberlain's claim in *Foundations of the Nineteenth Century* that Jews were a race; Zollschan disagreed even more emphatically that the Jews had degenerated. Zollschan, among others, championed a view of Jewish racial purity. In phrases not too far removed from Chamberlain's, Zollschan wrote that, "the interbreeding of totally different nations produces a bastard type whose character is far below the level of either parent."[20] Yet Zollschan's aggressive assertion of Jewish superiority did not obviate a need for apologetics. Having demonstrated the Jews' high racial value, as well as their racial purity, Zollschan claimed that the disappearance of the Jews would be an "irretrievable loss for the general culture." Reacting to the belief that Jewish endogamy had led to a disporportionately high degree of madness, cretinism, and neurasthenia (a belief held by scientists as reputable as Jean Charcot, Sigmund Freud's mentor) Zollschan contended that the damage caused by inbreeding was minor in comparison to outbreeding. Zollschan concluded that only by adopting a "great task" could Jewry be saved from degeneration through racial mixing. Thus Zollschan, "one of the most prominent race scientists of the day, came to embrace Zionism."[21]

Maurice Fishberg, Zollschan's principle antagonist in the area of Jewish race/anthropology, denied that there was such as thing as a Jewish race[22] (*The Jews*, pp. 179). Fishberg devoted a lengthy chapter of his treatise *The Jews: A Study of Race and Environment* to the contemporary intermarriage situation. He concluded that legalization of intermarriage had opened the floodgates to exogamous marriages, which could only be prevented by a return to the ghetto. Fishberg, born in Czarist Russia, agreed with Arthur Ruppin's verdict that, "no thinking Jew could desire a return to the ghetto" (*The Jews*, p. 209).[23] Fishberg, though he believed that assimilation in the west would continue unabated, threw in his lot with the mainstream liberal solution and dismissed the path of Zionism.[24] Zollschan's and Fishberg's respective treatments of the biological implications of intermarriage, aside from demonstrating that Jewish race "scientists" could no more agree on the issues of intermarriage and race mixing than their Gentile counterparts, also demonstrated how inextricably linked science and ideology were for fin-de-siècle Jewish academics, and how much weight they placed on the importance of intermarriage.

Lurking behind this discourse on race, blood mixing, and the viability of German Jewry lay that great bogeyman of fin-de-siècle thinking: degeneration. Popularized by Max Nordau's book of the same name, *Degeneration* (1892), this fear posited that the fatigue of the human organism, reified by the nervous excitement of the modern industrial society, was leading to a decline.[25] Whether of the individual character (Charcot/Freud), race, and/or national characteristics (Chamberlain, Zollschan), European society at large (Spengler), one could very well take one's pick of the offending ailment. For *völkisch* racists, as George Mosse explained, miscegenation often epitomized this degeneration. The Nazis, of course, took Jewish degeneration, criminality, and race characteristics as structural and final (Mosse, pp. 83–85). But scientists without any apparent anti-Jewish animus also considered the low birth rates, the high proportion of suicide, and the tendency to genius/madness "characteristic" of European Jewry; characteristics attributed to Jewish degeneration and Jewish endogamy or Jewish incest.[26]

I am aware that my discussion of context has led very far away from a discussion of text. Two tempting roads back present themselves, one biographical and one political. Mann wrote *Wälsungenblut* in 1905–1906, shortly after his engagement to Katja Pringsheim. His pursuit was long and frustrating and it is possible to read this story as a cathartic release of pent-up frustration and the aggression that invariably accompanies such release. How can one overlook the fact that Katja, like the fictional Sieglinde, also had a twin brother (Klaus), who chided Mann for his (goyish) lack of ardor (Walter, "Affair Wälsungenblut," pp. 465)? Or that von Beckenrath is pointedly described as thirty-five while Mann was thirty and Katja just nineteen at the time of their betrothal?

On the other hand, one could just as easily read *Wälsungenblut* as the reproach of "an unpolitical man" to the crude mechanism of racial anti-Semites. Certainly Mann's title is partly a spoof of Aryan pretensions to nobility. Mann would later rebuff his friend Ernst Bertram for "falling" for H. S. Chamberlain as follows: "I am simply more an artist, a melancholic, an enjoyer of contrasts and distinctions, than a judge and prophet who idolizes the one and damns the other." In 1925, however, the lines between barbarism and civilization were drawn more clearly; one should not read Mann's subsequent politics into the pre-World War I setting.[27]

Mann's sole concern for artistry in the novella *Wälsungenblut* stymies any definitive attempt to pigeonhole his position on the themes of race and intermarriage, themes that exercised so many of his less brilliant contemporaries. I am afraid, however, that this only underlines the evidence that Mann's genius transcended this unwholesome background, but did not escape from its influence, or the vocabulary of the fin de siècle. In retrospect, the objections of Alfred Pringsheim to the publication of *Wälsungenblut* seem justified: it is a very clever tale, but a very nasty one too.

## NOTES

1. Nor are these the only clues to the Jewish identity of the protagonists. Herr Aarenhold's origins are placed in a remote village in East Prussia; the children despise their father's origins, blood, and financial methods; the twins are marked by typically Jewish features; their speech is characterized as sharp, nervous and biting; they refer to von Beckenrath as "that German," etc.

2. Hans Rudolf Vaget, "'Sang reserve' in Deutschland: Zur Rezeption von Thomas Manns *Wälsungenblut*," *German Quarterly* 57 (1984), pp. 367–375.

3. Marie Walter, "Concerning the Affair Wälsungenblut," *Book Collector* 13 (1964), pp. 463–472. While Walter's reconstruction of the "affair" is quite ingenious, I cannot accept her verdict on the novella's original conclusion: "And we realize with electrifying clarity that Wälsungenblut, the blood of that preferred race, sired by Wotan himself, flows through the veins of these patiently forbearing Jews," p. 469. The story suggests neither superiority (except in an anti-Semitic sense) nor patient forebearing.

4. Sander Gilman, *Jewish Self-Hatred: Anti-Semitism and the Hidden Language of the Jews* (Baltimore: Johns Hopkins University Press, 1986), p. 292. Since Gilman's focus is Jewish self-hatred, his discussion of Mann's *Wälsungenblut* is appropriately but tantalizingly brief.

5. Thomas Mann, *Wälsungenblut. Gesammelte Werke* VIII, second edition (Frankfurt am Main: Fischer, 1974). All quotations come from the English edition of Mann, *Death in Venice and Seven Other Stories* (New York: Vintage, 1963). This edition contains the revised final sentence, which removes the telltale Yiddishisms.

6. George Mosse, *The Crisis of German Ideology* (New York: Schocken, 1981), pp. 126–145.

7. See Deborah Hertz, "Work, Love and Jewishness in the Life of Fanny Lewald," in Sorkin, ed., *From East and West: Jews in a Changing Europe* (Cambridge, MA: Blackwell, 1990).

8. Lothar Kahn, "Tradition and Modernity in the German Ghetto Novel." *Judaism* 28/1 (1979), pp. 31–41. Idem, "Neglected Nineteenth-Century German-Jewish Historical Fiction," in Mark H. Gelber, ed., *Identity and Ethos: A Festschrift for Sol Liptzin* (New York: Peter Lang, 1986), pp. 155–167. I have dealt with the literary treatment of intermarriage in my dissertation, *Jewish Reactions to Intermarriage in Nineenth Century Germany.* Columbus, Ohio State University, 1990.

9. "*Völkisch*" = populist. Lucy Dawidowicz, *A Holocaust Reader* (New York: Behrmann House, 1976), pp. 47–48.

10. Cf. Geoffrey Field, *Evangelist of Race*: *Houston Stewart Chamberlain* (New York: Columbia University Press, 1990).

11. Houston Stewart Chamberlain, *Foundations of the Nineteenth Century* I, (New York: Fertig, 1968), pp. 311, 329–340.

12. Heinrich von Treitschke, "Ein Wort über unsere Juden." The documents relevant to this phase of the anti-Semitic debate, including Theodor Mommsen's replies, have been collected in Walter Boehlich, *Der Berliner Antisemitismusstreit* (Frankfurt am Main: Fischer, 1965).

13. Ismar Schorsch, *Jewish Reactions to German Anti-Semitism, 1870–1914* (New York: Columbia University Press, 1972), pp. 53–78.

14. The principal works predicting the Jews' demise in the German context are Arthur Ruppin, *Die Juden der Gegenwart* (Berlin: Jüdischer Verlag, 1904, 1911); Maurice Fishberg, *The Jews: A Study of Race and Environment* (New York: Walter Scott Publishers, 1911); Ignaz Zollschan, *Das Rassenproblem* (Vienna and Leipzig: Böhlau: 1910, 1921); Felix Theilhaber, *Der Untergang der deutschen Juden* (Berlin: Jüdischer Verlag, 1911, 1921). Reactions to these works and to the Jewish Question in general are collected in Hans Oswald, ed., *Diskussion: Kultur Parlament* (Berlin: Verlag der Nation, 1913); *Judentaufen*, ed. Walter Sombart (Munich: Müller, 1912).

15. Eduard Hartmann, *Das Judenthum in Gegenwart und Zukunft* (Leipzig: Friedrich, 1885), p. 350; both Hartmann and Vacher de Lapouge favored intermarriage; the latter, as a means of destroying the Jews' will to survive. Quoted in George Mosse, *Toward the Final Solution* (New York: Harper, 1978), p. 61.

16. Max Marcuse, "Die Assimilation der Juden in Deutschland," *Diskussion: Kultur-Parlament*, p. 3–4. The historical presence of intermarriage justified some assimilationists who found baptism unpalatable.

17. Herbert Eulenberg, *Judentaufen*, p. 33. Along similar lines, the Sanskrit authority Albrecht Weber called intermarriage, "the best kind of *Judenmission*." Quoted in Barbara Suchy, "Die Vereine zur Abwehr des Antisemitismus," *LBIYB* 28 (1983).

18. Richard Dehmel, "Mischehen," in *Diskussion: Kultur-Parlament*, pp. 14–22.

19. Despite its anti-Semitic tone, Karl Marx's essay "Die Judenfrage" may be considered representative of this sort of presentation. Karl Kautsky updated and affirmed Marx's viewpoint in *Rasse und Judenthum* (Stuttgart: Insel, 1914). Dehmel, it should be noted, did not adhere to a materialistic philosophy.

20. Ignaz Zollschan, *Jewish Questions*, p. 36. John Efrom (*Defining the Jewish Race: The Self-Perceptions and Responses of Jewish Scientists to Scientific Racism in Europe, 1881–1933*, Dissertation (Ann Arbor: University Microfilms, 1992) carefully distinguishes the difference between the Jewish and non-Jewish uses to which "race" was put.

21. Zollschan, *Rassenproblem*, p. 468; *Jewish Questions*, p. 36. Zollschan makes this point most clearly in "Rassenproblem und Judenfrage," *Die Welt* 14 (25 August 1911), p. 34.

22. Fishberg was deeply influenced by the American sociologist Franz Boas who held that races intermingle quickly and create new anthropological types. Boas, "Race Problems in America," *Science* 29 (1909), pp. 830–849.

23. Zollschan would also have agreed that a Jewish return to the ghetto existence was undesirable.

24. Zollschan, *Rassenproblem*, Preface, p. ix. Zollschan wrote: "He [Fishberg] not only pleaded for total cultural assimilation of Jewry, but also for the assimilation of the blood (i.e. intermarriage and dissolution). I do not believe that Fishberg can be characterized as a proponent of intermarriage."

25. Max Nordau, *Degeneration* (New York: Columbia Press, 1968).

26. Nigel Hamilton, *The Brothers Mann* (New Haven: Secker and Warburg, 1979), p. 215.

27. Ibid., p. 215.

# The Negative German–Jewish Symbiosis

## Jack Zipes

> It is, after all, to a German Jew who had left Judaism—though, as he wrote, he of course knew that this was impossible—that we owe what a critic once called "the most naked exposures" of the Berlin Jewish bourgeoisie that exists anywhere and will endure as a sinister document of the German–Jewish reality; I am referring to the monologues of Herr Wendriner, written by Kurt Tucholsky.
> 
> Gershom Scholem, "Jews and Germans" (1966)

In his book *On Jews and Judaism in Crisis* (1976), Gershom Scholem refuted the existence of a productive German–Jewish symbiosis that, many intellectuals believe, played a vital role in the flowering of German culture, particularly during the Weimar period. According to Scholem, the Jewish enthusiasm for German culture was always one-sided and unreciprocated. The relationship between Germans and Jews was "never anything else than a fiction"[1] that had disastrous results for the Jews because it denied the possibility of emancipation.

Scholem's remarks have caused considerable debate about the meaning of a German–Jewish symbiosis that has never been resolved. However, as Dan Diner cogently demonstrated in his essay *Negative Symbiose*, it is most evident that a German–Jewish symbiosis developed after 1945:

> Since Auschwitz—what a sad twist—one can indeed speak about a 'German–Jewish symbiosis.' Of course, it is a negative one: for both Germans as well as for Jews, the result of a mass annihilation has become the starting point for their self-understanding. It is a kind of contradictory mutuality, whether they want it or not, for Germans as well as Jews have been linked to one another anew through this event. Such a negative symbiosis, constituted by the Nazis, will stamp the relationship of each group to itself, and above, all, each group to another for generations to come.[2]

Diner's essay endeavors to deal with the difficulties that Germans and Jews since 1945 have encountered as a result of the negative symbiosis while seeking to establish identities for themselves. However, I maintain that this negative symbiosis has always been at the basis of German–Jewish identity during the twentieth century. In fact, the contemporary questions posed by Scholem and Diner about the negative German–Jewish symbiosis were strikingly formulated by two of the most satiric critics of Germans and Jews during the Weimar Republic—Kurt Tucholsky and Mynona (Salomo Friedlaender), who were both assimilated Jews.

In 1922, in reaction to the assassination of Walter Rathenau, Tucholsky and Mynona began writing stories that had a direct bearing on the German–Jewish symbiosis. Tucholsky created his Wendriner sketches, which criticized the manner in which Jews obsequiously "Germanicized" themselves.[3] Mynona wrote "The Operated Goy" [Der operierte Goy], published in *Trappistenstreik* (1922) to mock anti-Semitism and posit a solution to the negative aspects of the German–Jewish symbiosis.[4] Unlike Tucholsky, Mynona tried to explore how extremes could be reconciled, and he continued to seek answers to the differences between Germans and Jews even during his Paris exile after 1933. His grotesque tale, "The Laughing Job" ("Der lachende Hiob," 1935), dealt with a Jewish and universal triumph over totalitarianism that enabled all individuals to form their own identities in keeping with Kantian ethics. It was also about this time that Tucholsky committed suicide and his last letter to Arnold Zweig denigrating Jews was published in *Neue Weltbühne*. In a strong response to the dead Tucholsky's remarks, Mynona/Friedlaender wrote a highly significant letter to his friend Fritz Lemke, commenting on Jewish self-hatred and anti-Semitism and the need to rise above racism if one wanted to establish the conditions that would further the development of authentic identity.

The Tucholsky–Mynona dialogue about German Jewish identity is extremely important for reflecting on the contemporary situation of Jews in Germany. In fact, given the negative symbiosis, a crucial ethical aspect of German identity depends on the degree to which Germans as well as Jews confront the questions that Tucholsky and Mynona raised during the 1920s and 1930s. The more the Germans try to avoid the Jewish question within the question of German national identity, the more German Jews are becoming anxious about their own identity and recall the quandary of Tucholsky and Mynona.

What exactly is this quandary? What is the negative German–Jewish symbiosis? Diner focuses on the period after 1945 to define the negative symbiosis, but, as I have remarked, it was always there and can perhaps be comprehended best by recalling an incident that affected Tucholsky and Mynona the same year that Rathenau was assassinated.

At the end of 1922 the case against the two men who had attacked and brutally beaten Maximilian Harden within inches of his life came to trial. Harden, whose real name was Felix Ernst Witkowski, was the perfect example of the assimilated Jew who came to believe that he embodied the German nation. Son of a Berlin businessman, who had supported the German revolutionary movement of 1848, Harden became alienated from his family as a young man and traveled about Germany as an actor between 1880 and 1885. At this point he settled in Berlin and began writing for various newspapers while taking courses at the university. By 1891 he was able to gather together enough money to start his own magazine, which he called *Die Zukunft*, and within a few years it became one of the most significant political journals in Germany. Although Harden did not align himself with any one party, he did support many of Bismarck's policies and became one of the most ferocious conservative critics of the Kaiser, claiming to speak on behalf of the German nation. In this regard, he was always critical of the "unassimilated" Jews in Germany. As early as 1900, he published an article by Walter Rathenau, who called for a mass conversion of all Jews to Christianity so that they could get rid of their outmoded East European customs and play a role as full-fledged Germans and help determine the future of Germany in modern European civilization. Naturally, Harden supported the German cause during World War I, but his journal fell into disrepute after 1919, and ironically he, like Rathenau, was singled out by the extreme right wing as a "Jewish" instigator and was beaten on the head with an iron rod by hired thugs during the night of 3 July 1922.

One of the attackers, Herbert Weichardt, was captured, and eventually his partner, a Lieutenant Ackermann, was arrested. Both were tried in Moabit during December of 1922, and it became apparent to all who witnessed the trial—and Tucholsky was there—that the two unscrupulous attackers tried to kill Harden mainly for money and not out of political convictions. Indeed, they had been in the employ of Albert Wilhelm Grenz, a bookseller and pornographer, who acted on behalf of a so-called "patriotic" party in Munich, concerned about the good name of Germany. However, the proceedings became a mockery of justice. Harden, the victim, was actually the man placed on trial, while his victimizers were treated with respect. The trial focused on Harden's alleged unpatriotic writings and his alien or Jewish provocation of "good" Germans. In the end, the defendants were sentenced to only one year in prison. This travesty of justice had a particularly grotesque side to it because the judge who delivered the sentence was Jewish. So were the two lawyers who defended the assailants. It seems that these Jewish jurists wanted to appear detached and objective before a Gentile jury, but Harden himself delivered a passionate speech toward the end of the trial, maintaining that a light sentence for his attachers would harm our reputation, that is, the German reputation in other countries, and then he corrected himself:

> No. It was a slip of the tongue. I didn't mean to say *we*. I meant *you*. If you do not want to have me because I was born into this world as a Jew, then so be it! I also told Rathenau often enough: Why do you always write and say 'We' Germans?—They do not want to count Jews as Germans. I love the Germans, but I don't want to force myself upon them. Let them justify the way in which they order their affairs of justice before their children and before what I have

termed the world conscience. If you want to acquit these mercenaries of the murder cooperative and to wine and dine them at the Prytaneum as a reward for their patriotic deed, then do it.⁵

But it is not the way justice is slighted in this case that is significant here. Rather it is the German–Jewish symbiosis that is of essence, the negative German–Jewish symbiosis. Theodor Lessing, whose book *Der jüdische Selbsthaß* (1930) is seminal for grasping this symbiosis, summarized Harden's case as follows:

> Here a German court of justice, presided over by converted Jews, favors the murderers of another converted German Jew, because these murderers assure everyone that they wanted to murder in the name and spirit of German convictions. And insofar as these men conduct themselves in an extremely 'German' way, they drive this other man, who until then had still been 'German' wherever possible, back into his 'being Jewish.' (Lessing, p. 204)

Bodies beaten. Justice taunted. Identities imposed upon bodies. Jew as stigma. Jews legislating laws of anti-Semites to determine their own identities. Prejudices that take the form of prescriptions and inscriptions that determine the internal and public discourse of German Jews, who claim to be German as a mark of distinction only to discover that the mark is the insignia of suicide and death. The trial of Harden's assailants was also a mark, one that showed how deep the imprint of the negative German–Jewish symbiosis was.

As can be seen in Rathenau's assassination and in the works of Tucholsky and Mynona, 1922 was stamped by this mark. The negative German–Jewish symbiosis wove its way through their writings between 1922 and 1935 as a dialogue that they held directly and indirectly with one another and other German Jews.

Tucholsky wrote sixteen Wendriner stories from 1922 to 1930. The immediate stimulus for the tales was Rathenau's murder and the response to it by German Jews.⁶ Tucholsky created the character of Herr Wendriner, an assimilated Jewish businessman, who avoided confronting the racism and class struggles in Germany, to demonstrate Jewish self-hatred and to show how Jews became instrumental in their own destruction. The very first sketch, "Herr Wendriner Makes a Phone Call" ("Herr Wendriner telefoniert"), illustrates the social and political attitudes of many wealthy and conservative German Jews that contributed to stereotypical notions of the materialistic Jew. Herr Wendriner attempts to make a business phone call on the day of Rathenau's funeral, when all mail and telephone service in Germany was suspended between 2:00 and 2:10 p.m. At first Herr Wendriner is respectful, but he becomes more and more annoyed that business as normal cannot continue, and during his monologue he lets slip various remarks that reveal his admiration for the right wing in Germany and also reveal that he blames the Jews or Rathenau himself for the assassination. For instance, at one point he comments:

> Shooting him from a car—outrageous! The police ought to . . . Operator! Guess the ten minutes aren't up yet. Must have been crack shots, those fellows. Officers, maybe. . . . Can't really imagine that, though. . . . Had all the boys from my son's regiment over for dinner that time, didn't I? Such nice, high-class people. Terrific personalities, some of them. I got a big kick out of it when the boy became a reserve officer. (*Tucholsky Reader*, p. 41)

And later:

> Let them kill each other or not but they've got to keep it out of our business! And another thing, a Jew shouldn't make such a spectacle of himself. That only stirs up anti-Semitism. Since the ninth of November we haven't had law and order in this country. Is it necessary to shut off the phones? Who's going to pay me damages if I don't reach Skalitzer? Operator! (*Tucholsky Reader*, p. 41)

There is a macabre if not grotesque twist to this monologue as Wendriner moves from stating his admiration for Rathenau to taking sides with the reactionary forces in Germany and condemning Rathenau the Jew for bringing upon his murder because of his success. In the genial monologues that Tucholsky published during the next eight years, "Herr Wendriner Goes Shopping," "Herr Wendriner Has Company," "Herr Wendriner Has his Hair Cut," "Herr Wendriner Deceives his Wife," etc., Wendriner exposes himself as being authoritarian, hypocritical, pretentious, coarse, cowardly, and conformist. In other words, he is the prototype of a German philistine, and by the time Tucholsky writes his final sketch, "Herr Wendriner under the Dictatorship" ("Herr Wendriner steht unter der Diktatur") he has become a full-fledged Nazi supporter. While attending a movie theater, he makes the following comments to a friend:

> Intermission now. Shush! Say, take a look at that dark-skinned fellow down there! Some Polish Jew I'll bet . . . lemme tell you something, with kikes like that there's a reason for anti-Semitism. Take a good look at him. Disgusting fellow. What surprises me is that he's still around; why don't they kick him out? . . . Well I can't complain. On our street everything's in perfect order. We've got a nice storm-trooper on the corner, a real nice fellow. When I go to work in the morning, I slip him a cigarette—he salutes as soon as he sees me coming; salutes my wife too. (*Tucholsky Reader*, p. 46)

What is perhaps most horrifying about all these Wendriner monologues is the fact that Wendriner is totally unaware of his own anti-Semitism. His assimilation and acceptance of Nazism is a form of suicide, and it was perhaps Tucholsky's feeling of shame about the "Germanized" Wendriners and recognition of his own dilemma as a German Jew that led to his own suicide, a suicide of protest. Interestingly, in one of his last letters to Arnold Zweig, shortly before he committed suicide, he focuses on Wendriner and his difficulties with his Jewish identity.

> In the year 1911 I 'withdrew from Judaism,' and I know that one cannot do this at all. Yet, the official formulation from the courts stated it that way. You know that this was not tied to any effort on my part to improve my economic or social situation—a Jew had a tolerable time in Imperial Germany, while someone who did not declare a religion had it difficult. (You were a suspicious dog in the military's eyes, suspicious.) So why did I do it?—I did it because I could never get rid of the disgust I felt very early in my childhood for the unctuous rabbi—because I felt the cowardice of this society more than I grasped it.... Wendriner had not yet been born at that time. That is, yes, he was, but he did not have a name. So that's why I withdrew from Judaism.[7]

And a few paragraphs later, he focuses his attack on the German Jews in association with Wendriner:

> The Emancipation of the Jews is not the work of the Jews. This liberation had been given the Jews as a present through the French Revolution, that is, from non-Jews—the Jews never fought for it, and they have to pay for this. (*Politische Briefe*, p. 118)

> It is not true that the Germans have become contaminated by Jews (*verjudet*). The German Jews have become 'krauts' (*verbocht*). You say: Yes, there are people like Wendriner. For me they are the exceptions.—They are deadly but... *I* say: There are also decent Jews, some, as shown by the number who emigrate, yet 10 percent.—They are the exceptions.—I have the greatest respect for them, for their silent suffering—I am not talking about them either—but... But—? The rest are not worth anything. (*Politische Briefe*, pp. 117–118)

Tucholsky's letter, which essentially charged the German Jews and German Leftists with cowardice and accused them of failing to organize a stronger resistance to Nazism, was published by *Neue Weltbühne* and then revised and published by the Nazis to stress Tucholsky's critique of the Jews. As such, it became, like the Wendriner stories, the means through which German Jews sought to define themselves and the German–Jewish symbiosis. Friedlaender was extremely angered by Tucholsky's remarks, and in a letter to his friend Fritz Lemke, he asserts:

> But what this Wendriner–Tucholsky does is vulgar empiricism and damaging in a sensory way. Certain Jews do not smell good to him—in a wink *the* Jew is fabricated, just like the mob loves to do it. 'Ghetto is not a consequence! Ghetto is fate.' He wants to say it is due to the *character* of the Jews. This Jewish character is an empirical product of the mob. I was not born to defend Jews. But

> I shall defend the sublime, beautiful, good, pious, intelligent *human being* that is just as much in the German as it is in the Negro and the Jew. I do not continually ask, like Hitler and Tucholsky, whether a human being is empirically and materially Jewish. It may be very interesting ethnologically, even though this science has not yet been fully developed. Humanly, politically, logically, and intellectually it is something a mob would do.[8]

Aside from this angry response to Tucholsky, Friedlaender had already conceived a different solution to the negative German–Jewish symbiosis in "The Laughing Job," published in Paris the same year that Tucholsky committed suicide. Friedlaender's approach to the quandary of the Jew faced with the possibility of losing his or her identity due to the instrumental forces of assimilation had always been different from Tucholsky's, though he, too, wrote in the satirical and ironic vein. (It was not by coincidence that, in 1922, the year Wendriner was created, Friedlaender wrote "The Operated Goy" in response to Oskar Panizza's "The Operated Jew" and to subvert and resist the negative German–Jewish symbiosis.) His last work of fiction or "grotesque," as he used to term his stories, was in effect a culmination of his final public response to Tucholsky and other German Jews who sought to define themselves through the discourse about the negative German–Jewish symbiosis. In "The Laughing Job" Joshua Zander, the rich Jewish owner of a mining company, is deprived of his property and abandoned by his family and workers. Arrested by the Nazis, Joshua's only response to threats and torture is laughter. Even when he is killed, his spirit remains indomitable, and this spirit becomes infectious so that Joshua eventually leads a rebellion against the *Führer* and shows how *Vernunftmenschen* or men of reason can control their bestial instincts and create a truly humane society.

Friedlaender's wish-fulfillment in "The Laughing Job" reflects a certain naive idealism if not mysticism that stamped this thinking. But, in this case, it is not the solution he proposes for overcoming Nazism that is important. Rather, it is the transformation of the Jew into a universal if not anonymous ethical ideal, the man of reason, that is significant. Ironically, it was more or less the same ideal that Tucholsky imagined in opposition to his character Herr Wendriner. In each case, Jewish identity is impossible to attain without overcoming the negative German–Jewish symbiosis. For both Friedlaender and Tucholsky, the goal is to avoid succumbing to Germanization without identifying with Jews as a race or religion. Paradoxically, then, Jewish identity is a secular sublation of the negative German–Jewish symbiosis, the avoidance of stigmatization, the sign that obliterates signs.

The dialogue concerning the negative symbiosis between Tucholsky and Friedlaender from 1922–1934 can be traced in the works and letters from many German Jews. Public and private, explicit and implicit, conscious and unconscious, this dialogue assumed many forms and was on the minds of most German Jewish intellectuals during the Weimar Republic. For instance, right before the assassination of Rathenau in 1922, Jakob Wassermann wrote *Mein Leben als Deutscher und Jude* [My Life as German and Jew, 1921], in which he tried to counter the raging anti-Semitism of the times and come to terms with what he regarded as the paradox of being German and Jewish at the same time.[9] Toward the end of the 1920s Leo Löwenthal published several essays on Moses Mendelssohn, Salomon Maimon, Ferdinand Lasalle, Heinrich Heine, Karl Marx, Hermann Cohen, and Sigmund Freud in congregation newspapers published in Frankfurt and Bavaria that sought to bring out the Jewish aspects of all these "German" writers.[10] In 1933, Arnold Zweig completed his book, *Bilanz der deutschen Judenheit. Ein Versuch* [A Balance of German Jewry], in which he argued that the "Jewish question" in Germany was a question for all nations, and if it were not resolved, then civil rights for all minorities would be threatened. The question of how the "Jewish question" was to be treated would be a measure of the humanity and the enlightenment of Western civilization.

As Friedrich Wolf demonstrated in his remarkable play, *Professor Mamlock* (1934), it was impossible to avoid the Jewish question. Though Mamlock, who is world renowned and head of a Berlin clinic, wants to remain above the political and anti-Semitic conflicts of the early 1930s, he is forced into taking a position when the Nazis pass the law that prevents Jews from being civil servants. The good doctor desperately wants to find a loophole in the law that will enable him to do so. However, when a Jewish assistant Simon is excluded, compelling Mamlock to realize that he is an exception, the doctor refuses to collaborate with the Nazis and commits suicide rather than sign a self-incriminating document. Wolf's Mamlock is Wassermann's German Jew come full circle. He is the paradox that can only be transcended through the universal Jew who obliterates signs.

In a penetrating essay, "The Irresolution of the Jewish Question" ("Die Unlösbarkeit der Judenfrage," 1932), Theodor Lessing, the Jewish critic murdered by the Nazis in 1933, wrote that the major contradiction for Jews was that they were expected to retain the nationality of the nation in which they were living and at the same time represent something else:

> As guest and stranger, merely tolerated, Jews will naturally sense human misery as their own fate and feel all human guilt as their own guilt. Thus they will feel drawn to everything that transcends a *Volk* and to everything between people. They will come logically and ethically to the point of losing their elements. At the same time, however, they are supposed to preserve a limited ethnic identity (*Volkstum*) and have a feeling for life that is different from other people (*Völker*).[11]

Lessing argues that this contradiction cannot be resolved, and anyway, it is not a "Jewish" contradiction:

> People may consequently learn: what they do to the Jews today will be their own fate tomorrow. . . . 'One cannot belong to two nations at the same time.' But the Jews must be able to do this! And tomorrow, and the day after tomorrow in the polynational states of the future everyone will have to learn what only the Jews today have wrested from their nature. (*Der Jud ist Schuld*, p. 411)

According to Lessing, the Jew is therefore a symbol for all humanity, for Jews are assigned to live through prejudice, anti-Semitism, negative stereotypes and to transcend them in a manner that will bring about a new universal human being.

Again echoes of Kant mixed with Marxist ideals are suggested in the works of Tucholsky and Mynona/Friedlaender. Lessing's essay was part of a large anthology, entitled *The Jew is Guilty . . . ? A Discussion Book about the Jewish Question* (*Der Jud ist schuld . . . ? Diskussionsbuch über die Judenfrage*, 1932) in which well-known German anti-Semites, German philo-Semites, and German Jews offered their comments about the situation of the Jews in Germany at the time. Lessing's contribution was the last in the volume, and as such it marked the culmination of the discussion about the German–Jewish negative symbiosis. That is, until 1933 German Jews in their dialogues with each other and with Germans were always aware that the distinction between assimilation into "Germanness" and the extinction of their Jewish identities was practically negligible, and many argued—especially the secular Jews—that this negative symbiosis could and would be sublated and lead to a new ethical identity that would contain the best elements of Germans and Jews as humanitarians. They were also aware that, without some kind of sublation, they would be literally faced with extinction. Such a possibility in the negative German–Jewish symbiosis was one that most German Jews did not want to face. But the Germans compelled them to face it by 1933 when Lessing was killed, and when Professor Mamlock's suicide on stage was only the beginning of many suicides to come in reality.

Whereas the focus of the negative German–Jewish symbiosis until 1933 had been the "Jewish question," i.e. how to morally reform Jews so they would be fit for German civilized society, the "new" negative German–Jewish symbiosis, as Diner has shown, now focuses on the "German question," or how to reform Germans so that they realize the problematic nature of provincial nationalism and xenophobia. This reform process is a difficult one for any nation, and it has encountered many obstacles and strong opposition in Germany. It is for this reason that the German–Jewish symbiosis will remain negative and needs to be negative as a positive force for reform.

## Notes

1. Gershom Scholem, "Against the Myth of the German–Jewish Dialogue," *On Jews and Judaism: Selected Essays* (New York: Schocken, 1976), p. 63. Cf. also Harold L. Poor, *Kurt Tucholsky and the Ordeal of Germany, 1914–1935* (New York: Charles Scribner's Sons, 1968).

2. Dan Diner, "Negative Symbiose," *Babylon* 1 (1986), p. 9. The translations are those of the author.

3. The Wendriner sketches can be found in Tucholsky's *Gesammelte Werke*, eds. Mary Gerold-Tucholsky and Fritz J. Raddatz, 10 vols. (Reinbeck: Rowohlt, 1975). In addition, there is an excellent selection in *Germany? Germany! The Kurt Tucholsky Reader*, ed. Harry Zohn (London: Carcanet, 1990).

4. See *Trappistenstreik und andere Grotesken*, illustr. Gustav Henselmann (Freiburg: Walter Heinrich, 1922). See also my translation and commentary in *The Operated Jew: Two Tales of Anti-Semitism* (New York: Routledge, 1991).

5. Quoted in Theodor Lessing, *Der jüdische Selbsthaß* (Munich: Matthes & Seitz, 1984), p. 204. The book was originally published in Berlin in 1930 by the Jüdischer Verlag.

6. Kurt Tucholsky's Wendriner Stories: "Herr Wendriner telefoniert" (1923); "Herr Wendriner kauft ein" (1924); "Herr Wendriner erzieht seine Kinder" (1925); "Herr Wendriner nimmt ein Bad" (1925); "Herr Wendriner hat Gesellschaft" (1925); "Herr Wendriner beerdigt einen" (1925); "Herr Wendriner läßt sich die Haare schneiden" (1925); "Herr Wendriner betrügt seine Frau" (1925); "Herr Wendriners Jahr fängt gut an" (1926); "Herr Wendriner kann nicht gut einschlafen" (1926); "Herr Wendriner in Paris" (1926); "Herr Wendriner erzählt seine Geschichte" (1926); "Herr Wendriner geht ins Theater" (1926); "Herr Wendriner diktiert einen Brief" (1928); "Herr Wendriner läßt sich massieren" (1929); "Herr Wendriner steht unter der Diktatur" (1930).

7. "Ich bin im Jahre 1911 'aus dem Judentum ausgetreten,' und ich weiß, daß man das gar nicht kann. Die Formel vor dem Amtsgericht lautete so. Sie wissen, daß damit keine Konjunkturkriecherei verbunden gewesen ist—ein Jude hatte es im Kaiserreich erträglich, ein Konfessionsloser nicht. (Militärhm verdächtiger Hund, verdächtiga.) Warum also tat ich das—? Ich habe es getan, weil ich noch aus der frühsten Jugendzeit her einen unauslöschlichen Abscheu vor dem gesalbten Rabbiner hatte—weil ich die Feigheit dieser Gesellschaft mehr fühlte als begriff ... Wendriner war damals noch nicht geboren. Doch—aber er hatte noch keinen Namen. Also heraus." *Politische Briefe*, ed. Fritz J. Raddatz (Reinbeck: Rowohlt, 1969), p. 117.

8. Salomo Friedlaender/Mynona, *Briefe aus dem Exil* (Mainz: Von Hase und Koehler Verlag, 1982), pp. 60–61.

9. In a very revealing, unpublished draft of the foreword of *Mein Weg als Deutscher und Jude*, Wassermann wrote: "Without taking care as I usually do in my creative spirit to write in images and figures, I want to render an account of myself for my contemporaries, my real or imagined friends about the problematic part of my life that concerns my Jewishness and my existence as Jew. To be sure, it is an existence not only within the non-Jewish society, a non-Jewish people, but also within the Jewish community itself. An endless theme, a typical case. For me, and it is ongoing for me, it is the only reality, and it has serious consequences that needed a great resolution on my part to depict in its entire scope with its large amount of misunderstandings, tragedy, contradictions, ugliness and suffering." See *Deutscher und Jude*.

*Reden und Schriften 1904–1933,* ed. Dierk Rodewald (Heidelberg: Lambert Schneider, 1984), p. 260.

10. Cf. "Judentum und deutscher Geist," in *Untergang der Dämonologien: Studien über Judentum, Antisemitismus und faschistischen Geist* (Leipzig: Reclam, 1990), pp. 26–82.

11. *Der Jud ist Schuld . . . ? Diskussionsbuch über die Judenfrage* (Basel: Zinnen, 1932), pp. 402–403.

# Historical Consciousness and Jewish Identity: Stefan Zweig and Wilhelm Speyer on the Way to Themselves

Luke Springman

Stefan Zweig (1881–1942) and Wilhelm Speyer (1887–1952), were progeny of assimilated, wealthy Jewish families of Vienna and Berlin, respectively. Their work calls for comparison, because both published popular books during the Weimar Republic that were based on instructive visions of history and read primarily by young people.[1] The anecdotal structure of Zweig's *Sternstunden der Menschheit* [The Tide of Fortune] (1927), focusing on isolated moments of glory that changed the course of history, compares with the way young students emulate the heroes from their lessons in history and mythology in Speyer's *Der Kampf der Tertia* [The Third Form Struggle] (1927). In the nineteenth-century German tradition of education and of building a state culture, history served to legitimate the nation through thorough pedagogical formulations: lessons of history ingrained personal identification with Germany among educated youth. By the late nineteenth century, no group of Germans more assiduously appropriated German culture and the virtues of education than the Jews, who in a newly secularized state with geopolitical aspirations continued their progress to full emancipation. Upper-middle-class Jews and descendants of Jews, especially those born during the Second Reich, contributed to German culture far beyond their demographic representation. In the period of historicism in art and architecture, the German national identity constructed historical legitimation for a unified culture. Therefore Jews entered German culture by conceiving of themselves as part of the national heritage and as progressing toward full acceptance as Germans.

Yet what order and progress could they imagine for civilization in the twentieth century after all reason descended into the utter barbarity of Nazism? Zweig's memoirs in *Die Welt von Gestern* [The World of Yesterday] (1943) contain less a personal history than a literary essay on the decline of European civilization in his own time. In contrast, Speyer based his autobiographical novel *Das Glück der Andernachs* [The Good Fortune of the Andernach Family] (1947) on one year of family history around the time when he was born in 1887. I shall first examine how Zweig and Speyer codify historical moments of glory as having significance for their own time, and then compare how these authors later comprehended the popular and political hatred of the Jews that overwhelmed their culture.

Originally the thin volume *Sternstunden der Menschheit* contained five historical "miniatures," portraits of decisive moments in history from 1805 to 1912.[2] As stellar moments of history, Zweig selected Marshal Grouchy's decision to not send Napoleon reinforcements at the Battle of Waterloo, Goethe's moment of inspiration and salvation in writing the poem cycle "Marienbader Elegie," the fate of Johann August Suter (sic!) after discovering gold in California, Feodor Dostoyevski's mock execution, and Robert Scott's expedition to the South Pole. Although the foreword denies embellishments upon the facts, Zweig applies poetic license in depicting the grand decisive moments of human action. The pathos emanating from these vignettes dramatizes events as the author divines the spiritual convulsions of his heroes down to their facial expressions. There appear, according to Zweig, only a constellation of those few and rare "moments of inspiration" that immutably and massively determine the future, yet these are not sparks of courage and genius of human agency, but rather intrusions from a mysterious, holy, and poetic force called history.[3]

Detractors of Zweig's vision of history criticize his formulation of a "mystified, aestheticized, and personalized power of fate," especially because it undervalues social and political forces.[4] Others, however, understand that the love of reason and faith in human progress that Zweig held before 1914 was shattered by World War I, causing him to perceive only inscrutable purpose in the seemingly arbitrary chaos of events. He therefore was responding to contemporary problems by seeking answers in the past, although admittedly motivated by subjective, emotional turmoil.[5]

Zweig identified three guiding principles in his selection of historical events and biographical subjects: he claimed to have no theory of history, and that in general he had no grasp of abstract categories, but could only apprehend the historical moment through persons and objects.[6] Second, he did not support political action or resistance in times of crisis because he was convinced that justice and moral superiority belonged to the vanquished, not to the victor, for defeat anticipates vindication in the future.[7] (This second principle determined Zweig's interpretation of Jewish suffering.) Finally, the moment of inspiration in the process of creative genius fascinated Zweig. His greatest avocation during his Salzburg years between the wars was collecting original manuscripts of great writers and composers, always seeking not completed work, but the work in progress, with all of the original corrections and notations.

Each of the five original historical miniatures of *Sternstunden der Menschheit* derives from isolated historical events the ultimate glory, and at times the genius, that a great downfall presages. Grouchy was cheated of his heroic moment by following Napoleon's order not to attack, yet following his own intuition he commanded an operation that saved the homeland. Goethe's sublime renunciation of the young Ulrike von Levetzov inspired nothing less than a moment of genius that Zweig hailed as the pinnacle of poetry: "The date is memorable, and even after the lapse of a century we may call it to mind with reverence, for German poetry has never reached sublimer altitudes than are attained in this magnificent 'Elegy'" (*Tide of Fortune*, p. 178). Zweig ascribed messianic redemption to the suffering of genius as he narrates in verse Dostoyevski's traumatic mock execution. Zweig's poetic imagination concludes with Dostoyevski's last laugh as the prophetic "yellow laughter of the Karamazovs" (*Sternstunden*, p. 112)[8] The portrait of Robert Scott suggests a contradiction to Zweig's professed dedication to a pan-European community. His narrative miniature stages the competition between Scott and his Norwegian challenger Admundsen as "a crusade of races and peoples."[9] In defeat and death, Scott's glory was his passion for the English nation and his source of greatness was his English breeding. Although Zweig's autobiography proclaims his ideal of a European culture and his abhorrence for nationalism, his praise of Scott's good British stock and upright sense of duty reveals that Zweig accepted and perpetuated the account of Scott's expedition as a British national legend and exemplum of human achievement. Zweig chose French, German, Russian, American, and British heroes, demonstrating on the one hand that genius does not favor any one nation. Yet he preserves the narratives as part of national lore as well as paradigms of tragedy and glory.

The human tragedies of *Sternstunden der Menschheit* demonstrate a paradigmatic example of what the philosopher Agnes Heller defines as a universal, world-historical consciousness. According to this view, humans and civilization depend more on a universalized historical person, a collective subject; the individual is subordinate to the world process. The following summary from Heller perfectly characterizes Zweig's conception of history:

> In this way man becomes the subject *of* history, but not the *person*. The person becomes the subject *to* history. Man is universal, but not the person. The person is identified with the universal called 'the man' only if he or she becomes the subject of history or *resigns* history completely. The person is either seen as contingent or as the *man of genius* or as the *man of resignation* (from history). This 'contingent person' pursues his or her goals, does his or her duty as a means for 'higher' aims (of the world spirit, of historical laws, of unconscious structures). It is through him or her that History, the unconscious, the 'laws' realize themselves. The protagonists of the nineteenth-century novels are mostly contingent persons. They are defeated by superior powers, and even their happiness is not their own deed, but befalls to them by the grace of the 'cunning of reason.' The genius, the great conductor of history, is not subject to rules, but is their arbitrary creator. Men of genius in politics, in art, or in abstract ideas are worshipped. Human sacrifice is welcome on their altars; contingent persons are so much raw material for them.[10]

Zweig projects an organic process of history that declares certain moments ripe for significant action, while the great expanse of human activity prepares the ground for the singular, rare, and fertile actions. Even the heroes act contingent to the "great conductor of history," and human genius is circumstantially dependent on the movement of world genius. Moreover, as Heller indicates, the world-historical consciousness is most characteristic of nineteenth-century Europe, whereas the trauma of rationalized mass death shook the foundations of the redemptive and secure course of history. World War I, however, did not topple Zweig's optimistic, yet deterministic conception of history, because before World War II he believed the word still had power.

> The historical vision of *Sternstunden der Menschheit* conceived of the progress of reason toward a goal in the future, even if humans cannot apprehend this end purpose. Still, in Weimar education, history written for young people had not even progressed to this post-Enlightenment stage, but most often resorted to history as a source for its mythology and paragons. Myth in this sense does not contain a past the way that the later world-historical consciousness projects past events as precursors to the present. Rather, history is always present, is continuously relived, and understands nature and social reality as one unified process.[11]

It was no accident that Nordic sagas and medieval legends became the preferred genres for young males in nineteenth-century Germany. The lines between myths and historical events became obscured as education appropriated history for the legitimization of the state, constructing a lineage from the ancient gods and heroes to Goethe and Bismarck. Wilhelm Speyer exploited the eternal present of myth and history in his adolescent novel *Der Kampf der Tertia*.[12] While Zweig's historical "miniatures" presume a loftier, more edifying literary posture than Speyer's novel, the adolescent struggles at a fictional boarding school nonetheless offer an ideal point of contrast through projections of the past on the present.

Wilhelm Speyer is still known primarily as the author of *Der Kampf der Tertia*, one of the most popular and long-selling adolescent novels in German literature.[13] The novel depicts the rural boarding school as the model for a primitive agrarian idyll of heroic young men (and one young woman). Speyer projects onto this fictional school, which was inspired by his years at Hermann Lietz's country boarding school (*Landerziehungsheim*) at Haubinda, an inflated allegiance to the specific culture and traditions of this school as its own tribal nation—a state within a state. Lietz's schools flourished because those who could afford the expense wished to spare their children the chaos and danger of the city, and also because the "romantic anticapitalism" that proliferated in Germany before World War I and during the Weimar Republic fostered ideals of a pre-industrial society.[14] Speyer's novel coupled such *völkisch* sentiments with a barely subdued eroticism, which, judging by the book's vast popularity, elicited a sympathetic response among German readers. Nevertheless, the National Socialist regime banned Speyer and his books after 1933 because of his Jewish lineage. Despite the apparent paradox, Speyer in his later work demonstrates how an author from an assimilated Jewish family in Berlin would have conceived a work that appealed to the very irrational primitivism and cult of rootedness that was integral to political anti-Semitism. It is telling, moreover, that one of the first teachers at Lietz's boarding schools, the philosopher Theodor Lessing, would later write a book on Jewish self-hatred and confront some of the contradictions of Jewish identity in European culture.[15]

For many years after leaving Haubinda, Speyer maintained a sentimental reverie for Hermann Lietz's Landerziehungsheim. Two main aspects of Lietz's philosophy elucidate how Speyer conceived of *Der Kampf der Tertia*. First, Lietz believed the school should govern its own affairs as a self-contained state, primarily in order to train healthy, enthusiastic patriots to lead Germany in the future. He hoped that self-sufficiency would weaken the control that bureaucrats and politicians could exercise over his schools. Second, instruction in history was central to the curriculum and the subject Lietz himself taught at Haubinda. For Lietz, history furnished parables for behavior and models for conducting affairs of state whether the state be a "horde" of young people or the German nation itself.

In Speyer's fictional construct, imitations of history and the state determine the organization, leadership, and purpose of the clique of pubescent males comprising the *Tertia*. The members of this school class excel in the art of pretension and hyperbole as they invest their initiative to rescue stray cats from extermination with world-historical consequence. Through this struggle, the author imbued the "horde" with the legendary strength and purity of a righteous *Volk*. Speyer inundated his novel with hackneyed analogies from history lessons, so that, for example, a soccer match replays the storming of Troy and student meetings imitate the ancient Roman senate. This contortion of history served only the violent self-affirmation in the students' battles with outsiders. Loyalty to the school flourishes on the "blood-and-soil" projections of pure "youth," holistic communalism, and primitive ties to nature. The narrator's incessant historical references serve to justify or to clarify by analogy the actions of the *Tertia*. The following represent only a small selection:

> Hannibal's troops had also bickered in Capua, as did the Ostrogoths in the Romagna when there was nothing to kill, storm, and plunder. (p. 7)

> The Grand Elector demonstrated once again his classic composure in the critical moments of the battle. He knew his Wellington and his Napoleon. (p. 36)

> "Gentlemen," he declared with a gesture, as if Wallenstein were turning Max Piccolomini over to the Pappenheim soldiers. (p. 45)

> Did they not say that Themistocles, out of patriotism, attempted to win over the king for the Athenians even after they had banished him from Athens? (p. 67)
>
> So they stood like the warriors of the Nibelung, with their backs against the wall of the house. (p. 143)[16]

A striking congruity emerges between the ways Lietz and Speyer understand and apply history and legends. The *Tertia* at Haubinda, after three years of folklore, legends, and mythology in the lower classes, received instruction in ancient Greek, Roman imperial, and German history.[17] In order to convey his world views most efficiently through history lessons, Lietz emphasized the monumental and legendary episodes in order to capture young imaginations and to make the lessons of the past endure in students' minds. For Lietz, the purpose of studying history was to cultivate love for the fatherland in children, developing in them an appreciation for so-called highest values. Indeed, he even maintained that historical veracity dulled the glory of fateful moments, which are to be recounted to young people in order to inspire them.[18]

Historical commonplaces pervade the text of *Der Kampf der Tertia* because they legitimize actions and determine the thinking of the characters. Correspondingly, the leader of the class is known not by name, but only as "The Grand Elector," and is distinguished by his "Caesarean chin" (p. 7), and commanding with his "Ciceronian manner of speaking" (p. 139). Each main character in the novel is confined by physiology, behavior, and speech to a determined role, so that the "Elector" rules only by virtue of those inborn qualities that purportedly distinguish leader types throughout history. However, the projection of types upon the courses of human events is in fact *ahistorical*. Projections remove history from dialectical processes to static emplotments; they create myths through notions of eternal correspondence. In this way, the Napoleonic and the Peloponnesian wars serve as preposterous analogies supporting the myth of human conflict—that violence and war are inevitable, righteous, glorious, and beautiful. The self-proclaimed righteous struggle of Fascism, and all its ignominy in splendor, appropriated such myth-building and projection for the National Socialist doctrine.

In *Der Kampf der Tertia*, Speyer projects stereotypes based upon historical, legendary, mythic, and animal prototypes, creating an imago of youthful power. As writers in exile fleeing before the debris of culture left behind in Europe, the violent conformity of Nazism, embodied especially in the Hitler Youth, mocked the youthful optimism of writers such as Speyer and Zweig. Therefore inevitable despair pervades the autobiographical self-examinations that each author undertook in the 1940s in order to comprehend their present. In Speyer's exile novel, *Das Glück der Andernachs*, the author becomes the reflecting subject of history, setting up the constellations of an assimilated Jewish family in the late nineteenth century, viewing their encounters with anti-Semitism on the wings of what Walter Benjamin, Speyer's schoolmate from Haubinda, described as the Angel of History.[19] In contrast, Zweig highlights the bright moments of his career, conceiving of his Jewishness as the tragic lot that fate issued to him and to other luminaries of European culture.

A reproduction of Stefan Zweig's suicide note appears on the cover of the Fischer paperback edition of *The World of Yesterday*. Although not part of the original autobiography, the reader begins with the end, preconditioned for the outcome of this chronicle and the underlying despair of its pages. The title anticipates the sentimental longing and mourning for a shining, extended stellar moment in European history. Fin-de-siècle Vienna proved not to be a golden age of peace and a flourishing high culture, but the dazzling light of a dying star. Seen through the lens of intervening years, the world of Zweig's youth appears as the thin ice of placid stability covering a seething reality of turmoil and hate. The ride through unknown danger and subsequent apprehension of the brush with disaster has become in German a proverbial image for the personal experience of history, "the horseman on thin ice."[20] Even if the reader adjusts for Zweig's penchant for superlatives, World War II caused Zweig to abandon hope, and at the outset of his memoirs he predicted nothing less than the end of the civilized world.[21] Yet by surviving exile and the alleged decline of European culture up to that point, Zweig claimed to have found the way back to himself, affirming in the foreword of *The World of Yesterday* his identity "as an Austrian, a Jew, an author, a humanist and a pacifist" (p. xvii).

More clearly stated by his biographers than by his own account, Zweig's attitude toward his Jewish identity is fraught with the contradictions that accompany Jewish assimilation to European culture.[22] His distaste for politics and his political naiveté firmed his conviction that the diaspora holds the rightful destiny of the Jews, for in their suffering and wandering they spread the highest values of civilization, sowing the seeds for a universal culture. Therefore, Zweig described assimilation as the Jews' crowning achievement, while persecution and homelessness conceal history's enigmatic and inexorable mission for them.[23] In the face of nationalism and imperialism in European politics, Zweig sought an identity as an international conciliator of cultural conflicts, which actually detached him from political realities. Many condemned Zweig's quietism as myopic fatuity, especially considering unfortunate statements such as his welcoming of Hitler's movement as the revolt of youth against "high politics."[24] However, in *The World of Yesterday* Zweig finally confronts his Jewishness, anti-Semitism, and the double-binds of assimilation, albeit in an understated and diffident manner.

Zweig consistently portrays the Jewish experience as having made great contributions to European cultures, while Jews never became insiders in those cultures. Looking back from the 1940s, he discerns blind tragedy and ironic prophesy. For example, the story of Theodor Herzl's adoption of Zionism supports Zweig's contention that Europe would never accept Jews and that the Jewish hero acts as pariah and unheeded prophet. Proclaiming Herzl in characteristic panegyric style as a man of "world-historical presence," Zweig continues the project of charting "stellar moments" of genius. Through Herzl, Zweig reminds the reader of the blind folly with which the Jewish bourgeoisie of Vienna viewed their own prominence and security, the same lack of understanding from which Zweig does not extricate himself.

> Are we not equal subjects, inhabitants and loyal citizens of our beloved Vienna? Do we not live in a progressive era in which in a few decades all sectarian prejudices will be abolished? Why does he, who speaks as a Jew and who wishes to help Judaism, place arguments in the hands of our worst enemies and attempt to separate us, when every day brings us more closely and intimately into the German world?

Zweig confirms Herzl's greatness, but only as a consequence for other Jews, not for those feeling secure in the social elite. Those who harked to Herzl's treatise *Der Judenstaat* (1896) came from among the less secularized persecuted Jews living in Slavic countries. Therefore, Herzl as the Cassandra for the assimilated bourgeoisie became at once the prophet for the downtrodden. Again, Zweig persists in his inclination to bathe historical figures, in this case Herzl, in the light of stellar moments:

> Whenever anyone—prophet or deceiver—throughout the two thousand years of exile plucked this string, the entire soul of the people was brought into vibration, but never as forcefully as upon this occasion, never with such a roaring and rushing echo. By means of a few dozen pages a single person had united a dispersed and confused mass. (*World of Yesterday*, p. 104)

Vienna, startled, became aware that it was not just a writer or a mediocre poet who had passed away, but one of those creators of ideas who disclose themselves triumphantly in a single country, to a single people at vast intervals (*World of Yesterday*, p. 109). Despite this late tribute to Herzl, Zweig dismisses the early political anti-Semitism of Germany and Vienna as relatively harmless pandering to lower-middle-class frustrations by unscrupulous politicians. For example, Zweig sees less a connection between the anti-Semitism of Vienna's mayor Lueger and Hitler than between the popular appeal of both politicians to the so-called abused "little man" of society.

In *The World of Yesterday*, Zweig even defends Lueger for upholding democracy and remaining loyal to his Jewish friends (pp. 30, 56). Even as late as the 1940s, Zweig perceived political anti-Semitism as incidental to opportunistic populism. The autobiography does not conceal the anguished discord when at one moment Zweig attributes Hitler's power to economic troubles (p. 228), yet finally nothing explains his lack of comprehension for the enormity of the German persecution of Jews.

Zweig strived to avoid the Jewish psychological paradox of identity, which he contended was a symptom of political consciousness. In Walther Rathenau Zweig felt the genius tortured by inner conflicts exemplified, "the tragedy of the Jew."

> His entire existence was a single conflict of constantly changing contradictions. He had inherited all imaginable power from his father and yet had no wish to be his heir, he was a merchant but fancied himself an artist; he had millions and toyed with socialistic ideas; he felt himself to be a Jew and flirted with Christ. He thought internationally and worshiped Prussianism, he dreamt of the people's rule and yet was highly honored every time he was received and consulted by Emperor Wilhelm, whose weakness and vanity he saw through intuitively without being able to master his own vanity. (*World of Yesterday*, p. 181)

Rathenau was assassinated in 1922 because he embodied the projection of hate for anti-Semitic associations such as the *Deutschvölkischer Trutz- und Schutzbund* [German Populist Protection Alliance], for the paramilitary *Freikorps* groups such as the *Stahlhelm*, and for segments of the bourgeois youth movement, such as the *Jungdeutsche Orden*. Despite the persistence and deepening of political anti-Semitism after World War I, Zweig perceived the Jewish "affliction" as a psychological disorder in the Jewish identity. Only at the end of *The World of Yesterday*, when recalling Sigmund Freud's reaction to National Socialism, did Zweig consider that the actual tragedy did not lie with Jewish mentality, but that German culture could not master its pathological drives.

Zweig's admonitions against political obsessions make one further leap in the character of the German Jewish nationalist. Ernst Lissauer illustrates the quintessential emulation of German nationalism by a Jew. Lissauer was a minor poet caught up in the patriotic frenzy of 1914. He became well known for his hymn "Haßgesang gegen England" [Song of Hate against England], a vicious incantation of hate that Zweig found most repugnant to a greater European vision. The tide of fortune soon turned against Lissauer, casting him into obscurity after 1919 and driving him into exile from his beloved Germany during the Nazi period (pp. 171–172). Anecdotes on the tragic failings of people such as Lissauer and Rathenau corroborate Zweig's conviction that politics spell the downfall of the cultured European, Jew or otherwise.

Stefan Zweig's review of his life and times carries a dreary optimism of perpetual catastrophe and redemption. Hannah Arendt criticized *The World of Yesterday* in an essay from 1948 and attributed Zweig's emotional crisis to the divestment of his fame and banishment into anonymity. She characterized his generation and class as an "international society of the successful," in which Jews held equal rights and wore their prestige "like a suit of armor." Only when events stripped Zweig of his mantel of success did he encounter the reality of the Jewish people.[25] But Zweig himself purports to have already apprehended Jewish reality through his pacifist drama *Jeremias* (1917), in which he portrays the epitome of his anti-heroes, those who acted against their time, resisted political struggle, and were vindicated by history. Zweig ascribes the fate of Jeremias as an allegory of Jewish history, guided by a mysterious, ineluctable, even divine force:

> But in choosing a Biblical theme I had unknowingly touched upon something that had remained unused in me up to that time: that community with the Jewish destiny whether in my blood or darkly founded in tradition. Was it not my people that again and again had been conquered by all other peoples, again and again and yet outlasted them because of some secret power—that power of transforming defeat through will, of withstanding it again and again? Had they not presaged, our prophets, this perpetual hunt and persecution that today again scatters us upon the highways like chaff, and had they not affirmed this submission to power, and even blessed it as a way to God? (*World of Yesterday*, p. 253)

Zweig describes the writing of *Jeremias* as a momentous event in his life: "I had thrown off the burden that had rested on my soul and had been restored to myself; in the very hour in which everything in me was 'No' against the times, I had found the 'Yes' to myself" (*World of Yesterday*, p. 254). As such, he inscribed this moment as one of his "Sternstunden," an allegory both of Jewish destiny and of the plight he shared with the scorned outsiders whose genius was misjudged. But Zweig's conception of history, unaltered by the events of Hitler and National Socialism, led ultimately to an unreconcilable dilemma. In the pageant of fateful moments that comprise history, both in *Sternstunden der Menschheit* and in Zweig's autobiography, the momentous vicissitudes in human fortunes strike like a bolt from heaven, with no manifest meaning to the subjects of history, but nevertheless invested with latent purpose. By narrating glories and cataclysms Zweig constructs a sense for the seeming peripateia in the stories of Western civilization. In the final analysis, however, Zweig despairingly no longer conceived any meaning for the "world tragedy" of the Jews. Freud's last days, when he was vainly preoccupying himself with questions about the victimization of the Jews, lead Zweig to a hopeless conclusion: "What was most tragic in this Jewish tragedy of the twentieth century was that those who suffered it knew that it was pointless and that they were guiltless" (*World of Yesterday*, p. 427).

Stefan Zweig's fin-de-siècle Vienna and sentimental longing for an aesthetic culture contrasts with the social and political issues in Wilhelm Speyer's Wilhelminian Berlin. In the 1940s, while living among other luminaries of German exile in California, Speyer confronted the issue of political anti-Semitism with an epic novel that traces in "Buddenbrooks" fashion the decline of his own, and, parabolically, of many other Jewish families. *Das Glück der Andernachs* (1947) portrays personal struggles with assimilation in a masterfully rendered portrait of Berlin culture at the juncture between the *Gründerzeit* and the reign of Wilhelm II. The contrast between this historical novel and his youth novel of twenty years earlier highlights the transformation in the author's historical consciousness, a revision that Stefan Zweig resisted. Whereas Zweig concedes that the fate of the Jew is to be a victim, Speyer undermined this resignation and anticipated later theories of Fascism by depicting anti-Semitism as a psychological malady of the Wilhelminian character.[26]

Speyer wrote his first historical novels in exile. *Im Hof der schönen Damen* [In the Court of the Beautiful Ladies] (1935) and *Das Glück der Andernachs* portray the daily lives of the social elite during periods of political transition in Germany, at the height of the Napoleonic era and the advent of Wilhelm II's accession to the throne of the German Empire, respectively. In *Das Glück der Andernachs*, Speyer blends autobiography into a fictional account set in the milieu of the *grande bourgeoisie* in Berlin during the Prussian Imperial age. Members of a wealthy German family in 1887, paradigmatic *Gründer* who bear the standards of Prussian Imperial Culture, begin to feel their marginalization as assimilated Jews. Speyer's turgid prose evokes the neogothic aesthetic through meditations on the emblems ornamenting Berlin and the house of Andernach, while authorial comments overtly connect the salon anti-Semitism of the Second Reich to the Holocaust of the Third Reich. The years from the "Antisemitismusstreit" in 1879–80 to the *Dreikaiserjahr* 1888, according to Speyer, convene the decisive period when anti-Semitism became fashionable among the aristocracy and in the academic circle around the historian Heinrich von Treitschke.[27]

Yet beyond locating the origins of political anti-Semitism, there lies within the text a tacit self-indictment of tragic denial and lack of foresight. The family portrait narrates one decisive year of transition, ending with the death of its ninety-year-old patriarch, just before the deaths of the emperors Wilhelm I and Friedrich III. Ephraim Andernach, an assimilated Jew, attained prosperity as the founder of a lucrative military uniform business, whose fortunes rose with Bismarck and expanded into an international market. He embodies the nineteenth-century ideal of cultivated respectability and remains staunchly loyal to the monarchy that emancipated him. Indeed, Ephraim feels a sympathetic bond with the health and spirit of the aged Kaiser. But above all, he is devoted to the genius of German Enlightenment and Idealism, revering especially the principle of tolerance. Despite his identification with the German state and its culture, Ephraim unexpectedly becomes the admonishing oracle, while his incredulous sons and daughters see only the progress of integration and the decline of bigotry.

The central conflict of the novel begins when Ephraim's granddaughter, Lotte, seeks his blessing to wed the grandson of Ephraim's Christian business partner and friend of sixty years. The patriarch's refusal to approve the union provides the vehicle to convey some of the ineffable complexities of Jewish history in nineteenth-century Germany. The business partner, Christian Rauch, accuses Ephraim of the very reactionary attitudes of the historian Heinrich von Treitschke and Adolf Stöcker, founder of the anti-Semitic Christian-Social Party. Rauch appeals to his friend's nearly religious ardor for the humanistic principles of Lessing, Herder, and Goethe; Lotte complains that her grandfather would have them return to the ghetto. Here the pleading collides against Ephraim's memory of serving in the Prussian army and being cheated of emancipation during the liberal movements of the Napoleonic years and of the 1848 revolution. With the formation of the North German Federation and the Prussian Constitution of 1869, which granted equal suffrage to the Jews, the progress of principled rationality appeared to move forward. Yet by the late 1870s, anti-Semitic demagoguery fomented in the Reichstag, in influential journals, and in the anti-Semitic petition of 1881, in which 267,000 signatures called for a halt to Jewish immigration and for reimposing the ban on Jews in civil service and government positions. Ephraim understood clearly that despite the conversions and assimilation of his family, despite their ardent desire to be truly German, and despite the relative marginality of anti-Jewish activity in Germany, the Andernachs occupied, in reality, a similar position to the barely tolerated court Jew. The elder Andernach strives in vain to convince Lotte that the current acceptance they enjoy in German society rests on an eroding foundation:

> Your ancestors also lived in the same country, even as far back as Roman times, probably on the Limes Germanicus. Your family name, that you will now give up, could be a testament to the great span of time we have occupied this glorious Germanic land. Nevertheless you have no patrimony here. Ferdinand has it, but you do not.[28]

> "Mark my words that things like this have happened in every century." "But not in ours." "In ours as well, which by the way is not over yet." Lotte looked at Ephraim and almost wanted to laugh. "You don't mean to say, grandfather, that one day Bismarck will take away our houses and business and have us killed." "It may go against the principles of the imperial chancellor's noble heritage and education, and against the sense of justice that he received from his experience as a conservative statesman. But if it should ever seem necessary to him, he would do it anyway." (*Andernachs*, p. 138)

In most of her talks with her elders, Lotte prefers to remain unaffected by Ephraim's pessimism and oblivious to the anti-Jewish sentiments past and present. Yet in one revealing exchange, she expresses her rebellion against the principles of suffering and sacrifice that had guided her father's class and generation of Jews. In Max Horkheimer's and Theodor Adorno's theory of anti-Semitism, the dialectical entanglement of enlightened liberalism, authority, and self-control drove the revolt against the double-binds of assimilation, an accommodation that transferred external domination into violent conformity.[29] Such a rebellion against accommodating injustice, as Ephraim's generation purportedly had done, wells up in Lotte when her grandfather suggests the nobility of being victims:

> "And what if I no longer want to be the victim, but the murderer?" Lotte asked petulantly. Jakob Ephraim cast the look of an old Jewish judge on his granddaughter. "You would not rather bear injustice?" "No. Then I'll take my lessons from Bismarck and from court preacher Stöcker and from the Tsar: I want to cause the suffering." "Cause suffering?" asked Ephraim as his wrath grew. "For whom? Perhaps for those to whom you previously belonged?" Lotte blushed. "I would cause suffering for anyone who would raise a hand against me or my children. Don't you think that is better than offering oneself up as a sacrifice to every century?" A ninety-year life did not seem to prepare Ephraim with answers to such questions. He said coldly: "I have nothing to do with this question. Whatever is significant in my century gives me no answer to this." Lotte was generally easy with apologies, but in this case she did not want to yield. In this case she seriously meant to advance in the hierarchy of crime from victim to perpetrator. (*Andernachs*, p. 139)

A recent article that discusses Walter Benjamin and his Jewish identity pointed out that Jewish assimilation and revolution do not exist so much as oppositional poles as intersecting tendencies.[30] Speyer underscores this entwining of so-called reason and rebellion in Lotte; so long as Germans accept her unconditionally there is no issue, but she rejects self-denial and sacrifice to assuage the forces of oppression. Whereas the house of Andernach prospered through assimilation and the timely suppression of its Jewishness, Lotte claims her German identity as a birthright (even her name is quintessentially German). Lotte's resistance to the cycle of victimization represents an unreflected rejection of her Jewish heritage, but at the same time she would protect those whom the anti-Semitic forces would disenfranchise.[31]

Yet Lotte's rebellious spark does not ignite any passions for defending Jewish rights. After her wedding she detects none of the animosity or stigmatization that she falsely interpreted as Ephraim's warning. There is no reason for her to believe that the anti-Semitic agitation would not abate and that the process of Jewish acculturation would not continue as indeed seemed the case until World War I.[32] And even in this "great" War, Speyer himself along with thousands of young Jewish men defended their German fatherland against the national enemy France. In the novel, brief authorial asides underscore the irony of Jewish-German patriotism by peering still further into the future, to the California coast where Lotte's nephew recounts these events in his exile (pp. 323–324), and to the Oranienburg concentration camp where Lotte's husband is imprisoned in 1934 (p. 206). Through these leaps in history, Speyer acknowledged Lotte's tragic, and perhaps necessary, disavowal of inescapable "otherness" that relates Jewish history to his own tragedy.

Lotte's denial of "otherness" does not imply that she rejects her family identity. However, among the scions of Ephraim Andernach, some of those who do understand themselves as "different" react by concealing all traces of Jewishness or, in extreme forms, by despising their own ancestry. In striving to be more monarchist than the monarchy, Lotte's father dropped his given name Salomon and adopted the name Friedrich Wilhelm. Few of Ephraim's sons and daughters, including Friedrich Wilhelm, actually converted to Christianity, yet Judaism plays no role whatsoever in their lives. Lotte's elder sister Malwine carried her denial further. She not only converted to Protestantism, but proclaimed herself to be a disciple of Stöcker and Treitschke (p. 112). Speyer locates the development of such hatred in Malwine's childhood, associating the seed of her loathing with the inculcation of Prussian values:

> Malwine went into the chamber next to her room, where the doll "Mommy's Pet" stood erect in the corner in its Prussian parade uniform, which was made from material the company used for military uniforms. (To lay the doll down to bed would have been soft and —*that*. Even quietly to herself she called everything Jewish "*that*," which is how she referred to something unspeakable, as in the way other children secretly talk among themselves about a traumatic sexual experience they cannot describe by name.) (*Andernachs*, p. 369)

That Malwine's shame wielded the force of sexual taboo indicates the irrational power of her self-hatred. Her father, Friedrich Wilhelm, the archmonarchist who advocates violent retaliation against all opposition to the throne, no doubt instilled in her a disgust for anything that smacked of Jewishness.

Speyer does not isolate Malwine's case, but points to disturbances in childrearing in general as the source of such irrational hatred. The novel's paradigmatic Jew-hating university student, Ewald Sawade, correspondingly transferred his father's contempt for Jews to his own sexually-laden revulsion against his projection of an inferior Jewish race:

> As a child Ewald had perceived a certain expression on his father's face the moment this clerk of the magistrate uttered the word "Jew" at the family table. The initial sounds of the "J" and "u" could pass; July, jury and jewel also began with this sound. But the way that word alone crossed his father's lips ultimately determined Ewald's hate. Whenever he uttered that word, he imitated his father's facial expression, as his father had imitated his grandfather at such moments, and so on through the course of centuries. And words such as Jew-church, Jew-bush, Jew-tree, Jew-town, and Jew-street evoked a fury in the Sawade men that manifested itself in sexual emanations. (*Andernachs*, p. 351)

In *Das Glück der Andernachs*, Wilhelm Speyer perceives political anti-Semitism not as an ineluctable confrontation of social groups, but as a psychosis inflicted upon people subjected to an absolutist repression within the family. Near the end of the novel, Ephraim's wife, the matriarch of the Andernachs, declares that anti-Semitism shows the symptoms of deeper social ills: "If I were a Christian and one morning woke up as an anti-Semite, then I would send for Uncle Martini. Something would be wrong in this body of mine. But a person or a people dies from sickness, not from its thermometer" (*Andernachs*, pp. 440–441). Malwine Werthern and Ewald Sawade suffer from the poison of child-rearing in an atmosphere of rigid intolerance. Therefore, Speyer conceives of anti-Semitism as a psychological disturbance in much the same way that Alice Miller analyzes hatred as the product of "poisoned pedagogy," that is, the systematic withdrawal of love and parental denial of a child's self-worth.[33]

On the one hand, the theories of "Jewish self-hatred" (Theodor Lessing, Sander Gilman) illuminate the psychological double-binds of assimilation and suggest compelling interpretations for the contradictions in Speyer's work. However, Speyer takes care to distinguish between Lotte's refusal to view herself as "other" and Malwine's malignant self-denial. I believe that Speyer identifies himself with his characterization of Lotte, and that the philosophical tension between the historical subject and the object of its perception underlie the discrepancies between Speyer's *Der Kampf der Tertia* and *Das Glück der Andernachs*. In the *Dialectic of Enlightenment*, also a product of Jewish exile published in 1947, Horkheimer and Adorno assess the epistemological constructs of Fascism and anti-Semitism. They maintain that with the domination by the subject, the "absolute self" projects a seamless reality upon nature until all phenomena either support the subject's perception or are obliterated. History is then perceived as an unreflected extension of the subject's world, as eternal repetition. Only the subject's critical reflection of the world as "other" holds some hope for redemption. Correspondingly, Speyer's earlier literary projection of a "heile Welt" in *Der Kampf der Tertia* conceived of a social reality that was cut from one cloth. The reality of National Socialism, however, jolted him into an awareness of the historical "other."

## NOTES

I would like to thank Professor Johanna W. Roden for allowing me access to her personal archival collection on Wilhelm Speyer.

1. Stefan Zweig himself characterized *Sternstunden* ... as youth literature that had become standard reading in German schools: "a small book [*Sternstunden der Menschheit*] was adopted by the schools and in a short time achieved 250,000 copies in the Inselbücherei." "Chancing to be in a book shop in Germany, I was touched on observing—unrecognized—a very young *Gymnasium* student enter and ask for *The Tide of Fortune*, paying for it out of his meager allowance." *The World of Yesterday. An Autobiography by Stefan Zweig* (New York: Viking, 1943), pp. 317–318, 322–323.

2. The current edition of *Sternstunden der Menschheit* adopts the posthumous 1943 edition, which added seven miniatures: "Flucht in die Unsterblichkeit" about Balboa's drive to the Pacific Ocean, "Die Eroberung von Byzanz" about the sacking of Byzantium in 1453, "Georg Friedrich Händels Auferstehung" about Handel's composing of the *Messiah*, "Das Genie einer Nacht" about the composition of *La Marseillaise*, "Das erste Wort über den Ozean" about the first transatlantic telegraphic communication, "Die Flucht zu Gott," a one-act drama portraying Tolstoy's death, and "Der versiegelte Zug" about Lenin's journey to Russia in 1917.

3. Stefan Zweig, *Sternstunden der Menschheit* (Frankfurt am Main: Fischer, 1964), pp. 7–8. English passages are quoted from Stefan Zweig, *The Tide of Fortune. Twelve Historical Miniatures*, trans. Eden and Cedar Paul (New York: Viking, 1940), except where otherwise indicated.

4. Hartmut Müller, *Stefan Zweig*, Rowohlts Monographien, ed. Klaus Schröter (Reinbek bei Hamburg: Rowohlt, 1988), pp. 78–83.

5. For example, see Lionel B. Steiman and Manfred W. Heiderich, "Begegnung mit dem Schicksal: Stefan Zweigs Geschichtsvision," *Stefan Zweig heute*, ed. Mark H. Gelber, *New Yorker Studien zur Neueren Deutschen Literaturgeschichte* 7, ed. Joseph Strelka (New York: Peter Lang, 1987), pp. 101–129 and Lionel B. Steiman, "Stefan Zweig und Franz Werfel: Humanism and Mysticism as Responses to Antisemitism and the Holocaust," *Holocaust Studies Annual 1990*, ed. Sanford Pinsker and Jack Fischel (New York: Garland, 1990), pp. 63–76.

6. "Without exception, my thoughts are developed by objects, events and persons, and the purely theoretical and metaphysical remains beyond my ken." *The World of Yesterday*, p. 96.

7. "I chose for my symbol the figure of Jeremiah, the man of futile warnings. I had no intention of writing a 'pacifist' play, or to set in words and verses the truth that peace was better than war, but to portray the man who in time of enthusiasm is despised as the weakling, the timid one, but who in the hour of defeat proves himself to be the only one able not only to endure it, but also to master it. From the time of my first play, *Thersites*, I had frequently occupied myself with the problem of the spiritual superiority of the vanquished. I was always tempted to depict the internal hardening which every form of power brings about in man, the spiritual numbness of an entire people which every victory entails, and to contrast it with the energizing power of defeat that plows through the soul so painfully and fruitfully. In the midst of war, while others, prematurely triumphant, were proving to one another the certainty of victory, I already threw myself to the lowest abyss of the catastrophe and was seeking the way out." *The World of Yesterday*, pp. 252–253.

8. The miniature on Dostoyevski does not appear in the English translation *The Tide of Fortune*. I offer the following content translation: "That in this one second he / was the other / who thousands of years ago hung on the cross, / and that he, as He, / Since that burning kiss of death / For all the suffering had to love life."

9. My translation. This passage in Stefan Zweig, *Sternstunden der Menschheit* (Frankfurt am Main: Fischer, 1970), p. 158, did not appear in the English translation.

10. Agnes Heller, *A Theory of History* (Boston: Routledge & Kegan Paul, 1982), p. 23. Also important for my interpretation of historical consciousness is the work of Hayden White, especially *Metahistory. The Historical Imagination in Nineteenth-Century Europe* (Baltimore: Johns Hopkins University Press, 1973) and *The Content of the Form. Narrative Discourse and Historical Representation* (Baltimore: Johns Hopkins University Press, 1987).

11. *Die Welt von Gestern*, p. 177. This definition of a mythological consciousness is discussed in Peter L. Berger and Thomas Luckmann, *The Social Construction of Reality* (New York: Anchor, 1967) and in Jürgen Habermas, *Theorie des kommunikativen Handelns*, vol. 2 (Frankfurt am Main: Suhrkamp, 1981), pp. 275–293.

12. I am not aware of any translation in English. The only English rendering of the title I have found refers to the novel as the "Third Form Struggle," using the British designation for the class level *Tertia*. "Children's Literature," *Encyclopedia Britannica* 5 (Chicago: William Benton, 1973), p. 522B.

13. I repeat here some points I made about this work in my book *Comrades, Friends and Companions: Utopian Projections and Social Action in Literature for Young People 1926–1934* (New York, Bern, Frankfurt, Paris: Peter Lang, 1989), pp. 109–128.

14. Even though Lietz's schools often furnished havens for conservative reactionism against the modern infringements of economy and technology, Haubinda counted among its alumni and faculty Jewish intellectuals and writers such as Theodor Lessing, Walter Benjamin, Bruno Frank, and Erich von Mendelssohn. Lietz was, however, anti-Semitic and eventually eliminated the Jewish presence from his schools.

The term *völkisch* refers to a specific conservative ideology, widespread from Wilhelminian times to the Nazi period, and in some respects, it may be argued, to this day. The abstract and often perplexing idea of *Volk* connected the German spirit to its natural landscape, indicating that the German's union with the land was sublime, mystical, and beautiful. The "romantic anti-capitalism" of *völkisch* thinkers refers to their disdain of the modern, urban world, blaming the alleged materialism and spiritual vacuousness of "capitalistic" civilization for the decline of Germany. This irrational primitivism is also an essential component of modern political anti-Semitism.

Cf. Peter Pulzer, *The Rise of Political Anti-Semitism in Germany & Austria*, revised edition (Cambridge: Harvard University Press, 1988; original 1964), pp. 63–70; George L. Mosse, *The Crisis of German Ideology. Intellectual Origins of the Third Reich* (New York: Schocken, 1964, 1981), especially pp. 4–5; Fritz Stern, *The Politics of Cultural Despair: A Study in the Rise of the Germanic Ideology* (Berkeley: University of California Press, 1961, 1974), especially pp. xviii–xxix. Although the *völkisch* ideologues were averse to the uses of technology in modern industrial society, many conservatives perceived that technical developments could aid nationalist causes, in particular that of warfare. Cf. Jeffrey Herf, *Reactionary Modernism. Technology, Culture and Politics in Weimar and the Third Reich* (Cambridge: Cambridge University Press, 1984).

15. Klaus Doderer puzzles over this contradiction in "'Solidarität oder Untertangeist.' Zu Erich Kästner's *Emil und die Detektive* und Wilhelm Speyers *Der Kampf der Tertia*," in *Klassische Kinder- und Jugendbücher*, ed. Klaus Doderer (Weinheim: Beltz, 1969), pp. 35–54. The only extensive literary/biographical article on Speyer is: Johanna W. Roden, "Wilhelm Speyer," *Deutsche Exilliteratur seit 1933*, vol. 1, part I, ed. John M. Spalek and Joseph Strelka (Bern: Francke, 1976), pp. 606–615. Theodor Lessing, *Der jüdische Selbsthaß* (Berlin: Jüdischer Verlag, 1930) had been reprinted with an introductory essay by Boris Groys in 1984 published by Matthes & Seitz Verlag in Munich. Hans Mayer discusses Theodor Lessing in his chapter on "Jüdischer Selbsthaß" in *Außenseiter* (Frankfurt am Main: Suhrkamp, 1977), pp. 414–421. For a history and penetrating analysis of the phenomenon, see Sander L. Gilman, *Jewish Self-Hatred. Anti-Semitism and the Hidden Language of the Jews* (Baltimore: Johns Hopkins University Press, 1986).

16. Wilhelm Speyer, *Der Kampf der Tertia* (Reinbeck bei Hamburg: Rowohlt, 1964), pp. 7, 36, 45, 67, 143. (My translation.)

17. Hermann Lietz, "Geschichtsunterricht," *Die Landerziehungsheimbewegung* (Bad Heilbronn: Klinkhardt, 1967), p. 30.

18. "The love for the fatherland does not need to be artifically cultivated, so that relatively insignificant moments of history are always dragged out and magnified with either stronger or weaker intention, even though they do not inspire anyone, while many significant aspects in the history of foreign nations remain neglected. One should learn to recognize the uniqueness and the essence of everything of value, which was and is." Lietz, "Geschichtsunterricht", p. 27. (My translation.)

19. "A Klee painting named 'Angelus Novus' shows an angel looking as though he is about to move away from something he is fixedly contemplating. His eyes are staring, his mouth is open, his wings are spread. This is how one pictures the angel of history. His face is turned toward the past. Where we perceive a chain of events, he sees one single catastrophe which keeps piling wreckage and hurls it in front of his feet. The angel would like to stay, awaken the dead, and make whole what has been smashed. But a storm is blowing from Paradise; it has got caught in his wings with such violence that the angel can no longer close them. This storm irresistibly propels him into the future to which his back is turned, while the pile of debris before him grows skyward. This storm is what we call progress." Walter Benjamin, "Theses on the Philosophy of History," *Illuminations*, ed. Hannah Arendt, trans. Harry Zohn (New York: Harcourt, Brace & World, Inc., 1968), pp. 259–260.

20. "*Der Reiter über den Bodensee*" refers to Gustav Schwab's ballad "Reiter über den Bodensee" (1826), and has become emblematic for the unawareness of impending danger. In the ballad, a horseman unwittingly rides across the thin ice of Lake Constance. Upon reaching shore, the shock of realizing his blunder ironically causes his death. Zweig evokes this image when he writes: "We must agree with Freud, to whom our culture and civilization were merely a thin layer liable at any moment to be pierced by the destructive forces of the Underworld" (*The World of Yesterday*), p. 4. Among others, Christa Wolf has also used this image, see *Kindheitsmuster* (Darmstadt: Luchterhand, 1979), p. 308.

21. "Against my will I have witnessed the most terrible defeat of reason and the wildest triumph of brutality in the chronicle of the ages. Never—and I say this without pride, but rather with shame—has any generation experienced such a moral retrogression from such a spiritual height as our generation has" (*The World of Yesterday*, p. xvii). "All the livid steeds of the Apocalypse have stormed through my life—revolution and famine, inflation and terror, epidemics and emigration. I have seen the great mass ideologies grow and spread before my eyes: Fascism in Italy, National Socialism in Germany, Bolshevism in Russia, and above all else that arch-plague nationalism which has poisoned the flower of our European culture" (*The World of Yesterday*, p. xx).

22. Cf. Müller, pp. 63–65, and Donald A. Prater, *European of Yesterday. A Biography of Stefan Zweig* (Oxford: Clarendon Press, 1972), pp. 190ff. I defer here to Peter Gay when using the problematic term "assimilation." "German Jews used [assimilation] quite indiscriminately to mean acculturation—comfortable integration into the larger social whole while retaining one's identity—or amalgamation—adoption of all the customs of the larger society through intermarriage, baptism, and change of name." Peter Gay, *Freud, Jews and Other Germans. Masters and Victims in Modernist Culture* (New York: Oxford University Press, 1979), p. 95.

23. Zweig goes so far as to describe assimilation as the path of liberation open to the

Jews: "This constant categorization, which actually was the main topic of every familiar and social conversation, at that time seemed to be most ridiculous and snobbish, because for all Jewish families it was merely a matter of fifty or a hundred years earlier or later that they had come from the same ghetto. It was not until much later that I realized that this conception of 'good' family, which appeared to us boys to be a parody of an artificial pseudo-aristocracy, was one of the most profound and secret tendencies of Jewish life. It is generally accepted that getting rich is the only and typical goal of the Jew. Nothing could be further from the truth. Riches are to him merely a stepping stone, a means to the true end, and in no sense the real goal. The real determination of the Jew is to rise to a higher cultural plane in the intellectual world. . . . A 'good' family therefore means more than the purely social aspect which it assigns to itself with this classification; it means a Jewry that has freed itself of all defects and limitations and pettiness which the ghetto has forced upon it, by means of adaptation to a different culture and even possibly a universal culture" (*The World of Yesterday*, pp. 11–12). Even beyond the practical ends of liberation and security, Zweig describes assimilation as an internal longing of the Jews: "Adapting themselves to the milieu of the people or country where they live is not only an external protective measure for Jews, but a deep internal desire. Their longing for a homeland, for rest, for security, for friendliness, urges them to attach themselves passionately to the culture of the world around them" (*The World of Yesterday*, p. 20). See also Prater, p. 190.

24. Klaus Mann, *Wendepunkt* (Munich: Ellermann, 1969), p. 249, quoted in Müller, p. 96.

25. Hannah Arendt, "Juden in der Welt von Gestern. Anläßlich Stefan Zweig, *The World of Yesterday, an Autobiography*," *Sechs Essays, Schriften der Wandlung* 3 (Heidelberg: Verlag Lambert Schneider, 1948), pp. 112–127. See also Volker Henze, *Jüdischer Kulturpessimismus und das Bild des Alten Österreich im Werk Stefan Zweigs und Joseph Roths* (Heidelberg: Carl Winter, 1988), pp. 301ff.

26. Among the classic studies on the psychological foundations of fascism are Wilhelm Reich, *Die Massenpsychologie des Faschismus* (Frankfurt am Main: Fischer, 1977, first published 1933); Theodor W. Adorno, Else Frenkel–Brunswick, Daniel J. Levinson, and R. Nevitt Sanford, *The Authoritarian Personality* (New York: Harper, 1950); Klaus Theweleit, *Männerphantasien*, 2 vols. (Frankfurt am Main: Roter Stern, 1977–1978).

27. See for example the collection *Der Berliner Antisemitismusstreit*, ed. Walter Boehlich (Frankfurt am Main: Insel, 1988). Regarding the Wilhelminian era as the period when modern anti-Semitism originated is a long-established thesis. Cf. Peter Pulzer.

28. Wilhelm Speyer, *Das Glück der Andernachs* (Frankfurt am Main: Fischer, 1983), pp. 136–137. (My translation.)

29. "The dialectical link between enlightenment and domination, and the dual relationship of progress to cruelty and liberation which the Jews sensed in the great philosophers of the Enlightenment and the democratic, national movements are reflected in the very essence of those assimilated. The enlightened self-control with which the assimilated Jews managed to forget the painful memories of domination by others (a second circumcision, so to speak) led them straight from their own, long-suffering community into the modern bourgeoisie, which was moving inexorably toward reversion to cold repression and reorganization as a pure 'race.' " Max Horkheimer and Theodor Adorno, *The Dialectic of Enlightenment*, trans. John Cumming (New York: The Seabury Press, 1972), p. 169.

30. "[T]he opposition between assimilation and revolution is actually a chiasmus, that there is an underlying intersection between these opposed tendencies and that repudiation of the goals of assimilated Jewry does not necessarily signal liberation from the matrix of Jewish psychosocial conflict." Beth Sharon Ash, "Walter Benjamin: Ethnic Fears, Oedipal Anxieties, Political Consequences," *New German Critique* 48 (1989), p. 11.

31. As a point of comparison, Theodor Herzl himself had no interest in Jewish affairs before he covered the Dreyfus affair as a journalist, which inspired him to join the Zionist movement. Herzl sought to provide a space for Jews who either could not or would not assimilate.

32. The anti-Semitism controversy of the 1870s and 1880s established a vocabulary and discourse that imbued racial theories with a semblance of scientific and scholarly legitimacy, and which persisted through the twentieth century. See for example the collection *Der Berliner Antisemitismusstreit*, and compare Shulamit Volkov, "Antisemitismus als kultureller Code," *Jüdisches Leben und Antisemitismus im 19. und 20. Jahrhundert* (Munich: Beck, 1990), pp. 13–36.

33. Alice Miller, *Am Anfang war die Erziehung* (Frankfurt am Main: Suhrkamp, 1983), pp. 17–123.

# *Bezwingt des Herzens Bitterkeit*:
# Hilde Burger's Return from "Paradise"

## Roslyn Abt Schindler

> Was hatred supposed to continue! Was it supposed to determine our lives? Did there not have to be people who were ready for reconciliation? Friedrich von Schiller said: "Overcome your heart's bitterness, hatred meeting with hatred does not beget a good fruit." [1]
>
> (Hilde Burger)

*For my mother and in loving memory of my father*

The canon of autobiographical works written by German women about their Holocaust experiences is growing because heretofore unknown women writers are increasingly being discovered or rediscovered. Moreover, these Holocaust accounts by and about women are being slowly integrated into the overall canon of Holocaust literature, while retaining their obvious human and historical uniqueness. Many of these now aging writers have only begun to publish in recent years: to "rush to print before they leave their stories to the distortions of history." [2] Most, in fact, could not or would not publish earlier. Renate Wiggershaus explains the phenomenon of memoirs written so long after the fact:

> There were . . . women who were capable only after decades of reporting about the horror and fright they suffered under the terror of National Socialism—for example Hanna Levy: *Vielleicht war das alles erst der Anfang* (1977) or Ingeborg Hecht: *Als unsichtbare Mauern wuchsen* (1984). Their books are like lighthouses towering over a sinister past. [3]

Vivid and constant recollections of the horror and the unspeakable, lack of energy, incapability, and unwillingness often prevented earlier publication, indeed, caused a kind of paralysis in these survivors and witnesses, related to the "dual and contradictory demands imposed by the Holocaust: response and silence." [4] Among the authors in this group are Lotte Paepcke, Hanna Levy,

Ingeborg Hecht, Cordelia Edvardson, and Ruth Elias. Each has made a lasting contribution to the canon, and each has broken her silence and the double obscurity of being a woman and a writer of Holocaust literature with a liberating and self-affirming response.[5]

The focus of this paper is Hilde Burger, who has much in common with the aforementioned survivor-authors but who has connections with a number of additional experiences as well. To date, no study of her work exists. In 1988 and again in 1991 I had the opportunity to interview Burger at her home in Bad Krozingen (near Freiburg im Breisgau, Germany), and I have engaged in an extensive letter correspondence with her since 1988. I have come to cherish my acquaintanceship, indeed friendship, with the author because she is a very special person who also represents a link with the past that my parents, their relatives, and their friends endured and, only in the case of a precious few, survived. This link has continued to encourage my own personal journey and scholarly inquiry into an area of Holocaust Studies that is authentic and that has become increasingly significant and acknowledged within the greater context of *"Zachor!"* [Remember!].

Individual stories or testimonies are critically important to enable us not to repeat history, to analyze the events of history, to remember for all time, and to provide future generations with the inheritance of remembering. Memoirs or autobiographies like Burger's are significant "human expressions of personal feeling and individual perception, imparting the aura and ambience of living reality to the historical record."[6] In a review of three such Holocaust autobiographies, Julie Zuckman appropriately concludes that these are stories which "we need to fortify ourselves, examine ourselves, know ourselves and our potential strengths and weaknesses. Part of the process of bearing witness, each story is also a prayer, an offering to the dead by those who lived" (Zuckman:15).

Burger's memoir, *Bezwingt des Herzens Bitterkeit* (1984),[7] is a significant contribution to the canon not only because it identifies and deals with issues and experiences common to most Holocaust survivors, but also because it is a special and unique individual portrayal. Hilde Burger is a *Mischling ersten Grades,* the offspring of a mixed marriage, a "half-Jew." A survivor of Theresienstadt, Burger, unlike most survivors of the Holocaust, made the decision to remain in Germany after 1945. Burger's book uniquely reflects her experiences as a female inmate in Theresienstadt as well as postwar realities. It has brought her increasing recognition and has inspired her to continue her efforts to "go public." Hilde Burger, who was seventy-five in May 1991, is ultimately one of many survivors who have demonstrated the courage to share brutal experiences that shaped their lives and those of all humankind forever.

The genesis of Burger's autobiography is a simple one. She wrote the book for her family, most especially for her two daughters and their children, "Dedicated to my dear family" (p. 5), so that they would know and remember their heritage and have an important legacy. The book is written with tenderness, love, and sensitivity, out of her mind's or memory's eye. It is also fresh, forceful, and compelling, as if she were telling the story for the first time. The details are absolutely vivid in her mind, typical of many such autobiographical accounts. But Burger has her own, unique story to tell. And it is significant that what began as a private purpose (her desire to leave a legacy for her family) has developed into something that she feels completely committed to: her role as witness, teacher, survivor-author. That metamorphosis has occurred in large measure because of the responses and reactions she has received from the growing circle of her readership as well as her listenership. She now considers it her responsibility to participate in the enlightenment especially of young people in Germany today, and she plays an active, conciliatory role in this regard by reading from her work in schools, in churches, and in cooperative Christian–Jewish circles and by initiating and engaging in constructive dialogue about her own individual experiences within the context of the horrific events of the Holocaust.

An overview of the structure of Burger's memoir shows a clear emphasis on the period from 1933 to 1945. Although she provides the "sequence" of her life at the outset, "When I think back on the years of my life it appears to me as if I had lived several lives" (p. 5). The book is divided structurally and substantively into four discernible sections or epochs: 1916–1933 (early childhood and education in Berlin); 1933–1943 (professional training and work as a nurse in the Jewish Hospital while experiencing an escalation of both personal and general discrimination); 1943–1945 (deportation to, experiences in, and survival from Theresienstadt); 1945–1984 (postwar realities, personal and professional experiences in Berlin, marriage and motherhood, conquering "the bitterness of the heart"). The first and fourth sections provide an effective frame for the thrust of Burger's autobiographical account, the actual twelve-year period of the Holocaust. The two major themes, however, are present throughout: Burger's relationships with her family, friends, and acquaintances; and the waxing and waning of the "bitterness of the heart" in relation to her status and experiences as a *Mischling ersten Grades*, although actually considered Jewish within the context of the 1935 Nuremberg Racial Laws.

Hilde Burger's technical status as *Mischling* is introduced immediately as the author documents her parentage: "My mother, Margareta Pohlmann, was born a Jewish woman in Berlin. . . . My father, Albert Kallenbach was born in Turkey, the son of a German father and an Armenian mother" (p. 5). Her parents were never married, and her father, in fact, later refused to acknowledge and verify her *Mischling* status at a time when she believed that this verification would have prevented her deportation to Theresienstadt. However, her belief would never have coincided with reality anyway. *Mischlinge ersten Grades* had a very specific place in Nazi Germany—a place wrought with negativism and terror, indeed eventual death. *Mischlinge* were a special "breed" with some seemingly special privileges because of their "half-Aryan" origin but with the same inevitable fate of all "full-blooded" Jews under Hitler. Premier historian Raul Hilberg, whose 1973 *The Destruction of the European Jews* is still considered a landmark comprehensive study of the Holocaust, devotes an entire chapter to the fate of this group:

> The *Mischlinge* were the recurring problem children of the German bureaucracy.... They comprised all half-Jews who did not belong to the Jewish religion and were not married to a Jewish person (the so-called *Mischlinge* of the first degree) and all quarter-Jews (*Mischlinge* of the second degree).[8]

In her classic *The War Against the Jews*, Lucy S. Dawidowicz also emphasizes the complexity of the various categories, definitions, and status of Jews and *Mischlinge*.[9]

Discrimination and restrictions against the *Mischlinge*, "this third race," varied in kind and intensity from the time of the adoption of the *Nürnberger Rassengesetze* in 1935 to the very end of the war. As time went on, discrimination and restrictions escalated and intensified, including various plans to sterilize, deport, and eventually murder the *Mischlinge ersten Grades,* who posed problems and were considered "unfinished business" when the "Final Solution" was at hand. "No solution could really be 'final' unless the 'Mischling' problem was also 'solved'" (Hilberg, pp. 418, 419). Also Ralph Giordano, the son of an Italian–German father and a Jewish mother, describes in his own family saga *Die Bertinis* (1985) the fate of the *Mischlinge*. He substantiates Hilberg's documentation and analysis in comments related directly to Ingeborg Hecht's *Als unsichtbare Mauern wuchsen*, comments that emphasize the significance of Hecht's personal, experiential account as a *Mischling*:

> Hecht's book confirms once again: For the destruction machinery of the State Security Service the entire difference between "Full Jews," "Half-Casts" of different degrees, and Jewish related persons there was only one difference, namely different timetables for the deportation to the gas chambers. In the framework of the murder plans in the Holocaust this group of people was never given any special consideration.[10]

Burger's status and fate as a *Mischling* are verified by the experiences of her contemporaries Hecht and Giordano and by that of the historical record, which is (to recall Dawidowicz's analysis) made real in feeling and perception by the author's memoir. Burger's early childhood and education were characterized by close family ties, especially to her mother and grandmother, and a relationship to Judaism amid growing anti-Semitism. Although Burger participated in Protestant religious instruction in school because neither she nor her mother felt uncomfortable with that decision, her grandmother insisted upon the continuity of her Jewish heritage as well. Burger went to synagogue as a young girl, observed major Jewish holy days, and celebrated her Bat Mitzvah in the largest synagogue in Berlin. Because of this observance and participation, she was "legally" regarded as a Jew although her parentage indicated otherwise.

It was to her mother, however, that Burger had the closest relationship: "Even after seventy-five years I still cry when I think of her."[11] Indeed, so many of the recollections recorded in the memoir relate to or focus on Burger's mother: family life in the tight quarters of their apartment; her mother's pride when Burger was eight and received a prize for a superbly written essay; her mother's love for birds (which became a political issue when the Nuremberg Racial Laws prohibited Jews from having pets); her mother's response to the escalation of laws that stripped Jews of their possessions, rights, friendships, education, and future. Burger's mother was, unfortunately, typical in terms of her denial response to the latter even as others began to emigrate: "No, no, nobody will harm us, after all, we were born here . . ." (p. 20). The end result: the family did not emigrate. Nevertheless, through a stroke of luck, while Jews and *Mischlinge* were being denied the right to study and access to a secure job, Hilde Burger secured a place in a Jewish hospital as a student nurse to fulfill her educational dream. Burger's "shelter" as a *Mischling* in a Jewish hospital was shortlived, however: "The Jewish hospital had been something like an oasis for Jews, but this changed quickly. . . . In September 1941 the ordinance was passed that all non-Aryans and *Mischlinge* of Jewish Faith had to wear the Yellow Star . . ." (p. 31).

After overcoming a serious illness and continuing to be victimized by new discriminatory laws, Burger passed both the theoretical and practical sections of her exams and was relegated to treating only Jewish patients. Through a good friend, Burger learned that her grandmother was on the list to be deported to the east while others awaited deportation to Theresienstadt, "a camp for the privileged, or people with Aryan relatives. Of course this was a deception, as I had to find out later" (pp. 39–40). Although her eighty-three-year-old grandmother was actually spared deportation, Burger's mother was deported to Riga: "Still today, forty years later, her words ring in my ear: 'My child, don't be frightened, I have just been arrested'" (p. 40). Griefstricken, Burger had to convey the news to her grandmother who died just a few days thereafter: "I received special permission to ride the streetcar to Weißensee where the funeral was held in the Jewish cemetery" (p. 44). After a failed attempt to get her father to verify her status as a *Mischling* ("I will not do now what I did not do twenty-six years ago," p. 44), continued indignities and loss of protection from the inevitable, Hilde Burger met her fate on 17 June 1942, with bitterness ("The bitterness in my heart was steadily increasing," p. 49) and calm: "I arrived in Theresienstadt. . . . I was completely calm. Nothing could distress me any longer. There could be no greater misfortune for me than my mother's deportation" (p. 49).

After parting with friends, possessions, home—the known—Burger arrived in Theresienstadt, only to experience one of the many indignities and violations—as a human being and as a woman—that were to follow:

> Now I knew that we had ended up in a KZ. An SS man pulled me aside: "Quickly, quickly, get undressed!" I was in total shock when he yelled: "Come on, get completely undressed." Crying I undressed in front of him until I was naked. I had to turn in front of him. He laughed scornfully and let me stand like that for a long time, until he ordered: "Put your clothes back on immediately." He took one of the two coats that I had worn one on top of the other. All of us had to line up outside. Because I had had to undress I was among the last ones. Those who marched in front of me went to the barracks and houses, women and men separately. We, the last ones, were distributed into the attic. (p. 52)

Joan Ringelheim's cogent and powerful 1985 study, based upon a series of interviews with survivors, confirms that women's experiences during the Holocaust were indeed different from men's in some fundamental respects. Ringelheim explains:

> In their descriptions of the tragedy of Jews during the Holocaust, the women interviewed discussed women's particular victimization. They spoke of their sexual vulnerability: sexual humiliation, rape, sexual exchange, pregnancy, abortion, and vulnerability through their children—concerns that men either described in different ways or, more often, did not describe at all. Almost every woman referred to the humiliating feelings and experiences surrounding her entrance to camp (for my interviewees, this was Auschwitz): being nude; being shaved all over—for some being shaved in a sexual stance, straddling two stools; being observed by men, both fellow prisoners and SS guards. Their stories demonstrate shared fears about and experiences of sexual vulnerability as women, not only about mortal danger as Jews.[12]

However, Ringelheim appropriately emphasizes that these aspects of the women's daily lives, which cannot be universalized as true for all prisoners, cannot either be generalized to characterize "the whole of women's sexual experiences during the Holocaust":

> Some women speak about heterosexual love relationships, great passions, or small romances in the ghettos, resistance groups, and even in the camps. They also speak of liaisons created out of loneliness, friendship, the need for help, or even through the desire to experience sex before one's death. (Ringelheim, p. 745)

Gender differences specifically related to the need for and ability to communicate, connect, and nurture manifested themselves in profoundly important survival strategies:

> Some of the differences perceived do appear as transformations related to gender: starving transformed into communal sharing of recipe stories; sex into food, rather than the reverse; rags into clothes; isolation into relationships or surrogate "families." Women were able to transform their habits of raising children or their experience of nurturing into the care of nonbiological family. Men, when they lost their role in the protection of their own families, seemed less able to transform this habit into the protection of others. Men did not remain or become fathers as readily as women became mothers or nurturers. (Ringelheim, p. 747)

Hilde Burger's experiences in Theresienstadt reflect the gamut of what Ringelheim outlines and emphasizes as human and as women's experiences. As a designated "showcase" or "utopia" of concentration camps, Theresienstadt was, in fact, "an imaginary and . . . remote place"[13] that included 50,000 men, women, and children at its peak and provided a gruesome, grotesque illusion of well-being to the outside world. It was within this context that Hilde Burger experienced hunger and illness, brutality and abuse, warmth, comfort, friendship, and love, pregnancy and abortion, real hope and false hope, nightmares and fantasies. Foremost among those fantasies was miraculously being spared deportation to Auschwitz. Hilde Burger was indeed spared even after she was already on the train bound for Auschwitz and certain death:

> The next day I arrived with my suitcase at the place in front of the train station, ready for the transport. The train was already waiting. We were 2,500 people, partly sitting on the ground, partly on our suitcases. We were called up once again according to the list, and woe to him or her who had not arrived! That person was searched and put into the luggage compartment. I had been told about the terrible place by Thea who was taken away a few weeks earlier and with whom I had stayed until the last moment. We were ordered to board the train. This meant that my life was over, and I asked God for a merciful death. The train started. Suddenly my name was called over the loudspeakers: "Nurse Herma Pohlmann, get out." I threw my suitcase out of the window. Everyone helped me to pull myself up to the window. No sooner had the train got in motion, did I jump out. My knee was bruised, but what did that matter! Kari took me into his arms. Dr. Metz was also there. He told me that he had taken advantage of the fear of contagious diseases among the SS. He had told them that there was another typhoid fever epidemic in the camp and that there were no qualified nurses left. So he was ordered to get the nurse from the train immediately. Later I found out that every one of the 2,500 people on the transport were gassed. Dear God, once again you had protected me. In the past years I have thought time and again of those minutes. (p. 67)

Having witnessed even more than she had actually experienced in Theresienstadt, Burger took her place among those who survived and were liberated. Yet with the news of her mother's probable extermination in Riga, she was totally numb and could not rejoice in her freedom. She became more and more distraught as the news of her mother's death became certain, and she attempted suicide on two different occasions. After the second and more serious attempt, she received counseling from a medical student assigned to her: "I promised him to join the last Berlin transport on 1 September 1945 and to make the attempt to put my life back in order by myself. It was in fact the very last transport leaving Theresienstadt" (p. 73).

Burger's immediate destination was her native Berlin because she had a faint glimmer of hope that her mother had survived against all odds and would seek her out there. Reunited with colleagues and friends, Burger began to overcome her broken spirit by returning to the Jewish hospital as an active, productive nurse and living in a small room in the nurses' quarters. Her immediate post-Holocaust experiences were positive and supportive: "The inner petrification of my hatred slowly started to melt" (p. 79). Her courtship and marriage in 1949 to Friedrich Burger, an internist whom she had met in the hospital, drew a negative reaction from family members who considered her marriage to a "German" a betrayal. However, despite her tragic experiences and losses, Burger's thoughts were directed toward the future: "Was hatred to continue to determine our lives? Did there not have to be people who were ready for reconciliation? As Friedrich von Schiller had said: 'Overcome your heart's bitterness, hatred meeting with hatred does not beget a good fruit'" (p. 83).

Burger's active conciliatory role actually began with a personal act. Because her parents-in-law were unhappy that their son had not married a Catholic and she did not want dissonance within the family, she converted to Catholicism in 1950. It is noteworthy that her husband preferred that she not convert, and in fact she confesses: "My heart adheres to the traditions and has remained attached to Judaism" (p. 84).

Burger and her husband raised their two daughters in Berlin while maintaining a medical practice. In 1979, after Friedrich Burger retired, they moved to Bad Krozingen, near Freiburg im Breisgau, where they are very happy and active members of the community. They miss only their daughters and their families who have remained in Berlin. Burger concludes her book with a final dedication to her daughters and four grandchildren:

> My husband and I have suffered and experienced a lot. In retrospect it was a full life. When we will close our eyes forever, then you, beloved daughters, Monika and Renate, and you, beloved grandchildren, Sarah, Tibor, Miriam, and Sonja, shall be able to form an impression of your parents or grandparents. (p. 87)

Burger's book, written for the sole, private purpose of leaving a legacy to her loved ones, has nevertheless achieved a broader goal, not only for the author herself but also for the canon of Holocaust literature and contemporary enlightenment about the Holocaust. When Burger wrote her book, she did not anticipate her new role as survivor-author, witness, and teacher. This role has evolved as the book has reached wider audiences and Burger has developed a greater level of comfort with "going public." Positive reinforcement of her book and of her experiences as a survivor and as a woman within that context has helped her make great strides. Her letters to me, beginning in October 1988, reflect those dramatic changes. Regular invitations to do readings and lectures regionally in Trier, Staufen, Salzburg, Freiburg, and Bad Krozingen have been further reinforced by supportive reviews of her book and the prospect of a second printing in 1992 by a publisher with a wider readership and circulation.[14] Although Burger retains cautious optimism, if not skepticism, about the older generation in Germany today, she feels very comfortable, indeed obligated, as a survivor-witness-teacher despite the strain she feels each time: "In the meantime I have read again at the high school in Staufen. It is hard work but I consider it an obligation.... An obligation of the witness of an era."[15]

In my most recent interview with Burger in July 1991, she expressed great pleasure and comfort about the ever increasing support and encouragement from her family and especially from the young people with whom she interacts during her school visits. Burger's spiritual, indeed mystical, ties to Judaism remain, and she indicated that these are shared by her daughters. On an intensely personal level and within the context of Holocaust enlightenment, her new role has been increasingly satisfying and rewarding. Student groups express great interest in her book and experiences and, through these, view history as more accessible and real. Burger teaches tolerance and mutual respect, trust and hope, and is a living example of these values. Hilde Burger talks about her life "not as an accusation, but as a warning for the living and a legacy for the young people."[16] As part of her mission to provide a warning and a legacy, Burger donates all of her honoraria to support education about the Holocaust.

Julie Zuckman maintains correctly that "few of the many women Holocaust writers have achieved fame and recognition on the order of Primo Levi, Tadeusz Borowski, Jerzy Kosinski or Elie Wiesel" (Zuckman, p. 14). Indeed, Hilde Burger is among those women writers who have emerged only recently and are just beginning to achieve recognition. She has contributed significantly to the canon of Holocaust literature but, even more importantly, to our growing understanding of a period in history that unfolds in ever greater complexity before us: "a separate universe, with laws of its own, the Holocaust defies every 'final solution' to the problems it engenders" (Sherwin and Ament, p. 1). Hilde Burger's reality was and is complex and is a critical chapter in our understanding not only of the Holocaust but also of the special place that survivor-authors have in contemporary Germany, especially in light of questions and concerns raised subsequent to the recent unification. Burger has chosen to play a constructive role and has made a vital contribution toward mutual, Jewish and Christian, understanding and enlightenment. She has been particularly successful in reaching the younger generation and is earning increasing recognition for her book and for her public efforts. Hers is a voice that will continue to be heard and heeded. Hers is a story that will continue to be told as an individual portrayal, as an offering, as a prayer, as a contribution to the inheritance of remembering.

## NOTES

1. "Sollte denn der Haß immer weitergehen! Sollte er unser Leben bestimmen? Mußte es nicht Menschen geben, die zur Versöhnung bereit waren? Friedrich von Schiller sagte: 'Bezwingt des Herzens Bitterkeit, es bringt nicht gute Frucht, wenn Haß dem Haß begegnet.' " These and the following translations are those of the editors.

2. Julie Zuckman, "Survival Strategies," *The Women's Review of Books* 6/9 (June 1989), p. 14.

3. Renate Wiggershaus, "Neue Tendenzen in der Bundesrepublik Deutschland, in Österreich, und in der Schweiz," in Hiltrud Gnug and Renate Möhrmann, eds., *Frauen–Literatur–Geschichte: Schreibende Frauen vom Mittelalter bis zur Gegenwart* (Stuttgart: J. B. Metzler Verlag, 1985), p. 419.

4. Josephine Knopp and Arnost Lustig, "Holocaust Literature II: Novels and Short Stories," in Byron L. Sherwin and Susan G. Ament, co-eds., *Encountering the Holocaust: An Interdisciplinary Survey* (Chicago: Impact Press, 1979), p. 268.

5. Paepcke's *Ein kleiner Händler, der mein Vater war* (1972), Levy's *Vielleicht war das alles erst der Anfang* (1977), Hecht's *Als unsichtbare Mauern wuchsen* (1984), Edvardson's *Gebranntes Kind sucht das Feuer* (1986), and Elias's *Die Hoffnung erhielt mich am Leben* (1988) were all published decades after the experiences detailed in each autobiographical account. For a discussion of Paepcke, see my chapter, " 'Ohne Heimat': The Problem of Exile in the Works of Lotte Paepcke," in Uwe Faulhaber et al., eds., *Exile and Enlightenment: Studies in German and Comparative Literature in Honor of Guy Stern* (Detroit: Wayne State University Press, 1987), pp. 131–139. For a discussion of Hecht, see my chapter, "The Writings of Ralph Giordano and Ingeborg Hecht: Toward a New Enlightenment," in Sara Friedrichsmeyer and Barbara Becker–Cantarino, co-eds., *The Enlightenment and Its Legacy: Studies in German Literature in Honor of Helga Slessarev* (Bonn: Bouvier Verlag, 1991), pp. 195–207.

6. Lucy S. Dawidowicz, ed., *A Holocaust Reader* (New York: Behrman House, 1976), p. 1.

7. Freiburg: Gutenbergdruckerei, 1984. All references will be given parenthetically in the text with page number(s).

8. Raul Hilberg, *The Destruction of the European Jews*, volume II, fifth edition (New York: Holmes & Meier, 1985), p. 417.

9. Lucy S. Dawidowicz, *The War against the Jews* (New York: Holt, Rinehart, and Winston, 1975), pp. 68–69.

10. Ralph Giordano, "Foreword," in Ingeborg Hecht, *Als unsichtbare Mauern wuchsen: Eine deutsche Familie unter den Nürnberger Rassengesetzen* (Hamburg: Hoffmann und Campe, 1984), p. 18.

11. Interview with Hilde Burger, 25 July 1991. I am especially grateful to Hilde Burger for her permission to include quotations from my interviews with her and from her letters to me in this essay.

12. Joan Ringelheim, "Women and the Holocaust: A Reconsideration of Research," *Signs: Journal of Women in Culture and Society* 10/4 (1985), pp. 743–744.

13. *Webster's Ninth New Collegiate Dictionary* (Springfield, MA: Merriam–Webster, Inc., 1988), p. 1300.

14. The book will be published by Waldkircher Verlagsgesellschaft in Waldkirch im Breisgau, Germany.

15. Letters of 1 June 1989 and 1 May 1991.

16. "'Lebendige Quelle' einer grauenvollen Vergangenheit," *Badische Zeitung*, no. 198 (13 May 1986).

# The Legacy of the Holocaust

# "You Who Live Safe in Your Warm Houses":
# Your Role in the Production of Holocaust Testimony

## Irene Kacandes

> You who live safe
> In your warm houses,
> You who find, returning in the evening,
> Hot food and friendly faces:
> > Consider if this is a man
> > Who works in the mud
> > Who does not know peace
> > Who fights for a scrap of bread
> > Who dies because of a yes or a no.
> > Consider if this is a woman,
> > Without hair and without name
> > With no more strength to remember,
> > Her eyes empty and her womb cold
> > Like a frog in winter.
> Meditate that this came about:
> I commend these words to you.
> Carve them in your hearts
> At home, in the street,
> Going to bed, rising:
> Repeat them to your children,
> > Or may your house fall apart,
> > May illness impede you,
> > May your children turn their faces from you.
>
> (Levi 8)

I begin this article by quoting in full the epigraph from Primo Levi's *Survival in Auschwitz* (*Se questo è un uomo*, the original title of the memoir, as well as a line of the poem), not only because of its eloquence and its searing evocation of the contrasts betweeen our own comfortable lives and the brutal misery of Holocaust camp internees, but more importantly because its injunction is as appropriate for us today as it was for Levi's first readers. Levi's poem thematizes testimony; not only must the survivors tell, they must also be heard, their story repeated. As both its form and content indicate, this poem could not have been written without "you"—that is: not without *us*. And yet, have we listened? Have we retold?

A perusal of almost any German or American newspaper on almost any day of the last year or so would probably force us to answer these questions with a collective "no." It is hard to deny that anti-Semitism is on the rise in the Western world once again: the video game "KZ Manager" circulates widely among Austrian and German youth; Elie Wiesel is renounced in Romania as a liar; neo-Nazi gangs attack foreigners in the newly reconstituted Federal Republic; David Duke, former Ku Klux Klan leader and founder of the National Association for the Advancement of White People, conducted a viable campaign for the governorship of Louisiana; and the so-called "Committee for Open Debate on the Holocaust" undertakes a national advertising campaign in American university newspapers to urge reexamination of the "Holocaust legend."

In light of such news, one could reframe a question of Martin Walser's, originally posed in response to the obsessive interest in the Frankfurt Trials of 1965—the same trials that inspired Peter Weiss's drama *Die Ermittlung* [The Investigation]—"Have these brutalities reached our consciousness?"[1] I fear we once again would have to answer, "no." Our compatriots, like Walser's a quarter century ago, seem more interested in details of the atrocities than in the victims (cf. Walser, p. 194). But in implying through these parallels that we need a profound reexamination of the Holocaust now, precisely when so many would like to forget about Nazi crimes or pretend they never happened, I would take to heart Walser's astute comment, that it is both "senseless" (*sinnlos*) and "gratifying" (*befriedigend*) to get caught up in the historical specificity of "Auschwitz" rather than in its implications for contemporary life (Walser, p. 200). Walser, like Levi in "You who live safe," I suggest, is asking for a different type of response to the Holocaust—not a sensationalistic one, but a responsible, personal one. This message is communicated explicitly through the content of Walser's essay and Levi's poem, and also implicitly through their rhetoric; Walser enacts his involvement through use of the first personal plural: "*Unser* Auschwitz"; and Levi solicits our help through direct address: "You who live safe ... You who find ... Consider ... Meditate ... Repeat."

This interactional imperative has shaped some recent Holocaust scholarship. In the last decade or so, enormous energy and resources have been dedicated to preserving testimony from eyewitnesses to and victims of the events of the Holocaust. A growing body of literature, films, and videotaped testimony based on interviews aids our meditation "that this came about." The most famous example may well be Claude Lanzmann's prodigious film and subsequent book, *Shoah* (1985). But one could also point to the plans for the United States Holocaust Memorial Museum in Washington, DC, or to books such as Claudine Vegh's collection of interviews with survivors who were children during the Holocaust, *Je ne lui ai pas dit au revoir* [I Didn't Say Goodbye] (originally published 1979), or to Peter Sichrovsky's volumes about the second generation, *Wir wissen nicht was morgen wird, Wir wissen wohl was gestern war* (published in English as *Strangers in Their Own Land*, 1985), and *Schuldig geboren: Kinder aus Nazifamilien* [Born Guilty. Children from Nazi Families] (originally published 1987), interviews with the children of Jewish victims and Nazi perpetrators, respectively.

Perhaps less well known are the myriad recording efforts around the world to get the experiences of literally thousands of survivors onto cassette- or videotape.[2] The motivations for such a flurry of recording activity at this particular point in time are probably as various as the number of interviewing projects, but certainly one of the most compelling is demographic: the imminent loss of eyewitnesses as the last generation of victims who were actually in camps or hiding places. From a psychological perspective, it has been observed that more survivors may be willing to come forward now than previously because as they have gotten older, and in many cases retired from fulltime careers, they have entered a phase of self-examination and thus naturally are reflecting on their own life stories.[3] Finally, the collection of personal Holocaust narratives undoubtedly has been aided also by the development, proliferation, and relatively low cost of video technology.

If the motivations for giving and collecting Holocaust testimony are various, the value attributed to the documents produced is perhaps even more diverse. Vonnie Gurewitsch of the Center for Holocaust Studies in New York, for example, has argued that these testimonies make a significant contribution to the historical record about the Holocaust and are as valid and valuable as eyewitness testimony in a court of law.[4] David Roskies, on the other hand, in reviewing the first full-length study of the Fortunoff Archive for Holocaust Testimony at Yale University, Lawrence Langer's *Holocaust Testimonies: Ruins of Memory* (1991), maintains that these tapes have little to contribute to historical knowledge.[5]

Whatever the final verdict on the historiographical role of these testimonies, I suggest they offer insight into a related, though distinct debate: In what ways do the participants and the circumstances of telling a story structure the stories that emerge? The interactive format of the Holocaust testimony-interview foregrounds the *addressee's* participatory role, which other media and genres may obscure. Dr. Dori Laub, cofounder of the project that developed into the Fortunoff Archive, himself a survivor and interviewer of more than one hundred fellow survivors, identifies witnesses not only as those who live through a particular trauma, but also those who witness the witnessing, in other words, the recipients of the testimony (Roskies, p. 75 *et passim*). And those who perform this second type of witnessing include not only the immediate interviewer, but also anyone who views or listens to the testimony. In presenting below two segments of particular personal Holocaust narratives I have heard, I thus aim not only to follow Levi's edict to "repeat," but also to demonstrate how "you" are involved, that is, how the shape and meaning of a story are produced interactively by the actual survivor *and* the multiple addressees. The word "testimony" may obscure this interactional component, but once one views a tape (or, I hope, reads a detailed transcript, as you will below), one does not hesitate to recognize these video testimonies as a speech exchange genre in which the addressee plays a significant part. Thus with this article, I also aim to create more recipients, more coparticipants in Holocaust witnessing, to make these tapes more accessible to other scholars and teachers who share with me a concern for understanding more about life as the Other during the darkest chapter of German history.

## I. Description of the Videotapes

Below, I will analyze excerpts from two testimonies in the Fortunoff Archive for Video Testimony at Yale University, segments from the personal narratives of Leon S. (tape T–45) and (Rabbi) Baruch G. (tape T–295).[6] The Yale archivist characterizes interviews produced by the archive as "non-directed" and "non-interventionist," that is to say, the archive's stated goal is "simply allowing survivors to speak" (Rudof, "Organizing," 16 December 1990).[7] Trained interviewers usually make contact with a potential (volunteer) witness by telephone before the actual taping to elicit a small amount of factual information such as where and when the person was born, names and occupations of family members, length and locations of internments or hiding, etc. They also mention to the interviewee that they would like him or her to describe earliest personal memories, life during the War, and life after Liberation, thus suggesting a roughly chronologically-shaped personal narrative, though as will be seen below many interviewees are unable or unwilling to narrate strictly chronologically. The actual interview occurs shortly after initial phone contact; one or two interviewers are present who are usually unacquainted with the former victim. The length of the testimonies varies enormously, but is most typically between one and three hours. While the immediate addressees of the testimony are the one or two interviewers present, it is also important to mention that both witness and immediate receiver are aware of the production of the tape for an unspecified "other audience," whom I refer to as the external recipient or addressee, researchers like myself, or perhaps students and the general public who might view the tapes. Additionally, there is a technician in the room who usually speaks only to announce the commencement or changeover of a tape. The camera is focused solely on the witness, though at the beginning of some tapes, the interviewers are shown as they introduce themselves; their voices can be heard throughout.[8]

The shared orientation of speaker and listener to particular generic constraints of the interview become most apparent in what conversation analysts refer to as the nature of its "turn-taking": who talks when and for how long (Sacks, Schegloff, Jefferson, p. 696 *et passim*).[9] The Holocaust testimonies are unlike spontaneously occurring ordinary conversation in which the order, length, and content of turns by coparticipants varies widely. Rather, they typically contain extended multi-unit turns on the part of the witness, and the interviewer usually just asks questions and avoids evaluation of the victim's testimony. In this respect they are somewhat like television news interviewing in which the interviewee is assumed to have something worthwhile to say and in which the primary audience is considered to be the viewing audience at home.[10] On the other hand, unlike in television news interviewing or in witness testimony in a court of law, the Holocaust interviewee does not necessarily answer all questions posed by the interviewer, nor necessarily wait for the interviewer to ask questions, but rather might pose and answer questions him/herself.[11] A striking characteristic of Holocaust video testimony as a speech exchange genre is silence; there are numerous and occasionally long pauses—inconceivable in the expensive world of broadcast news and rare in the competitive economy of spontaneous conversation. Interviewers are encouraged to allow the survivor to resolve these silences or to break in only when it seems the speaker cannot continue without a verbal prompt.[12]

These guidelines and roles were developed over a period of time, of course, and with the traumatic nature of the subject of the testimonies in mind. Furthermore, many of the witnesses are survivors who have never spoken about their experiences before. It is understandable that generic features would develop that privilege survivors' turns. Even so, one interviewer writes that: "The questions always seem impertinent, or gratuitous, or insensitive; the answers always seem incomplete, like shadows that are simultaneously real and unreal. Nothing is certain, no words adequate, every statement seems equivocal and leaves the impression that it is simultaneously true and not true" (Bolkosky, p. 33).[13]

And yet, interviews do take place, archives do develop. (The archive at Yale contained videotapes of approximately 2,500 interviews during the summer of 1992.) Despite the horror of the subject, despite the awkwardness and unfamiliarity of the video testimony as a speech exchange genre, stories do get recorded.[14] Precisely because of these two seemingly contradictory facts—that the events of the Holocaust seem beyond human experience and thus resistant to verbal description and that somehow personal narratives of Holocaust experience do get told—it would be worthwhile to analyze "successful" storytellings: interviews, or more accurately sections of interviews, in which personal experience is communicated as a coherent narrative unit. This happens through negotiation and cooperation. What I hope to demonstrate is the striking *commonality* of these testimonies with less formal verbal exchanges, in which "the form and content of talk is continuously reshaped by the coparticipants, through their ability to create certain alignments and suggest or impose certain interpretations."[15] I aim to demonstrate that the description of these interviews as "non-directed" and "non-interventionist" is not particularly accurate. This is both because more than one person is involved in the speaking and because interaction seems *required* to narrate and interpret what happened. A more accurate description of the discourse situation would be that it maximizes the opportunity for storytelling. In the testimony of Leon S., for example, a question from one interviewer extends the length of the narrative and reframes its significance. In a second example, from the testimony of Baruch G., the effects of interaction are even more profound, though also more elusive. The survivor does not even seem to be recounting a personal event at the point when a factual question posed by the interviewer triggers a private story whose shape neither interviewer nor witness seems to fully control. A more precise connection between the question and the personal narrative perhaps can be recognized only in retrospect. Thus the production of narrative requires not only the witness and interviewer at the time the words are produced, but also *you*, the witness who will later create the "significant narrative," transforming a listing of events into a single story.[16]

## II. A Note on Transcriptions and Tapes

I have purposely limited myself to segments of tapes that could be viewed by readers of this article. Therefore, though my analysis is based on work with the noncirculating full tapes of both testimonies, the segments on which I will focus below are included in the circulating edited versions.[17] I have borrowed the transcription methods of conversation analysis in order to capture on paper some of the aural and visual aspects of the videotapes. The words and sounds actually produced by speakers are transcribed as faithfully to their sound quality as our alphabet permits. Stress is indicated through underlining; embedded laughter is indicated by: (h). An "h" preceded by a raised dot (•) indicates an inbreath; multiple symbols indicate length of sound. Colons indicate the extension of the sound they follow. An arrow just before a sound indicates a rise in pitch. Sideways chevrons indicate that the enclosed speech is spoken more quickly than surrounding speech. Silences are recorded in parentheses; a period represents a short pause; longer silences are measured in seconds and tenths of seconds. Brackets are used to indicate overlapping utterances. Single parentheses enclosing words indicate transcriber doubt. Punctuation marks do not indicate syntactical units, but rather prosody: a hyphen indicates a stopping of sound; a question mark indicates rising pitch; a period, sliding or falling pitch; and a comma, subtle intonational completion. Gestures are noted in double parentheses. At this point, you may want to read the transcriptions aloud to familiarize yourself with the sound of these narrators.

The quotations in my analyses below and the transcripts produced in Appendices A and B are not easy to read, especially for those who are encountering this system for the first time, but the advantages of using this transcription method include your enhanced ability to test my hyphotheses against your own experience of the data. A potential disadvantage is the superfluity of data; there are many features of the exchanges that there is simply not space to comment on here. Those unfamiliar with this system might also receive the false impression that the speakers are illiterate. Though most are not native speakers of English, the appearance of incoherencies are more a feature of transcribing oral discourse than of the individuals' linguistic abilities.

### III. LEON S. AND THE RESHAPING AND REINTERPRETATION OF PERSONAL NARRATIVE

I would like first to demonstrate how the shape (content, length, etc.) and meaning of a story—even one based on personal experience—is cooperatively constructed.[18] Leon S. is interviewed by two psychoanalysts, Drs. Hillel Klein and Dori Laub, both of whom are also Holocaust survivors. Leon S. speaks very slowly, making many pauses, rarely gazing directly at his interlocutors. In short, he seems to be in much emotional pain throughout his interview.[19] After a confusing opening sequence in which Leon S. attempts to speak immediately of his experiences in the camps—a fairly typical opening in the tapes I have viewed[20]—the interviewers succeed in getting him to give some background information; the rest of the interview proceeds mainly chronologically.

Born in Cracow, Poland in 1921 to middle-class parents, Leon S. speaks of enjoying a comfortable childhood as an only son. He is separated from his family when the Nazis select the strong young men from his town for a work camp and "resettle" the others in the Eastern territories. He never sees his family again. His description of his arrival at "Julag" (which Leon S. himself glosses as "Judenlager"), in the town of Plaszow outside of Cracow, consists of rather typical expository statements about the length of his internment there, the nature of the work he and other inmates were required to perform, and the characterization of the experience as "torture." In a standard narrative move, Leon S. then proceeds from summary to scene:[21] "But let me give you an example of actual experience." In the first part of this illustration, Leon S. describes how the food inmates were given, particularly the watery soup, induced a constant need for urination.[22] But those who went to the latrine at night were shot. So internees tried to find a bottle into which they could urinate without leaving the barracks. If, however, one was discovered by the guard with a bottle, he was shot. So, Leon S. summarizes, "you were in constant pain and the alternative was not to eat anything, not to eat or suffer tremendously." He concludes this sequence with the coda "and this kinds of a torture we were endured," thus bringing him and his listeners back to the topic that had launched this sequence: torture.

Leon S. then initiates another multi-unit turn, beginning with the clear turn signal of an inbreath after a short pause (during which the interlocutors could have taken a turn, but do not).[23] He narrates:

> *Leon S*: There was an epidemic of (.) typhus that broke out there (3.5) but you were afraid to go to the uh (7.0) which I couldn't even call dispensary but whatever it was (3.0) because we were afraid that people would be ki̱lled who were reported there (1.0) so people with: temperature of (.) hundredfour hundredfive degrees were working. (4.5) And I ((raises eyebrows)) was working when I had that high (.) fever (1.4) and of course the other uh (0.3) inmates tried to protect you ((glance to interviewers)) (1.7) in other words if you re(were) reported for work (0.8) and there was an opportunity to uh (1.0) hi̱de ((glance to interviewers)) (2.0) they did the work for you and you were hiding ((glance to interviewers)) (1.6)

Leon S.'s glance to his addressees and pause at this point in his recital seem to solicit an aligning interlocutor, a recipient response that someone is following the exposition to his narrative and perhaps also that he is being given permission to continue another long turn.[24] There are pronomial cues that he is indeed in the middle of a story of personal experience (the shift from the nonspecific "people"—"*people* with temperature of hundredfour hundredfive degrees were working"—to the personal "And *I* was working when I had that high fever").[25] But his use of the ambiguous second person ("the other inmates tried to protect you"—a locution he employs in the prior sequence on the soup and urination problem) perhaps obscures his intent; does he mean "one"/"anyone" or "I"?[26] At least one of his addressees appears not to recognize this as orientation to a personal narrative. Hillel Klein interrupts Leon S. with a question designed to get him to talk about himself: "Could you tell me more about it, about your friendships and colleagues." That Leon S. perceives this as an interruption is obvious from both his verbal and nonverbal reactions: he flutters his eyelids while quickly responding:

> *Leon S.*: >>I just want to finish that<< (1.0) episode with: (0.8) the typhus (0.4) because I remember it like today.

The faster pace with which he begins this turn also indicates his rejection of an interruption. Leon S. does then go on to a personal narrative that conforms to the outline he had given before Klein's question:

> *Leon S*: I had (.) was just the onset of that (1.2) disease and I had a very high temperature and we were <u>un</u>loading (3.0) a (.) freightcar full of coal (3.4) and I was just <u>s</u>itting by the s(.)side because I couldn't work (3.0) :hhhh and a German railroad (.) policeman came by (1.0) and he <u>saw</u> me and he took out the gun (2.3) and he made me (5.5) <u>ju</u>mp up on that (.) car which was: (2.0) sixseven ((shakes head)) feet off the ground and down (again) and I had to do it probably twentythirty times (2.0) ((glances at interviewers)) and I knew if I didn't do it he would have killed me there, (0.4) >>cause he had his<<gun out of his holster (1.2)

At this point, Dori Laub, Leon S.'s other interlocutor, poses a question: "And that was <u>not</u> an <u>SS</u> man (0.5) and <u>not</u> a Gestapo, just a regular (.) Ger[man]." This query is not received as a potential derailment of the narrative in the sense that Klein's was, not only because Leon S. immediately answers the question rather than rejecting it, but also because it shows that the recipient registers the connection to the immediately prior testimony: this is gratuitous torture excessive in and of itself and inappropriate in that it comes from someone who has no direct charge to torture the prisoners. This structural interpretation is confirmed by the other interlocutor's subsequent demonstration that he understands precisely whom Leon S. means; Klein provides the German appellation, and Leon S. confirms that his knowledge is correct:[27]

> *HK*: =Ostbahn?
> (0.3)
> *Leon S:* <u>O</u>stbahn, ((shakes head up and down))(0.1) Ostbahnpolizei

That the climax of the story has been reached, its point understood, is confirmed by Leon S.'s use of a coda, preceded and followed by a pause:

> (6.0) ((Leon S. looks down, shakes head back and forth))
> *Leon S*: And (0.4) I remember (0.8) after he (1.0) left ((tilts head to left)) me there (0.8) I just passed away ((flutters eyelids as says "passed away"; eyes down)) (6.0)

Leon S. reinforces the point of the story—the excessive cruelty of the railroad officer's command—through his linguistic slip, "I just passed away" (instead of "passed out").[28] He verifies this as the last piece of this narrative segment with his next statement: "Well we stayed in that camp." This summary/coda gets repeated almost verbatim when he finally does go on to the next major event in his life ("We moved from that camp (3.0) in fortythree (1.0)"). That he considers this piece of personal narrative concluded is also signaled by the pronominal switch from "I" to "we." And that he is proceeding to another episode is confirmed by the inappropriate timing of Hillel Klein's next question. Klein does not wait for a transition-relevance place; he does not wait for

Leon S. to drop his voice (Sachs, Schegloff, Jefferson, pp. 702–710), because he might lose his chance to ask about the narrative Leon S. is leaving behind:

*HK*: How (were) you helped

(0.3)

*Leon S*: Pardon me?

*HK*: How have you been helped (.) when you passed (out)

(1.2)

*Leon S*: They took me to thee uh (0.2)

*HK*: =Who's they?

(1.2)

*Leon S*: ((raises eyebrows)) Other people who worked with me, (.) my friends (2.2) They took me to a (0.4) shack nearby (2.5) ((sniffle)) and (.) revived me and uh I (1.3) I went back to the camp (.) at the end of the day
(7.0)

Klein's question at this point causes Leon S. to both extend the reach of his story (including some events that he does not seem originally to consider part of the story) and to provide a different "meaning." Though Leon S. first tries to reject any backtracking ("Pardon me?"), he does, in fact, answer Klein's question this time and reconciles the story in a way that accommodates a new interpretation. That all three coparticipants agree to this conclusion and to the altered interpretation is indicated by Leon S.'s ability to proceed: to announce the end of this series of memories and narrate the move to the next camp.

The "point" of the story, I suggest, shifts from torture in the form of impossible choices (a frame by which the typhus segment serves as a second example to the immediately prior section of the testimony, the dilemma of eating versus urinating at night) to how friendship operates even under the most adverse conditions. To speak of Klein as misunderstanding or to claim one interpretation more valid than the other or to speak of the truth of one version or the other is to misunderstand oneself: because the second fits as a continuation of the original rather than a retelling of it, and also because the emphases foregrounded in each version do not exclude each other. Even more remarkable, however, is the way that this account of individual experience is in fact constructed by teller *and* addressees.[29] No one can relive the events on that day in Julag; what we can do is observe the way in which the event comes to exist for Leon S., his interlocutors, and us through satisfaction with the negotiated shape of the narrative, with its "narrative truth" (Spence, p. 31 *et passim*).

## IV. Baruch G., the Emergence of Personal Narrative, and Recipients' Roles

Like Leon S., Baruch G. grew up in Poland and experienced the invasion of the Germans as a young man. Although he, too, was incarcerated in several labor and extermination camps, the section of his testimony I would like to examine here occurs as he narrates the events at the beginning of the war, shortly after the German army and then the Gestapo and SS enter his hometown of Mlawa. His speaking style is much more fluid than that of Leon S. His single interlocutor, Dana Kline, has conducted more than one hundred interviews for the Fortunoff Archive over a period of many years, and is one of the main trainers of other interviewers, though at the time of this interview she was still relatively new to the experience. A factual, impersonal historical question of hers seems to trigger forgotten private events for Baruch G., and though neither speaker nor interlocutor comments on the storytelling *per se* (as Leon S. does with his statement, "I just want to finish that episode"), Baruch's eventual (unacknowledged) return to the issue Kline had raised, and a subsequent question of Kline's allow us to recognize ten minutes of the testimony as a narrative unit, even if the exact order of events remains obscure. Kline's question does not ask for a story; the recognition of it as the narrative trigger belongs to the external addressee who can come to understand the connection between narrative pieces in retrospect. Thus this example illustrates particularly well our role in this genre. In sharing my own sometimes desperate search for narrative coherence as a recipient of this testimony, I demonstrate one way in which you and I are coparticipants in the storytelling.

After relating the events of the German invasion of his home town, Baruch G. remembers that his first impressions of the German army were pleasant. He then goes on to distinguish between the friendly attitude of the German combat troops and the sinister behavior of the SS and Gestapo personnel who arrived soon after. A first sign of their malevolent intentions is the arrest of the town's rabbi and other prominent Jewish citizens. Though they are released unharmed, they are made responsible for a series of progressively restrictive laws. Baruch G.'s enumeration of these laws is animated, but impersonal. Initially he uses the present tense, almost as if he were quoting the laws themselves, rather than narrating his past experience of them:

> every uh Jew uh must register (2.5) •h Every Jew must have a number. (2.2) •h U:h later on a Jew must carry, a uh (.) must ((points to spot on chest)) must uh have a wh a white a white at first it was white round sign that he's a Jew, on the front and on back, (1.2) later on (it) was changed to a yellow (1.8) U:h, later on a::n announcement was made that a Jew must u::h walk if he sees a German, must (1.0) wa- must u:h go off the sidewalk and must go in the middle of the

street (0.8) •h A Jew must u:h take off his hat ((makes gesture doffing hat)) when he sees a German (1.2)

When Baruch G. mentions the ubiquitous practice of Germans commandeering Jews to perform any task at any time, he begins to stumble on his words even more:

A German has the right to call on any Jew any tim:e for work, any kind of work he wants to. (1.4) And then, supposedly through the repre<u>sen</u>tatives which ultimately became the J<u>u</u>denrat, (1.0) :hh they uh issued laws that uh every Jew 200 Jews every day ev twohundred Jews must appear in the market place for Germans to come in the morning to:: •hhto pick d- <u>o</u>ut people to work
(0.5)

*DK*: Who chose the two hundred men

Congruent with the factual tone of Baruch's reporting, Kline asks for elaboration of the institutionalization of this practice. She queries: "Who chose the two hundred men." Her question could be labeled an interruption, however, since Baruch is completing his sentence. Note the overlap and Baruch's "pardon":

*DK*: Who chose the 200 men

[

*Baruch G*: (for their work)

(0.3)

*Baruch G*: Pardon

*DK*: Who ch<u>o</u>se the two hundred men

[

*Baruch G*: =•hhh O.K., so then: this developed into a uh numbers, first it was by numbers (.) ((hand gestures only partially visible; seems to be pointing in various directions))

Baruch's next turn after hearing the question is *not* a coherent response to it—"okay, so then." But his "answer" does underscore the chronological character of what is about to be related that was minimal in the prior listing of laws. These hints at the emergence of a personal narrative multiply quickly, as seconds later Baruch G. places himself on the scene for the first time in many minutes:[30]

*Baruch G*: =:hhh okay, so then: this developed into a uh numbers, first it was by numbers (.) ((hand gestures)) number so and so must appear (1.0) and <u>that</u> uh (0.5) almost immediately:: (1.0) ((adjusts his glasses)) beca:me became a uh a source of income for some, hum (1.2) ((looks at interviewer)) as: strange as it may seem (1.2) if someone didn't want to appear, he would ask me (.) ((gestures to self)) if I wanted to go for him he would pay me for the day's work(4.5) ((looks straight at the interviewer in this pause))

Never answering her question directly, Baruch remarks on people buying off their turns with the evaluative comment: "strange as it may seem." Coupled with his subsequent pause and direct gaze to the interviewer, I interpret this as a request for alignment with his storytelling.[31] Kline's silence may be primarily the product of the principles of "noninterventionist" interviewing mentioned above or it may be her vague awareness that Baruch is in the process of relating a personal narrative.[32] But whatever its cause, its effect is that Baruch continues his turn. In conversation-analytical terms, what he has said thus far has not been received as the possible climax of the story, and thus must be " 'negotiated' through retries" (Mandelbaum, p. 124).

Baruch launches his next multi-unit turn with "In my case [ . . . ]." Enigmatically, what follows this phrase, however, is not about himself (directly), nor about the institutionalization of forced labor in Mlawa, but rather about the disappearance of his father:

In my c:ase u:h (12.0) my father managed to: save some of his merchandise and he was able t:o (1.0) •h have to carry on:, throughout that period (1.0) •hh u:h although he was caught one day and di- disappeared (1.2) with all of us going crazy=
=I remember ((stares ahead, slightly to left of interviewer)) my: mother pra-practically risked her life, (1.0) pleading with the German authorities there in the city hall, (1.2) to: try to send him back, to find out where he is, (0.6) no avail, (0.4) to no avail, (1.0) •h except uh after a month he came back (1.2) my father was (not) never the same. ((blinks; eyes move right then left; hand on face)) (4.0)

This does not relate his father's participation in the lottery, but rather a kidnapping. Nor does it explain how or why Baruch would hire himself out in other men's stead. In terms of the whole sequence and the interaction between Baruch G. and his immediate interlocutor, we can observe that a factual question—"Who chose the two hundred men"—causes him to shift from impersonal reporting of events that affected the whole town to narration of a personal family event. But why these two are connected in his mind, and how this provides an explanation for his relationship to conscripted labor remain mysterious.

At this point, however, I will indulge in some personal narration of my own. Baruch G.'s testimony was among the first I viewed at the Fortunoff Archives, and this moment in the tape captured my attention. Baruch's almost instantaneous association of the procedures of labor conscription with personal tragedy perplexed me; his obvious need for confirmation from his interlocutor of the strangeness and injustice of the rich buying off their turns and the interlocutor's lack of verbal response pained and puzzled me. And though other incidents narrated on this tape, as well as the episode related by Leon S. and analyzed above are ultimately more tragic, it is these words which are carved into my heart, to borrow from Primo Levi once again. This drove me to view and review the tape, to show it to my classes and colleagues, to write on it. I have now viewed the tape more than a dozen times, and listened to this sequence and what follows it scores more times. What I present to you below is a narrative in whose creation I participate as co-storyteller to an even greater extent than I have above.

Baruch continues immediately from the sequence about his father with some general comments on topics like availability of food and reports people's thoughts on the war: that it was not so bad and soon it will be over. This is followed by several additional narrative sequences—which I do not have the space to include here—relating his parents' attempts to hide him from the authorities, his being caught one night as he is on his way to a clandestine worship service, his being forced to work on the Sabbath, refusal to eat nonkosher food while working. Baruch mentions again his own experiences with substituting for other men whose turn it was to work for the Nazis, but he does not mark it as a return to a topic that had already been discussed, nor does he connect it to his father's disappearance[33]:

> *Baruch G.*: And perhaps you could say there was already a kind of routine. Call it normalcy established. Yes, my fath- my brother myself would go out to work whenever our turn come >>of course by that time there was already a Judenrat established<< And they were to supply x number of laborers every d<u>a</u>y. And y<u>e</u>s I could go work for somebody and those who were had means of su would pay off they would pay and I would go out and do my work and come home and uh and hoping (and uh and they was and uh) (.) And then rumors started to uh that in Mlawa too a ghetto will be established. Of course in between we had heard of ghettos being established in other cities and towns.

The narrative connection between his father's disappearance and Baruch's substitute labor began to come into focus for me when I realized that his father did *not* participate in the lottery. Baruch does a self-repair: not his father, but he and his brother would go: "Yes, my fath- my brother myself would go out to work whenever our turn come." The two "yesses" in the passage above ("Yes, my fath-", "And y<u>e</u>s I could go work"), I interpret as a belated reply to Kline's questions, or as a reply to an internal reliving of a discussion that might have taken place (with his mother in his father's absence?) about whether he could earn money by hiring himself out or about the necessity of his working for his father when the father's turn would come. The painful trailing off at the end of this sequence ["I would go out and do my work and come home and uh and hoping (and uh and they was and uh)(.)"] reminds me of Baruch's apparent distress minutes earlier when relating that there was something amiss about buying off one's turn in the lottery.

I am now able to reconstruct the sequence of historical events as follows: Baruch's parents try to shield him from Nazi authorities and provide for him and his siblings; once his father disappears, Baruch has to substitute as provider, a role he connects with his own loss of innocence ("I was a rather sheltered young man") and the injustice and impropriety of others being able to buy off their turns. Forced labor was horrible for him, not so much because of physical harm—though he describes being beaten up—but because of the loss of values it represents (the Nazis wouldn't explain how to do something, they would just throw punches if one wasn't doing it right), the loss of his ability to study Torah, to keep the Sabbath, and to adhere to dietary laws. The exact order of events—the institution of forced labor; his father's continuation of his business; his father's kidnapping; Baruch's own arrest for work duty; the commencement of his need to accept other people's money in exchange for labor; the establishment of the *Judenrat*—remains obscure due to absent and conflicting chronologies.

But this confusion should be expected. One should actually anticipate—as I suspect Kline does—Baruch's inability to produce a clear chronology of events. Experts such as Caruth tell us that the true nature of trauma "lies precisely in its belatedness, in its refusal to be simply located, in its insistent appearance outside the boundaries of any single place or time."[34] Though Baruch himself comments that later events were so horrible that "these things [initial experiences with forced labor] are forgotten," I surmise these first events were also traumatic *because* they were forgotten. Due to the eventual loss of his parents, Baruch is unable to frame the story as one in which his father is partially to blame. And yet a subconscious link obviously can be detected through his narrative association of hiring himself out and his father's disappearance.

I now consider a lengthy segment of the interview (approximately ten minutes) as belonging to a single narrative unit that covers the time period between the institution of restrictive laws against the Jews to the creation of a ghetto in Mlawa when Baruch's family is expelled from their home and transported to another town's ghetto. Though filled with facts about life in Mlawa at the beginning of the war, this segment is also rife with references to Baruch's loss of innocence, his transformation from protected oldest son into protector. I create this larger narrative by my own desire for narrative coherence, by my own desire to explain the connection Baruch G. makes between the public selection of two hundred men for the Germans to exploit, and the mysterious disappearance of his father. My construction is confirmed, or perhaps prompted, by the reactions of Baruch's immediate interlocutor. Kline not only allows Baruch to relate these narrative pieces with relatively little interruption, but she also shows her comprehension through a question in the next segment (about the family's experience in the other ghetto, and Baruch's decision to return to Mlawa illegally). Kline asks: "What was your intention?" Like Hillel Klein's query to Leon S.: "Ostbahn?"; Dana Kline's question shows that she understands the point of the story. Baruch decided to go back to Mlawa because he needed to continue serving as the provider of the family, and the economic opportunities in Mlawa were better than in the town where they were resettled. I cannot claim any historical accuracy for my narrative, I can only relate that my narrating it to you allows me to align with Baruch G. and Kline, the narrator and the immediate narratee, and to conclude my search for narrative coherence, which I now do.

### V. "If You Would Talk to Me—Just Talk to Me"

I began this article by quoting Primo Levi's injunction to meditate on the horror of the Holocaust and to repeat what we have learned to others, connecting it with my own observation that elements in our current society seem to be doing the opposite: denying and silencing. The danger of doing so is not just that of historical ignorance. Rather, even in the process of being silent, of not repeating, we are reenacting Nazi behavior. If we refuse to become coparticipants in the storytelling, we deny survivors one aspect of their humanity: the ability to communicate.

Toward the conclusion of Baruch G.'s testimony, he returns to his experience of liberation and subsequent time spent in a displaced persons camp in Italy. When asked by Kline how he felt there, he responded:

> *Baruch G.*: So, feelings was just existing. If you would talk to me- just talk to me, I would start crying. Why? Because as I- I said to myself, is it true that you're talking to me? Why should you talk to me? It's probably not true. There was all confusion around that whole thing of existence. Obviously, at least to my way of thinking, that (.) they [the Nazis, author's gloss] got us to at least they got me to think of myself so little, that nobody should talk to me, what this does, it takes years (.) and again, here if I may interject a religious thought, is the idea that it's the potential of the human being (.) he can't pull himself up even with his own bootstraps.

The camps had dehumanized Baruch G. to the point where he did not consider himself worthy of being engaged in conversation.[35] Baruch G. then relates how fortunately he met his wife and they quickly married and started a family: You can't pull yourself up; you need another.

The value of these tapes lies not so much in their ability to document the past as it "really happened"—an unprovable task in any case—as in their capacity to produce interaction, interaction that the Nazis denied their victims.

## APPENDIX A

Excerpted from the testimony of Leon S. (Videotape unedited #T-45, edited #A-25, Fortunoff Video Archive for Holocaust Testimony at Yale University). Leon S., interviewed by Drs. Hillel Klein (HK) and Dori Laub (DL) on 25 April 1980. [Leon S. has just finished relating the circumstances of his separation from his family in Sept. 1942; he never saw them again.] Note: the passage appearing between double brackets is not included on the edited videotape.

*Leon S*: And I was taken to a camp called (2.2) Julag which was a (3.2) a abbreviation for Judenlager, a Jewish camp (4.0) in the town of Plaszow (4.5) which is a suburb of Cracow (7.0). I spent there (1.8) a little over a year (4.0) working with (.) a few thousand of other Jews (6.0) on building a (5.3) a railroad station, a freight station (1.6) ((sniffle)) building viaducts (2.3) storage facilities for coal (5.2) working six days a week (5.0) tentwelve hours a day (4.2) constantly on the move (5.5) under very horrible conditions (2.5)

(2.5)

And we were tortured (6.5) :hh not a physical torture. [[But let me give you an example of ((clears throat)) actual experience. ((clears throat)) The guards in the camp were (2.0) Lithuanian and Latvian volunteers. (7.5) The food that we were getting (.) ((clears throat)) consisted of a watery soup (3.2) and a few pieces of bread, and of course the watery soup gave you at night (4.5) constant need for urinating. (4.5) But you couldn't go out at night to the latrine. >>Whoever went out at night to the latrine was shot<< (2.0) pushed into the latrine. (5.5) So what people tried to do, ((clears throat)) you secured a bottle and you tried to urinate into the bottle (.) but then these um Lithuanian and ((clears throat)) Latvian guards (.) walked into the barracks and if they found a bottle, they shot the people. So you were in constant pain and the alternative was not to eat anything, not to eat the soup or suffer tremendously and this kind of a tortures we were endured.

(5.0)]] ((quick sniffle on an inbreath))

There was an epidemic of (.) typhus that broke out there (3.5) but you were afraid to go to the uh (6.0) which I couldn't even call dispensary but whatever it was (2.4) because we were afraid that people would be killed who were reported there (1.2) so people with: temperature of (.) hundredfour hundredfive degrees were working. (4.5) And I ((raises eyebrows)) was working when I had that high (.) fever (1.4) and of course the other uh (0.3) inmates tried to protect ((glance to interviewers)) you (1.7) in other words if you re(were) reported for work (0.8) and there was an opportunity to uh (1.0) hide (2.0) ((glance to interviewers)) they did the work for you and you were hiding ((glance to interviewers))

(1.6)

*HK*: Could you tell me more about it, about your friendships and colleagues

(1.6)

*Leon S*: >>I just want to finish that<< ((Leon S. flutters eyelids while uttering previous phrase)) (1.0) episode with: (0.8) the typhus (0.4) because I remember it like today ((looks down))

(2.4)

I had (1.2) was just the onset of that (0.8) disease and I had a very high temperature and we were <u>un</u>loading (3.0) a (3.4) freightcar full of coal (3.4) and I was just <u>s</u>itting by the s(.)side because I couldn't work (3.0) :hhhh and a German railroad (.) policeman came by (1.0) and he <u>saw</u> me and he took out the gun (2.3) and he made me (5.5) j<u>u</u>mp up on that (.) car which was: (2.2) six seven ((shakes head)) feet off the ground and down (again) and I had to do it probably twenty thirty times (2.0) ((glance to interviewers)) and I knew if I didn't do it he would have killed me there, >>cause he had his<<gun out of his holster

(0.4)

(1.2)

*DL*: And that was <u>not</u> an <u>SS</u> man (0.5) and <u>not</u> a Gestapo, just a regular (.) Ger

[

*Leon S*: It was a

*Leon S*: It was a <u>rail</u>road policeman=

*HK*: =Ostbahn?

(0.3)

*Leon S*: <u>O</u>stbahn, ((shakes head up and down))(0.1) Ostbahnpolizei

(6.0) ((looks down; shakes head back and forth))

And (0.4) I remember (0.8) after he (1.0) left ((tilts head to left)) me there (0.8) I just passed away ((flutters eyelids as he says "passed away"; eyes down))

(6.0)

*Leon S*: <u>Well</u> we stayed in that c<u>a</u>mp

*HK*: How (was) you helped

(0.3)

*Leon S*: Pardon me?

*HK*: How have you been helped (.) when you passed (out)

(1.2)

*Leon S*: They (.) took me to the uh (0.2)

*HK*: =Who's they?

*Leon S*: ((Raises eyebrows as HK asks question))

(1.2)

*Leon S*: Other people who worked with me, (.) my friends (2.2) They took me to a (0.4) shack nearby (2.5) ((sniffle)) and (.) revived me and uh I (1.3) I went back to the camp (.) at the end of the day

(7.0)

But these are some of the episodes (.) and uh I probably don't recall all of them, but some of them that s: (2.4) stand in my mi:nd

(9.2)

We moved from that camp (4.0) in fortythree (1.0) ((sniffle)) (2.5) after a (3.6) few day transfer through a (1.5) c<u>a</u>mp on the Arizalimska (2.0) We went to Skarzysko–

Kamienna (2.0) where we were working on a (6.3) a ammunition factory (hasag), and this ((looks at interviewers)) was quite an experience. (4.5) As usually [[...]]
[[this narrative sequence then continues]]

## APPENDIX B

Excerpted from the testimony of Baruch G. (Videotape unedited # T–295, edited #A–50, Fortunoff Video Archive for Holocaust Testimony at Yale University). Baruch G., interviewed by Dana Kline (DK) on 6 September 1984. [Baruch G. has been talking about his experience of the first days of World War II when the Germans invaded Poland; he lived in the town of Mlawa at the time where the first contact with German soldiers "was uh rather a pleasant one".]

*Baruch G*: •hhh It was da only a few days after when they settled into (.) hometown they arrested the rabbi of the community.

*DK*: They, meaning who?

*Baruch G*: German Gestapo (the uh)- Uh he was arrested with a number of prominent citizens and not knowing what's going to happen and uh (.) •h And uh, they announced that uh if uh any Jew does anything wrong, (0.4) these are going to be shot to death.

(2.0)

So here is a frightening thing uh, (.) then after a few days they let them go, (0.8) and making them responsible (1.4) •hh for a number of laws which they instituted (1.0) immediately after that >>Not all at once<< One u::h that uh every uh Jew uh must register (2.5) •h Every Jew must have a number. (2.8) •h U:h later on a Jew must carry, a uh (.) must ((points to spot on chest)) must uh have a wh a white a white at first it was white round sign that he's a Jew, on the front and on back, (1.2) later on (it) was changed to a yellow (1.8) U:h, later on a::n announcement was made that a Jew must u::h walk if he sees a German, must (0.8) wa- must u:h go off the sidewalk and must go in the middle of the street (0.8) •h A Jew must u:h take off his hat ((makes gesture doffing hat)) when he sees a German (1.2) A German has the right to call on any Jew any tim:e for work, any kind of work he wants to. (1.6) And then, supposedly through the representatives which ultimately became the Judenrat, (1.0) •hh they uh issued laws that uh every Jew 200 Jews every day ev 200 Jews must appear in the market place for Germans to come in the morning to:: •hh to pick d out people to work

(0.5)

*DK*: Who chose the 200 men
[
*Baruch G*: (for their work)
(0.3)
*Baruch G*: =Pardon
*DK*: Who chose the 200 men=

[

*Baruch G*: =•hhh okay, so then: this developed into a uh numbers, first it was by numbers (.) ((hand gestures only partially visible as if pointing?)) number so and so must appear (1.0) and that uh (.) almost immediately. (1.0) ((adjusts his glasses)) became became a uh a source of income for some (hhh) (1.2) ((looks at interviewer)) as: strange as it may seem (1.2) if someone didn't want to appear, he would ask me ((gestures to self)) (.) if I wanted to go for him he would pay me for the day's work

(4.5) ((looks straight at the interviewer in this pause))

In my c:ase u:h (2.0) my father managed to: save some of his merchandise and he was able t:o (1.0) •h have to carry on:, throughout that period (1.0) •hhu:h although he was caught one day and di- disappeared (1.2) with all of us going crazy=

=I remember ((stares ahead, eyes slightly left of interviewer)) my mother pra, practically risked her life, (1.0) pleading with the German authorities there in the city hall, (1.2) to, try to send him back, to find out where he is, (0.6) no avail, (0.6) to no avail, (1.0) •h except uh after a month he came back (1.2) my father was never the same. ((blinks, eyes move right,then left; hand on face)) (3.5)

*DK*: Where had they sent him?

(1.0)

*Baruch G*: Uh he never talked about it. (1.0) Obviously it was a labor camp of some sort. They uh needed him for harvesting the potatoes or whatever it was, so he worked very hard there, (1.4) They cut his beard. ((knits eyebrows)) And he he became a differ- a different person=

=While I know him to be the dynamic, •hhhall knowing, hah, strong (1.6) u:h he became very much reserved ((second syllable previous word voiceless))

(2.0) ((looks at interviewer))

Since then although he took well care of his family >>there were the five of us<<, my two grandmothers moved in with us and one cousin of ours so we were eight (1.8) And we stayed in the apartment, he managed to uh do business, secretly (.) wi against the law, (06) with uh people who came in to buy things and they would knew him customers who knew him before, so he was able to: sell some merchandise and (.) provide for for (.) his family (1.0) U::h food at that time you know (0.3) it was bad, but when we look back (1.2) it was great. huh (1.2) It was good >>It was good<< (.) the family was together. And there was a feeling also the war will be over an:d uh. There was no inclination no idea of (1.2) no que- no question about survival. I mean it's a question of hard times. (1.2) Okay uh, so it's •h hard times.

## NOTES

1. Martin Walser, "Unser Auschwitz," *Kursbuch* I (1965), pp. 189–200; here p. 195. The translation of this quotation and of others from Walser's article are my own.

2. The two largest and most prominent collections are at Yad Vashem in Jerusalem and at the Fortunoff Archive for Holocaust Video Testimony at Yale University. In addition to recording testimonies themselves, these collections receive tapes from local projects in many countries, including Argentina, the former Yugoslavia, France,

and throughout the United States, to name just a few. There is also a substantial aural testimony collection of cassette tapes at Gratz College in Philadelphia. And there are said to be videotaped interviews at UCLA, though I have had no direct experience with this collection. Cf. James E. Young, *Writing and Rewriting the Holocaust: Narrative and the Consequences of Interpretation* (Bloomington and Indianapolis: Indiana University Press, 1988), p. 157.

3. Henry Krystal, "Integration and Self-Healing in Post-Traumatic States: A Ten Year Retrospective," *American Imago* 48 (1991), pp. 93–118; here p. 95.

4. Bonnie Gurewitsch, "Holocaust Oral Testimony: When is it Oral History?" Association for Jewish Studies Convention, Boston, 16 December 1990.

5. David Roskies, "Through a Lens, Darkly," review of Lawrence Langer, *Holocaust Testimonies. Commentary* (November 1991), pp. 57–59.

6. Sections of these taped interviews have been transcribed and published with the express permission of Yale University. Much of what follows would not have been written without the inspiration and encouragement of the Monday afternoon viewing group of the College of Communication at the University of Texas at Austin. Special thanks to conversation analysts and superb colleagues Robert Hopper, Madeline Maxwell, and Jürgen Streeck for sharing what they know and responding to my ideas; extra thanks to Robert Hopper for his assistance with the transcripts themselves, though the responsibility for their limitations remains mine. This article could not have been written without the financial support of the University of Texas in the form of a University Research Institute Grant for Summer 1991. Responses to the first draft of this essay were graciously shared with me by Katherin Arens, Philippe Carrard, Peter Jelavich, Ruth Kluger, Otto Lippmann, and Eric Santner.

7. Joanne Rudof, Informal training session of an interviewer. Yale University, 18 June 1991.

8. The preceding information and much of what follows in the next section is based on my own viewing of several score of tapes, the viewing of the recording of a testimony (at Yale University on 17 June 1991), and my presence at an impromptu training session for a volunteer interviewer whose aid had been solicited because of his knowledge of Yiddish (also Yale University, 18 June 1991). Additionally, I have spoken with the head archivist of the Fortunoff Archive, Joanne Rudof on numerous occasions, and with one of the chief interviewers, Dana Kline, on several occasions.

9. Harvey Sacks, Emanuel A. Schegloff, and Gail Jefferson, "A Simplest Systematics for the Organization of Turn-Taking for Conversation," *Language* 50 (1974), pp. 696–735; here p. 696 *et passim*.

10. On television news interviewing see John Heritage and David Greatbatch, "On the Institutional Character of Institutional Talk: The Case of News Interviews," *Discourse in Professional and Everyday Culture*. Seminar Proceedings (Department of Communication Studies, Linköping University, Linköping, Sweden, 1989) pp. 47–98; here p. 86 *et passim*. The most typical utterances of interviewers in the Holocaust videotapes are questions that ask for clarification of facts, for example, place names or years in which an event occurred. But additionally, the interviewers often pose questions that are designed to lead the speaker back to an event in his or her personal experience. The archivist's comment quoted above—that the survivor is "simply allowed to speak"—is part of a philosophy that acknowledges those giving testimony as experts only of the self. Thus when the interviewees extensively recount general historical fact, an interviewer is likely to attempt to lead him or her back to personal history. The most frequent signs of awareness of the "overhearing audience" (Heritage

and Greatbatch, pp. 65–68 *et passim*) are the glossing of foreign words by interviewer or interviewee. In the testimony of Leon S. (to be discussed below), for example, the witness glosses the abbreviation "Julag."

11. In training a new interviewer, the head archivist commented that one does not want the survivor to be waiting for the interviewer to ask a question (oral communication, Rudof).

12. On silences see Sidney M. Bolkosky, "Interviewing Victims Who Survived: Listening for the Silences that Strike," *Annals of Scholarship* 4 (1987), pp. 33–51; here p. 50 *et passim*. See also Nanette C. Auerhahn and Dori Laub, "Holocaust Testimony," *Holocaust and Genocide Studies* 5 (1990), pp. 447–462; here p. 457. Holocaust testimony shares this characteristic of long silences with the speech exchange genre of psychotherapy. But, of course, it is also distinctly unlike therapy in that the interviewer, in contrast to the analyst, is discouraged from analysis of the witness's speech. In training a new interviewer, Rudof has commented with regard to gaps and silences: "It is very important to wait. You don't have to jump into the silence" (oral communication, Rudof).

13. See also Langer, *passim*. Of course what is ironic about both Langer's book and Bolkosky's article is that, despite the authors' protestations of unanalyzability or general indescribability, they provide eloquent analysis.

14. I use the word "story"—and below "storytelling"—to emphasize the process of the production of personal narrative; I am NOT implying anything about the truth content of the discourse.

15. Alessandro Duranti, "The Audience as Co-Author: An Introduction," *Text* 6 (1986), pp. 239–247; here p. 242. Though the exact descriptions of the processes at work differ significantly, psychotherapists, sociolinguists, anthropologists, and conversation analysts (among others) have necessarily been aware of ways in which the addressee shapes the discourse of the speaker. Cf. for example Dédé Brouwer, "The Influence of the Addressee's Sex on Politeness in Language Use," *Linguistics* 20 (1982), pp. 697–711; Dédé Brouwer, Marinel Gerritsen, and Dorian de Haan, "Speech Differences Between Women and Men: On the Wrong Track?" *Language in Society* 8 (1979), pp. 33–50; Donald Spence, *Narrative Truth and Historical Truth: Meaning and Interpretation in Psychoanalysis* (New York: W. W. Norton, 1982); Charles Goodwin, "Audience Diversity, Participation and Interpretation," *Text* 6 (1986), pp. 283–316; "Notes on Story Structure and the Organization of Participation," *Structures of Social Action: Studies in Conversation Analysis*, J. Maxwell Atkinson and John Heritage, eds. (Cambridge and New York: Cambridge University Press, 1984), pp. 225–246; Marjorie Harness Goodwin, *He-said-She-said: Talk as Social Organization among Black Children* (Bloomington: Indiana University Press, 1990); John B. Haviland, " 'Con Buenos Chiles': Talk, Targets and Teasing in Zinacantán," *Text* 6 (1986), pp. 249–282; Jennifer Mandelbaum, "Recipient-Driven Storytelling in Conversation," Diss. University of Texas at Austin, 1987; etc. Primarily as a result of the work of Bakhtin on dialogism and Prince on the addressee, literary critics have also begun to recognize the importance of the addressee or narratee (cf. esp. M. M. Bakhtin, *The Dialogic Imagination. Four Essays*, trans. Caryl Emerson and Michael Holquist, ed. Michael Holquist (Austin: University of Texas Press, 1981); *Speech Genres and Other Late Essays*, trans. Vern W. McGee, ed. Caryl Emerson and Michael Holquist (Austin: University of Texas Press, 1986); Gerald Prince, "Introduction à l'étude du narrataire," *Poétique* 14 (1973), pp. 178–196; idem, "The Narratee Revisited," *Style* 19 (1985), pp. 299–303; idem, "Notes Towards a Categorization of

Fictional 'Narratee,'" *Genre* 4 (1971), pp. 100–105. Meir Sternberg, "The World from the Addressee's Viewpoint: Reception as Representation, Dialogue as Monologue," *Style* 20 (1986), pp. 295–318; Irene Kacandes, "Narrative Apostrophe. Case Studies in Second Person Fiction," Diss. Harvard University, 1990. But the model of the solitary writer sitting in a room composing a story has interfered, I believe, with more complete recognition of the influence of the addressee on the production of all discourse, including literary.

16. I borrow this term from Donald Spence's stimulating work, *Narrative Truth and Historical Truth. Interpretation in Psychoanalysis* (New York: W. W. Norton, 1982). Spence borrows the term from Walsh to signify "an account of the facts 'which brought out their connection' " (as quoted in Spence, p. 291).

17. Edited versions of the testimonies of both Leon S. and Baruch G. can be rented from the Fortunoff Archive for a minimal processing fee (#A–25 and #A–50, respectively). The edited or unedited tapes can be viewed at Yale in the Archive offices (Sterling Library, Rm 331 C).

18. On the basis of my research with these tapes I find I have to disagree rigorously with Mary Louise Pratt who, in commenting on Labov's work, concludes that narratives of personal experience are *least* vulnerable to influence by an interlocutor (Pratt, p. 104).

19. It should perhaps also be mentioned that Leon S. was reluctant to be interviewed. It appears that Dr. Klein may have known Leon S. prior to the interview and convinced him to give testimony. I have not been able to confirm this, and do not think that it is relevant to the structural part of my analysis of this segment, though it may provide some explanation for why Klein reframes Leon S.'s discourse in the ways that he does, i.e. urging him toward seeing the personal connections between himself and other people in his life. This interview could be described as closer to a psychoanalytic session than most others in the archive.

20. In the opening of the testimony of Baruch G. the speaker briefly answers the interviewer's questions about his childhood, but then comments rather extensively on the experience of liberation and the loneliness he felt. His interviewer asks an explicit question to bring him back to his memories of the period of Hitler's rise to power. Some witnesses find themselves totally incapable of speaking of events before the Holocaust. (Cf. comments of Bessie K., Tape T–206.)

21. It is interesting to note that in this kind of oral narrative one finds the same alternation between the summary and scene that Genette describes as typical of literary narrative. Gérard Genette, *Figures* III (Paris: Editions de Seuil, 1972), p. 142. Cf. Erving Goffman, *Frame Analysis. An Essay on the Organization of Experience* (New York: Harper & Row, 1974) and Labov's categories for describing narratives of personal experience in his chapter, "The Transformation of Experience in Narrative Syntax," in *Language in the Inner City* (Philadelphia: University of Pennsylvania Press, 1972), pp. 354–396. On the basis of his experience with oral narratives primarily those told by youths in American inner city ghettos, Labov discerns the following main parts of personal narratives: an *abstract*, which usually provides some kind of short summary of the story, encapsulating its point (pp. 363–364); an *orientation* section, providing names, places, dates, or times, etc. (pp. 364–365); the *complicating action*, the heart of the narrative; *evaluation*, "the means used by the narrator to indicate the point of the narrative" (pp. 366ff.); the *result* or *resolution*; and the *coda*, which closes off the sequence of complicating action, and signals that the narrative is finished (p. 365). This similarity might not be surprising since most of Labov's data

was produced in response to the question: "Were you ever in a situation where you were in serious danger of being killed, where you said to yourself 'This is it'?" (p. 354) But unlike Labov, I will demonstrate how much these narrative features are negotiated by both speaker and addressee, not merely produced by the storyteller.

22. This part is not included in the edited version of the videotape, but directly precedes the section I will discuss in detail below; it is included in the transcript found in Appendix A.

23. On the concept of "transition relevance place," the point at which another speaker might make a bid for a turn, see Sacks, Schegloff, and Jefferson (esp. p. 705). See also Mandelbaum.

24. On the necessity of response for storytelling see Goffman (p. 541); cf. also Pratt (p. 60); Mandelbaum (pp. 126ff); C. Goodwin "Story Structure," p. 236 *et passim*.

25. Note too that Leon S. raised his voice as he uttered the first person pronoun and raised his eyebrows as well, a gesture he rarely made during the course of this long interview.

26. See Kacandes (esp. pp. 41, 59, 62–63 *et passim*).

27. Klein's question translates as: "East Rail;" and Leon S.'s confirmation as "East Rail. East Rail policeman." They are both referring to the railroads that ran to the "Eastern territories," including Poland where this camp was located. For ways in which linguistic registers are also subject to collaborative negotiation, see Haviland (p. 278, note 13).

28. Although Leon S. is not a native speaker of English, his command of the language includes good idiomatic use, as can be judged from other parts of the interview. Therefore I would call this a Freudian slip, unconscious, though purposeful: the punishment was so cruel, he truly almost died.

29. In this I agree fully with the emphasis of Mandelbaum, (esp. pp. 124, 238, and 239). The recipient "may play an instrumental part, not just in bringing the storytelling to the floor and sustaining it, but also in working out, with teller, what the storytelling is about. In this way, the character of the reported event is collaboratively constructed by recipient and teller working together" (p. 239). On creating an alternative framework for events see also C. Goodwin, "Audience Diversity" (p. 300 *et passim*).

30. Baruch G. opens his testimony with some personal comments. Upon being prompted by Kline he speaks, for example, of his brother and sister. But this sequence reporting the events after the invasion of the Germans in September 1939 has mainly been in a more neutral style. Even when clearly speaking of a personal experience, for example, reaction to behavior of the German invasion troops, he uses a first-person plural: "to *our* surprise." This is the first time he evokes himself exclusively, and, as we will see below, even this mention of the self is bound up inextricably with the father.

31. Cf. Charles Goodwin, "Notes on Story Structure and the Organization of Participation," p. 236.

32. I have spoken to Kline about this sequence, and though she understandably does not have a clear recollection of her own thoughts at the time, she finds my analysis plausible.

33. This section is not on the edited version of the tape. I suspect that the editors recognized this as a repetition of a topic already covered, whereas, again, neither Baruch G. nor Kline specifically orient to it as such.

34. Cathy Caruth, "Introduction. Special Issue on Psychoanalysis, Culture and

Drama," *American Imago* 48 (1991), p. 8. See also Shoshana Felman, "Education and Crisis, or the Vicissitudes of Teaching," *American Imago* 48 (1991), pp. 13–73.

35. Primo Levi writes of the same process of dehumanization through the denial of ability to be a speech partner in the second chapter of *Survival in Auschwitz* (London: Collier McMillan, 1969). Levi describes the attempt of the deported Italians to find out what is going to happen to them after their arrival at Auschwitz. One Italian who knows German asks the guard some questions: "We all look at the interpreter, and the interpreter asks the German, and the German smokes and looks him through and through as if he were transparent, as if no one had spoken" (p. 19).

# Social Darwinism in Edgar Hilsenrath's Ghetto Novel *Nacht*

## Dagmar C. G. Lorenz

"Social Darwinism assumes inequality—of groups, of peoples, nations, classes and races. This inequality may seem harsh, since in the struggle for survival the weak are the losers. But if one takes a loftier view one will note that those who survive are stronger and better: 'the survival of the fittest.'" This is how Piet de Rooy characterizes the ideology at the root of the "tremendous Western growth of technology and science, wealth and culture," as well as two world wars and Nazi Germany.[1] In his first novel *Nacht* [Night] the German-Jewish Holocaust survivor Edgar Hilsenrath examined the misery, poverty, and barbarism brought about by this ideology.

*Nacht* was published in West Germany by Kindler in 1964 and rejected not only by the public, but by its own publisher who refused to release more than a ridiculously small edition.[2] While German-speaking survivors of the Holocaust traditionally had difficulties in making their voices heard in postwar Germany, Hilsenrath's assessment of the genocide committed by the Nazis presented particular problems to German readers.[3]

Hilsenrath views the Holocaust neither in the light of European anti-Semitism as an event involving Germans and Jews exclusively nor as a disaster that defies the rules of the civilized world. Rather, he considers it as a twentieth-century population elimination program, of which another example would be the genocide of Armenians perpetrated by the Turks during World War I. In his recent novel, *Das Märchen vom letzten Gedanken*, Hilsenrath links this earlier mass murder with the latter even by name.[4] Hilsenrath does not "belittle, misjudge, or shrug off the significance of the Holocaust for sociology as the theory of civilization, of modernity, of modern civilization," which according to Zygmunt Bauman those do who present the Holocaust exclusively as a unique event in *Jewish* history, nor does he describe it merely as an example of undesirable social behavior taken to its extreme.[5]

Hilsenrath insists that the dynamics which caused the Holocaust are an integral part of the modern world, the product of a scientific mentality that wants to control the development of human and animal life, and to determine who can live where under which conditions.[6] His work suggests that in view of the conditions prevailing in the twentieth century, other genocides are not only likely, but inevitable. Richard Rubenstein considers the "overproduction" of people and programs for their elimination an intrinsic feature of modern civilization. He writes that:

> in a modern economy the 'overproduction' of people and goods can be regarded as a greater threat to economic and political stability than their destruction. Obsolescence and destruction can form the basis of future prosperity, as indeed was the case in both Germany and Japan after World War II. A surplus of either goods or people can lead to mass unemployment and depression. The most radical form of population elimination is outright extermination.[7]

In her 1951 study, *The Origins of Totalitarianism*,[8] Hannah Arendt had shown that, in Rubenstein's words, the Jews of Europe had become a "surplus" population in competition with the Gentile middle and lower-middle classes who feared downward mobility and unemployment. Rubenstein aptly notes that "anti-Semitism rose as the stock market fell." While the intentions of the Nazis did not differ from those of earlier persecutors, their means of extermination and their rationale did. Twentieth-century bureaucracy and technology made it possible to kill as many as ten thousand people per day in one camp.[9] Racial theory based on pseudo-science and utilitarian capitalist theory provided the ideological impetus.[10] After the *Kristallnacht* pogrom Edgar Hilsenrath fled with his mother and brother from Germany to Romania. In 1941 he was among the Jews who were deported to the ghetto Moghilev-Podolsk. Prokow, where *Nacht* is situated, reflects the burned-out ruin city on the Dnjestr River where the author arrived as a fifteen-year-old boy. At the gates of Prokow, the destination of the regularly arriving transports, civilization and technology come to a stop. Yet, one may argue, this ghetto is a no less efficient place for mass murder than an automated death camp. As was the case in Turkish Armenia, those captives not massacred on the transport are left to starve. In their futile struggle for survival they victimize and kill each other.

Unlike most German Holocaust fiction, Hilsenrath's novel does not clearly distinguish between perpetrators and victims, good and bad. Hilsenrath's characters are caught up in a Social Darwinist system whose dynamics determine the role and behavior of every individual. His protagonist Ranek acts ruthlessly when he is strong. As he grows weaker, he displays gentler traits, while other men are waiting to assume his position of power. Social behavior in Hilsenrath's text is determined by position and opportunity.

*Nacht* is situated exclusively among Jewish ghetto prisoners whom the Nazis had designated as "surplus people." Although the Nazis are the cause of suffering in Prokow, no Germans are in sight. The people imprisoned in the hermetically sealed-off ghetto are left to starve unless they are caught during the nightly raids. Those who are rounded up, because they cannot find a place to sleep, are either killed or put to work. In spite of the fact that the majority of the prisoners have no chance to find lodging, there is a curfew that makes it illegal to be outdoors at night. Those who are not summarily slain or slowly worked to death, fall victim to epidemics and starvation.

A major difference between Prokow and a concentration or death camp is the fact that the captors do attempt to feed the prisoners. The conditions remind the reader of descriptions of Bergen-Belsen at the time of its liberation by the British. There is no administration, no employment program, let alone rituals such as role calls or institutions such as prisons or hospital blocks. All the captives are Jews and of the categories in the Nazi camp system, they rank the lowest. Among themselves, their status is determined by brute force and cunning. In the absence of regulations, "survival of the fittest" is the law they live by. Short of becoming a traitor, a ghetto policeman, or enlisting as a prostitute in the ghetto brothel, the prisoners cannot influence their position vis-à-vis the Romanian Nazis.

According to Hilsenrath it did not matter whether the people enclosed in Moghilev-Podolsk were Jewish, nor did their social background and education make a difference.[11] In a personal interview Hilsenrath revealed that he observed that individuals with a criminal past or those used to physical labor could achieve the highest status in the ghetto hierarchy.[12] Often they had the ability to amass food and goods through which they were able to influence others and ensure their own survival.[13] Survival in Prokow depended on the individual's ability to abandon the luxury of bourgeois values. Those who were raised outside of the traditional moral system, those who rejected it, and those who were too young to be indoctrinated by it, were at a distinct advantage.

Other authors and critics have advanced similar concepts about life during the Holocaust, for example death camp survivor Jean Améry, and the novelist Ilse Aichinger who survived the time of persecution in Vienna.[14] However, few reveal such disturbing insights as blatantly as does Hilsenrath. According to him the Nazi ghetto and extermination camp system is the rule rather than the exception, not only in the Western capitalist but also in the Eastern socialist context. The concentration camp state does not contradict Western culture, but is its logical conclusion.

As early as 1848 Karl Marx and Friedrich Engels formulated *The Communist Manifesto*, a treatise about the most advanced developmental phase of Western world capitalism. In keeping with their theses, the ghetto society recognizes no other values than material ones. In Prokow, an ethnic and social melting pot, there is no room for sentimental considerations. All relationships have been reduced to their exchange value, with the exception of male sexuality, which above all is a show of strength that establishes rank among males. The ability to perform sexually presupposes a measure of physical well-being and this, in turn, shows that the individual has the means to feed himself. Lina

Werthmüller makes precisely this point in her film *Seven Beauties,* which Bruno Bettelheim criticized so virulently.[15] The symbolic meaning of male sexuality is displayed in Ranek's futile attempt at copulation with a strange woman for whom he feels no desire, and the act he is unable to consummate. Since he will let her sleep in his spot, he feels that she owes him his due. The bodies of women and children, on the other hand, are commodities with which they compensate their adult male protectors on whom they depend for their survival.

Hilsenrath shows that the absence of goods creates the most ruthless material greed and capitalism. The "rich" people of the ghetto, such as the owner of the makeshift coffee house and his wife, wield the power over life and death, for they decide who is to leave the premises at night to be picked up and killed. In the absence of goods the body becomes merchandise and means of payment. Only wealthy prisoners can afford a semblance of family life, augmented, to be sure, by the casual exploitation of the starving poor. Monogamy as a lifestyle has gone by the wayside, because, as Hilsenrath shows, it takes a certain stability and affluence to support it. In this sense Ranek is right when he laments that all women are whores. Yet he overlooks the fact that he and the likes of him are responsible for this situation by becoming whoremasters. Chastity is not among the priorities in the ghetto, because the chaste eliminate themselves.

A weaker person is lucky if he or she finds a permanent protector. The other option is prostitution. The latter, although discussed in derogatory terms among males, has become a lifestyle, as the example of the old woman prostituting herself to protect her dying son illustrates. Scenes like these bring to light Hilsenrath's insight that not only the distant instigators of the Holocaust, but also its victims apply the psychology of domination to each other. These, in turn, are already contained in the elitist and sexist concepts of Judeo-Christian culture.[16]

Joan Ringelheim's observations about sexuality in the ghetto confirm Hilsenrath's often grotesque, often tragicomical descriptions. She describes sexuality in the ghetto as a commercial service, which for many women presented the only opportunity for survival.[17] Accordingly, in a state of colonization women suffer from a more profound oppression than men.[18] The basic factors that determine the power structure in the ghetto are the same ones that shape post-Holocaust society. As Ringelheim states, women are hesitant to write about rape and prostitution during the Holocaust, while men, frequently uncritically, discuss these topics. Hilsenrath shows brutal sexuality as an important aspect of the ghetto, the creation of the Social Darwinist Nazi regime.

*Nacht* is told in the third person, mainly from Ranek's point of view, and focuses on the protagonist's demise. Hilsenrath's black humor shows an affinity with Jerzy Kosinski in *The Painted Bird.* Sidra Ezrahi compared him with Tadeusz Borowski.[19] Like these authors Hilsenrath shows the ghetto as a segregated realm where the normal life-expectancy has been reduced to a few months. While his descriptions and psychological explanations allow insight into other characters as well, the narrator empathizes with Ranek, who is by normal standards a young man but is considered already old in the context of the ghetto society.

Ranek is an illustration of Hermann Langbein's thesis that people imprisoned for an indefinite period of time suffer from a psychological reduction, hence Hilsenrath's insistence on the graphic description of physical functions.[20] Eating, be it the ability to eat and digest, be it the availability of food, decides who survives. Digestion and excretion are discussed in more detail than psychological and spiritual processes (Ezrahi, p. 65). However, the interdependency of body and mind are shown as well: through his imprisonment Ranek, the son of a Jewish middle-class family, has lost his values and his religion. As he grows increasingly hungry, he loses his stamina and with it his ability to think rationally. The guests of the makeshift coffee house in the ghetto are greedy for life, information, and entertainment. Even a dying man who lies hidden under the rubble of a porch has not lost his basic desires. In Hilsenrath's novel religion is not among them. How well an individual meets his or her physical needs determines survival. The daily concern for the body is shown in haunting images. Hilsenrath describes desperate men, women, and children lingering around the ghetto brothel hoping to grab some edible garbage, fighting for a place to sleep on or under a bed, in rooms, or in crawl spaces.

*Nacht* is void of the conciliatory tone characteristic of other Holocaust fiction. It shows neither enemy images nor a hopeful perspective for the future. The ghetto police—desperate and hungry men recruited from among the prisoners—do the Nazis' dirty work. The Nazis are manifest only by the effect they have on the environment. Their prisoners are left to their own devices; it appears, however, that those of them who do not live by the rules established by the conquerors' policies are the first to die. Whoever refuses to reproduce the system, perishes first.

The ghetto population is controlled by extreme need: deliberate pauperization, intentional starvation, and the suppression of information. In terms of Social Darwinism their inferiority is indicated by their appearance and living conditions alone, while the Nazis' ability to reduce the Jews to such a level may be taken as proof of their superiority (de Rooy, p. 8). Ranek serves as a case in point in examining the attitudes resulting from rule by humiliation, hunger, poverty, and the constant threat of death.

In some ways Ranek has to force himself to act against his bourgeois conscience, but in other ways his patriarchal values help him to do so. He already believed in male superiority when he entered the ghetto, as well as in his right to fend for himself as an individual. The chaos of the ghetto allows even him to act for a short while without restraint either on his misogyny or on individualism. The price for such a chance at attaining almost unlimited power over other human beings is the absence of any protection whatsoever. Others, who in turn will briefly have the opportunity to be stronger than Ranek, oppress him while exercising their right as "the fittest."

The ghetto laws reproduce the structures that shape Nazi Germany. Both realms are male-dominated, utilitarian societies that reduce people to their functional value. Here, as there, life is divided into life worth living and "unworthy" life. In Prokow, as in Nazi Germany, no one has a "right" to live. Being alive is a privilege that can be revoked at any time. The ghetto, much like Nazi society, has its own "surplus people": the weak, the old, and the sick (cf. Rubenstein, p. 27). The ghetto has no safe place for children. Only those born to powerful fathers have a chance to survive.

In concentration camps and established ghettos such as Theresienstadt, the Nazis practiced forced abortion, and, in the case of pregnant Jewish women, instant murder. However, in Prokow the Nazis do not need to persecute the children, because the living conditions and the rules the imprisoned live by are such that they do their killing for them. Also the loyalty among prisoners is based on usefulness. Individualism has been taken to the extreme and become crass selfishness. Since children are of no immediate value, they are killed by neglect. Mothers and pregnant women are a burden to men in search of a sex object and consequently they are among the most at risk in Prokow.

Hilsenrath's female characters display more altruism than his male figures. This portrayal corresponds with Joan Ringelheim's study of women in the ghetto. Even when Ranek thinks that he loves someone—as is the case with Deborah, his brother's widow—he remains ambivalent. He is ready to reject her when he realizes that she presents a responsibility in his life (*Nacht*, p. 427).[21] As Ranek's alter ego Deborah also represents an alternative. Throughout the novel it is unclear if she is a hallucination, an *anima* figure that becomes stronger as Ranek grows weaker, or if she is, indeed, a separate character. Against Ranek's prediction Deborah adheres to her religious and social values even in the ghetto. She displays reverence for the dead, while Ranek on the first pages of the novel transgresses against this basic rule of civilization by taking the dead man's possessions and wearing his hat. Deborah respects life, no matter if it is that of a stray dog or a fatherless child. She nurtures those in need with her and Ranek's meager supplies. She attempts to create a community in a place where loneliness and hostility are the basic experiences.

Hilsenrath shows the fragility of civilization. Conditions that counteract basic survival create dehumanized people. Prokow serves as an example of the problems created by need and hunger. It seems only too natural to collapse in a situation of misery. In *Nacht* social standards such as morals, religion, good manners, as well as the ties of friendship and family depend on the supply of basic goods. Thus the interdependency of individual destiny with the fate of the collective becomes manifest. Conception, birth, disease, relationships and love, all of which are, in the discourse of the bourgeoisie, "private matters," appear as dependent on the economy.

In the same way convictions, philosophies, religions, as well as ethnic identity only begin to matter once a certain economic comfort level is reached. Hilsenrath shows that social categories based on them are part of the "bourgeois smokescreen" distracting from the physical reality of the body on which the reality of life is based. The males in *Nacht* are the most alienated from this reality and thus most likely to embark on a path that leads from the destruction of others to self-destruction. In this regard the prisoners of Prokow are similar to their captors. Counter to notions generated by middle-class sentimentality, suffering does not ennoble them. However, Hilsenrath does not fuse them into the amorphous mass of martyrs frequently referred to in Holocaust literature. Hilsenrath's hungry and poor are eminently dangerous due to their unfulfilled needs and desires. At no point, however, are they portrayed as animalistic. *Nacht* is a powerful accusation of the invisible engineers of the Holocaust who commit murder at their desks by destroying people whom they have never met. In this sense Hilsenrath's Romanian ghetto also represents the slums of the world's metropolitan areas and the poverty of the Third World, whose fate is decided by politicians and functionaries thousands of miles away. *Nacht* opens up dimensions of horror without invoking images of physical cruelty, the stock scenes of beating and torture found in traditional Holocaust literature.

The figure of Deborah suggests a different approach to survival. Her dignity and altruism represent an alternative that is closed to dominant men in a male-dominated society. The more Ranek's strength fails, the more he recognizes Deborah as the symbol of a different way of life. As she assumes the dimensions of a Madonna or a Great Mother, Ranek realizes that universal competition leads to universal death.

The fact that Ranek can recognize the necessity of mutual nurturing as the key for survival suggests that buried within him is the ability to behave as a social being. The desperate response of the dying man to Deborah, the embodiment of wifely, motherly, and sisterly love, demonstrates man's inability to survive, even to die, alone. Ranek comes to understand that the short-term gratification gained by a life of self-seeking carries a high price: the rejection and extermination of the weak, old, sick, and helpless—conditions that not even the strongest can escape in the end.

Hilsenrath does not criticize the prisoners in the ghetto as Jews or as corrupt people by way of Deborah's alternative. Rather he criticizes a system that makes human beings the victims of their own weaknesses. To dismiss the prisoners in the ghetto would amount to following Fascist thought by condemning the victims of manmade misery. The people of Prokow are not dehumanized, but their living conditions are such that only a saintly apparition such as Deborah can cope with them.

*Nacht* was so uncomfortable to the postwar reader in Germany because it questioned values on which Germany continued to rely even after the demise of Nazism. Hilsenrath showed the Holocaust as "another face of the same modern society whose other, more familiar face we so admire" (Bauman, p. 7). Racial nationalism, which "offered the promise of wars of conquest against inferior peoples in which the declining fortunes of the lower middle class would be reversed as they shared in the spoils of a triumphant racial empire" (Rubenstein, p. 148), has, once again, asserted itself in Germany's association with its former enemies, the United States and the Soviet Union. In addition to having become a powerful ally of the Western block superpowers, West Germany has created an underclass of Mediterranean foreign workers who are stereotyped by the same images that previously had been applied to the Jews.

Hilsenrath's novel also invites a closer look at the reestablished patriarchal family values, which in the form of clannishness and in- and out-group thinking promote cutthroat competition and sexism. By treating the Holocaust as "a rare, yet significant and reliable, test of the hidden possibilities of modern society," he reveals the dynamics that the ghetto has in common with the new societies (Bauman, p. 12).

The character of Deborah suggests a way out of the vicious cycle of Darwinist and crypto-Fascist social dynamics. The qualities implied in this utopian figure coincide remarkably closely with the solutions Richard Rubenstein envisions for the debacle of Reaganomics (Rubenstein, pp. 224ff.). Rubenstein demands a full employment policy regardless of age, sex, and education that would reduce competition as the basis of social interaction and prevent the problem of "surplus people."

Hilsenrath was aware of the utopian quality of his Deborah. So is Rubenstein as he outlines his "Way Out," suggesting that it would take no less than a religious transformation for the realization of his vision. In no other way can he conceive of "a society of universal otherhood" becoming a society of "universal brotherhood" that would allow room for bonding, as defined in Wilson's thesis on the function of homosexuality (Rubenstein, p. 229; Wilson, p. 144). In view of the ongoing ethnic and economic strife worldwide, both the German Holocaust survivor and novelist and the American theorist ultimately admit that there is no end in sight to the dictate of state-controlled procreation and mass slaughter, the mandatory production and elimination of "surplus populations"—Social Darwinism.

## Notes

1. Piet de Rooy, "Ernst Haeckel's Theory of Recapitulation," in Jan Breman, ed., *Imperial Monkey Business. Racial Supremacy in Social Darwinist Theory and*

*Colonial Practice* (Amsterdam: VU University Press, 1990), p. 9. Edward O. Wilson's study *On Human Nature* (Cambridge, MA: Harvard University Press, 1978) is but one example that to this day Darwin's views on human 'nature' are accepted by experts.

2. Edgar Hilsenrath, *Nacht* (Frankfurt: Fischer, 1980; Cologne: Literarischer Verlag Braun, 1978; Munich: Kindler, 1964).

3. Peter Jokostra, "Brief an Landau," *Börsenblatt für den deutschen Buchhandel* 2.4 (1965); idem, "Offener Brief," ibid. 24.3 (1965). Susann Moeller, *Wo die Opfer zu Tätern werden, machen sich die Täter zu Opfern. Die deutsche und amerikanische Rezeption der beiden ersten Romane von Edgar Hilsenrath*, dissertation (Ohio State University, 1991). After the success of Hilsenrath's second novel, *Der Nazi und der Friseur* (1977), *Nacht* was published by the small Literarischer Verlag Braun.

4. Edgar Hilsenrath, *Das Märchen vom letzten Gedanken* (Munich: Piper, 1989), p. 174: "They [the historians] will call the great massacre the murder of a people or mass murder, and the scholars among them will say that it should be called 'genocide.' Some know-it-all will say that the proper term is *Armenocide*, and the last of the idiotic experts will consult dictionaries and finally come up with the term *Holocaust*." (Translations by Lorenz.)

5. Cf. Zygmunt Bauman, *Modernity and the Holocaust* (Cambridge: Polity Press, 1989), pp. 1–2.

6. Jan Breman, "Introduction," in Jan Breman, ed., *Imperial Monkey Business*, p. 2. Peter Morton, *The Vital Science. Biology and the Literary Imagination 1860–1900* (London: George Allen & Unwin, 1984), discusses the impact of Darwinism on literary discourses.

7. Richard L. Rubenstein, *The Age of Triage. Fear and Hope in an Overcrowded World* (Boston: Beacon Press, 1983), p. 8.

8. Hannah Arendt, *The Origins of Totalitarianism* (New York: Harcourt, Brace and Co., 1951).

9. Rubenstein, p. 32: "Hitler's 'solution' included genocide and wars of enslavement and extermination. He also had as little compunction about eliminating those Germans he considered superfluous as he did Jews, a fact demonstrated by his 'euthanasia' program. Moreover, his 'solution' was 'rational' in the narrowly defined sense in which we use the term, namely, the most efficient, economical and morally neutral method of solving a 'problem.' As such, genocide represents the ultimate expression of the revolution of rationality with which the problem of population redundancy began in the first place." Cf. also pp. 26 and 145.

10. Darwin held that "the various races, when carefully compared and measured differ much from each other." He refers not only to physical but also mental characteristics. *Human Nature: Darwin's View*, Alexander Alland, Jr., ed. (New York: Columbia University Press, 1985), p. 185.

11. Wilson, *On Human Nature*, p. 159, observes: "The primacy of egocentrism over race has been most clearly revealed by the behavior of ethnic groups placed under conditions of stress. For example, Sephardic Jews from Jamaica who emigrate to England or America may, according to personal circumstances, remain fully Jewish by joining the Jews of the host society, or may abandon their ethnic ties promptly, marry gentiles, and blend into the host culture."

12. My interview with Edgar Hilsenrath in Columbus, Ohio on 15 May 1986.

13. Cf. Jean Améry's account of his survival in Auschwitz, *Jenseits von Schuld*

*und Sühne. Bewältigungsversuche eines Überwältigten* (Stuttgart: Klett–Cotta, 1977), p. 21. Améry explains that intellectuals like himself and his fellow prisoners Primo Levi and Viktor Frankl were the *Lumpenproletariat* of the concentration camps. They not only lacked manual skills, but also the ability to cope with the concentration camp structures. Neither did they possess the cunning to manipulate the powers that be nor the daring and courage to fend for themselves.

14. Ilse Aichinger, *Die größere Hoffnung* (Vienna: Bermann–Fischer, 1948; Frankfurt am Main: Fischer, 1974).

15. Bruno Bettelheim, *Surviving* (New York: Knopf, 1979).

16. Breman, p. 2, discusses the importance of the sexual factor in the theory and practice of racism.

17. Joan Miriam Ringelheim, "Women and the Holocaust: A Reconsideration of Research," *Signs* 10/4 (1985), p. 744. On sexual mores and oppression in Colonialism, cf. Ann Stoler, "Making Empire Respectable," in Breman, ed., *Imperial Monkey Business*, p. 37.

18. According to Breman, p. 2: "Racist theorists and politicians modelled an image of the European in which typical 'masculine' characteristics such as leadership ability and intellectual power had pride of place, while levity, lack of discipline and other 'feminine' traits were said to be characteristic of the colonized people."

19. Sidra DeKoven Ezrahi, *By Words Alone. The Holocaust in Literature* (Chicago and London: University of Chicago Press, 1980).

20. Hermann Langbein, *Menschen in Auschwitz* (Vienna: Europa, 1972), p. 92.

21. Wilson, *On Human Nature*, attributes the quality of altruism that Hilsenrath codifies as feminine, to homosexuals. He regards its preservation as the reason for homosexual bonding. "Homosexuals may be the genetic carriers of some of mankind's rare altruistic impulses" (p. 143).

# Politics to Pulp a Novel:
# The Fate of the First Edition
# of Edgar Hilsenrath's Novel *Nacht*

## Susann Moeller

When asked about the position and function of his protagonists in general, Hilsenrath explained that they were anti-heroes. This concept holds particularly true for *Nacht*, as reviewer Hubert Nachtsheim pointed out.[1] Nachtsheim assumed that the novel was rejected by its readership on the grounds of there being no hero in the traditional sense. "The sensitive reader," he argued, "may be nauseated by some passages."[2] Any skepticism induced by and toward the anti-hero in this novel is undoubtedly increased by the confrontation with images of decay and provocative words such as "pus," "blood," "vomit," "excrement," etc. Yet, Hilsenrath's vocabulary leads to a reconstruction, however imperfect, of the protagonist's experience in the reader's mind. Nevertheless, to counteract possible controversies arising from Hilsenrath's choice of words, publisher Helmut Kindler decided to furnish the first edition of *Nacht* with an explanatory preface and epilogue.

In this epilogue Hilsenrath pointed to an allegedly biographical character of his work, a feature that not only misleads the reader but frequently formed the basis of literary discussions on *Nacht*. The epilogue did not reflect the author's opinion but that of Kindler, who, by his reference, confined the claim to the validity of *Nacht* to its author. In order to secure the publication of this novel, which had already led to controversies within the publishing house, Hilsenrath saw himself forced to accept Kindler's conditions. It was not until many years later that Hilsenrath could correct this misunderstanding: "The Kindler publishing house coerced me into writing this epilogue. *Nacht* is one hundred percent novel, not an autobiography. Of course, I did live in a ghetto. But this is not my story, it is an invented truth."[3] The Kindler publishing house feared that a Holocaust novel such as *Nacht* would meet with too many objections if it claimed validity beyond an autobiographical content.

However, the epilogue did not prevent a growing animosity against the book within the publishing house. B. Graubard of the *Association of Israelite Cultural Communities in Bavaria* advised against the publication of *Nacht*.

He based his opinion on his conviction that the Jews in *Nacht* would not arouse sympathy but rather the contrary.[4] He doubted that readers would have the ability to understand those circumstances created by a system in which any human being, Jewish or otherwise, can sink into an abyss such as Hilsenrath described. Marion Gid, editor-in-chief of the *Neue jiddische Zeitung* in Munich contradicted Graubard: "I do not believe that any intelligent reader will tend to be permeated with anti-Jewish prejudice against Ranek and Red, characters in this book, and assume that their actions were a result of their being Jewish."[5] Yet, Gid's opinion reflected on the "intelligent reader," while regarding any "unintelligent reader" as an anti-Semite.

The question remains, whether anti-Semites reacted to the novel in the way Kindler had anticipated. Although anti-Semitism refutes all rational perception and argument as a kind of pseudo-religion, a review of the pertinent documents reveals that *Nacht* had not been exploited to stir up anti-Semitic baiting. However, some reviewers did consider this possibility when responding to an opinion poll, initiated by Ernest Landau, the head of Kindler's publicity department. The correspondence that developed thereafter between the author, the publisher, the publisher's wife, the chief editor, the head of publicity, and several reviewers illustrates the fate of the first edition of *Nacht*. A chronological examination of these letters shows the process of opinion forming toward the novel.

In 1963 Henry Marx, the chief editor of the *New Yorker Staatszeitung und Herold*, advised Hilsenrath to send his manuscript *Nachtasyl* to Hans-Geert Falkenberg, the chief editor of the Kindler publishing house. There the working title of the manuscript was changed into *Nacht* so as not to be confused with Maxim Gorki's novel.[6] On 9 December 1963 Falkenberg wrote to Hilsenrath that he considered his novel an outstanding contribution to German postwar literature, since he had "nowhere met with such merciless, harsh, yet simple description of a Jewish ghetto."[7] On 2 March 1964 Henry Marx sent a letter directly to Helmut Kindler, calling his attention to *Nacht*. Marx concluded his recommendation "in the belief that you are the publishing house most suited for this book," an assumption that did not prove correct.[8] After Falkenberg had recommended the novel for publication and Kindler had given his approval, Landau launched a readers' poll. In a cover letter accompanying promotional copies, Landau's request for commentaries implied that *Nacht* supported anti-Semitic tendencies.

On 31 July 1964 the Jewish historian and camp survivor Joseph Wulf submitted the first reply. In an unconcealed criticism of Landau's insinuations he responded: "I am at a loss to understand why the publication of such a novel should be damaging."[9] Hugh Elbot's letter of 10 August 1964 also indicated that Landau's objections were untenable. The editor of *Radio Free Europe* thought *Nacht* to be a document "of a more or less determinant nature of all peoples and eras."[10] In his letter dated the same day, Ernst G. Löwenthal regarded Landau's veiled implications with great displeasure. Although he was the first to admit the possibility that publication "under certain circumstances could be damaging," his very next sentence made it clear that he did not share Landau's reservations at all. He believed that, rather than producing an anti-Semitic effect, Landau's insinuations could at best refer to the "sometimes excessive elaboration on the intimate sphere."[11] Yet Löwenthal regarded such scenes as credible and necessary.

The first to fall in with Landau's reservations was B. Graubard who commented in detail on Landau's question. His letter of 14 August 1964 revealed that he did not want to be reminded of his own past as a survivor of a Polish ghetto. Therefore he preferred descriptions "of the moral solidarity" as demonstrated by the ghetto uprising in Warsaw and the resistance of the Oneg Schabbat Circle around Ringelblum.[12] Considered as a personal reaction, Graubard's view is understandable. Contrary to Hilsenrath, he was not capable of using "writing as therapy" to come to terms with his ghetto experience. For Graubard, coming to terms with his past was by way of reading, inducing a less therapeutic effect, since receiving information is more of a passive process than the active endeavor of generating information.

Readers of *Nacht* who have gone through similar horrors experience a mental and emotional repetition. Many Holocaust survivors choose selective oblivion over reminiscence, which is to say that events are not annulled but put in a new order, thus making it possible, at least for a period of time, to live with them.[13] Therefore, it seems appropriate to examine the novel's impact especially on readers who are not affected as Holocaust survivors. To be sure, Jewish criticism should have been taken into account—as did Landau—but having made the publication of *Nacht* solely contingent upon those voices did deprive the novel of its intended impact. *Nacht*, written in German, i.e. in the language of a majority of non-Jewish readers in Germany, is above all addressed to a public to whom the unimaginable reality of the ghetto is rendered imaginable by Hilsenrath's unsentimental presentation.

On 18 August 1964 Emil Jakob in Nuremberg confirmed: "Nobody can be expected to read this novel on demand; all the same, people should be informed of its content and read it after all."[14] Here, too, there was not the faintest suspicion of an anti-Semitic impact. The memo Landau submitted to the Kindlers on 20 August 1964 reflected an unsubstantiated bias based on the selected reviews he had solicited. Landau informed the publisher and his wife that Hermann Lewy, the editor-in-chief of the *Allgemeine Wochenzeitung der Juden in Deutschland* "was unable to pass any favorable judgment on *Nacht*." Either this was Landau's assumption, or else the editor-in-chief changed his mind when nearly a year later he penned a detailed review that gave Landau the lie.

On 28 August 1964 the management of the Dürer Haus in Bremen also supported the publication of *Nacht* as it demanded: "This [*Nacht*] must be made available to a large number of readers." Despite the positive reception,

Landau continued his negative information policy. One week after his first international notice, he informed Kindler anew: "The Jewish press unanimously rejects the book." Landau believed his opinion to be supported by Karl and Lilly Marx, the publishers of the Jewish newspaper *Allgemeine*, and Moses Lustig, the head editor of the *Münchner jüdische Nachrichten*. But again, not one of these three references was concerned with any anti-Semitic effect. Instead, they were offended by the blatant "sex" in *Nacht*, which, in their opinion and contrasting to Löwenthal's, rendered the novel "unbelievable." Apart from the fact that their criticism did not reflect the reception of *the* Jewish press, as Landau maintained, the Kindler publishing house had only internal knowledge of the reviews, none of which had been published. By 28 August 1964 no reviews on *Nacht* had been published. The first ones did not appear until the end of that year in *Siegener Zeitung* and *Freiheit und Recht*. The only negative review in a periodical of a Jewish community was published nine months later in Israel in *Jedioth Chadashoth*.

On 8 September 1964 Paul Arnsberg was the first one to endorse Landau's projected reception. Arnsberg vented his objections as follows: "To expose to the public these awful phenomena of decay, for which the persecutors are to be blamed, could lead to false conclusions." The same day, Marion Gid, correspondent of the *Forward* in New York and editor-in-chief of the *Neue jiddische Zeitung* in Munich, contradicted Landau's fears by pointing to the symbolic nature of the novel. Gid emphasized that Ranek's fate was neither specifically Jewish nor individual, rather he and all the other protagonists represented a victimized group of people. By referring to the name of each protagonist in the plural, Gid endowed all characters with their intended content and reflected the message imminent in the novel: *Nacht* reaches beyond the bounds of singularity.

Six months later Hilsenrath received another letter from Gid in which the latter deplored the fact that Kindler was not promoting any public interest in *Nacht*. As of 21 February 1965 Gid was unaware of any advertisement for or reviews of *Nacht*, and he recommended its translation into English: "Once your book finds an echo in America, its success in other countries, especially in Germany, is assured, irrespective of the misgivings certain people may have about it." Gid encouraged Hilsenrath to approach the New York resident Kurt Grossman, the former Secretary General of the German League for Human Rights. Gid hoped that Grossman, a winner of the Albert Schweizer Literature Prize and later chairman of the Austro-German Jewish League, could stimulate public interest in *Nacht*.

On 12 March 1965 Hermann Kesten, later president of the German PEN club, informed Hilsenrath that he had sent *Nacht* to Georg Ramseger, the editor of *Die Welt*, and he had also submitted a praising review to Kindler. On 24 March 1965 the freelance writer and author Peter Jokostra voiced his criticism of Landau's manipulative request in a letter to Kindler's public relations department: "In reading this novel I have not allowed myself to be influenced by any recommendations!" He informed Landau that he had contacted *Die Welt der Literatur*, the *Rheinische Post*, and the radio station *Süddeutscher Rundfunk* and had called their attention to this "necessary" novel. He had also requested the opportunity to write his own review with *echo der zeit*. Jokostra was the first to put *Nacht* in the context of the ghetto literature published hitherto and on a par with its most important testimonies by such authors as Leon Uris, Elie Wiesel, and Adolf Rudnicki. Landau, however, remained partial and ignored *Nacht*'s place within the larger framework of literary history.

Following Gid's advice, Hilsenrath wrote to Kurt Grossman and on 27 March 1965 he received an answer. Grossman's statement hardly differed from the rest of all the comments from the United States. Grossman, just as Marx, Gid, and Kesten, was convinced that *Nacht* deserved wider publicity. In their opinion, both content and language of the novel went beyond any known comparable literary contributions. Grossman was particularly awed: "I was most amazed at the fact that you left Germany at the age of twelve when you could not have had much schooling, and yet, you derived your language and gift of presentation from an intuition, both powerful and artistic."

Landau could no longer ignore these prominent voices from the United States. On 31 March he asked the *dpa* correspondent Gerty Agoston for a review of *Nacht*. In light of Landau's effort to obstruct the success of the book, his recommendation to Agoston is surprising: "This man has a story to tell and he can write."[15] Landau's letter to Hilsenrath on the following day suggests that basically he was not opposed to the publication of *Nacht*. Therefore, his negative propaganda must have been intended to collect rejections for the German market only.[16] Landau blamed the lack of sales of *Nacht* on the cultural and political situation in Germany. He avoided drawing any connection between poor sales figures and the low number of copies published. In fact, after 791 copies of the low edition of 1,200 books had been sold, Kindler withdrew the remaining copies from the market in mid-April 1965 as a bill submitted by Eugen Leer, Hilsenrath's lawyer, indicates.[17] Landau justified this measure of the publishing house by asserting that a latent anti-Semitic trend existed among the German population of the Federal Republic. By way of proof, he referred to a Federal Decree of the extension of the statute of limitation of Nazi crimes. This 'act of reparation' was passed only because of worldwide pressure on the *Bundestag*. It led to the establishment of diplomatic relations between Germany and Israel, which were not even initiated by Erhard, but rather by Ulbricht. According to Landau this political attitude reflected a tendency toward an unofficial anti-Semitism, springing from a growing right-wing radicalism. He argued that publishers and publishing houses working against such trends "quite frequently have to pay for their opposition with substantial financial losses."[18]

To be sure, a publishing house of the size of Kindler is hardly financially affected by the risk caused by the publication of a single controversial novel. The structure of Kindler's budget provides for losses to be balanced by profits from Kindler's large section of anthologies and reference works. Moreover, it is puzzling that Landau, a survivor of several concentration camps, allowed publishing houses to adopt a conformist attitude toward a tendency that had led to the Holocaust thirty years earlier. In addition, his reference to right-wing extremism as an explanation for 'unofficial' anti-Semitism in the 1960s is one-sided. His rejection of *Nacht* coincided with political controversies arising within the academic discussion of Fascism, evincing that anti-Semitism springs not only from right-wing radical thinking, but is also rooted in the Marxist tradition.

Among scholars of the political cultural situation in the Germany of the 1960s, Jack Zipes examined what prompted intellectuals from the left as well as from the right to differentiate between "good Germans" and "bad Germans" in order to cope with their past. "By dividing Germans in such a manner the Federal Republic could once again claim respect for Germany and Germans if it could only emphasize the 'good' and at least contain, if not extirpate, the 'bad.'"[19] Landau was following this model of thought when he used the same discrimination principle for Jews. To him, only the 'good,' upright Jews existed in Germany—Hitler's machinations had no influence on them whatsoever.

Against the backdrop of the philo-Semitic attitude favored in some conservative Jewish circles, Landau arrived at a political and cultural decision that does not seem to correspond with his personal view on *Nacht*. Had he rejected the novel outright, he would have hardly endeavored to engage prominent reviewers in New York. His recommendations, sent not only to Gerty Agoston and Kurt Grossman but also to the German Jewish journalists Paul Freedman and Samuel Gringhaus of the United Restitution Organization, confirm that his reservations applied to the place of publication, rather than to the novel itself.

On 2 April 1965 the *Börsenblatt für den deutschen Buchhandel* published Jokostra's letter to Landau.[20] In this issue as well as in the issue of 9 April 1965, a full-page advertisement of the Kindler publishing house appeared for *Nacht*. However, as can be taken from Landau's letter of 1 April 1965, the fate of the novel had already been sealed at that time and the advertisement served only *pro forma*. On 14 April 1965 Nina Raven–Kindler countered Hilsenrath's disappointment by rebuking him for not showing fitting gratitude: "I do not know if you realize that you would probably never have found a publishing house in Germany that would have published your book."[21] This patronizing assumption bears no grounds for an argument since Hilsenrath, upon the advice of Henry Marx, had not submitted his manuscript to anyone except Kindler. Subsequently, Raven–Kindler reiterated Landau's position, which, according to her statement, reflected not only her own and her husband's view, but was also shared by Geert Falkenberg. By including the chief editor, Raven–Kindler gave the impression that the management of the publishing house had unanimously backed the decision to withdraw the book.

Bearing Falkenberg's testimony in mind, in which he recommended the novel highly, there is no evidence of his complicity in the subsequent countertrend in the Kindler publishing house. Raven–Kindler's mention of Falkenberg served her own purpose: She argued that both Falkenberg and Landau belonged to the same group of victims as Hilsenrath. Thus she implied that Hilsenrath, by not agreeing with Landau and allegedly Falkenberg, would stand outside their union of suffering. Placing Hilsenrath beyond the pale enabled Raven–Kindler to undermine his objections. Her arguments aimed at indebting Hilsenrath to the publishing house, causing him to feel guilty for his lack of gratitude, and demonstrating her own positive attitude toward the Nazi victims beyond a shadow of a doubt. Her deliberations culminated in the reproach that publishers could not be blamed if a book did not turn out a bestseller: "As a publisher one is, of course, bound to hear and bear this again and again." Since Kindler never gave the novel a chance to reach readers in any number, this accusation turns the perpetrators into the victims.

On 27 April 1965 Alfred Joachim Fischer was the last to reply to Landau's request. The journalist and foreign correspondent in Canada described *Nacht* as "a masterpiece of literature and humanity." However, he declined to review the novel for the general public, "albeit with a heavy heart." In his opinion, "the average German was still far from being mature enough for this material."[22] Fischer feared that the novel's "realistic representation" would not create sympathy, but rather anti-Semitic reactions. Contrary to the works of Friedrich Torberg, Stephan Hermlin, or Bruno Apitz, *Nacht* lacks any positive Jewish or socialist hero; nor are there any potential role models as in Jurek Becker's *Jakob der Lügner*, Albrecht Goes's *Das Brandopfer*, or Alfred Andersch's *Efraim*. Instead of confronting the heroes with criminals, Hilsenrath describes the reproduction of exploitative and oppressive Nazi tactics among the victims. Consequently, Graubard commented: "I am afraid that it [Hilsenrath's outlook] emanates from the spirit of the well-meaning, but naive Hannah Arendt."[23] Both Graubard and Fischer objected to the presentation of a ghetto that reflected the success of a totalitarian system celebrating its greatest triumph when duplicated by the oppressed in their conduct toward one another.[24] Ghetto survivors such as Gerty Spies and Jurek Becker deliberately avoided the presentation of moral corruption. Consequently, Friedrich Torberg, who presented a Nazi stool pigeon in *Hier bin ich mein Vater*, met with sharp criticism.

Hilserath's anti-heroes pose a problem to those Germans who think that the earlier hatred for Jews can now be compensated with a special love for them, and thereby continue to allocate to them the slot of "the other."[25]

Hilsenrath is convinced that it is out of keeping with the new Semitophile pattern in Germany "to show Jews as human beings and to not glorify them."[26] Gid expressed himself similarly: "Maybe—it is just an assumption—the Kindler Verlag has after all become afraid of its previous courage to publish your book and took to heart the opinion of a certain prominent Jewish leader in Germany who has advised against its publication on the grounds that it may show Jews in an unfavorable light (which is, of course, sheer idiocy and a result of an acute inferiority complex")."[27] Hilsenrath's portrayal of the past was therefore not only "too controversial for the Teutonic readership"—as the *Neue Zürcher Zeitung* put it[28]—it was also too controversial for some members of the Jewish community in Germany.

With his cover letter accompanying the review copies of *Nacht* Landau prevented any unbiased reading and at the same time he convinced the publishing house "that such a book must be published in Germany."[29] By misrepresentation, i.e. that German Jewish critics unanimously rejected *Nacht*, Landau not only convinced semitophile circles, but also enabled covert anti-Semites to do likewise. Their joining opinions reveals a continuity of literary thought that from 1941 onward remained unchanged for twenty years when Bertolt Brecht wrote in his *Anmerkungen zum aufhaltsamen Aufstieg des Arturo Ui*: "You generally hear nowadays that it is inadmissable and pointless to ridicule capital political criminals, living or dead. Even the common herd, we hear, would be touchy on this point, not only because it was involved in those crimes, but also because those left in the ruins found nothing to laugh about."[30] Indeed, "those who are left," and reject *Nacht*, do so because its portrayal of reality is out of step with their own conception of *the* Jew. Their ideas are complied with in literary works where: "the old cliché is covered up from shame or by new images resulting from the desperate attempt to find an alternative, distorting any real dialogue with the Jewish experience."[31]

The fate of *Nacht* proved the poignancy of Brecht's commentary when Hilsenrath reflected accordingly: "But Kindler was afraid to publish the book precisely because it broke a taboo, and therefore he had it disappear."[32] That taboo was characteristic of the German way of dealing with the past and explains why Hilsenrath was rejected in Germany, but praised overseas. German Jews living abroad were not subjected to the pressures of a society directly in their debt, trying to forget its guilt by pointing to historical justifications, inventing new heroes, or stereotypically glorifying the Jews. Since such pressures hardly existed abroad, there was little necessity to match German heroes with Jewish heroes. The 30,000 or so Jews in Germany, comprising less than 0.1 percent of its population, form a relatively small minority by comparison with the 6,000,000 Jews in the United States or 500,000 in France. Arising from the history of the Third Reich, being a German national of Jewish descent presents a conflict unknown to an American Jew, for example. In Germany, Jews are facing the problem of reestablishing their identity within a society in which hatred of foreigners has either replaced the hatred of Jews or coexists with it in equal intensity. Günter Wallraff's studies reveal that latent racism is concentrated on groups that have remained culturally unintegrated. As they appear ethnically different they become a target of the public's attention.[33] Nowadays, the Jewish minority of Germany consists mainly of East Europeans cast ashore there in the wake of the Holocaust. According to Sander Gilman, that minority tolerates the literary concept of "the exemplary Jew" because it takes a reserved stand toward issues of its own in order to avoid confrontation.[34] In contrast, American Jewry forms a union that rests upon "the acknowledgment of pluralism within their creative groups."[35]

German reviewers unafraid of the allegedly anti-Semitic effect of *Nacht* regarded the novel as a portrait of the battle for survival. "Morals laws no longer count and human beings turn into animals," observed Bernd Lubowski.[36] That battle, appropriately apostrophized by Lubowski as "one against all and everybody against his neighbor," is, as Walter Herzog puts it, "no longer a question of Jew or Gentile."[37] "Anti-Semitism as a Literary Reproach," the title Edwin Hartl chose for his review, conceives of and mirrors *Nacht* in only a limited way.[38] Rather, the novel addresses observations regarding the psyche of the individual within a group mercilessly hunted and persecuted for racist, religious, or political reasons. Based upon these farther-reaching implications of *Nacht*, Gid noted: "The book does not read like an autobiographical work.... It is a great book ... not only about the Holocaust, but in general."[39] He saw in Prokow a symbolic ghetto, not to be found on any map, a place of which its author claims: "Its ruins could be anywhere and its people could live anywhere."[40]

Most reviews on the first edition of *Nacht* contained similar observations, proving how unfounded Kindler's fears were and the conjectures of those pulling the strings to get the book pulped. Despite, or perhaps because of, his renunciation of all sentimental pathos, as pointed out by critics time and again, Hilsenrath was able to move his readers deeply. This so baffled most of his reviewers that they focused on assembling and scrutinizing a variety of criteria that they believed to hold the answer to the question of how *Nacht* could produce such an effect. Most of them revealed the dilemma in which their literary yardstick of conventional categories and classifications turned out to be a hackneyed cliché against the backdrop of *Nacht*. The majority of those reviews show an absence of any weighing up of the strengths and weaknesses of the novel; instead, one was either for or against *Nacht*.

NOTES

1. Edgar Hilsenrath, *Nacht* (Munich: Kindler, 1964).
2. Hubert Nachtsheim, "Buch der Woche. Edgar Hilsenrath: *Nacht*," *Kölnische*

*Rundschau* (26 September 1965): "Sensitive readers may feel sick when reading certain passages." (Translations by editor.)

3. Peter Wapnewski, "Der neunte Autorscooter," *Second Program, German Television* 1978. Hilsenrath described in detail in a letter to me and during the interview with Peter Wapnewski the pressures and politics that forced him to agree to this preface.

4. B. Graubard, Letter to Ernest Landau, Munich, 14 August 1964.

5. Marion Gid, "Edgar Hilsenrath's *Nacht.*" Forward, New York, 17 November 1964.

6. Confusion with Elie Wiesel's novel entitled *Nacht* (New York: Avon, 1969) was to occur later anyway.

7. Hans-Geert Falkenberg, Letter to Hilsenrath, Munich, 9 December 1963.

8. Henry Marx, Letter to Helmut Kindler, New York, 1 March 1964.

9. Letter to Ernest Landau, Berlin, 4 August 1964.

10. Hugh G. Elbot, Letter to Ernest Landau, Munich, 10 August 1964.

11. Ernst G. Löwenthal, Letter to Ernest Landau, Frankfurt am Main, 10 July 1964.

12. B. Graubard, Letter to Ernest Landau, Munich, 14 August 1964. Although Graubard did not mention any specific titles, his argument points toward works such as Philip Friedman's *Jewish Resistance to Nazism*, Stanislaw Kohn's *The Treblinka Revolt*, Zvi Goldfarb's *Hehalutz Resistance in Hungary*, and Rachel Auerbach's *The Jewish Uprising in Warsaw.*

13. Although Jean Améry, Jerzy Kosinski, and Paul Celan survived the Holocaust, they found life afterward more difficult than their survival during the Third Reich and eventually committed suicide.

14. Emil Jakob, Letter to Kindler, Nuremberg, 18 August 1964.

15. Ernest Landau, Letter to Gerty Agoston, Munich, 31 March 1965.

16. Similarly, Austrian presses, publishers, and the cultural establishment tend to suppress the publication of books on the Holocaust as well as Jewish history, yet they seek outlets for them in the United States.

17. Louisa Leer, Letter to Edgar Hilsenrath, Munich, 3 March 1968.

18. Ernest Landau, Letter to Edgar Hilsenrath, Munich, 1 April 1965.

19. Jack Zipes, "The Vicissitudes of Being Jewish in West Germany," *Germans and Jews Since the Holocaust. The Changing Situation in West Germany*, ed. Jack Zipes and Anson Rabinbach (New York: Homes & Meier, 1986), p. 32.

20. Peter Jokostra, "Brief an Landau." *Börsenblatt für den deutschen Buchhandel* (2 April 1965).

21. Nina Raven–Kindler, Letter to Hilsenrath, Munich, 4 April 1965.

22. Alfred Joachim Fischer, Letter to Hilsenrath, Montreal, 27 April 1965.

23. B. Graubard, Letter to Ernest Landau, Munich, 14 August 1964.

24. Hannah Arendt, *The Origins of Totalitarianism* (New York: Harcourt & Brace, 1973), p. 45.

25. Cf. Wolfgang Paulsen, "Theodor Fontane the Philosemitic Antisemite," *Leo Baeck Yearbook* 26 (1981), pp. 303–322.

26. Marianne Wagner, "Edgar Hilsenrath," *Studiowelle Saar* (18 April 1978, 2:30 p.m.).

27. Marion Gid, Letter to Hilsenrath, Munich, 21 February 1965.

28. Alfred Starkmann, "Scherz mit dem Entsetzen und die Lesegewohnheiten der Briten. Literaturbrief aus London," *Neue Zürcher Zeitung* (24 February 1976).

29. Uwe Naumann, "Zwischen Tränen und Gelächter. Ein Gespräch über Satire

und Faschismus," *Jahrbuch für antifaschistische Literatur und Kunst. Sammlung I* (Frankfurt am Main: Röderberg, 1978), pp. 133–146.

30. Bertolt Brecht, *Gesammelte Werke in 20 Bänden* XVII (Frankfurt: Suhrkamp, 1974), p. 1176.

31. Christiane Schmelzkopf, "Zur Gestaltung jüdischer Figuren in der deutschsprachigen Literatur nach 1945," *Juden und Judentum in der Literatur*, ed. Herbert A. Strauss and Christhard Hoffmann (Munich: dtv, 1985), p. 279.

32. Andreas W. Mytze, "Präzedenzfall der deutschen Literatur. Interview mit dem Schriftsteller Edgar Hilsenrath," *Tagesspiegel* (31 August 1977).

33. Günter Walraff, *Ganz unten: mit einer Dokumentation der Folgen* (Cologne: Kiepenheuer & Witsch, 1988). Anti-Semitic and Nazi hate jargon are currently used to denote foreign workers as "subhumans," such as the terms *Kanake*, which originally applied to deserted USSR soldiers.

34. Sander Gilman, "Jüdische Literaten und deutsche Literatur: Antisemitismus und die verborgene Sprache der Juden am Beispiel von Jurek Becker und Edgar Hilsenrath," *Zeitschrift für deutsche Philologie* 107 (1988), p. 272.

35. Leo Trepp, *Die Juden, Volk, Geschichte, Religion* (Reinbeck: Rowohlt, 1987), p. 242.

36. Bernd Lubowski, "Schicksale im Getto: Edgar Hilsenraths Roman *Nacht*," *Berliner Morgenpost* (7 September 1978).

37. Walter Herzog, "In einer Ruinenstadt am Dnjestr," *Mühlheimer Tageblatt* (11 May 1965).

38. Edwin Hartl, "Antisemitismus als literarischer Vorwurf," *Salzburger Nachrichten* (29 May 1965).

39. Marion Gid, "Edgar Hilsenrath's *Nacht*," *Forward* (17 November 1964 (New York)).

40. Edgar Hilsenrath, Cover Text, *Nacht* (Munich: Kindler, 1964).

# The Case of Jakob Littner: Authors, Publishers, and Jewish History in Unified Germany

Dagmar C. G. Lorenz

Soon after Athenäum Publishers and their Jewish branch went out of business, Suhrkamp founded a Jewish publishing company. Suhrkamp and the media did not indicate that Athenäum's Jewish branch was the immediate predecessor of the Jüdischer Verlag im Hause Suhrkamp, but they proclaimed a direct link between the first German Jewish publishing house, the Jüdischer Verlag, founded by Martin Buber, Chaim Weizmann et al. in 1902, as if Athenäum's Jewish publishing house had never existed.

It is preposterous to compare Buber's enterprise with the new Suhrkamp branch. Buber created an autonomous forum for Jewish writers to express their concerns. After *Kristallnacht* the Nazis eliminated all Jewish publishers on German territory. Claiming the legacy of Buber's company for the new Suhrkamp branch means ignoring the years between 1938 and 1945 when Jewish presses were outlawed in Germany. The failure to acknowledge the hiatus created by the Holocaust constitutes historical revisionism.

Since the Nuremberg Laws Germany's Jewish population was increasingly ghettoized. For their cultural needs they depended on designated Jewish publishers, as well as on the activities of the Jewish *Kultusgemeinden*. Despite tight supervision by the Nazis, Jewish organizations developed a great variety of cultural programs. Their activities were whenever possible resumed in ghettos and KZs such as Theresienstadt.[1]

At the turn of the century creating a publishing house to articulate Jewish concerns had been an expression of self-confidence. During the 'Third Reich' the Nazis appropriated the Jewish media to facilitate segregation. Jewish authors had to publish in 'Jewish' presses; 'Jewish' presses were not allowed to print works by non-Jews. To the Germans classified as 'Jewish,' 'German' journals or books were off-limits, and so-called Aryans were not allowed to purchase books by Jews.[2] Despite the restrictions imposed on the Jewish communities, their achievements must not be underrated. The authors whose works were accessible to the Jewish public until November of 1938 belonged to the German intellectual elite—Alfred Döblin, Martin Buber, Else Lasker-Schüler, Gertrud Kolmar, Nelly Sachs, and Gershom Scholem, to name only a few.

Athenäum's Jewish publishing company reflected the newly awakened interest in German Jewish culture during the 1970s. At the same time it was sensitive to the fact that there were Jewish communities in post-Holocaust Germany and that German Jewish intellectuals continued to play a decisive role. Suhrkamp's Jewish branch, on the other hand, made a surprising debut with a novel by Wolfgang Koeppen, which had already been published in 1948 in Munich by Herbert Kluger as the memoir of Jakob Littner, *Aufzeichnungen aus einem Erdloch* [Notes from a Hole in the Ground].

From a literary point of view the work does not come close to the achievements of the authors mentioned above, nor to those of many contemporary Jewish writers. *Aufzeichnungen* does not even constitute a contribution to German Jewish literature. As stated on the dust jacket, at the age of eighty-five Wolfgang Koeppen finally disclosed his authorship of the supposed Holocaust account. According to several reviewers Koeppen was inspired by the founding of Suhrkamp's Jewish branch to reveal that not Littner, but he himself had written this hard-to-classify book.

The first titles in a series or press are programmatic. Thus Suhrkamp's Jewish publishing house ignored contemporary Jewish authors and current issues from the outset. Since German literature and media have traditionally portrayed Jews and Jewish culture in antagonistic terms without factual knowledge, it would be the mission of a Jewish publishing house to promulgate Jewish literature and to keep the Jewish heritage alive. This mission is undermined when in the framework of a Jewish press the discussion of Jewish identity and the Holocaust experience is relegated to a non-Jewish author, as is the case in *Aufzeichnungen*. To this day the stereotypes of anti-Semitic literature are reproduced in the works of German writers.[3] Jewish authors after 1945 were no more able to communicate their assessment of the Nazi past and of their precarious position in Germany and Austria to the mainstream than their predecessors had been in combatting anti-Semitism.

There are many German Jewish writers whose works would have provided a fitting introduction to a German Jewish publishing house. The often-repeated notion that the destruction of German Jewish culture by the Nazis was total—as total as the 'total war'—was never more than a catch phrase. It is true that under Nazi rule Jewish authors were forbidden to publish, but many of them wrote in secret. Outside of Germany exile authors published with international presses even after the destruction of their cultural network in Europe. After World War II both groups published in German, be it in their countries of exile, be it in the new German states, Austria, or Switzerland. Many younger people had begun to write as a reaction to persecution and mass murder and entered the literary scene after 1945.[4]

In post-Holocaust Germany, the topic of German Jewish identity was taboo, but there can be no question about the continuity of German Jewish literary traditions. To be sure, literature by Jewish authors in the German language does not conform with any narrow definition of German literature.[5] Their works form a multicultural discourse in German that transcends the boundaries of a national literature.

Works by authors such as Grete Weil, Edgar Hilsenrath, Jean Améry, Gerty Spies, Jurek Becker, Peter Edel, or Ruth Klüger, who were directly affected by the Holocaust, but also books by younger writers who, like Henryk Broder, Jeanette Lander, Lea Fleischmann, Rahel Hutmacher, Ruth Beckermann, Barbara Honigmann, and Wolf Biermann, have experienced the longterm effects of the genocide, belong in the context of a Jewish publishing company. The novel by a non-Jewish author, no matter how much he tried to immerse himself into the "Jewish fate," does not. Assigning Koeppen's *Aufzeichnungen* such a prominent position places Suhrkamp's Jewish branch outside of the tradition of German Jewish publishers. Also its next titles, a specialized Scholem edition and the planned edition of Gertrud Kolmar's *Susanna*, bypass modern German Jewish literature.

The genesis of Koeppen's novel poses an even more serious problem. The cover text cannot conceal that the work was a forgery, even though it uses the euphemistic term "pseudonym" to express the fact that Koeppen represented his novel as someone else's autobiography.[6] Koeppen's late 'revelation' is as ambiguous as the publication history and the book itself. "Pseudonym" suggests that Littner and Koeppen are identical and relegates the historical Littner to a position of nonexistence.

The quality of Koeppen's novel is not the topic of this article—it is a readable book because, as is to be expected, it is free of the inhibitions and the horrifying details of concentration camp accounts and novels by Holocaust survivors, for example Peter Edel's *Schwester der Nacht* [Sister of the Night] (1947), Edgar Hilsenrath's *Nacht* [Night], Bruno Apitz's *Nackt unter Wölfen* [Naked among Wolves], and Gerty Spies's or Rahel Behrend's memoirs.[7]

Holocaust literature by Jewish authors was controversial and unpopular with the German public—the majority of the existing memoirs never left the archives. Some were published privately or by small presses. They soon disappeared from the market although they contribute more to the understanding of German Jewry and the Holocaust than the more or less sympathetic Holocaust fiction by non-Jews.[8] The latter still constructs Jewish fantasy characters from the traditional stereotypes, which accommodate the public's expectations in accordance with the political trends of the time. Koeppen's novel is no exception.

*Aufzeichnungen* addressed a non-Jewish audience that preferred Holocaust stories by Christian authors such as Luise Rinser, Albrecht Goes, or Elisabeth Langgässer over the literature and documentaries written by Jews. Unlike his obscure model, Koeppen's Holocaust survivor is in control of his language—so much so, that the real Littner protested against *Aufzeichnungen*. But he was in New York and unable to affect the way in which Koeppen represented him.

The scanty introduction on the dust cover of *Jakob Littners Aufzeichnungen* formed the basis for the reviews, which began to appear in January 1992. This media discourse was symptomatic of the way in which post-unification Germany deals with her history. The following analysis of representative reviews reveals why Koeppen and his publisher were safe in assuming that the time was ripe to resurrect a book that had been unsuccessful under the name of a Jewish author who was now dead.

The media discourse largely ignored the controversial aspects of Koeppen's novel. An early review in *Forum Politik-Unterricht*, for example, does not even mention that *Aufzeichnungen* was the first title of Suhrkamp's new Jewish branch.[9] The novel is praised as a literary historical document of the highest quality without asking on what basis and for whom Koeppen constructs history. Suhrkamp's statement that Littner was Koeppen's pen name goes unquestioned. A few days later a review in *Buch Journal* discusses Littner as a historical person. On the basis of the novel's history the reviewer, fjg, addresses the problem of authorship. fjg is not critical of the fact that *Aufzeichnungen* was initially published as Littner's memoir, but s/he does correct the impression that Littner was "a German and a Jew" as is asserted by the majority of the critics who applied insights gleaned from prominent German Jewish autobiographies such as Jakob Wassermann's *Mein Weg als Deutscher und Jude* [My Life as German and Jew] to Littner. Littner, fjg explains, was born in Budapest in 1883, became a Polish citizen after the demise of the Austro-Hungarian Empire. At the age of twenty-eight he, his wife, and his daughter moved to Munich. Clearly the point of view of an immigrant who was doubly marginalized as a foreigner is not that of a German Jew.[10] Littner's inability as a writer is not necessarily the result of the Holocaust trauma, as numerous critics claim. The 'Case Littner' does not lend itself to substantiating one of the favorite concepts of German Holocaust criticism, namely that the Nazi victims were incapable of articulating their experiences in a literary form. More likely it was Littner's lack of experience as a writer and his possibly less than perfect command of German that prevented him from becoming an author.

The edifying account of the Suhrkamp dust jacket is repeated by fjg, who maintains that Koeppen spontaneously volunteered to take charge of Littner's story, which Kluger was eager to publish. According to this version of the background history, Koeppen fulfilled a Holocaust survivor's wish of having a professional author write and publish his story. If one accepts this interpretation, Koeppen is more than redeemed because he gave a voice to someone who otherwise would have been condemned to silence.[11]

In keeping with this interpretation, Florian Illies smoothes over the genesis of *Aufzeichnungen* in "Eine kleine literarische Sensation" [A Small Literary Sensation]. Declaring Littner, the intended Nazi victim, incapable of self-expression was easy enough, since the ongoing debate focused on the sensational discovery of the author and the significance of *Aufzeichnungen* in the context of Koeppen's work. Illies concurs with a statement made by Siegfried Unseld: "From now on Koeppen's novel trilogy, written in the 1950s, and his prose text 'Youth' (1976) will have to be evaluated differently."[12] The Swiss critic Urs Bugmann expanded this theme further in "'Über mein Dasein wurde nun nach der Nummer verfügt'" [My Existence Was now Run according to a Number]. To his unproblematic plot summary he adds reflections about the nature of memory in *Aufzeichnungen* and Koeppen's autobiographical account *Es war einmal in Masuren* [Once Upon a Time in Masuria].[13] Hans Jansen's later review comes closer to the dilemma of *Aufzeichnungen* by asking specific questions about the role of the "nameless Jew" such as: "Who is Jakob Littner? He is no other than Wolfgang Koeppen." But also here the critical attempt ends in formulaic statements, for instance: "Koeppen wrote an account of terror." Despite his reservations Jansen recommends the book as required reading in schools.[14]

In "Biedermänner und Bestien," published a few days later in *General-Anzeiger*, Marion Löhndorf tried to come to terms with the relevance of *Aufzeichnungen* within the framework of Suhrkamp's Jewish branch, taking the discourse begun by fjg and Illies as the point of departure. Löhndorf claims that the novel was based on Littner's "authentic biography," that is, documents written by Littner, which Koeppen had somehow had at his disposal.[15] Portraying Suhrkamp's new enterprise as the direct successor of Buber's Jüdischer Verlag whose "reestablishment" (*Neugründung*) prompted Koeppen to disclose his authorship, Löhndorf tries to steer clear of disharmony. In an attempt to explain why Suhrkamp's Jewish publishing company differs so radically from its supposed precursor, she argues that the role of a Jewish publisher in post-Holocaust Germany is by necessity different from that of the original *Jüdischer Verlag*. This assessment can hardly be disputed, because of the size and role of the Jewish communities in post-Holocaust Germany and Austria.

Numerous later reviewers accepted Löhndorf's speculation that the new edition of *Aufzeichnungen*, Koeppen's late revelation, and the foundation of the Jewish publishing company, were acts of restitution. Löhndorf quotes Unseld: "Today—after the destruction of European Jewry by Germans—the situation of the Jewish publishing company has undergone a basic change. Aware of what has happened, the company considers as its mission to provide a forum for the religious, political, social and artistic life of the Jews." In his statement Unseld assumes the posture of a protector and spokesman for German Jews, a role into which many critics have cast Koeppen. Indeed, the pattern underlying Koeppen's book corresponds with the structures of its publishing company. Littner's story as retold by Koeppen is a 'Jewish' story with neither a Jewish author nor a Jewish character. The Jüdischer Verlag im Hause Suhrkamp is a 'Jewish' publishing house without Jews. Its director, Thomas Sparr, like Unseld, is neither Jewish nor a scholar of Judaica. Under their direction the legacy of Germany's Jewish past is transformed into a gentrified museum culture.

Less ambitious reviews such as Holger Schlodder's "Ein Geheimnis wird gelüftet" [A Secret is Revealed] and Martin Meyer's "Todesspirale" [Death Spiral] highlight formal aspects and discuss aesthetic issues in the stock terminology of journalistic literary criticism.[16] Schlodder mentions stylistic shortcomings only to qualify them by an allusion to the "Winter of Hunger 1946/7" when *Aufzeichnungen* was written. He goes on to praise Koeppen's sensitive, unsentimental diction, appropriate to a subject that touches on the "limits of language." Schlodder is primarily interested in Koeppen's book as a historical document. He is so surprised that in 1946 Germans could have already known "what had happened" that he forgets that Koeppen merely pretends to be an eyewitness.

Also Schlodder intimates that Koeppen's disclosure was prompted by the transformation of *the* Jewish publishing company into a branch of Suhrkamp. Why, one may ask, did the Suhrkamp author Koeppen and his publisher insist on placing *Aufzeichnungen* into an ostensibly Jewish press? Was the announcement of Koeppen's identity intended to right an earlier wrong? Or did Unseld and perhaps Koeppen not find a single work by a Jewish author that they considered a fitting literary introduction for the Jüdischer Verlag?

Andreas Thiemann criticizes the sensationalism of Unseld's revelation and mentions Littner's protest in his generally positive article, "Haß und Rache führen zu nichts. Beklemmende Zeugnisse über den Holocaust" [Hatred and Revenge Lead to Nothing. Uncomfortable Documents about the Holocaust]: "Littner was ultimately deeply disappointed by the novel about his Jewish fate; he felt misrepresented."[17] In the end, however, Thiemann concedes that from today's perspective Littner's objections are "beside the point" and asserts that the "documentation" of the "incomprehensible historical tragedy" and Koeppen's profound understanding of the "fate of Jewish victims under National Socialism" are the pivotal aspects of the "diary-like" novel. Thiemann does not even question Koeppen's ability to write in a "diary-like" manner about the life of a man whom he knew only from hearsay.

Werner Thuswaldner seems convinced of the validity of the call for mutual forgiveness on the part of Koeppen's Littner and maintains that Koeppen devoted himself selflessly to a greater mission.[18] Thuswaldner alleges that it is possible for a German author to assimilate the suffering of a Jew through the process of writing to such a degree that his identity and that of the former victim merge. Hence he does not question Koeppen's right to appropriate Littner's story, and even praises it as a strategy by which a German author contributed to the lessening of the German collective guilt.

*Aufzeichnungen* was rarely discussed in the context of international Holocaust literature as is suggested by Peter Jokostra, who places the work into a broader context by mentioning Jean Francois's *Treblinka* (1966) and Edgar Hilsenrath's *Nacht*. In contrast to Jokostra's enthusiastic review of *Nacht* (1965) and his repeated support for Hilsenrath, this radio review of *Aufzeichnungen* appears remarkably detached.[19] Jokostra explains the novel's failure to affect him emotionally by the fact that "as literary topics pogrom and Holocaust are exhausted."

On 26 March 1992 *Aufzeichnungen* climbed to the second place of the list of outstanding books of the press of Upper Hessia (*Oberhessische Presse*). At this time the reviews became more detailed and critical. In "Das Ghetto hieß Zbaraz, Galizien" [The Ghetto Was Called Zbaraz, Galicia] Herbert Wiesner contrasts Koeppen's underhandedness with the decision of the concentration camp survivor Eugen Kogon to publish his documentation of Nazi extermination politics under his own name.[20] By this contrast Wiesner criticizes Koeppen's duplicity—rather than appropriating someone else's story, he could have told his, that of a deserter who went into hiding toward the end of the war. Wiesner stresses that Kogon rejected anonymity for moral reasons.[21] As Wiesner suggests, Koeppen seems to have been ashamed to publish *Aufzeichnungen* as his own work, and the "non-Jew who was no victim in the sense that Littner was" may have had reason to be ashamed. Wiesner questions Koeppen's integrity even more directly: "When listing his previous publishers Koeppen mentions Henry Goverts as his rediscoverer 'after Hitler.' He repressed Herbert Kluger, and it is incorrect when he suggests today that Kluger became a publisher because of Littner's account."

He also criticizes the lack of documentation provided by Koeppen. He intimates that Koeppen suppressed source materials and that Koeppen used documents made available to him by his publisher Kluger. However, also this analysis breaks off when it threatens to compromise Koeppen and his publisher. In a reversal of his previous position, Wiesner proclaims Koeppen's honesty, citing passages where Koeppen uses a third-person narrator. However, this narrative distance is the exception in the 150-page-long novel in the course of which the author's identity is nowhere spelled out.

Wiesner considers *Aufzeichnungen* as paradigmatic of the production and reception of German Holocaust literature. Rejecting Yoram Karniuk's assertion that German authors did not confront the Holocaust, he indicts the German public for its unwillingness to confront the past. According to Wiesner, "unliterary" accounts like *Aufzeichnungen* and the extensive anti-Semitism scholarship are a body of literature that the public refused to take notice of. However, he does not differentiate between Koeppen's bogus memoir and actual Holocaust documentaries. Still, his point is well taken when he criticizes the traditional genre categories, which exclude Holocaust texts from literary debates. Wiesner is correct in suspecting that *Aufzeichungen* suffered from the fact that its supposed author was a "nobody," a "'mere' victim"—also the Berlin edition of 1985 under Littner's name remained obscure. In the guise of a Jewish memoir *Aufzeichnungen* was ignored.

The detailed analysis by Thomas Meyer, published about four months after the first reviews, restates the major themes of the previous media discourse, for example the justification of the use of Littner's name as a strategy to give the novel the appearance of a historical account and the notion that the book served the purpose to inform the public about the reality of the Holocaust at a time when the Warsaw Ghetto, Auschwitz, and Bergen-Belsen were unfamiliar to the public. Like other critics Meyer seems ignorant of the fact that as early as 1933 atrocities were known to be committed in Nazi concentration camps[23] and that immediately after 1945, prior to *Aufzeichnungen*, literature by Jewish survivors about the KZs and the Holocaust had already appeared, for example Peter Edel's Auschwitz novel *Schwester der Nacht* [Sisters of the Night] (1947), the memoir *Teufel und Verdammte* [Devils and the Damned] by Benedikt Kautsky, *Zeit ohne Gnade* [Time without Pardon] by Rudolf Kalmar (1946), and the diary-like analysis of the Nazi jargon by the philologist Victor Klemperer, *LTI* (1946). Eugen Kogon's documentation *Der SS-Staat* [The SS-State] appeared as early as 1946.[24] One of the most informative studies on the 'Third Reich,' *Behemot. The Structure and Practice of National Socialism* by Raul Hilberg's teacher Franz Neumann, had been published in the United States as early as 1942.

The relationship between Littner and Koeppen gave rise to the most bizarre speculations, because most critics failed to address the attitude of Koeppen and his publishers vis-à-vis Littner. Andreas Müller states in "Eine Überlebensgeschichte" [A Survival Story]: "In all likelihood it was his regard for Littner's feat of survival that caused Wolfgang Koeppen to attribute this book to him."[25] Müller considers Littner's 'story' as the real sensation. Pointing out that Koeppen spent the last months of World War II hidden in a basement, he suggests a parallel between the two men's fates. As if this analogy could solve the authorship problem, Müller compares the persecuted Jew with the German deserter, intimating that Koeppen possesses the qualifications to be a generic representative of all Nazi victims, no matter if they were Jews or marginalized non-Jews, because he had to hide in order to avoid combat. To make his generalizations work, Müller adds epic detail to his account.

From the start critics were fascinated by the extraordinary story of a Jew who asked a German author to become his ghostwriter for an honorarium of two Care packages per month. Most reviewers treated this 'deal' as proof that Littner had 'sold' his story to Koeppen. In a peculiar reversal of facts, they overlooked that customarily not the resource person but those who reap the benefits—Koeppen and his publishers—pay the honorarium.

Schlodder may have inspired Müller to speculate that Koeppen used "notes taken by his publisher," but "because he respected this human being [Littner] he was painstakingly careful not to turn this story into a work of art" (Müller). He maintains that Koeppen wrote in a purposely simple style to create the impression of authenticity—as if Holocaust survivors were necessarily bad writers. Ultimately Müller himself is taken in by Koeppen's strategies and discusses Koeppen's Littner as one would a factual self-portrait. He is particularly impressed by the way in which Koeppen constructed Jewish identity.

However, the Jakob Littner created by Koeppen does not sound Jewish at all when he proclaims: "What does that mean: the situation of the Jews? I do not feel a part to a special and foreign group within the German people." It seems unlikely that a man who was neither a German by birth nor the holder of a German passport, a man who witnessed the radicalization of the German public since World War I and was persecuted as a Jew and foreigner, would have gone to such length to deny his Jewishness. Müller, in agreement with Koeppen's fantasy of how someone in Littner's situation feels and thinks, states: "Koeppen deserves the credit for having preserved this life, this agony. ...As Wolfgang Koeppen wrote in the preface, he made the story about a German Jew's suffering his own story. It seems impossible to come any closer to this German Jew, to do his suffering greater justice."

Using a motif from Wiesner, Ernest Wichner investigates the history of *Aufzeichnungen* in "Vielleicht aus Schamgefühl verschwiegen?" [Possibly not Mentioned Out of Shame?].[26] He reports that Koeppen was already suspected of being the author of *Aufzeichnungen* when it was reprinted by Kupfergraben in 1985.[27] Koeppen denied ever using a pseudonym and the matter was dropped. Passing over Littner's disapproval, Wichner elaborates on a theme from Thuswaldner, namely *Aufzeichnungen* represents a "gesture of personal restitution." He, too, praises Koeppen for having appropriated "the identity of those victims ... on whom the Germans inflicted the greatest suffering" as early as 1947, particularly since at that time making such an identification was probably not easy for Koeppen.

Bernhard Fetz identifies a common denominator between the Holocaust survivor and his 'ghostwriter' in "Berichte aus der Hölle" [Reports from Hell]: On the basis of the biographical parallels between Koeppen and Littner, which Müller established three weeks earlier, he claims that neither one of the two men was a hero—Littner was deported and Koeppen did not want to return to the war.[28] Like Bruno Bettelheim in his controversial study on Anne Frank's family, Fetz implicitly blames the victims of the Holocaust for having been victimized.[29] Unlike the critics who treat *Aufzeichnungen* as a documentary, Fetz emphasizes its fictional character, but questions if Koeppen's is a novel in view of its genesis. Fetz's review ends with highest praise for this "unique literary document" and "story of human suffering paradigmatic for this century."

Hans Bertram Bock's unabashed criticism of Koeppen's "ghostwriter activity" is based on a right-wing nationalist ideology. In "Die Flucht in die

Todeshölle" [Escape to the Hell of Death] Bock accuses Suhrkamp and the press for having distorted the facts.[30] Bock rejects particularly the final paragraph, "Only God can judge that which is void of humanity," maintaining that there is no need for gestures of reconciliation because the "Allies did take revenge on the Nazis in 1947 in Nuremberg." Bock's irritation stems from the fact that Koeppen's novel was published at all, reminding the public that many Germans still repress their Nazi past.

Also Frank Dietschreit in "Ich hasse niemanden. Wolfgang Koeppen bekennt sich zu einem fast verschollenen Buch" [I Hate Nobody. Wolfgang Koeppen Acknowledges an Almost Forgotten Book] takes issue with the conciliatory gesture. He considers it the cause of Koeppen's and his publishers' secrecy. Dietschreit argues that in 1948 a non-Jewish author could not have been generous and forgive "seinen Peinigern" [his tormentors]. This utterly illogical statement—Koeppen does not forgive *his* but Littner's tormentors—implies that a change has occurred between 1948 and 1992 that enables a non-Jew to pardon the killers of the Jews.

The most comprehensive review essay about *Aufzeichnungen*, Eberhard Falcke's "Literarisches Carepaket" [Literary Care Package], was published in *Die Zeit* on 8 May 1992.[31] Falcke characterizes *Aufzeichnungen* as a moving (p. 6) but also strangely ambivalent book (p. 7), written concurrently with the Nuremberg Trials. He takes a critical look at the language conventions of those years: "It [the usage that was most popular] implied that the German people had been raped by its Nazi dictators and that everyone who had become a monster had merely followed orders from above and reluctantly so" (p. 6). Falcke regards *Aufzeichnungen* as a prime example of the spirit of reconciliation and the relinquishing of hatred that Germans generally expected from Nazi victims. He describes Koeppen's novel as an integral part of the dominant post-Holocaust and shows that Littner, as constructed by Koeppen, is one of many fictional Jews contrived to indulge the wishful thinking of the German public.[32] Koeppen's Littner is designed to alleviate German guilt: He advocates forgiveness and, by stressing the help he received from average Germans, he allows his readers to feel good about themselves. Falcke exposes the bigotry with which German Holocaust literature was received: "One reads the accounts of the tormented people as if they were messages from a strange, horrible world about which no one claimed to have known, in which none of the perpetrators ever admitted to have been" (p. 7).

Falcke's discussion of Littner's objections against his portrayal by Koeppen—and ultimately the misuse of his name—reveals the causes for Koeppen's anonymity: "Jakob Littner wrote a letter from New York in which he expressed his anger about the fact that he was unable to recognize himself in the memoir published under his name. This fact, however, remained the secret of the publisher Herbert Kluger and another man—the author who had actually written the book." Falcke's analysis makes Koeppen's and Kluger's ruthlessness evident. Never did they take Littner's wishes and intentions into consideration: "It [*Aufzeichnungen*] became his [Koeppen's] story not only through an act of narrative appropriation and identification, but for another reason: there was no detailed account by Littner and none was requested. All there was were some notes the publisher had taken down after his conversations with Littner. This is how the book was produced, which was presented to the public as a factual account. And it was and is, there can be no doubt, a good and moving work.... Initially Koeppen did not want to have the secret of the book disclosed until after his death—possibly in an attempt to rectify the problem-ridden history that made his novel an exceptional case."[33]

Falcke also addresses the problem of genre, stating that *Aufzeichungen* is clearly a work of art—an artefact. Therefore the "transformation of the factual account (as which the work was still received in a new edition of 1985) into a newly-discovered novel" was difficult to make—Koeppen had so completely appropriated the victim's story. Falcke exposes particularly the sections where Koeppen puts authoritative statements into the mouth of his character, for example the way in which he has the fictitious Jew proclaim his political ignorance and his disapproval of hatred and revenge.

This decisive review had almost no impact on the media discourse in general. Most critics continued to belabor ostensibly innocuous points. The reviewer K. K.'s "Auferstehung aus der Grube" [Resurrection from the Pit] in *Freizeit Kurier* consists of a biographical sketch and an unproblematic work history.[34] Naive statements like "the first-person narrator is, like many others, primarily a German and only then a Jew" attest to the reviewer's eagerness to embrace Koeppen's point of view. K. K.'s statement that "the account sounds authentic" proves that Koeppen had calculated his readerships' expectations correctly. K. K. confuses Koeppen, Littner, and himself when during a *salto mortale* of projection—he declares that "death" was the only alternative to Koeppen's writing about "the life of these Jews suffering from rheumatism in their humid quarters."

It is true that many concentration and death-camp prisoners discovered writing as a survival strategy. To this day many Holocaust survivors have a need to speak and write about their experiences.[35] However, to assume that the same existential need compelled Koeppen to deliver *his* soul from *Littner's* experience borders on the ridiculous.

Superficiality and arrogance characterize best Karl Birkensei's "Zeuge der Unmenschlichkeit und der Finsternis" [Witness of Inhumanity and Darkness].[36] Rephrasing the Suhrkamp cover text, he declares *Aufzeichnungen* the "story of a Munich postage-stamp dealer who became a Jew by the 'coincidence of his birth' and absurd political circumstances that made him the holder of a Polish passport." But rather than natural forces it was the territorial politics of nineteenth- and twentieth-century Germany and Austria that made people like Littner Poles and Hungarian emigrés. The notion that someone is Jewish by birth reproduces a kind of racist thinking that negates the religious and cultural tradition of European Jews and a person's right to self-definition.

Birkenser's image of Littner as Koeppen's 'employer' is a travesty of the actual situation. It is hardly true that the Holocaust survivor commissioned a German author, paying him for services rendered. Rather the German author, encouraged by his German publisher, took charge of the name and the story of a Jewish Holocaust survivor who was unable to defend himself against his 'benefactors,' because he had left the country. Several decades later, the time had come for the same author and another German publisher to strike again: This time they got rid of the name of the unknown Jew altogether, replacing it with that of the German bestseller author who had written the 'memoir' in the first place. In contrast to other German veterans, Koeppen, as a deserter, had a relatively clean past. It is not surprising Birkenser does not mention Littner's disappointment about his role in Koeppen's text.

Other reviewers such as Karin Wieckhorst followed the established patterns.[37] Also radio programs added little to the by now established discourse. Many of them, like Jürgen Manthey in "Das Buch der Woche" [Book of the Week], invite the listener to identify with Koeppen's narrator.[38] Here and elsewhere the author's point of view blends with that of his character, fact with fiction. Manthey, like Wiesner, observes inconsistencies in Koeppen's narrative. According to him it is the author, stepping outside his fiction, who asks, representative of all Germans: "What could we have done, how could we have defended ourselves.... What would have happened... if Germany, the old Germany, would not have followed the orders of her monstrous leader." (p. 5).

It is a question persecuted Jews have also asked themselves. Holocaust survivors were confronted with this question by the postwar generations.[39] Asked from a Jewish point of view, this question might lead to topics that elude the reviewers of *Aufzeichnungen*, for example the issue of German Jewish identity, the relationship between German Jews and non-Jews, assimilation, Zionism, and Jewish renewal, in other words, issues similar to those raised by the Jüdischer Verlag of 1902. These issues are relevant to this day, but books like Koeppen's *Aufzeichnungen* suppress them.

The treatment of Jewish topics by Gentile authors often creates a dilemma, for instance Brigitte Schwaiger's version of Eva Deutsch's memoir, *Die Galizianerin* [The Galician Woman].[40] Not unlike Koeppen, Schwaiger told a Holocaust story from the point of view of a survivor, possibly with the intention to lend her voice, the voice of an established Austrian author, to a Polish woman with a less than perfect command of German who, like Littner, had ended up in a German-speaking country. Although Schwaiger and Koeppen seem to have used materials written by their informants, they did not document their sources. As a result their works are overshadowed by title and authorship problems indicative of a deep-rooted ethical dilemma.

German and Austrian authors who pose as the protectors of former Nazi victims cannot but usurp the stories of the victims and attribute their own opinions and viewpoints to them. Koeppen and Schwaiger wrote passages that read like apologies for Nazi perpetrators. Occasionally their supposedly Jewish narrators criticize from the point of view of his/her 'privileged' knowledge of Jewish customs and rituals or assume the position of crown witnesses against Jewish collaborators. These themes also appear in the works of Jewish authors such as Edgar Hilsenrath or Friedrich Torberg, but they are placed in a larger context. At no time is the narrator (and hence the reader) unaware of the fact that the Nazis rather than their insignificant and occasionally even Jewish errand boys were responsible for the Holocaust.

*Aufzeichnungen* facilitates the repression and distortion of the past by validating the viewpoint of the German mainstream through an alleged Jewish author. In today's Germany the book continues to serve its original purpose by its very place of publication, an ostensibly Jewish context. However, members of the German mainstream can under no circumstances speak for the Nazi victims nor emulate their experience. Wherever they attempt to do so, they take advantage of the plight of the Holocaust victims in intellectual, emotional, and material terms. This kind of exploitation is reminiscent of the total utilization of all raw materials that was practiced in the concentration camps: the spoils of the Holocaust are transformed into German products. The history of *Littners Aufzeichnungen* clearly shows that such acts of appropriation can be carried on in post-unification Germany with impunity under the acclaim of those who control media opinion.

## NOTES

1. Cf. Josef Bor, *Theresienstädter Requiem* (Gütersloh: Mohn, 1963).
2. Silvia Schlenstedt, "Suche nach Halt in haltloser Lage...," *Sinn und Form* 41/4 (1989), p. 728, mentions journals such as the *CV Zeitung*, *Der Morgen* (since 1933 *Monatsschrift der Juden in Deutschland*), *Jüdische Rundschau* (Berlin), and the activities of the Jewish Museum.
3. Cf. Susan E. Cernyak–Spatz, *German Holocaust Literature* (New York, Bern, Frankfurt: Peter Lang, 1985); Christiane Schmelzkopf, *Zur Gestaltung jüdischer Figuren in der deutschsprachigen Literatur nach 1945* (Hildesheim, Zürich, New York. Olms, 1983).
4. Cf. Sander Gilman, "Jüdische Literaten und deutsche Literatur. Antisemitismus und die verborgene Sprache der Juden am Beispiel von Jurek Becker und Edgar Hilsenrath," *Zeitschrift für deutsche Philologie* 107/2 (1988), pp. 269–294; Jack Zipes, "The Holocaust and the Vicissitudes of Jewish Identity," *New German Critique* 20 (1980), pp. 155–176.
5. Cf. Guy Stern, *Literatur im Exil: Gesammelte Aufsätze 1959–1989* (Ismaning: Hueber, 1989).
6. Cf. Littner's *Aufzeichnungen*, dust jacket.

7. Peter Edel, *Schwester der Nacht* (Vienna: Erwin Müller, 1947); Edgar Hilsenrath, *Nacht* (Frankfurt: Fischer, 1980; Munich: Kindler, 1964; Cologne: Literarischer Verlag Braun, 1978); Bruno Apitz, *Nackt unter Wölfen* (Halle: Mitteldeutscher Verlag, 1958); Gerty Spies, *Drei Jahre Theresienstadt* (Munich: Kaiser, 1984), based on "Ein Stück Weges (ein Gedanke an Jahre schmerzvoller Reifung)," ms. Leo Baeck Institute, New York; Rahel Behrend, *Verfemt und Verfolgt* (Zurich: Büchergilde Gutenberg, 1945); also: Else R. Behrend–Rosenfeld, *Ich stand nicht allein. Erlebnisse einer Jüdin in Deutschland 1933–45* (Frankfurt: EVA, 1964).

8. For instance Norbert Troller's portfolio of drawings, watercolors, and texts, Leo Baeck Institute, New York; Hans Winterfeld's *Deutschland, ein Zeitbild 1926–1945: Leidensweg eines deutschen Juden in den ersten 19 Jahren seines Lebens*, ms., Yonkers, NY, 1969, Leo Baeck Institute, New York; Nina Weilovàs, "71978 Jude. Erinnerungen," Österreichisches Dokumentationsarchiv der Widerstandsbewegung, Vienna, or Elisabeth Freund's *Zwangsarbeit für Hitler. Berlin 1941*, ms. no date, Leo Baeck Institute, New York.

9. *Forum Politik-Unterricht*, ed. Vereinigung für Politische Bildung Landesverband Bayern 1, January 1992.

10. fjg, "Koeppen oder Littner," *Buch Journal* (January 1992). Cf. Jakob Wassermann, *Mein Weg als Deutscher und Jude* (Berlin: S. Fischer, 1921). Items 4 and 5 of the program of the NSDAP specify that only ethnic Germans qualify as citizens of the state. "Volksgenosse kann nur sein, wer deutschen Blutes ist, ohne Rücksicht auf Konfession. Kein Jude kann daher Volksgenosse sein. . . . Wer nicht Staatsbürger ist, soll nur als Gast in Deutschland leben können und muß unter Fremdengesetzgebung stehen." Helmut Krausnick, "Judenverfolgung," *Anatomie des SS-Staates* II (Munich: dtv, 1982), pp. 11ff. The laws concerning foreign workers in Germany follow these principles to this day.

11. The impossibility of articulating the Holocaust experience was a *leitmotif* of postwar criticism, sanctioned supposedly by Adorno's statement that writing poetry after Auschwitz was barbaric. In the case of Paul Celan, who was considered the paradigm of a Holocaust poet, this thesis proved useful. It was not in the case of lesser-known Holocaust authors represented in such anthologies as *An den Wind geschrieben. Lyrik der Freiheit. Gedichte der Jahre 1933–1945*, ed. Manfred Schlösser, Hans-Rolf Ropertz (Darmstadt: Agora, 1960).

12. *Fuldaer Zeitung/Hünfelder Zeitung/Kinzigtal-Nachrichten* 35 (11 Feb. 1992).

13. *Luzerner Neuste Nachrichten* 54 (5 March 1992).

14. Hans Jansen, "Buch der Woche. Protokoll des Grauens," *Westdeutsche Allgemeine Zeitung* 87 (11 April 1992).

15. Marion Löhndorf, "Biedermänner und Bestien," *General-Anzeiger* (14–15 March 1992).

16. *Hannoversche Allgemeine Zeitung* (14 March 1992); *Neue Zürcher Zeitung* (27 March 1992).

17. *Westfalenpost* (19 March 1992).

18. Werner Thuswaldner, "An der Grenze des Erträglichen. Leidensfähigkeit eines Menschen. Wolfgang Koeppen ist der Autor des Romans 'Jakob Littners Aufzeichnungen aus einem Erdloch,' " *Salzburger Nachrichten* (21 March 1992).

19. Peter Jokostra, "Ex Libris" ORF 1, 22 and 29 March 1992, 3:15 p.m., ms. 2 pp.; P. J., "Brief an Landau," *Börsenblatt für den deutschen Buchhandel* (2 April 1965); P. J., "Offener Brief," ibid. (24 March 1965). Cf. also Susann Moeller, "How to Pulp a Novel," this volume.

20. *Süddeutsche Zeitung* (26 March 1992).

21. Cf. Eugen Kogon, *Der SS-Staat* (Frankfurt: Verlag der Frankfurter Hefte, 1948; Europäische Verlagsanstalt, 1946).

22. *Deutsche Tagespost* (28 March 1992). Cf. also fjg (cited in note 10 above), Illies (note 12), Bugmann, Löhndorf (note 13), etc.

23. Martin Buber in *Jüdische Erneuerung* (1934) and Alfred Döblin in *Flucht und Sammlung des Judenvolkes* (1935) interpreted the Nazis' rise to power as an opportunity for a Jewish *renouveau* but other texts appeared since 1932 discussing the plight of German Jews. Cf. Werner T. Angress, "The German Jews, 1933–1939," *The Holocaust: Ideology, Bureaucracy, and Genocide* (The San José Papers), ed. Henry Friedlander, Sybil Milton (New York: Kraus International, 1980), pp. 69ff. Kurt Grossmann's *Juden hinter Stacheldraht* and *Deutschland am Hakenkreuz* appeared in 1933, Alfred Kerr's *Die Diktatur des Hausknechts*, Georg Hermann's *Ruths schwere Stunde* und *Eine Zeit stirbt* in 1934. Lili Körber, *Eine Jüdin erlebt das neue Deutschland* (1934) and Willi Bredel, *Die Prüfung* (1934) are eyewitness reports about concentration camps. At the same time Lion Feuchtwanger wrote *Die Geschwister Oppenheim* (1933), Arnold Zweig *Die Bilanz der deutschen Judenheit* (1934), Karl Kraus *Die dritte Walpurgisnacht* (posthumously 1965), and Friedrich Wolf, *Professor Mamlock*.

24. Frankfurt: Europäische Verlagsanstalt, 1946.

25. "Es wird die Achtung vor der Überlebensleistung Littners gewesen sein, die Wolfgang Koeppen dazu brachte, ihm dieses Buch zuzuschreiben." Andreas Müller, "Eine Überlebensgeschichte," *Darmstädter Echo* (20 March 1992).

26. *Basler Zeitung* (10 April 1992).

27. Of 3,000 copies only 1,200 were sold in five years. The remainder was bought by Suhrkamp.

28. Bernhard Fetz, "Berichte aus der Hölle," *Falter* 15 (10–16 April 1992).

29. Bruno Bettelheim, "The Ignored Lesson of Anne Frank," *Surviving* (New York: Knopf, 1979), pp. 246–257.

30. Hans Bertram Bock, "Die Flucht in die Todeshölle," *Nürnberger Nachrichten* (14 April 1992). "Als der Suhrkamp-Verleger Siegfried Unseld kürzlich das neue Programm des renommierten Jüdischen Verlages präsentierte, lüftete er bei der Neuedition des Littner-Werkes das Geheimnis. . . . Jakob Littner wanderte 1947 nach New York aus. Koeppen ist dem 'Wohltäter' nie begegnet."

31. *Die Zeit* 20 (8 May 1992), "Literatur," pp. 6–7. Translations by D. C. G. Lorenz.

32. Karin Wieckhorst, "Aus dem Erdloch," *Zitty* 12 (28 May–10 June 1992), pp. 210–211.

33. "Ich aß die amerikanischen Konserven und schrieb die Leidensgeschichte eines deutschen Juden. Da wurde es meine Geschichte" (Falcke, p. 7).

34. *Freizeit Kurier* 138 (9 May 1992).

35. Cf. Gertry Spies, *Drei Jahre Theresienstadt* (Munich: Kaiser, 1984); *Ein Stück Weges (ein Gedanke an Jahre schmerzvoller Reifung)*, ms., no date, Leo Baeck Institut, New York; *Theresienstadt. Gedichte* (Munich: Freitag, 1948); Ruth Kluger, *weiter leben* (Göttingen: Wallstein, 1992).

36. Karl Birkenser, "Zeuge der Unmenschlichkeit und der Finsternis," *Mittelbayerische Zeitung*, "Das Neue Buch" (9–10 May 1992), p. 2.

37. Karin Wieckhorst, "Aus dem Erdloch," pp. 210–211.

38. Ibid.

39. Bruno Bettelheim, *The Informed Heart: Autonomy in a Mass Age* (New York: Avon, Glencoe, Free Press, 1960); "Eichmann: The System, the Victims," *Surviving* (New York: Knopf, 1979), pp. 258–273.

40. Brigitte Schwaiger, *Eva Deutsch: Die Galizianerin* (Vienna and Hamburg: Paul Zsolnay, 1982).

# The Glory of Austrian Resistance and the Forgotten Jews

## Ruth Beckermann

Two events in recent times have changed the cultural climate in Austria: the election of Kurt Waldheim in 1986 and the so-called commemoration year of the *Anschluß* in 1988. The commemoration year would have gone by quietly for the most part if it had not been for the furor caused by the Waldheim affair. The *Anschluß* by the Third Reich fifty years ago would have been celebrated with the usual lie about how Austria had been occupied by the Germans. Moreover, the November pogrom of 1938, which had been much worse in Austria than in Germany, would have been neglected as usual.

But the Waldheim affair made it necessary to improve the tarnished image of the country and to counter the attacks against the glory of Austrian resistance through an enormous number of events and television programs. In other words, the Waldheim election and the commemoration year led to a paradoxical situation for the Austrians and the Jews who live there today. While anti-Semitism became more rabid than ever before, Austria experienced a widespread discussion about its Nazi past for the first time, and a more active Jewish community began to assert itself and come to terms with its identity.

In order to understand why Austrians have only recently begun to speak about Austrian guilt, anti-Semitism, and the fate of Jews as the primary victims of the Nazis in response to massive pressure from abroad, one must understand the specific Austrian situation forty-five years after the end of World War II. Up until the Waldheim affair the Austrians had either been considered in the same boat as the Germans (and this was mostly the case) or they were exculpated from any kind of guilt and regarded as though they were charming figures from the film *The Sound of Music*.

I would like to outline the specific conditions that led to this view of the Austrians, especially in light of their relations to the Jews since 1945. Then I will analyze how Jewish life changed due to the Waldheim affair and its consequences. After the defeat of the Third Reich, the situation in both Germany and Austria was the same, but only at the beginning. Soldiers of the allied forces occupied both countries, no mention was made of the fate of the Jews in the first declarations by the governments, and there was no reaction of the people to what happened in both Germany and Austria. Visitors were struck by the inability of the Germans and Austrians to feel and by the manic way in which they devoted themselves to the reconstruction of their countries.

By the 1950s, however, the situation in Austria changed. That the relationship of the Austrians to the Jews took a different shape than that in the Federal Republic was not due to different notions of morality, nor was it due to a different perception of guilt. The Germans simply did not have the Austrian excuse that would allow them to pose as victims. (Of course it was different in East Germany, where state doctrine claimed that the German people had been taken over by the Nazis.) The Austrian attitude toward their own past was similar to the attitude in the GDR, which had declared itself free of any historical guilt.

In Austria, Jews were permitted to live again after 1945 if they behaved and kept their mouths shut. To be sure, as the first chancellor Figl emphasized, Jews were permitted to practice their religion, but he warned them not to demand any compensation or privileges, otherwise there might be a new kind of anti-Semitism. Their special fate under the Nazis was posthumously taken away from them. Jews were not needed politically in the Second Republic. The representative role that they played in West Germany as a sign of a new democracy was given to the political resisters. Accordingly the only victims of the Nazi regime immediately recognized after 1945 were those people who had been politically persecuted. As a result, an archive that documented the Austrian resistance was founded, but to this day there is no special archive in which documents concerned with Austrian Nazi crimes and Austrian persecution of Jews can be found. Although the removal of the Nazi regime in Austria came essentially from the outside, the role of a patriotic resistance had to be exaggerated afterward in accordance with the glorious myth about how the republic was founded. The Austrian Left and the Right came to an unspoken agreement about this after 1945. They formed a coalition that lasted twenty years. The truth is that this resistance had not been greater than that in Germany. In both ruling parties the politicians would refer to the glory of the resistance to prove the legitimation of an independent Austrian state.

As is well known, Austria was occupied by the four allied powers, but it was also recognized as the first victim of German aggression at the Moscow meeting of 1943. After the war politicians used the Moscow declaration to legitimate themselves. Their legitimation determined Austrian politics, which successfully led to complete independence in 1955. Once again Austrians had proof that opportunism pays off and had shown that it is easy to deceive the entire world if one does it with the right amount of charm. Indeed, in order to make their role as victims halfway credible, it was necessary to emphasize and embellish the resistance.

Yet the Austrian people always recognized such interpretations of the past for what they were—a necessary way to conform to the conditions of the time and a necessary means to get rid of the consequences of the defeat of 1945. The words chosen by the Austrians make it clear that in their consciousness the liberation took place in 1938 and the occupation in 1945. The liberation in 1938 was from a hated Catholic–Fascist regime that defeated and prohibited the mighty workers' movement; it had ruled for four years in a dictatorial way. The occupation was by the Allied Powers in 1945 after the dream of a great German Empire had exploded. The new image of Austria was thus created from the perspective of the perpetrators, who pretended to be the victims.

Now it was fortuitous for the Austrians to be able to distinguish themselves from the Germans. People spoke dialect. The schools taught not German, but *Unterrichtssprache*, school-language or language of instruction. The Austrians dressed in quaint local costumes and found that this made a good impression on the rest of the world. As a result Austria received a special treatment in comparison to Germany: the country was not divided, Austrians were not stigmatized, and they did not suffer from massive forced emigrations. The reparations Austria had to pay were insignificant and the payments slow. In addition, the withdrawal of all foreign soldiers and national independence were guaranteed. No wonder that the Austrians rejoiced and subscribed to a new patriotism that was founded only in retrospect on the struggle against the Nazis for a free Austria. Typical of the situation are the newspaper *Neues Österreich* and its editor-in-chief, the Communist Ernst Fischer, who wrote: "The graves of the past should not come between us, for the grave is gigantic in which the dead martyrs of Austria lie, one body next to the other, Communists, Socialists, Catholics, all who died in a struggle for a free, independent, and democratic Austria."

In the first two years after the war the anti-Fascists still hoped for a radical change in Austria. But in 1949 during the first elections in which former Nazi party members (in Austria a third of the population had been in the Nazi party, more than in the other parts of the Reich) were allowed to vote again and therefore were wooed by all parties, a hypocrisy began that lasted until the election of Waldheim. Outside of Austria the glorious victim version of history was presented. However, in the election speeches in Austria, addressed to the Austrian people, more popular slogans were offered. The Austrians understand with a wink of an eye that the official discourse about victims is a necessary masquerade. Austrian politicians in particular know very well how to condemn anti-Semitism during their visits to the United States, and after their return to Austria they complain about the WJC (World Jewish Congress). These two discourses have existed peacefully side by side during the forty years of Austria's existence. This hypocrisy characterizes the fundamental lie of Austria.

It was Waldheim who exploded the lie, actually with just one sentence. When he said "I only fulfilled my duty," he mixed both discourses together. Indeed, if he did fulfill his duty as an officer in the German *Wehrmacht*, then all those who had refused to serve, who had emigrated and resisted, had not fulfilled their duty in fighting for a free Austria. It was with just this one sentence that Waldheim achieved great success. At first he only uttered it incidentally at an election meeting and achieved spontaneous applause, and thanks to this response he began to use this sentence more and more in the center of his campaign speeches.

There was a feeling of great relief among the listeners who from a certain age onward had fulfilled the same duty. The cowardly Waldheim was in their eyes a courageous man who did not want anything to do with hypocrisy. The conspiracy of silence and the implication that each and every person could interpret history according to his or her taste vanished. Waldheim turned history back on its feet. To be sure, the Austrians had fulfilled their duty in the Wehrmacht, and they had even tried to outdo the Germans. . . .

Of course the Waldheim affair had a great and shocking effect on the Jews in Austria—I shall now turn to the Jewish community. Suddenly the Austrian Jews were the focus of international attention. Suddenly the WJC was supposedly acting in their interest. Yet, suddenly, they were excluded very openly from the collective memory that was being honestly articulated for the first time, and they became the target of anti-Semitic rage. The real gap in the memory of Jews and non-Jews showed. Even before this no one had paid special attention to their feelings and had ignored them—as the quote by Ernst Fischer shows. Of course, it must be said, they, too, had been involved in the consensus of silence. They had played along. Most likely they had no other choice but to play along, if one considers their lack of numbers and level of consciousness.

Some facts: In 1946 there were 6,428 registered Jews accounted for by the Austrian Jewish community. This number remained about the same until today. Naturally there was a strong fluctuation of members until the end of the 1950s. Many emigrants who had returned left Austria after some time. Many East European Jews who came out of the Austrian DP (Displaced Persons) camps went to Israel. However, some could not establish roots in Israel, returned to Austria, and tried to develop a new life there. Of the 126,500 Jewish emigrants who left Austria, only 4,500 came back; relatively very few returned from the United States, but a relatively large number came back from Palestine/Israel. The wish to return was strongest on the part of the emigrants who had gone to Shanghai, Karaganda, and Mauritius, because they could not get used to the climate and the foreign culture.

Emigrants who had returned to Austria formed the majority of the Jewish community right after the war. This was only for a short time. A Communist faction under the name of *Einheit* [Unity] received the majority of the Jewish vote and took control of the first community (*Kultusgemeinde*). It published a remarkably good journal, *Der neue Weg* [The New Way], which supported restitution for Austrian Jews (in other words, reparation) and very rarely carried Communist propaganda. In order to understand the success of the Communist Party among the Jews, one must consider that a great success of the Communist Party in general had been expected during the first elections in Austria in 1949. The political elite believed, like the Jews and naturally the Communists themselves, that the Austrians would thank the Russians for having freed Vienna and the eastern part of their country. They also thought that the Austrians would welcome Socialism after Fascism. However, from the perspective of the majority of the Austrian population, the Russians had occupied Vienna, raped women, etc. The relief of the other parties and the disappointment of the Communists were great when the Communist Party (KPÖ) received only a small portion of the votes and began to sink slowly into oblivion, a situation that has remained unchanged ever since.

Since that time the KPÖ has played no role whatsoever in the Jewish community. From the early 1950s until the middle of the 1980s the Jewish community has voted Socialist. In fact, for a long time the Jews voted against their economic interest by voting for the Socialist Party (SPÖ) and not for the Conservatives, the Catholic *Volkspartei* (ÖVP). In the mid 1980s, it is significant to note, the thirty-year-rule of the Socialist Party was broken in the Jewish community by a group called *Junge Generation* [Young Generation], which consisted of young entrepreneurs who no longer had any illusions about anti-Semitism in Austria's Socialist Party. They were not involved with the SPÖ and voted either according to their economic interests, which are conservative, or for the Greens, or not at all.

In 1948/49 the makeup of the Jewish community was clearly in favor of an East European majority. Polish, Rumanian, and Hungarian Jews, who had remained in Austria as DPs or refugees from Stalinism, formed the majority of the community and are still dominant today. It is estimated that there are about 10,000 Jews living in Vienna today (Austrian Jews live exclusively in Vienna). Most recently the Jewish population has increased by 5,000 due to the new arrivals of Russian Jews. That is, there are again at least 15,000 Jews in Vienna, and Vienna has the largest population of Jews in German-speaking cities.

There is very little contact between the Viennese Jews who had returned, and the East European immigrants. The Viennese had a difficult time in reestablishing themselves in an Austrian society that had changed, in a city without Jews in which almost 200,000 Jews had lived before 1938. In addition, these Viennese Jews retained their old prejudices against the East European Jews. But what is more important to consider is the different experience these groups had during the Nazi period and their fundamentally different connection to Vienna. The president of the Jewish community, Paul Grosz, is of the opinion that the Viennese Jews of the first generation are to this day divided into *Landsmannschaften* or associations by place of origin. They have social contact with people of the same language and the same roots. The East European Jews did not have their traumatic experiences in Austria and/or with German-speaking Nazis, but rather with local Fascists in the Ukraine, Romania, and Hungary. They did not have any experience with Austrian anti-Semitism before the war or with the attitudes of the population after the *Anschluß*. On the contrary, they brought a romantic and glorified image of the *Kaiserstadt* [Imperial City] with them—Vienna had remained a center of attraction for them even after the collapse of the monarchy. Their experience was different from that of Jews in West Germany, for the East European Jews who remained in Vienna after the war feel even today a strong bond with the cultural tradition of the former Austrian Empire. One should not forget that, despite the suffering and losses they underwent, their childhood dream had been fulfilled: they had left their *shtetl* and settled in the *Kaiserstadt*, the capital of their former country. It seems no coincidence that for the Jews who stayed in Vienna after the liberation, the very places that corresponded to their image of the former monarchy became favorite meeting places. Beautiful *Schönbrunner* yellow buildings were the background scenery in front of which people with similar prewar experiences and a similar fate during the Nazi period came together once more.

Despite all this, they always felt that their stay in Vienna was temporary. The East European Jews did not decide to remain in Vienna, but rather kept postponing their departure. From time to time, at any rate after each anti-Semitic incident, they promised themselves and their friends that they would soon leave. It is in this provisional condition that most Jews have been living for forty years, even though it would appear that they are firmly established in Austria due to their families, work, and property. There has never been an inner decision to remain.

This condition distinguishes these Jews from the earlier Jewish settlers from other parts of the monarchy, and it also distinguishes their children's identity from that of the Jewish immigrants at the beginning of the century and after World War I. But precisely these distinctions must be pushed aside as far as possible and redirected toward "the Germans" or "the anti-Semitic Poles." They are distinctions created by the experience of the Nazi era and the failure to achieve "normalcy" thereafter. It was easier for the East European Jews to achieve normalcy in Vienna than in their countries of origin. It is easier to be a foreigner in a foreign city than to feel alien and undesired all of a sudden in a familiar environment.

The Hungarian and Romanian Jews had no connection to Austria except a romantic, imaginary one. They had no connection to the history of the Viennese Jewish community before 1938. These East European Jews were interested primarily in developing an existence for themselves, but had no inner need to proclaim their patriotism and their eagerness to participate in the reconstruction of the Austrian *Heimat*. They left this role to the few Viennese Jews who had returned, and who regarded it as their task to represent the Jewish community to the outside world as if it were not merely the remains of the community destroyed by the Nazis, but as if by its makeup it were Austrian through and through. Up to the present it has been unthinkable to have an East European Jew as president of this community. The major qualification for this office seems to be the ability to speak good German, and in this context a Viennese accent is permitted. In this and other ways Viennese Jewry has attempted to avoid anti-Semitic clichés; even well-intended Jews, who equate anti-Semitism with racism or the hate of foreigners speak of the Jews as if the majority of them had been rooted in Vienna for generations. No Jews who speak German with a strong Jewish accent appear on the television and radio programs which have aired in the postwar period at regular intervals.

Jewish life in Austria is burdened by a plethora of identity problems. It is a wobbly house of cards held together by painful experiences and dreams of hope. While the experiences continue to happen, no matter what, forming dreams of hope demands that the disturbances be repressed or at least minimized. All of this demands a great expenditure of energy. The Jews create myths about their own history, cling to the great musicians and poets who gave rise to the famous Jewish Vienna, and forget the dark side of emancipation and assimilation. They imagine themselves back in the beautiful days of the past, without realizing that the beautiful days of the past were those that led to the yesterday of Nazi persecution.

No sooner did the survivors feel themselves to be respected citizens than they forgot that nobody wanted them to be in Vienna, even after the collapse of the Nazi Reich. They are ashamed of their vitality, which helped them build an existence out of nothing. Their ideas, their virtues, and their intelligence appeared to them to be less valuable than good citizenship. They downplay the everyday anti-Semitism and say there are more important things to consider. They are successful in doing this, in part because they have cultivated a certain feeling of superiority that enables them to regard the Austrians as stupid conformists. They have convinced themselves that the Austrians are actually too dumb to be really evil. The general distinction between evil Germans and good-natured Austrians has been taken over by the Jews themselves in order to legitimate their existence in Vienna. The ability to tolerate the Austrians is made possible by certain fantasies of Austria: the retrospective wish for a positive Jewish–Austrian symbiosis, the glorification of a condition that lasted only about seventy years, from 1867 to 1938, a period in which Jews were equal citizens before the law. Both sides of this symbiosis, which gave birth to psychoanalysis and modern music, have been retrospectively idealized. In the process one forgets that the Jews achieved their works in spite of the petty attitude of the Viennese environment and that they also produced their works as a reaction against this environment. "Vienna has no right to claim any part of Freud's fame," Marthe Robert has written, "for during the seventy-eight years that he spent there, Vienna made his life only unpleasant and despised him, and when Vienna could no longer make him look ridiculous it ignored him with mean indifference."

The yearning for symbiosis has produced great works for the price of the dissociation of real experiences from an image that needed to stay intact. Conflictual feelings must exist side by side, since their convergence might lead to the collapse of the house of cards. Painful experiences must be pushed aside repeatedly, while signs that reinforce the fantasy are being emphasized dramatically. The current president of the community, for example, makes much of a few supportive letters that he received during the anti-Semitic rumblings around Waldheim's election, and considers them indications of progress. Simon Wiesenthal speaks forever about his trust in the younger generation. One wonders what happened to the generations in which he placed great hopes only ten and twenty years ago. How young do you have to be not to be an anti-Semite?

Dissociating those painful experiences means considering them as a private affair rather than thematizing them publicly. By playing Yiddish music and telling Jewish jokes the consensus of silence can be maintained. The illusion that people have nothing against Jews is comforting. Most Jews find it incomprehensible that even flaming anti-Semites have a good time in a typically Viennese Jewish cabaret. They take this as the beginning of a dialogue and don't even notice that in doing so they accept the following conditions: to remain silent about the events during the Nazi period; to repress the humiliating experiences of postwar Austria; and to downplay the day-to-day anti-Semitism of the present.

The anti-Semitic wave of 1986 evoked memories of anti-Semitic scandals during the past forty years as well as of personal slanders that were mostly ignored by the Jews. As a result, the question of Jewish existence in Austria had to be posed anew. Most of the decisions along with all the compromises that had been made in order to live there were now unmasked as illusions. Over the years people had tried to draw a rather dense veil over their memories. According to Gerhard Bronner, a well-known cabaret artist in Austria, people acted as if nothing had ever happened in this country, which was obviously easier than in Germany, thanks to the Austrians' skill at denying their guilt. "For a half century I carried memories along that I thought I needed to forget in order to live in this country." He concludes: "Nothing has changed in Austria since 1938. Even the victims would like to forget that, but they are not given a chance."

How do we explain the unique position of Austrian Jewry? Until 1986 the Jewish community was quite isolated from the German communities as well as from those of the former Austro-Hungarian Empire, primarily the Hungarian one. Nobody showed any interest in how one could live as a Jew in Vienna, while the German Jews were precious for Germans and Americans alike. Even though the American television film *Holocaust* was shown on Austrian television in 1979, it did not provoke shock or discussion in the Austrian population, in contrast to West Germany. It was not until the discussions around the election of Waldheim that the relationship between Jews and Austrians became a topic.

The election campaign with the subsequent triumph of Kurt Waldheim and the commemoration year of 1988 changed the consciousness of the Viennese Jewish community profoundly. Now indeed we can speak of a new era of Jewish life in Vienna. For the Jews, despite the anti-Semitic outbursts, the second half of the 1980s marked the end of their provisional existence, the end of their postwar period. For the first time a collective and public discussion of Austria among Jews was triggered by these events. Those who decided not to leave in response to the Waldheim election were now forced to confront their lives in this country, and those who were willing to engage in this effort tied themselves to this country, even if negatively. The public discussions about Austria's contributions to Nazism created the climate for the Jewish coming out, approximately ten years later than in West Germany. Ten years later, that means a time in which both Zionist and Socialist options have become irrevocably unattractive and thus a concrete and pragmatic involvement in Austria was called for. Dramatic proclamations of the intent to emigrate, as in the cases of Henryk Broder and Lea Fleischmann, have become unthinkable. On the contrary, quite a few families who had emigrated to Israel are now returning before their children are drafted into the army.

And again this shows that the question so often posed abroad cannot be answered. It is probably better to ask instead, "How do Jews live there?" Possibly the Austrian Jews need to be grateful to Mr. Waldheim and the changes his election brought about. It might just have created an atmosphere in Austria in which Jews are now forced to face the realities of living there along with its past, present, and future.

*Translated by Jack Zipes*

Gender and Ethnicity
in Films of the 1980s

# Ethnicity, Sexuality, and Politics in István Szabó's *Colonel Redl* and *Mephisto*

## Dagmar C. G. Lorenz

István Szabó's films *Mephisto* (1981), *Colonel Redl* (1984), and *Hanussen* (1989) form a trilogy. Klaus Maria Brandauer stars in all three films as an amoeba-like and yet charismatic character. The works center on the issue of identity—self-definition and definition by others in ethnic, political, and sexual terms. In *Mephisto* the protagonist's sexual ambivalence concurs with his political opportunism; in *Colonel Redl* the same characteristics are amplified by an oscillating ethnic and class identity.[1]

Szabó was born in Hungary in 1938. He began his career as a film director in 1961. Reflections of World War II and the Hungarian uprising of 1956 already dominated his earlier works, *The Age of Day-Dreaming* (1964), *Father* (1967), and *Love Film* (1970). In *Mephisto*, *Colonel Redl*, and *Hanussen* Szabó expanded his scope, exploring the forces that shaped his cultural sphere and time: the Weimar Republic and the rise of Fascism, the decline of the Austro-Hungarian Empire, the Hungarian and Austrian republics, their absorption into Nazi Germany, and Nazi Germany itself. Szabó perfected the techniques of his earlier films, particularly the subtle creation of moods by elaborate soundtracks and understated editing and carefully chosen accessories and interiors, which underscore the historical significance of individual scenes.[2] The sensual quality of his scenery shows an affinity with Milos Foreman's *Amadeus*; his brand of historicity is reminiscent of Menachem Golan's *The Magician of Lublin*.[3]

*Mephisto*, *Colonel Redl*, and *Hanussen* are cultural critical works whose apparent realism is created by authentic European settings and period costumes.[4] *Colonel Redl* and *Hanussen* deal with historical figures, a notorious Austro-Hungarian officer and a magician of the 1920s. *Mephisto* is based on Klaus Mann's *roman à clef* of 1936 and deals with historical events.[5] Mann's novel and Szabó's film reflect the rise of the Nazis during the Weimar Republic. Both works show the fates of the liberal, leftist, and Jewish German artists and intellectuals of this era: persecution, exile, and murder. In *Colonel Redl* Szabó names John Osborne's play *A Patriot for Me* (first produced at the Royal Court Theater, London in 1965) and "events of this century" as his sources.[6] Here, as in *Mephisto*, Szabó's film is a critical comment on the text in the light of contemporary discourses.[7] Moreover, Szabó seems to have been familiar with Egon Erwin Kisch's journalistic account of the previously hushed-up Redl scandal.

His choice of protagonists enables Szabó to steer clear of the "great men" philosophy of history. At the same time his characters possess the very qualities on which the success of twentieth-century dictators was based. Hendrik Höfgen and Alfred Redl are careerists who climbed into prominence from the same lower socioeconomic strata that generated Mussolini, Hitler, Stalin, and Nasser. Both represent the aspirations of their social class, however, without the notoriety that surrounds the larger-than-life dictators.

Szabó's critical method resembles that of Elias Canetti.[8] Like Canetti, Szabó develops an authoritarian personality profile by which he generalizes and expands the problem of Fascism. Who exactly the leader is appears accidental. Göring, or for that matter Höfgen, could and would have played the same role as Hitler; Redl would and could have taken the place of Franz Ferdinand. Szabó explores the psychological makeup of the petit-bourgeois dictators by way of their class-specific aspirations: their persecution complex, the desire to get even with real or imagined oppressors, their feelings of inadequacy, their ambitions to be 'someone,' their repressed sexual desires, their education marked by discipline and corporal punishment.[9]

The occupations of Alfred Redl, Hendrik Höfgen, and Eric Jan Hanussen, show business and the military, have traditionally appealed to social climbers and gay men. In these careers class barriers are relatively fluid and there is an opportunity to mask and at the same time act upon one's sexual preference.[10] For example, Alfred Redl had risen to the rank of senior staff officer at the Austro-Hungarian Eighth Corps Headquarters in Prague and to the head of the Counterespionage Section of the General Staff Intelligence Bureau. He was considered one of the most brilliant military officers.[11] The model for Mann's and Szabó's Hendrik Höfgen was Gustav Gründgens, an actor whose interpretation of Mephisto in Goethe's *Faust* was considered exemplary during the Nazi era and beyond. In spite of their alibi marriages, both Alfred Redl and Gustav Gründgens were known to be homosexual.

So was Klaus Mann who, like his sister Erika, made no secret of his sexual orientation. His family background—his mother, Katja Pringsheim, was Jewish—his sexual orientation, and his politics made him a misfit in the eyes of the Nazis. Erika and Klaus Mann had intimate ties with Gründgens, which are also alluded to in the novel. In contrast to Mann, however, Gründgens managed to make an arrangement with the Nazis and made a brilliant career as an actor and as a cultural functionary.

John Osborne's interest in Alfred Redl seems to have been of a less personal nature than Klaus Mann's interest in Gründgens. Osborne wanted to write a play about the "ambiguity of homosexuality," hence his choice of

Redl as a subject, someone about whom surprisingly little was written in spite of the fact that the scandal he was involved in was second in notoriety only to the Dreyfus affair. Osborne explained his fascination with gay life not without homophobic overtones: "I've been surrounded by queers; betrayed by them and disliked by them, and have had friends who were queer. It's not a particular obsession, it's just something one lives with."[12] Even so, there is a good deal of ambivalence about John Osborne, who so desperately wanted to succeed in marriage, the heterosexual institution par excellence. Between 1951 and 1978 he was married five times.[13]

A Patriot for Me shows Osborne's familiarity with the British gay subculture. While Osborne does not recreate the atmosphere of the turn-of-the-century Austro-Hungarian monarchy, he comments on his own time by way of pseudo-historical masquerade.[14] There is a marked difference between Klaus Mann's, John Osborne's, and István Szabó's portrayal of homosexuals.[15] Osborne's Redl comes to accept his sexual orientation at the price of his social position and, ultimately, his life.[16] Being gay leaves him vulnerable to abuse and extortion as is indicated in the gay-bashing scene that concludes Act I. In Mann homosexuality is not the central issue, but rather the lack of integrity. Höfgen is an authoritarian personality reminiscent of Heinrich Mann's *Professor Unrat* (*The Blue Angel*) who crawls before authority and oppresses his inferiors.[17]

Klaus Mann does not associate homosexuality with corruption and Nazism, as has been done by most straight critics with the exception of Klaus Theweleit.[18] He portrays Höfgen as heterosexual, although those familiar with the circumstances may interpret his relationship with the African German dancer Juliette as symbolizing forbidden sexuality in general and homosexuality in particular. The stigma of the latter is represented by interracial sex, which was likewise outlawed by the Nazis. Such a "generic" representation of homosexuality is, however, problematic because it disregards both partners' male socialization as well as their social oppression. As Richard Dyer points out: "We, on the other hand, have nearly always been condemned even for having gay desires, and no real social legitimacy (in a wider sense than mere lack of legal constraints) has ever been allowed us."[19]

István Szabó, moreover, transformed Mann's ugly stripper into a good-looking black woman whose common sense and honesty leave no room for the shock effect intended by Mann.[20] Szabó makes it obvious that Juliette stages her *domina* act upon Höfgen's request. Thus he removed the taint of decadence from the homosexual and the black woman, placed it on the white male, and downplayed sexuality as a problem altogether.[21] In both the novel and the film Höfgen's friendship with Otto Ulrich, Bock, and the Airforce General (a reflection of Hermann Göring), as well as the intense conflicts between these men, suggest a homosocial if not repressed homosexual universe. The Nazi system is shown to be based upon a paradox: it prescribes homophobia and is at the same time a self-proclaimed state of men.[22] Indeed, while the majority of homosexuals were rounded up in concentration camps, others, like Gründgens, became celebrities and were as such above the law, as were the drag parties attended by Nazi leaders.[23]

Mann and Szabó avoided the overt representation of homosexual acts. Only Juliette's body and in *Colonel Redl* that of the prostitute are shown in close-up. Gay relationships and desires are only alluded to or signaled at times by the body language, for instance Höfgen's all-too-real demonstration of the cancan as his wife watches with sudden awareness and shock. Also his giggles, his hysterical fits, his prancing about and play-acting, his hand on Ulrich's shoulder, his intimacy with Bock are indications. In addition to Mann, Szabó underscores the motif of same-sex love by showing images suggesting lesbian relationships. These tend to be socially less visible, transparent through the body language and facial expressions of the partners of female couples.[24]

While in *Mephisto* Szabó adheres rather closely to the plot of Mann's novel, he all but disregards John Osborne's play in *Colonel Redl*. His reference to the play seems little more than a recommendation to compare his and Osborne's approach to the same material. The similarities between the writer's and the filmmaker's characters are superficial—Schorm is somewhat reminiscent of Kupfer, Katalin and Velochio of the Countess Delyanoff, Roden of Möhl. There are no models for Kristóf von Kubinyi and Archduke Franz Ferdinand. The significant childhood episodes in *Colonel Redl* and the film's impressive images are entirely Szabó's. However, he was inspired by Osborne's dialogues, some of which he incorporated verbatim.[25]

Another source for the film goes unmentioned. It is the Dreyfus affair. Alfred Redl and Alfred Dreyfus have more in common than their first names. Their Jewish background made them vulnerable despite their military rank. Neither the French nor the Austrian authorities hesitated to expose and frame these Jewish officers while protecting the traitor—in the French espionage affair it was a Hungarian major named Esterhazy who had sold information about the artillery to the German Colonel Max von Schwarzkoppen. It is a well-documented fact that papers were forged to bring about Dreyfus's downfall.[26] Such documentation about the Redl affair never surfaced—Vienna was not Paris and, moreover, Alfred Redl's homosexual connections possibly involved the innermost circles of German and Austrian nobility.

In *Colonel Redl* anti-Semitism is a recurrent theme, but Szabó does not make it the cause of Redl's demise, thus differentiating clearly between the French and the Austrian scandal: in France the rehabilitation of Dreyfus was possible, he could even become a member of the *Légion d'Honneur*. In Austria, however, the homosexual Alfred Redl, of uncertain ancestry, was forced into suicide and the discussion of his case was forever silenced. In Szabó's film the discussion of anti-Semitism goes hand in hand with that of homophobia, although at this time the Jews still enjoy a respite: the Archduke is careful not to frame a Jew at this time because of the recent Dreyfus affair. However, the writing on the wall is clear: it is a matter of time before the Jews as a group will be made the public scapegoat.

Szabó's assessment of the situation corresponds with accepted historical as well as social and psychological interpretations. Redl was a known homosexual, but the Nazis appear to have been the first to stress his Jewish background after 1938, thus linking homosexuality, Jewishness, and decadence.[27] Neither here nor in *Mephisto* did Szabó eliminate any of the associations evoked by the names of his protagonists. However, he prioritized his interests by placing his own emphases. In *Colonel Redl* he highlighted sexual and gender issues.

Szabó motivated Redl's sexual orientation psychologically and socially.[28] Insights from his own childhood experience of World War II, his familiarity with the works of Alain Resnais and anti-Fascist criticism, for example Adorno, Foucault, and Theweleit, inform his ideological framework.[29] The inclusion of what is made to appear as historical footage in the end underscores the historical, the mood-evoking impressions of the intimate scenes his psychological intent.[30]

The images of Redl's home village convey the cultural dilemma of the Austro-Hungarian multination state and the subjective plight of the individual. The camera approaches and scans Redl's isolated birthplace in the plains of Eastern Europe, the house of a simple *k. und k.* [Imperial and Royal] railroad official painted in *Schönbrunner* yellow, the color of Emperor Franz Joseph's residence in Vienna. Patriotism, piety, and an abundance of children are the norm in these remote territories of the Danube Monarchy. From an outsider's point of view, the Redls' poverty rather than their ethnic or religious identity is the most striking feature. The film remains ambiguous about the family's ethnic background. They live in Galicia, close to Lemberg, which was known for its sizeable Jewish population living among Poles and Ukrainians. The Redls' house overflows with children, in contrast to the barrenness of Redl's later life. At the time of Redl's secret visit before his downfall, the house is deserted, an image of his lost opportunities.

Unlike in *The Age of Day-Dreaming* where the protagonist's father, a soldier missing in the war, is the object of his son's fantasies, the father in *Colonel Redl* is physically present, but never as a role model. The boy is only too willing to accept Emperor Franz Joseph as his father ordained by God, a notion that is nurtured by his family, the Catholic state church, and the military academy. Redl's estrangement from his family becomes evident when he participates at the academy in the cadet's dedication as Imperial God Sons and the Emperor's birthday ceremony rather than attending his father's funeral. Redl's laudation of Emperor Franz Joseph, a pathetic but successful attempt to gain recognition, is an indication of his fierce ambition. At the same time, it is obvious that resorting to such demeaning adulation is his only chance to escape poverty and obscurity.

In *Colonel Redl* Szabó develops a concept of otherness in social and economic, ethnic and sexual terms. While poverty appears as a handicap that can be overcome by connections and hard work, being born a commoner and a Jew are handicaps the individual cannot escape. The frequent allusions to Redl's suspected Jewishness and the attacks on Jews, be they motivated by anti-Semitism or, as is the case with Schorm, self-hatred, are indicative of the racial tensions in pre-World War I Central Europe. They foreshadow persecutions of the Nazi era.[31]

Szabó's Redl is vulnerable because of his class, his homosexuality, and his Ukrainian, and perhaps hidden Jewish identity; thus he represents the ideal scapegoat. Archduke Franz Ferdinand sacrifices him because he wants to create a public-enemy image to avert ethnic unrest. At the same time he needs a cover for his own corruption and his criminal and possibly sexual involvement with Kristóf von Kubinyi. Lavender Cassels referred to the historical Franz Ferdinand's "complex personality," his unpredictable temper, ungovernable rage, particularly vis-à-vis his protégé Conrad during the Redl affair. However, Cassels claims that Franz Ferdinand had no detailed knowledge of the Redl case.[32] Stephan Verosta considered Redl's guilt a proven fact—Redl was convicted of being a Russian spy on 25 May 1913. According to Verosta he made a full confession. Verosta explains Conrad's behavior as an understandable hesitation to put an active officer on trial for espionage, because of the demoralizing effect on the public and the general staff. He mentioned that Redl possibly sold German military secrets as well. Moltke, who was known to be gay as well, reassured the German Emperor William II that no details of the Schlieffen Plan nor the German–Austrian pact had been betrayed. The Austrian Heir Apparent, a confirmed Catholic, was reportedly upset about Redl's forced suicide, but obviously not enough to allow Conrad to resign from office.[33]

Archduke Franz Ferdinand, like the Air Force general in *Mephisto*, is a key figure in Szabó's film. He is modeled on the ambivalent character of the historical Archduke (cf. Cassels, p. 54). Both the highest commander and Redl are quick-change artists. Franz Ferdinand moves as gracefully on the dance floor as he does in the garrisons, appealing to men and women alike. Redl has a similar androgynous appeal and can pass as a Jew in Galician taverns, but blends in with the Austrian officers as well.

If his environment perceives something "different," something "Jewish" about Redl, it is the odium of his low class origins. As a gay man of obscure birth who aspires to professional and social status, Redl faces similar obstacles as Jews, the workers, and women. Having been subject to constant oppression, he developed survival strategies that caused psychological deformities. As deviants from the norm of privileged white Christian males, the oppressed groups have developed traits that define them as "other."

Because of his otherness in terms of gender, ethnicity, and class, Redl has learned the art of dissembling. His opportunism assumes the form of hypocrisy, flattery, diplomacy, self-aggrandizement, or self-denial, whichever one seems called for and includes lying and spying on others. These patterns are traditionally associated with women, gays, and Jews who depended for their survival on the benevolence of others. As witch hunts and pogroms throughout the centuries show, the members of these groups could never take their safety for granted. On the other hand, those of Redl's traits which appear vulgar—his assertiveness to the point of brutality, his crudeness when he feels at ease or in control of his opponent—are generally associated with rebellious peasants and proletarians.

Redl makes the ranks, but cannot cast off the emotional makeup of his class. When his peasant-like sister Sopherl visits him at the garrison, he is well on his way to success. He gives her some money and frantically sends her away, because she embodies all that he does not want to be associated with: the premature aging of poor people, the ugliness and tedium of country life, family attachment, and heterosexuality. Moreover, he cannot cope with Sopherl, because deep down he shares her notions of love and commitment, no matter how often he transgresses against them to get ahead. At the time of his last crisis he returns to his roots. In the church *Maria am Gestade*, close to Vienna's old Jewish quarter, Redl, as if in an offering, burns his aristocratic friends' photograph. After this "Holocaust" [offering by fire] he walks past the Biedermeier façade of Vienna's main temple, the *Stadttempel* in the Seitenstettengasse to face his end at the Hotel Klomser.[34]

The aristocrats at the military academy consider homosexuality an activity without emotional and social significance and as such it is tolerated. The piano teacher is known to seduce boys. This becomes obvious during Schorm's interrogation. Redl's sexual orientation and his relationship with Kristóf do not concern Roden, but rather the possible public scandal.[35] As is to be expected in patriarchal society, and, according to Freud, in any normal child, male bonding and same-sex love precede Redl's heterosexual interests as is revealed in the episode when Redl in a pre-military training session breaks Kristóf's club—a surrogate sword and phallic symbol. The children, deprived of any other form of intimacy, have jousted with passionate fervor. As a result of their accident they are publicly flogged. Being singled out as delinquents, enduring shame and pain together, nakedness and wearing the same uniform constitute a bond of equality between the peasant and the aristocrat.

This experience has lasting impact on Redl. He falls in love in a manner characteristic of the middle and lower middle classes who, after all, popularized the notions of undying love and friendship along with the equation: love, marriage, family—a love progression impossible to achieve by a gay man and, as Katalin's experience shows, one that does not necessarily feature in the lifestyle of the aristocracy.[36]

Kristóf, on the other hand, becomes a lady's man, as is confirmed by the prostitute at the officers' brothel. It may be argued that his sporadic encounters suggest that he has no real interest in women at all. Until the fainting spell at the very end, after he has delivered the suicide weapon to Redl, Kristóf is aloof, even vis-à-vis Redl. The latter, however, in spite of his emotional awkwardness, thrives on intimacy. In one-on-one encounters, gay or straight, he is shown as a profoundly sexual and emotional being.

Redl is unable to shake his fixation for Kristóf. In his conversations with the prostitute as well as Katalin, he revels in his knowledge of Kristóf's body, deriving his stimulation from listening to reports about his friend's exploits. In the love scene with Katalin he closes his eyes admitting, when asked, that he is thinking of her brother. Neither friendship nor a common bond with his lover tie Redl to his wife, Clarisse, whose fragility is a symbol of how little consequence she is to him and society in general.

The sex scene with the whore—the girls suggest that this may be Redl's first heterosexual encounter—is followed by a passionate encounter in the staircase with Kristóf, who grasps Redl with the same aggression he displayed toward his girl and kisses him vigorously on the mouth.[37] Redl wipes his mouth while his friend observes him. He leans against the wall with the same provocative posture as Velochio in a later scene.

Szabó avoids flagrantly gay public scenes like Osborne's drag ball. This episode, however, corresponds in *Colonel Redl* roughly with two scenes: firstly the orgy at the bordello with whores dressed in bridal white, the dance where the officers and Galician civilians meet once again, the women, here the daughters of consequence, are dressed in white, and secondly the imperial masked ball where Katalin introduces Velochio to Redl. By changing these details Szabó indicates that gay life in turn-of-the-century Vienna was more discreet than portrayed in *A Patriot For Me*. However, the conversations during the ball suggest a multifaceted society reminiscent of Arthur Schnitzler's Vienna, a more enticing environment than Osborne's drag ball.[38]

Allusions to an all-pervasive homosexual underground in *Colonel Redl* are abundant. During Kristóf's and Redl's visit at the Kubinyi residence the camera focuses on Kristóf's grandfather, the way he glances at the boy, and the old man's hand coming to rest on Redl's. There can be no doubt that after young Redl's performance of his mother's vulgar Hungarian song, the grandfather knows that the boy is of an inferior class. His praise of him must refer to something very special: "Il est gentil, ton copin."[39] Under the tender and forgiving eye of the old gentleman, Redl experiences another humiliation that signifies the boy's separation from his class and his loss of self-determination: trying to serve coffee to his protector he is not able to stop the running samovar. The aristocrats stare at the boy, who must stand by and watch servants, people of his own class, clean up his mess.

The piano teacher's desirous glances and his hand caressing Redl's leg provide yet another example of homosexual desires on the part of authority figures. Redl neither reciprocates nor rejects the approach. The appreciation of Redl's superior Roden is more restrained. However, both men's glances and Roden's presents—the billfold and briefcase, which he buys back after Redl's death—indicate love between mentor and protégé. The ultimate manifestation of their complicity is Roden's advice to Redl on how to get Kristóf to join him.

Franz Ferdinand's repressed erotic fascination with Redl, although or because he decides to destroy him, is evident as early as the Heir Apparent's visit at the garrison. Here and elsewhere Franz Ferdinand appears provocatively relaxed, like a cat playing with a mouse. Redl in turn, encouraged by Roden's wink, glances suggestively at the Archduke. Shortly after this encounter Roden asks Redl upon the request of Field Marshall Konrad, Franz Ferdinand's confidant, if he is homosexual—an inquiry that prompts his sudden marriage. Franz Ferdinand's interview with Redl at Belvedere Castle, a male bastion without women, is more intense than Redl's honeymoon after a flashy wedding at Vienna's St. Stephen's Cathedral.[40] Publicly, Clarisse remains as invisible as the Archduke's morganatic consort, who is seen only in the brown-and-white footage of the assassination at Sarayevo. At all functions the Heir Apparent appears by himself with an entourage of officers. He flirts with men and women alike.[41]

In Franz Ferdinand's and Redl's conversation about power, the topic is less important than the seductive glances, as both men stand close to each other. The prince softly whistles the *Radetzky March*. His allusive statements and movements are seductive. Since Kubinyi, now Redl's adversary, left the prince's suite before Redl was asked to enter, a sense of danger heightens the excitement. Redl is known in his circles as a dangerous man, but this encounter proves that he is only a pawn. In the presence of the prince Redl is dwarfed in the same way as is Höfgen in *Mephisto* by the Air Force general: He is more brutal and ruthless, more powerful and suave.[42] As he talks to Redl he already has him trapped in his own web. For a while it appears as if the Archduke represented the ultimate power and evil incarnate. In the last frame, however, also his power is shown to be limited.

Szabó's Franz Ferdinand knows that Redl is no traitor. Moreover, his conversation with Konrad reveals his appreciation for Redl as a male whom in other scenes he lures with his sensuous smiles and an open shirt collar while casually destroying him. The viewer is led to suspect political considerations, but also Franz Ferdinand's inability to overcome his Catholic upbringing and his involvement with Kristóf. All these may be reasons for his not taking Redl as a lover.

To Redl Franz Ferdinand represents the ultimate challenge, a larger-than-life Kristóf whom he fears and desires, as he admits to Katalin. Kristóf and Franz Ferdinand, in fact, are the antithesis of the benevolent men in Redl's life, the old teacher, Roden, and the imaginary Emperor Franz Joseph. In his interaction with Franz Ferdinand, Redl's authoritarian bent and his paranoia reach their apex. He even lashes out at Katalin as his eagerness to please the Archduke increases while the latter mocks and dismisses him like a schoolboy. Redl randomly persecutes and brutalizes citizens to satisfy Franz Ferdinand's request for a show trial.

The raid of the Ullmann household is staged like a Gestapo *Aktion*. The choice of word, *Aktion*, is not accidental. As a part of the Nazi jargon the term denotes the terrorist attacks against political opponents and Jews during the Nazi era.[43] Not only Redl, whom Szabó carefully constructed as a proto-Fascist military type, but also Franz Ferdinand is a man of the Fascist future: ruthless and selfish without regard for traditional ties and values. Both variants of this type are shown as the root of the problems that lead to World War I and, by implication, World War II. However, these victimizers themselves suffer an untimely violent death.[44]

When Franz Ferdinand studies Redl's photo together with Konrad, he inadvertently describes himself—merciless, brutal, and sensual. The effect of this scene is intensified by the fact that Redl keeps a photo of Franz Ferdinand on his desk, supposedly to understand him, but more likely because he is drawn to him. Love and death are close allies in the demise of the homosexual Redl, to whom same-sex relationships are more than casual encounters. In his conversations with men Redl blossoms with warmth and affection, for instance with Sonnenschein and Schorm. Redl's eyes are filled with rapture as he watches Velochio asleep in bed. In such moments a Redl different from the man deformed by heterosexual oppression shines through, the man he might have been had it not been for his culture's gender and class structures.[45] There could not be a greater contrast between Redl, the lover of military men, and the careworn civilian Redl walking across the ruins of Rome with his mistress Katalin, or, for that matter, Redl the uneasy husband. Yet another, equally warm and relaxed Redl emerges in the company of Jews, be it in the Galician tavern, be it with the Jewish army doctor Sonnenschein.

Redl's story is about the waste of love and constructive energy because of social and political norms that create unsurmountable moral and psychological dilemmas. Ultimately all the individuals Szabó protrays in his films fall victim to man-made structures that are too inhuman for humans to cope with. In particular, Redl is placed by his ambition into a double-bind: being who he is he cannot succeed. At the academy, the Colonel extorts information from him by threatening to remove his beloved Kristóf and exploits his inferiority complexes as a commoner. Having acted as a spy, the boy Redl wails as he stands by the door: "I am a Judas," . . . "a treacherous peasant." However, he does not hesitate later to employ the same tricks to make others work for him.

During the visit at the Kubinyi residence Redl's homosexuality is awakened along with his heterosexuality. Kristóf's sister Katalin takes a liking to him. In an advance no less physical than that of her grandfather she pinches Redl's upper leg. In this scene Szabó codifies aggressive sexual behavior as class- and not gender-specific. To the aristocratic female Redl is, once again, a sex object. There is a degree of intimacy between Redl and Katalin during their Viennese affair, although it is based on frustrated desires. Seconds before their love-making, Redl raves about having seen the Emperor by the roadside while Katalin reminisces about her husband whom she can no longer tolerate. "Let's drink," are the last words before the sexual encounter. The following frame shows Redl and Kristóf on horseback in the midst of their soldiers.

Redl would prefer Kristóf as a lover if Kristóf could love him. Katalin, on the other hand, married in much the same way as Emperor Franz Joseph's Elisabeth, is ready for a commitment on Redl's part.[46] Suffering and frustration unite the adulterers, but adultery offers no solution. When Katalin asks whom Redl prefers, he diplomatically dodges the answer: "I like both of you very much." Redl appreciates Katalin's friendship, but he cannot love her, as is obvious during their vacation. He refuses to elope with her because he rejects heterosexuality and the nuclear family as much as he hesitates to start a new life away from the men he loves.

Szabó depicts the structures of Redl's society as homosocial and homosexual, dominated by ostensibly Christian heterosexual structures. They conceal, but do not squelch the underlying dynamics. Instances of drunkenness, for instance, reveal the desires underneath the surface. At the ball in Galicia, for example, an officer is shown dancing alone, then with a comrade, and only under pressure with one of the ladies, soon before he collapses on the floor. This scene signifies *in nuce* the fate of Redl and his peers.

The approved values, heterosexuality, the family, Catholicism, patriotism, and the social hierarchy provide a surface harmony, while they segregate classes, nationalities, religious groups, genders, friends, and foes. Oppression is the pillar on which this social fabric rests: that of the poor by the rich, of one ethnic group by another, women by men, gays by heterosexuals. Szabó focuses on the stunted growth of homosexual men within these repressive structures and the devastating results of denying male–male relationships the potential of love and partnership.[47] He develops the theme of gay oppression in conjunction with concerns of class, ethnicity, and gender. Redl's bigoted world semi-tolerates, semi-repudiates gayness. However, there is no chance for the social and sexual underdog to live with dignity, adhering to his own moral standards—not even Franz Ferdinand has such a chance.

On the basis of their physical and intellectual attraction and qualities, the Archduke, Redl, and Kubinyi seem singularly fated to be lovers. Deformed by social pressures, however, they become traitors, killers, and at the same time victims. Demanding that they deny themselves, their society produces spineless monsters. While these men's loveless and sexless marriages remain without issue, their frustrated desires turn into psychological time bombs.

Redl and Franz Ferdinand cannot but reproduce in business and politics the dishonesty demanded of them in their sexual life. Franz Ferdinand's corruption is a mirror image of the situation: just as homosexuality is arbitrarily defined as a crime, the Archduke invents crimes and criminals to serve his means, picking whom he wishes to accuse arbitrarily by social rank, origin, and ethnicity. Already before World War I, the stage is set for the libels and crimes of the Nazi era among whose first victims were, in fact, gays, who by their very presence undermined the Fascist gender and class structure. In comparison with the Archduke, Redl appears like an old-fashioned villain. Unaware of the magnitude of his inner conflicts, he envisions himself as a guardian of the monarchy. Franz Ferdinand needs no such pretexts, because he has no scruples.

In *Mephisto* the sexual and gender issues become increasingly less important as the Nazi system thwarts the expression of gay and straight sexuality alike, creating a general level of frustration, the source of powerful sadistic energies. The repression of homosexuality here results in the displacement of all forms of sexuality and the ultimate death of libido. All that remains is violence. The immediately visible result is the cultural and political decline after the liberal era of the Weimar Republic and the legalized brutality, which is soon to culminate in genocide and total war.

## NOTES

1. The three films have received little critical scholarly attention although *Mephisto* won the 1982 Silver Bear at the Berlin Festival, the Hungarian Critics Award, and the 1981 Academy Award for Best Foreign Film. *Colonel Redl* was supported by German and Austrian television. The films are available on video cassettes with English subtitles in the United States: *Mephisto*, director István Szabó. Produced by Mafilm-Objektiv Studio in Cooperation with Manfred Durniok Productions, 1981. Cassette: Thorn Emi Video, New York; *Oberst Redl*, director István Szabó. Produced by Mafilm-Objektiv Studio in Cooperation with Manfred Durniok Film and ZDF/ORF, 1985. Cassette: Pacific Arts Video, Beverley Hills, CA, 1987; *Hanussen*, director István Szabó. Columbia Pictures Industries, Inc., 1990. [Produced in 1989.]

2. Graham Petrie, *History Must Answer to Man. Hungarian Cinema Today* (Gyoma: Kner, 1978), p. 109.

3. In *Mephisto* the opening frames with excerpts from Carl Millöcker's operetta *Gräfin Dubarry* sung by Magda Kalmar in a rococo costume are particularly stunning. In *Colonel Redl* it is the alternation between march and waltz music, specifically Strauß's *Emperor Waltz* and the *Radetzky March*, which recaptures the morbid gaiety of turn-of-the-century Vienna, while in *Hanussen* the ambiance of Berlin of the 1920s is recreated. *The Magician of Lublin*, directed by Menachem Golan. Golan Globus (1978). The film was based on Isaac Bashevis Singer's novel with Alan Arkin as the magician Yasha in the lead role.

4. In *Mephisto* Szabó abandoned the surrealistic touches of *Concert* (1961) with the exception of a few emotional effects, for example the last scene. The protagonist Hendrik Höfgen (Klaus Maria Brandauer) is shown in the floodlight of the Berlin Olympia stadium asking what "they" want from a mere actor like him. This scene corresponds with an equally eerie one in *Colonel Redl*: After the departure of his friend and lover, Kristóf von Kubinyi is hunted by a pack of dogs. Shooting one of them he yells in despair: "What do you want from me?" Both scenes indicate the protagonists' isolation and disorientation.

5. Szabó preserved Klaus Mann's allusions to Gustav Gründgens's interpretation of Goethe's Mephisto in Brandauer's stage makeup and costume, which are identical to those which made Gründgens famous.

6. Klaus Mann, *Mephisto*, tr. Robin Smyth (New York: Penguin, 1977). John Osborne, *A Patriot For Me* (London: Faber & Faber, 1965), a play in three acts. Malcolm Page, *File on Osborne* (Methuen: London and New York, 1988), p. 43 lists performances: Royal Court Theater, London, club performance, to circumvent Lord Chamberlain's ban on the play on 30 June 1965. Maximilian Schell as Redl, Jill Bennett as the Countess, 4 December 1973, Palace Theater Watford. Marianne Faithfull as Countess. Chechester Festival, 12 May 1983, also Haymarket Theater, August 1983. New York: Imperial Theater, 5 October 1969. Schell as Redl.

7. A. L. Rowse, *Homosexuals in History. A Study of Ambivalence in Society, Literature and the Arts* (New York: Macmillan, 1977), p. 251: "The Great War of 1914–18 is the Great Divide."

8. Elias Canetti, *Masse und Macht* (Frankfurt: Fischer, 1980), pp. 487–522, explores magistrate Schreber rather than Hitler to expose the desires of a paranoid personality.

9. Klaus Theweleit, *Männerphantasien* II, "Zur Psychonalyse des weißen Terrors" (Hamburg: Rowohlt, 1980), pp. 336–338, discusses the role of physical punishment in the Wilhelminian and Franz Josephinian generations. He states on pages 256–257 that flogging and beatings in all likelihood became the most important acts of education in Central Europe during that time and assumes that the average German man received a secondary ego through flogging (a primary one could not be established because of the physical abuse) and made to operate this way. Szabó is clearly familiar with the Fascism studies that became the center of critical discourse in the 1960s, for instance: Wilhelm Reich, *The Mass Psychology of Fascism* transl. L. T. Wolfe (New York: Orgone Institute, 1946), Theodor W. Adorno, Else Frenkel–Brunswik, Daniel J. Levinson, Newitt R. Sanford, eds., *The Authoritarian Personality* (New York: Harper, 1950).

10. Hendrik Höfgen, the protagonist of Mann's *Mephisto*, is a type and the representation of a historical individual, the actor Gustav Gründgens, who made a name for himself as one of Germany's most prominent stage actors during and after the Nazi era in his role of *Mephisto* in Goethe's *Faust*. The allusions were so obvious that Gründgens's adopted son managed to have the book banned in Germany when an attempt to publish it in Germany was made in the late 1950s.

11. Lavender Cassels, *The Archduke and the Assassin* (London: Frederick Aruller, 1984), p. 157; Stephan Verosta, *Theorie und Realität von Bündnissen* (Vienna: Europa, 1971), p. 435.

12. A. Alvarez, "John Osborne and the Boys at the Ball," *New York Times* (28 September 1969), II, pp. 1, 5, quoted by Page, *File on Osborne*, p. 44.

13. In an age of greater sexual permissiveness the problem of sexual identity has

become more complex than at Redl's time. Martin Bauml Duberman, *About Time. Exploring the Gay Past* (New York: Sea Horse, Gay Presses of New York, 1986), p. 249, observed that "bisexuality" has become an ideal that is "increasingly touted as the standard against which all who aspire to *bona fide* membership in the Sexual Revolution must measure themselves." He asserted that anthropology proves that sexual behavior results from cultural, not genetic, imperatives, p. 253. From 1951–57 Osborne was married to Pamela Lane, 1957–63 to Mary Ure, 1963–67 to Penelope Gilliatt, 1968–77 to Jill Bennett, and after 1978 to Helen Dawson. Herbert Goldstone, *Coping with Vulnerability. The Achievement of John Osborne* (Washington: University Press of America, 1982), pp. 12f., discusses Osborne's affairs with actresses such as Stella Linden, as well as his marriages.

14. Martin Bauml Duberman, *About Time. Exploring the Gay Past*, p. 7, marks as the beginning of the modern gay liberation movement the year 1969 and the riot at the Stonewall Bar in Greenwich Village. James Fenton, referring to Molnàr's *Olympia*, remarks that Osborne's Empire is both historically based and imaginary. Malcolm Page, *File on Osborne* (Methuen: London and New York, 1988), pp. 44–45, quotes Frank Marcus: "These are Prussian, not Austrian, soldiers. In Vienna, callousness and brutality were covered by a veneer of geniality and false charm."

15. Emmanuel Cooper, *The Sexual Perspective. Homosexuality and Art in the Last 100 Years in the West* (London and New York: Routledge and Kegan Paul, 1986), p. XIX, observes that the "homosexual artist's response is governed by concerns which heterosexuals do not have. The knowledge that an artist was or is homosexual is not intended to 'explain' their work nor is it to suggest a particular context within which to view it. It is, rather the start of a process to look again and recover what has traditionally been omitted from the history of art using this to inform the present. What we can do most profitably is re-examine the work and lives of artists to search out from secrecy, prejudice, distortion and myth the homosexual presence and its wider significance in identifying homosexual expression."

16. Simon Trussler, *The Plays of John Osborne* (London: Victor Gollancz, 1969), p. 140: "The historical Redl was estranged both as a homosexual and a Jew: but his Jewishness does not particularly concern Osborne, and it is revealed (almost incidentally) only in the penultimate scene of the play.... Indeed, it is not till the climax of the first of the play's three acts that Redl is even aware of himself as a homosexual—and Osborne seems pedantically determined that his audience's awareness shall be similarly slow to develop."

17. Theodor W. Adorno, Else Frenkel–Brunswik, Daniel J. Levinson, Newitt R. Sanford, eds., *The Authoritarian Personality* (New York: Harper, 1950), developed a similar character profile for the Facist and authoritarian personality.

18. Theweleit, *Männerphantasien* II, p. 351, points out that there is no connection between homosexuality and Fascist forms of behavior. On pages 368f., he observes that homosexual relationships were attractive also to Fascist men because they offered a kind of love that was separate from the socially downgraded female realm. In volume 1, pp. 76f., he elaborates that the notions of what constitutes homosexuality are diffuse and full of denial. He characterizes the notion of the homosexual "tough guy" as a homophobic enemy image. By showing a black mistress and lesbians instead of male lovers, Mann does not elude the problem of representing gayness, because his public is aware of his and his protagonist's homosexuality. By equating marginalized expressions of sexuality, which his contemporary German readers were trained to perceive as criminal, he potentially feeds into popular prejudice. Parker Tyler, *Screen-*

*ing the Sexes. Homosexuality in the Movies* (New York, Chicago, San Francisco: Holt, Rinehart and Winston, 1972), pp. 70ff., observed that in popular films homosexuals, like drugs and prostitution, are used to symbolize the "bad habits" of humanity and to supply the motivation of a tough melodramatic plot. The homosexual is traditionally portrayed as a sick person, "like a pathological murderer, only commensurately less punishable."

19. Richard Dyer, "Rejecting Straight Ideals: Gays in Film," Peter Steven, ed., *Jump Cut. Hollywood, Politics and Counter Cinema* (New York, etc: Praeger, 1985), p. 290: "What this boils down to in films is that if you are representing sexual and emotional relationships on screen, it does make a difference whether they are gay or straight. One will not do as metaphor for the other. Nor will either do as general metaphors for human sexuality and relationship."

20. Mann, of course, participated in the socially involved discourse of the 1920s and 1930s, which had opened up to the problem of the black minority. These texts appear to the reader of the 1990s often rather racist, but were not recognized as such at the time. For example Claire Goll, *Der Neger Jupiter erobert Europa* (Basel: Rhein Verlag, 1926).

21. Also in other works Klaus Mann represented gay lovers by androgynous female characters following a sexual typology reminiscent of Otto Weininger, *Geschlecht und Charakter. Eine prinzipielle Untersuchung* (Munich: Matthes & Seitz, 1980), p. 60: "Fragen wir unsere Formel nach dem Komplemente des Konträrsexuellen, so erhalten wir vielmehr das allermännlichste Weib, eine Lesbierin, die Tribade. Tatsächlich ist diese auch nahezu das einzige Weib, welches den Konträrsexuellen anzieht, das einzige, dem er gefällt."

22. Cf. Alfred Rosenberg, *Der Mythus des 20. Jahrhunderts. Eine Wertung der seelisch-geistigen Gestaltenkämpfe unserer Zeit* (Munich: Hoheneichen Verlag, 1943; first published 1930), pp. 512–513.

23. Mann, *Mephisto*, p. 13: "The delicate Gallic admirer of German heroism, strapping German youths, the Führer's great thoughts and aristocratic flesh took alarm at the heaving proximity of so much womanly flesh." Theweleit, *Männerphantasien* II, p. 380, mentions that Göring had appeared at a reception in drag; however, he is quick to add that probably no homosexual activity took place. He assumes that the reason for the same sex attraction among men was at least in part the social structures. Women were excluded from public activity, adventure, esprit, and freedom, and appeared therefore less glamorous than men. Heinz Heger, *Die Männer mit dem rosa Winkel* (Hamburg: Merlin, 1972), a gay concentration camp survivor, describes the paradoxes within the camps where homosexuality was widespread. Many of the dominant males such as the Capos actively took part in homosexual exchanges, but dissociated their homosexual activity from being 'gay.'

24. Duberman, *About Time*, p. 254.

25. For instance the exchange in Möhl's office: "Sir, my own experience is that genuine merit rarely goes unnoticed or unrewarded, particularly in the Army." Osborne, *A Patriot For Me*, p. 22. In Szabó this dialogue takes place in Roden's office after the duel. Also here it constitutes an example of military double-talk. While Redl is reprimanded for having acted as the second in a duel, he is actually promoted.

26. Historical details such as the involvement of Oscar Wilde on behalf of Dreyfus are interesting in connection with Szabó's gay theme. Hellmut Andics, *Die Juden in Wien* (Vienna: Kremayr & Scheriau, 1988), p. 387.

27. Andics, *Die Juden in Wien*, p. 217: "Nach 1938 überraschte eine Wiener

Zeitung ihre Leser mit der Enthüllung, jener unglückselige, homosexuelle österreichische Generalstabsoberst Alfred Redl, der vor 1914 Aufmarschpläne der k. u. k. Armee an den russischen Geheimdienst verkauft und nach seiner Entlarvung im Wiener Hotel Klomser Selbstmord begangen habe, sei ein getaufter Jude gewesen."

28. Dyer, "Rejecting Straight Ideals: Gays in Film," p. 293, on the merits of certain kinds of stereotyping and the pitfalls of insisting on well-motivated, "rounded" characters such as E. M. Forster's, a "method that has inscribed the dominant values of western society above all individualism." While seemingly affirming these traditional belief systems, Szabó subtly undercuts them.

29. Petrie points out that Szabó's films are not about the autobiography of an individual, but autobiographies of generations. Petrie, *History Must Answer to Man*, pp. 107–108, 194. For instance Adorno, Frenkel–Brunswik, Levinson, Sanford, *The Authoritarian Personality*; Michel Foucault, *Discipline and Punish. The Birth of the Prison* (New York: Vintage Books, 1979) (*Surveiller et Punir; Naissance de la prison* (Paris: Gallimard, 1975)); Theweleit, *Männerphantasien*.

30. René Prédal, "Vie et Mort d'un Mythe," *Études cinématographiques* 73–77 (1970), pp. 183–198, 184. Szabó included historical footage in *The Age of Day-Dreaming*. Petrie, *History Must Answer to Man*, pp. 106ff., delineates the influences of the Polish cinema of the late 1950s, later influence of Truffaut, Resnais, and Godard on Szabó's early films.

31. Also in *A Patriot For Me*, p. 126, Redl's Jewish ancestry was an issue, however, without the representation of the larger social framework of *Colonel Redl*. Osborne makes allusions to the Nazi era and introduces a Freud figure. "Deputy: Is it not true that he was, in fact, the son of one Marthe Stein, a Galician Jewess? (Uproar.) Why was this fact not taken note of?"

32. Lavender Cassels, *The Archduke and the Assassin* (London: Frederick Aruller, 1984), pp. 157f. In 1913 it was discovered that Redl had clandestinely received money for selling military secrets to a foreign power. Informed of "the incontrovertible evidence" of this, Konrad ordered Redl's interrogation. Redl admitted having worked for the Russians. He was handed a gun and left alone. Forty-five minutes later he shot himself. Next day a search of his flat in Prague revealed that he was a homosexual, and produced evidence that his espionage activities were far more extensive than he had admitted. Franz Ferdinand summoned Konrad to the Belvedere and castigated the Chief of Staff.

33. Stephan Verosta, *Theorie und Realität von Bündnissen* (Vienna: Europa, 1971), p. 435.

34. This temple, founded in 1826, was the only Viennese synagogue spared during the Holocaust, perhaps because of its inconspicuous façade.

35. This theme is reminiscent of Joseph Roth's 1939 novel *Die Geschichte von der 1002. Nacht* (Cologne: Kiepenheuer & Witsch, 1981), which became widely known through the popular film version with Johanna Matz and Helmut Qualtinger.

36. Steven, ed., *Jump Cut. Hollywood, Politics and Counter Cinema*, p. 291, discusses this issue and the problems involved in the cinematographic representation of gay relationships.

37. Tyler, *Screening the Sexes*, pp. 176–177. It is the same pose as in Tyler's example shown in the illustration "Professional kiss" from *The Boys in the Band*.

38. Page, *File on Osborne*, p. 45, quotes John Simon: "You might expect a play whose high point is a drag ball to be a bore; what you would not expect is that even the drag ball is a drag."

39. It is significant that also in *Mephisto* the protagonist's singing is mentioned as a moment of great embarrassment.

40. The castle was built by one of Austria's most renowned military men, Prince Eugen, who defeated the Turks. Before Redl joins his bride in the honeymoon suite, Redl shuts out the world. He follows her request to come inside slowly and with displeasure. He closes the blinds, the double windows, and the curtains as if he wanted to make sure not to see her. Being married does not change his lifestyle.

41. Theweleit discusses the anonymity of the wives of military men in proto-fascist societies in *Männerphantasien* I, "Frauen, Fluten, Körper," pp. 19ff., and the topic of male couples in *Buch der Könige* I (Basel: Stroemfeld/Roter Stern, 1988).

42. Like the Air Force general in *Mephisto*, Franz Ferdinand is at one point shown in underwear and suspenders. Rather than diminishing the atmosphere of impending danger in Szabó's iconography, this apparent relaxation on the part of these figures heightens the impression of their monstrosity.

43. Another phrase that connects Franz Ferdinand with central European anti-Semitism and exposes his moral corruption is his statement, "Wer Verräter ist, entscheide jetzt ich" [Now I decide who is a traitor], reminiscent of Karl Lueger's "Wer ein Jud' ist, bestimme ich" [I decide who is Jewish], characterizing the autocratic behavior of Vienna's most powerful mayor and Franz Ferdinand's contemporary.

44. Tyler, *Screening the Sexes* shows in his illustrations between pages 176 and 177 as examples of "Homocult Plots" flirting with guns as typical *topoi* in gay film.

45. Cooper, *The Sexual Perspective*, p. XVIII, points out: "In patriarchal societies in which men have the greatest access to power, to be a male homosexual is to be 'less than a man,' or to be 'like a woman.'"

46. The Empress's apartment at the Vienna Hofburg bears quiet testimony to Elisabeth's plight. Hers is the only place with a bathtub. There is no actual bedroom; she preferred to use a simple folding bed. The doors connecting her suite with Franz Joseph's are furnished with gigantic bolts.

47. Tyler, *Screening the Sexes*, p. 22, points out that much of homophobia rests on a concept of natural sexuality "to regularize and maintain the higher (that is more complex) concept of the family."

# Rosa von Praunheim's Celebration of the Victim as Survivor: Jews and Gays in *Anita, Dances of Vice*

## Gabriele Weinberger

Since Fassbinder's death in 1983, Rosa von Praunheim has been Germany's single most prolific gay filmmaker with about forty films to his name. Asked by a viewer how he compares to the director of such films as *Berlin Alexanderplatz* and *Querelle*, Rosa von Praunheim quipped that "Fassbinder was perverse and wanted to be bourgeois whereas I am bourgeois and like to be perverse."[1] With this comment the filmmaker, who came from a middle-class Catholic background and started his career as an art student, alludes to his love for images that oppose the bourgeois categories of good taste. The director's joking comment hints at the very different way in which his and Fassbinder's films are camp.[2]

Rosa von Praunheim's 1987 film *Anita, Dances of Vice* is based on the life of Anita Berber, a film actress and the first woman to dance nude for the Berlin public in the 1910s and 1920s. Bisexual and a user of cocaine, she died young of tuberculosis. In Praunheim's film the forgotten star comes alive in the visions of an old woman who claims to be Anita. The police commit her to a mental institution, where in the old woman's dreams and exchanges with the staff, scenes from the life of Anita Berber appear. As the film offers images of the dancer's great era—Expressionist, silent, but in shimmering colors—the captive remembers her wild, short life to its bitter end.

All of Rosa von Praunheim's films offend against the code of color-coordinated propriety. Especially in his earlier films the images scream at the viewer loudly and a "queer and irritatingly flickering sensuality"[3] plays in a frantic manner with the ban on kitsch imposed by the bourgeoisie. Praunheim's works are characterized by excess, by a monstrous mass of signs, since to this director moderation would imply accepting the dictatorship of the taste of the repressive mainstream culture. Praunheim's views on love and sexual difference—the main parameters of his work all along—have culminated in *Anita, Dances of Vice* in a phantasmagoric dream of androgyny and transcendence, which through its 1920s time frame gives a historical dimension to the discourse on gender and sexual difference of the 1980s.

The operative terms "bourgeois" and "perverse" mark the constructedness of the categories that delineate the boundaries of our life experience. Praunheim assigns "taste" the same rank as class in its double appearance as a person's aesthetics (that is, in particular, visual design as expression of emotions) and a person's sexual preferences. He defines the parameters of class, possibly ethnicity, and taste as mutually depending on each other, constituting together inner and outer markers of a person's identity. Thus, his reference to "bourgeoisie" and "perversity" points to the fact that these two terms become *opposites* only through the sublimation of emotions.

The film director Praunheim is known for casting actors with strong personalities and for allowing them a great amount of creative input throughout the process. Praunheim's films of the early 1980s are open forms that incorporate a diversity of theatrical genres reminiscent of stage productions of the 1920s. While a direct connection with Expressionist art is most prominent in the 1984 film *Horror vacui*, this influence on the director was there all along and only surfaced to different degrees.

Evidence of his fascination for the arts and creative people of the 1910s and 1920s is abundant already in his earlier work. For example, it shows in scenes such as the one in which Maria Christiana Leven is performing a Mary Wigman dance routine on the roof of the "Kommunale Kino" in the 1977 film *The 24th Floor*. In *Our Corpses Are Still Alive* it also shows in Leven's second role and more generally in the focus on the woman of the 1930s. This 1981 film brought Rosa von Praunheim together with the Jewish actress and dancer Lotti Huber, the star of *Anita, Dances of Vice*. Praunheim's rootedness in this period in terms of not only artistic, creative influence, but also in terms of emotional and personal grounding, is central to my argument.

A number of gay filmmakers share Praunheim's fascination with strong women. For example, Fassbinder was famous for his constructed female figures that epitomized the mainstream German society to the extreme and demonstrated how it turned itself on its head. Praunheim, however, disinterested in the women of mainstream society, always had a fascination for older female or transsexual stars on the decline and strong women exiles, many of them beyond the age where they become invisible (of no consequence) in the eyes of mainstream society. Particularly unconventional old women often create their own post-menopausal identities, pursuing happiness against the demands of society.

Expressionist culture is unthinkable without Jewish contributions, particularly those of the strong Jewish actresses (e.g. Elisabeth Bergner) and poets (e.g. Else Lasker–Schüler) of the 1920s. In this bohemian culture, strong older post-menopausal Jewish women played an important role. Particularly Else Lasker–Schüler and her claim to desire and eroticism as a middle-aged woman comes to mind. Lotti Huber is another incarnation of this female mode of existence.

Eight of the director's works since 1981 explicitly ask questions of gender and sexual identity of such exceptional women, e.g. *Horror vacui* (1984), *Dolly, Lotte, and Maria* (1986), *Anita, Dances of Vice* (1987), his New York dance theater production, the film *Surviving in New York* (1990), and especially his 1990 film about Lotti Huber, *Affengeil*, subtitled "A Trip through Lotti Huber's Life," which he calls his "most personal film,"[4] and the 1992 film *Ich bin meine eigene Frau*.

*Anita, Dances of Vice* brought to a culmination both Praunheim's artistic cooperation with Lotti Huber and his central themes: strong women, sex, death, and survival. Openly sexual and older women have in common with gay men their isolation, the absence of respect granted by mainstream society, the closeness to death. Rosa von Praunheim, Lotti Huber, and Anita Berber in a similar way are able to embrace death. They share the fascination for death since the bourgeoisie excludes it from the specter of life. For Rosa von Praunheim their transgressions are heroic.

Anita Berber, the personification of Weimar depravity, danced naked at the White Mouse cabaret and appeared in a number of films, including a dancing role in Fritz Lang's *Dr. Mabuse*.[5] Praunheim sees her as a symbol of the decadence, the perversity, the bisexuality, and the drug culture of her time. Praunheim's direct inspiration for the film on Anita Berber came from Lothar Fischer's book, which documents her life and work. During the height of her short career she became a central figure in the creative circles of Berlin, and although she herself is not Jewish[6] some of the people who were most instrumental to her success in photography, dance, and theater and film productions were Jewish, as Fischer points out.[7] Most important for her career was the Berlin film director and producer Richard Oswald who made a number of films about sexuality and prostitution, and in collaboration with Dr. Magnus Hirschfeld[8] the film *Different from the Others* about gay love. In his revolutionary modern convictions concerning sexuality and gender roles Oswald had crucial influence on Anita Berber. Believing that "The principle of modernity is the public" (Fischer, p. 36), Richard Oswald promoted sexual freedom by making it a public topic and advancing a sexual community until his works were censored and banned by the Nazis.

In many respects Praunheim is continuing Oswald's work through his own films on gay men's and older women's sexuality and by documenting the sexual license of the period as in *Anita, Dances of Vice*.[9] In addition to the film itself documenting the 1920s, Praunheim toured German cities where the film was showing, with his star Lotti Huber giving live performances, thus reviving the live dance performances Anita Berber had given at the opening of the film *Unheimliche Geschichten*.

Whereas Berber died, Lotti Huber, the Jewish woman, survived the Fascist purge and called herself "an up and coming star" at age seventy-five. She exudes creative force, strength, and vitality. What won her the director's admiration is her optimism, which "(in contrast to Berber) seems to stem from a categorical refusal to be victimized by her time."[10] Lotti Huber, the Jewish exile, who returned as an old woman to Germany after many years in Cyprus, is as much at the margin of German society as the gay artist. Whereas Anita Berber only lives in pictures,[11] Lotti Huber becomes Praunheim's living link to the Weimar Republic. She not only recreated the Expressionist excess of the 1920s and herself as a would-be star of the 1920s but also assumes the role of a big star of the 1980s.

In the film *Anita, Dances of Vice* Praunheim sought for a second time (after *Horror vacui*) artistic communion with the two women he admires most: Lotti Huber and his friend of many years, the camerawoman and filmmaker Elfi Mikesch. He turned the film into a kind of worship of their creative life force. Through the work of the actress Lotti Huber and Elfi Mikesch's camera, Anita Berber turns into the starting point from which the creative transformation takes off. As the director concedes, the film is not his alone, and he credits these two women with the creation of this dream of gender and sexual discourse[12] (similar to the process envisioned in Expressionist drama, which leaves ample room for different theatrical realizations). As a result of Lotti Huber's input, the tragic downside of Berber's life and the 1920s social turmoil are overcome through her reenactment and reliving of Anita Berber's life.

The title *Anita, Dances of Vice* misleads the audience into thinking that Rosa von Praunheim's film is about Anita Berber, raising the question of dream versus reality, when in fact its foremost focus is Lotti Huber, who incarnates the equation life = sex = death, androgyny/sexual difference in present and past. Most of all, however, the film is about surviving, optimism, and creativity in the face of existential threat both in the repressive 1920s, when the Nazi ideology first gathered massive momentum, and the regressive, proto-Fascist 1980s with the threat of mass annihilation through AIDS and a growing right-wing agenda.

Long before Praunheim learned about Anita Berber from Lothar Fischer's book, he became fascinated with the Expressionist period at the beginning of his own artistic career as a painter and a student of Oskar Kokoschka in 1962/3. Since 1983 Praunheim again paints in an Expressionistic style. As a film director, Praunheim shares with Kokoschka the preoccupation with death, the often joyful visions of apocalypse, and a taste for the exotic, even aggressive use of the same primary colors. Praunheim's films mix stylistic elements from painting and art of the periods between the turn of the century and the 1930s, such as *Jugendstil* (arabesque excess in decor), Kitsch, and *Neue Sachlichkeit*. Like his Expressionist predecessors, Rosa von Praunheim combines in his films various art forms such as musical revue, performance art, pantomime, and harlequin figures.

Praunheim copied many of the authentic but not entirely unique poses and costumes in which Anita Berber dazzled her audiences. Some of the looks and costumes can be found in other work of this period, such as Charlie Chaplin's classic *Women*[13] and Rudolph Valentino's movies, as well as old vampire films.[14]

In *Anita, Dances of Vice* Praunheim reconstructs the Expressionist cinema as it represents urban mass society of the post-World War I years, with all its thematic and visual elements that have earned it its ban by right-wing ideologists. As the following paragraphs show, the director assembles a collage of structural elements of Expressionist art (not just cinema) as well as social and artistic themes that figured prominently in all anti-Semitic propaganda. It remains to be seen how Praunheim uses them and what functions these elements have in his work.

In both, *Anita, Dances of Vice* and Praunheim's 1984 *Horror vacui*, the city is the location in which the paradigmatic existentialist conflicts are experienced. The most symbolic meeting place and urban battleground between bourgeoisie and "the other" is the street. *Anita, Dances of Vice* begins and ends in the street; the street is where Anita Berber lands periodically for prostitution, in food lines, and as a sick performer without engagement. Even Expressionism's anti-militarist, pacifist theme is not missing in this film, as her artistic partner Droste escapes his fate as a soldier to become a dancer. In this film the city is marked as the locus of liberalism, progress, modernity, and the avant-garde as well as the struggle of the masses to survive.

Expressionist theater and literature made again fashionable the romantic idea of the "double" or split personality. *Anita, Dances of Vice* centers on this theme. Anita Berber is doubled twofold—once in the actress Ina Blum as part of the Berber role and the second time when the nurse (also played by Ina Blum), as nurse, discovers her affinity to the dancer toward the end of the film. Droste and the doctor are in a double constellation that appears less complex at first, since the latter remains alienated and separate from the bisexual dancer's role. Nevertheless, it proves to follow the oedipal pattern of, on the one hand, the partner/positive father figure, on the other hand, the physician in the asylum/negative repressive authority figure. Both male and female personae vacillate between present and past and between the poles of, on the one hand, the androgynous bisexual life of vice and, on the other hand, mainstream homophobic bourgeois authority.

The old woman had been committed to the asylum because of her sexuality. The people controlling her, trying to deaden her desires with drugs in the institution, are played by the same actors. In other words: what differentiates them from the characters who possess a sexual identity is only the narrowness of imposed restrictions on their desire and their bodies. By implication they appear as alter egos. Following her male/female double role of Prof. Kutowski/Madame C. in *Horror vacui* Lotti Huber continues in this film as Kutowski, only this time the female is doubled with the female role of A. Berber. By shaping Lotti Huber's character as more-dimensional through this technique, Rosa von Praunheim explodes the one-dimensionality of anti-Semitic stereotypes. As they are laid open as such, their contradictions are made obvious. In my opinion a major reason for Rosa von Praunheim's fascination with Expressionism is the multidimensional depth of personality structure and the concern with aspects of the human condition that were traditionally seen as separate.

Hostile feelings toward clergy and other father or authority figures, typical of Expressionist films, are introduced through Anita's Freudian relationship with her father, the police, and the personnel in the asylum, and finally in a short scene with a priest. The filmmaker marks gender as an artificial construct in the scene about Anita's rejection by her father. The doll-like "little woman" Anita is clearly marked as the mother's creation. In this scene, Lotti Huber as child in a pink baby-doll outfit is a similarly-forced construct, as is the wild-eyed Bette Davis as Baby Jane.[15] In contrast to this artificial female identity, the evolving androgynous identity is not marked especially but presented as a natural development as she grows up outside the bourgeois restraints of a father's love and acceptance.

Androgyny as a concept transcends the gender roles. The viewer is confronted with the grown Anita, as a bisexual socialite, later to be notorious for her nude dance routines with Sebastian Droste. It is significant, however, that he is presented as a man who has been afflicted by the traumas of heterosexual male gender roles and the duties of a macho man. In a quite lengthy scene he transforms himself into the androgynous bisexual dancer with makeup, demonstrating the dramatic break and the fact that one construct replaces the other: Droste is an ex-soldier and, implicitly, an alter ego of Hitler and *Freikorps* men. Intercut scenes of World War I fighting represent the heterosexual macho male role. However, he refuses this role and becomes an image of the androgynous man. Whereas the androgynous man represents the battle to achieve this androgynous identity, the women are not made obvious in the same way as gender constructs; on the contrary, they are rather natural beings who evolve and fade, their main characteristic being their inherent lightness. While quite limited in scope, Droste is a much more dramatic figure, as is visually expressed in his dances and in his conflicts, which make him sacrifice his partner. In keeping with the traditional dichotomy between woman as a quintessential natural being and man in the heroic battle against nature, Anita is made to fade into nothingness through consumption (tuberculosis) whereas his death (although caused by tuberculosis, like hers) is visually lifted out in scenes of shootings and hangings. Droste can have the idealized androgynous body in aesthetically highlighted dance scenes only for a short duration. Anita, however, in all her transfigurations of age and class throughout the film, in representations by both actresses, inherently possesses the desirable qualities that are nostalgically celebrated in this character.

The questions of sexual difference and their implications for today's society are confronted foremost in the scenes in which the identities of the later Anita and her young image are constructed through an encounter between the two women—first as nurse, then with Ina Blum taking on the role of Anita, and finally when the nurse reveals her homoerotic desire and closeness to the nude dancer on the woman's deathbed in a lesbian love-dance scene. In this scene the black and white in which the aged dancer appears in the asylum is mixed/intercut with the symbolism of dreamlike color scenes earlier on.

Rosa von Praunheim refuses a fixed and permanent quality (as Scott had argued) of the binary opposition male and female. Through the fluidity of their metamorphosis the five Anita/Droste personae demonstrate a potential of both male and female characteristics, changing with different situations and encounters.

Dance in *Anita, Dances of Vice* mirrors the function it had in the 1920s as a resistance to or escape from intellectualism.[16] Dance stands in opposition to rational linguistic discourse/communication. Not only are these scenes without dialogue, but even intertitles do not interfere with their effect on the viewer. However, Rosa von Praunheim focuses on the nude dance as a symbol for the ultimate (i.e. sensual, tactile, and aesthetic) opposition to bourgeois norms, which lies in the perversity of embracing the shunned sectors of human existence: lust, ecstasy, death. The only people really *alive* in the film's scenes from the past are the two dancers, as their movements symbolize *life* (versus the middle class's pseudo-life). The majority of dance scenes are Lotti Huber's. Central to the function of dance in the film is her particular style, underscored by her live performances in conjunction with film shows. In her comments on dance and her movements she stresses the opposition of mind and body and the necessity to do the body justice. Dance signifies sensuality, lust, ecstasy, i.e. life and death.

*Anita, Dances of Vice* emphasizes backdrops and stages action with the actors always facing the public. Its scenography is as rudimentary as in medieval morality plays. Although Rosa von Praunheim is familiar with the coloration code of the films of the 1920s, his use of color stems from the graphic arts, but is also informed by Expressionist painting, for example Franc Marc's use of colors to indicate emotional and existential qualities. He purposely heightens the trivializing/vulgarizing effect of color that was perceived in the 1920s (in contrast to "noble black"). The director equates sex with life through bright colors, which contrast with the relative colorlessness of the passive, sexually repressed middle class. Thus colors are markers for sexual identity within the central categories of class and taste (bourgeois versus perverse). Blue (pure, metallic, light, bright indigo) and red (full, bright, signal red) are reserved mainly for the two dancers, the representatives of free bisexual love, the "androgynous" beings. Anita and her male dance partner Sebastian Droste are made as gender-neutral as possible through their costumes and makeup, and share male and female characteristics. The same color scheme is shared by the poor hungry masses lining the streets for scarce food supplies. Their faces have androgynous traits as hard work and deprivation have rendered the women's appearance more masculine or gender-neutral than the gender-coded middle-class females. Simultaneously they are marked as sexual beings as they lack the sexually repressive mechanisms of the bourgeoisie. (Desperate for pleasure out of life, they seek it through sex, the only gratification that is free.) In contrast, the mainstream society is in greens, browns, orange tones, their round, plump faces in a sickly yellow. "Natural" lighting distinguishes them from the artificial lighting on the sexual beings.

Both representations of Anita by Lotti Huber and Ina Blum display the shimmering and glistening of Klimt paintings; Blum's red pantsuit and the pantsuit Huber wears in the asylum give them a harlequinesque appearance. In her red outfit, with a bluish-white face, Huber has the dramatic features of a clown whose act is funny despite his predicament.

In great part due to Elfi Mikesch's camera and control over lighting (which Praunheim adores: "Elfi makes wonderful light with very simple means. Her images are warm and her frames unusual"[17]) single frames often have the appearance of a Cubist painting set in motion: a composition of shapes in rhythm. Color is injected into a dark frame. It combines with motion to create the life force. In most frames with Anita and Droste, the black of the background and floor serves as a foundation for livid, blue and white light that throws the surface of the image into dramatic tension. In sharp contrast to this strongly rhythmic composition, green, yellow, brown make the middle class a slow moving or static blob that has a contained amorphous roundness.

Rosa von Praunheim sculpted body shapes in Cubist tradition by accentuating certain sensual body parts: eyes, mouth, movements of hands, body shape. Just as *Dr. Caligari's* Cesare (the symbol of subconscious aggression) is associated with triangular forms, Sebastian Droste is similarly angled and linear in his red loincloth, and his makeup very much resembles Cesare's. The same effect of angled, linear lines and shapes is reached in the character of Anita through Ina Blum's and Lotti Huber's costumes and makeup. Most dramatic is the expression of the eyes: Anita's and Droste's stare exposes the white of the eye and creates a hallucinating gaze à la Otto Dix.

Central to Praunheim's attraction to Lotti Huber as his friend and a pivotal part of her roles in *Horror vacui* and *Anita, Dances of Vice* is the fact that she does not follow purely female gender stereotypes. Her androgynous appearance can be read as both masculine and feminine. Huber seems to heighten her being the "Other" to everybody (Gentiles, males, pre-menopausal sexually-conforming women) into a defiant identity apart outside any category. She embodies the opposite of the powerless, "sad" Jewess as quintessential victim, a stock character of Holocaust fiction from Anna Seghers and Leonhard Frank to Peter Edel and others. Lotti Huber becomes the epitome of the survivor defying all the myths of society.

While sharing the eclectic range of facets and elements that comment on the world in both times of social crisis and change (the 1920s and the 1980s), what differentiates the director's models in Expressionist art from his own postmodern images is above all the difference in their outlook: while death has been acted out in her performances, the old woman is as chipper as ever in the end as she walks away hollering for a taxi. Through her ironic death Praunheim plays the opposition "bourgeois versus perverse" to the hilt as she chooses to "die" when pressured by the nurse to conform to the middle-class restrictions and become like an Inge Meysel (Edith Bunker). This death is no surrender, however, since the nurse who demands this conformity of her is the one whom we see as her lover at her deathbed, while the old woman is as alive and lively as ever in the last images. Thus the director does not quote his original (neither Berber's life story nor Expressionist cinema's storylines) directly but transforms them to create new meaning.

Rosa von Praunheim breaks up simple dichotomies of all categories and at the same time gives his scheme an ironic twist by relegating the androgynous state to the vision of a madwoman. The director's comment of self-irony seems to be: you have to be a fool to believe you can get away with it as Lotti Huber does in the end; there is a simultaneity of the traditional diagnosis of homosexuality as disease and vice (mainstream 1920s discourse) and the fear of not being taken seriously and being dismissed as crazy (the discourse of the 1980s).

Furthermore, the film structurally reveals what authors and critics of Fascism have maintained, namely, that none of the structures underlying Fascism have changed. The same homosocial structures, anti-Semitism, repressive authoritarianism prevail, only they have not (yet?) been formalized into a Nazi state. Probably the shock effect of Praunheim's films in the 1980s is as great as Anita Berber's dance was in the 1920s. At the time Praunheim made the film, there was hope. Lotti Huber has survived and has not (yet?) been seriously threatened, neither as a Jewish woman, a mental deviant, a bisexual person, or a woman rejecting standard role models.

Praunheim's film celebrates all the values contradicting the past and present repression of otherness. At the same time he expresses his awareness of the Reagan–Bush–Kohl era threat preceding unification. As if seeking allies, Praunheim's film, the film of a member of a doubly marginalized group, gay, but not butch like Fassbinder, turns to others in an equally precarious situation: Lotti Huber, Jewish, bisexual, like him an artist. . . .

## NOTES

1. Discussion with audience after showing of the film *Anita, Dances of Vice* at Cornell Cinema, Ithaca, NY, 27 September 1988.

2. On 'Camp' see Jack Babuscio "Camp and the Gay Sensibility" and Richard Dyer, "Rejecting Straight Ideals: Gays in Film," in Peter Stevens, ed., *Jump Cut. Hollywood, Politics and Counter Cinema* (New York: Praeger, 1985).

3. Cf. Klaus Kreimeier, "Das große hermaphroditische Tableau-Theater," *Rosa von Praunheim*. Reihe Film 30 (Munich: Carl Hanser Verlag, 1983), p. 38.

4. Rosa von Praunheim, *Sex und Karriere* (Rogner & Bernhard bei Zweitausendeins, 1991), p. 344.

5. Jonathan Kalb, "Lotti Da," *Village Voice* (19 January 1988). For documentation of her film career cf. Lothar Fischer, *Tanz zwischen Rausch und Tod. Anita Berber 1918–1928 in Berlin* (Haude & Spener, 1988, second edition).

6. Fischer describes her as surrounded by a whole collection of Madonna and Christ figurines on her deathbed (Fischer, p. 89).

7. Fischer, p. 32; e.g. the director of a number of her films, Richard Oswald.

8. Viennese-born famous sexologist Dr. Magnus Hirschfeld was the director of the Institute of Sexology in Berlin and author of numerous books on sexuality including writings on homosexuality. A victim of an anti-Semitic attack in 1921, he died in 1935 from injuries incurred in that incident.

9. In his 1976 film on Marianne Rosenberg, Rosa von Praunheim makes an issue of the Jewishness of the singer and her life in post-Holocaust Germany.

10. Jonathan Kalb, see note 5.

11. Most of them are available to the general public in Fischer's documentation and include numerous stills from her twenty-odd film roles and photos of her modeling poses (cf. the director's comment in his *Sex und Karriere*, p. 329). Some of them are in archives and private ownership like the ones taken by the famous photographer Dora Kalmus (a.k.a. Madame D'Ora).

12. Discussion with director after showing of the film *Anita, Dances of Vice* at Cornell Cinema, Ithaca, NY, 27 September 1988. See also his comments on the creative input of Lotti Huber, Inge Stiborski, und Hannelore Limpach in Kreimeier, pp. 242–245, and Rosa von Praunheim, *Sex und Karriere*, p. 330.

13. Rebecca Bell–Metereau has documented that drag roles were quite common in the 1910s and 1920s. Her book *Hollywood Androgyny* provides numerous examples, e.g. such notable early drag roles as Charlie Chaplin in *Women*.

14. Some scenes in *Anita, Dances of Vice* such as Anita Berber in pearl costume are directly reminiscent of specific images, in this case Bobby Vernon in drag (pearl costume) in a spoof of Theda Bara's successful version of *Cleopatra* and the Ben Turpin spoof of Rudolph Valentino, "the biggest sex star of the twenties" (Hans Scheugl in *Sexualität und Neurose im Film: Kinomythen von Griffith bis Warhol*, Munich: C. Hanser, 1974, p. 35) as alluring houri in *The Sheik of Araby* (1923). The scenes with Droste and Anita (played by Ina Blum) also warrant a comparison with Rudolph Valentino in *The Young Rajah* (1922), half-naked and only clad in pearls and a scarf around his loins. While his erotic character is underlined by the very decorative costume, his female partner in veil is marginalized. Valentino's rolling eyes are mimicked by both of the dancers in *Anita, Dances of Vice*. Rudolph Valentino's erotic effect on the audience was maximized by scenes of dressing and undressing. Praunheim replaced this function with dramatic movement and colors.

Rosa von Praunheim draws on the genre of the vampire film. Through his physiognomy and movements Anita's partner Droste is reminiscent of the count in Murnau's *Nosferatu* (1922) and Christopher Lee's Dracula in Terence Fisher's 1960 *The Brides of Dracula*. Not unlike the classical horror films in which "the vampire usually starts as male, but ends up embedded within the female, who, in turn, is then made an object of terror and fear" (Sheridan Morley, *Horror and Fantasy in the Cinema*, p. 60), a similar transference of power takes place between Droste and Anita, with the two dancers appearing like the living dead, preying on each other and the public. The playful interaction of homosexuality and vampirism in a blur can be read as a spoof of Jimmy Sangster's *The Lust for a Vampire* (1971).

15. Cf. Morley. In Robert Aldrich's *What Ever Happened to Baby Jane* (1962), which Lotti Huber seems to parody in one move.

16. Jost Hermand and Frank Trommler, *Die Kultur der Weimarer Republik*, p. 217.

17. Kreimeier, p. 245.

# The Tenuous Continuity:
# Contemporary German Jewish Culture

# The Legacy of Jewish Vienna

## Dagmar C. G. Lorenz

According to legend, a Jewish empire, Judaysapta, was founded in Lower Austria soon after the Great Flood. The sixteenth-century *Chronik Hagen*, written by the scholar and physician Wolfgang Lazius and the *Paulaner* monk P. Matthias Fuhrman, mentions that Jewish dukes held court at Tulln, Stockerau, and Korneuburg. These accounts about the origins of Vienna, which throughout history has been one of the most significant Jewish centers in Europe, seemed validated by tombstones with Hebrew letters that were found outside the city walls. In all likelihood these stones belonged to a Jewish cemetery that was first documented in 1244, and was abandoned after the destruction of the first ghetto Am Hof (Vienna I) in 1421.[1]

Since the arrival of the first Jewish merchants in the area of Vienna, together with the Roman legions, and immigration to Austria and Bohemia, which began during the first Crusade, Vienna's Jewish history has been one of persecution, oppression, and massacre. However, Jewish settlement in Vienna never ceased. Its centers, surprisingly, remained the same: the earliest one is documented close to the church St. Ruprecht and Seittenstettengasse, which is also the location of the present main synagogue, the Stadttempel (built in 1826). The second center was built around the Judenplatz, in the vicinity of what later became the "textile district" (*Textilbezirk*), a predominantly Jewish neighborhood.

In the seventeenth century, Vienna's Second District, Leopoldstadt, was the location of the second ghetto and became a major center for Jewish immigration from Eastern Europe after the Russian pogroms in the late 1800s. Until the destruction of the Jewish communities in 1938, Leopoldstadt was the quarter with the highest percentage of Jews in the area. However, it had an overall multicultural character, as vividly described in Joseph Roth's account of the migration of Eastern Europeans to the west, *Juden auf Wanderschaft* [Flight without End] (1927) and Veza Canetti's novel, *Die Gelbe Straße* [The Yellow Street] (1933/4).[2] Today, once again, a number of Jewish bookstores, hotels, and restaurants are located here and Jews from Eastern Europe, particularly from Russia, have begun to settle in this quarter along with large numbers of immigrants from Turkey and Arabic countries, as described in Ruth Beckermann's photo documentary *Die Mazzesinsel*. Until 1938, Vienna had about 200,000 Jewish inhabitants, 20 synagogues, 100 prayer houses, a rabbinical seminary, a Jewish school of education, Bible and Talmud schools, museums, one Jewish daily as well as approximately 20 weekly and monthly papers. The *Israelitische Kultusgemeinde Wien* was among the largest and most heterogeneous in the world.

Approximately five thousand Viennese Jews survived the Holocaust. Only the main synagogue in the inner city, the Stadttempel, remained intact, because its plain Classicist façade concealed the dome of the main building and made it less conspicuous than the other synagogues and temples. In 1945 the Vienna Jewish Community, the *Israelitische Kultusgemeinde*, was reorganized and services were resumed there as soon as possible. However, the postwar *Kultusgemeinde* was intended as an interim solution, a stepping stone toward *Aliya* to Israel or emigration to other countries, particularly the United States, because after the Holocaust the majority of Jews considered Germany and Austria inappropriate to live in. Most Austrian Holocaust survivors left, but a large number of Displaced Persons from Eastern Europe stayed in Vienna. They did not associate the Holocaust with the Germans and Austrians, but rather with the countries where they had lived when the ghettoization and deportations to labor- and death-camps began. Since the Gentile population of Eastern Europe, with a few notable exceptions such as the Bulgarians, had willingly assisted the Nazis, many Holocaust survivors had no contact with German or Austrian Nazis at all. In recent years, due to the immigration of Jews from Russia, the Jewish population of Vienna increased significantly.

The rededication of the Stadttempel in 1988, new Orthodox and Sephardic prayer rooms, kosher restaurants and hotels, regular publications such as the paper *Heruth*, a Jewish community center, and a museum attest to the continuity of Jewish life in Vienna, even a new diversification. However, the size and character of the postwar community is different from the one before *Kristallnacht*. The Jewish population in Vienna had been sizeable and diverse enough to support an entire cultural network. Outside of the religious establishment, secular political and cultural organizations such as the Jewish soccer club HAKOA, Zionist clubs, religious associations, Jewish schools, and so forth existed in abundance. Franz Weintraub/West describes the vibrant, diverse Jewish life of this time vividly in his film interview with Ruth Beckermann.[4]

Many Jewish or Jewish-identified Viennese were a part of the international intellectual and cultural elite and had considerable influence on other Jewish communities, for example in the United States, particularly in New York and California. Assimilated middle-class authors and artists played a leading role in Austrian public life, setting intellectual and aesthetic trends not only in Vienna but in Western culture in general. By virtue of its outstanding cultural achievements, the influence of prewar Vienna extended into the postwar years; one need only to mention Billy Wilder's American films, Arnold Schönberg's music, and the far-reaching implications of Freud's psychoanalysis.

Many members of this avant-garde of Jewish descent had abandoned their faith or become indifferent to it. Nevertheless, like for example Gustav Mahler, they continued to be perceived as Jews. The "Jewishness" of some was based exclusively on the perception of Gentiles. Independent of their own self-definition, personalities such as Arthur Schnitzler, Sigmund Freud, Peter Altenberg, Arnold Schönberg, Fritz Kreisler, Johann Strauß, Max Reinhardt, Karl Kraus, Stefan Zweig, Hugo Bettauer, Jura Soyfer, Elias and Veza Canetti, Vicki Baum, Franz Werfel, Joseph Roth, Hermann Broch, and Hugo von Hofmannsthal are to this day considered paragons of Viennese and, particularly, Jewish Viennese or Jewish Austrian creativity. In its extended sense the term "Austrian" applies to all German-speaking authors who were born in the former Austro-Hungarian territories and continued to display a strong affinity for the Imperial multination state.[5] Phenomena such as the literary coffee house, modern journalism with Egon Erwin Kisch as one of its foremost representatives, social and political satire, and Austro-Marxism are associated with Vienna's Jewish intellectuals.

Restoring this tradition and its cultural networks after 1945 was impossible. The Nazis had almost succeeded in annihilating European Jewry and had all but destroyed the Yiddish-speaking culture. In Vienna, persecution, expropriation, and deportation had met with widespread popular support, but the attempts to compensate those persecuted by the Nazis and restore them to their positions proceeded slowly, if at all. Despite strong tendencies in both Germanies to gloss over or even rewrite the Nazi past, many Holocaust writers of Jewish background such as Paul Celan, Ilse Aichinger, Jakov Lind, and Erich Fried, whose roots were at least partly Viennese, found the West German and even the Anglo-Saxon public more receptive to their works and consequently published rarely in Austria.

While many of these authors visited Vienna frequently, only few moved back to live there. Ilse Aichinger established residency in Vienna only recently. For several decades she had lived in the Federal Republic of Germany. A number of exile intellectuals, for example Elias Canetti, Jean Améry, Frank Zwillinger, and Egon Schwarz, received high honors from Austrian institutions but continued to live abroad. The journalist and novelist Hilde Spiel ventured to return several times, but, for external and personal reasons, resorted to a kind of commuter existence. The well-known poet Theodor Kramer returned to Vienna a dying man, when his works and achievements were almost completely forgotten.

Despite widespread hesitation, even apprehension on the part of former refugees and exiles to revisit their former hometown even for a short time, some came back to Vienna to live and work there, such as Viktor Adler and Hans Thalberg. Simon Wiesenthal, who is often mistakenly and slanderously referred to as a "Nazi hunter," deliberately chose Vienna, the cradle of both anti-Semitism and Zionism, as the location of his now famous archive and research center on Nazi crimes and perpetrators.⁶ After 1945, the authors and critics Hans Weigel and Hermann Hakel played an important role as mentors of young writers. As early as 1946 Weigel suggested reestablishing cultural relations between Germany and Austria on an egalitarian, democratic basis.⁷

To this day the terms "Jew" and "Jewish" have a negative connotation in the German language. In Austria they are used as insults. Austrian anti-Semitism is still a force to be reckoned with. It is not surprising that members of the older generation such as Austria's long-term chancellor Bruno Kreisky often displayed an uneasy attitude toward their Jewish heritage. The traditional ambivalence attributed to assimilated Jews remained characteristic of several personalities who, like the diplomat Hans Thalberg and the chansonnier Georg Kreisler, had returned to Vienna to participate in Austrian public and cultural life.⁸ Like Jakob Wassermann and Karl Kraus before them, most of them considered their Austrian identity as primary, their Jewishness as secondary.

After World War II, the artistic and literary circles at the Café Havelka and the Art Club planted the seed not only for the careers of a number of now prominent authors and artists of Jewish origin who, like Jakov Lind and Paul Celan, eventually left Austria. Also Friedrich [Friedensreich] Hundertwasser and Ernst Fuchs, two representatives of the *Wiener Schule* and "Fantastic Realism," are Holocaust survivors. Unlike their older colleague Rudolf Hausner, they were too young to have experienced the book burnings and the outlawing of their works by the Nazis, but, like the novelist and poet Ilse Aichinger, they witnessed the horrors and experienced the dread of the Holocaust. Fuchs, the group's spiritual mentor, was classified as a *Mischling*, a "half-caste," and survived together with his mother in underground hiding places. Hundertwasser, whose original surname was that of his Gentile father, Stowasser, was forced to become a member of the Hitler Youth to avoid raising suspicion while his Jewish mother's family was deported and murdered.⁹

Fuchs's provocative, more-than-life-size sculpture of a heavy-set, non-European looking Black woman entitled "The Great Queen Esther" in front of his Art Deco mansion built by Vienna's foremost turn-of-the century architect, Otto Wagner, is a celebration of the resilience of the Jewish people and signifies Fuchs's confirmation of the centrality of Jewish culture in Vienna. At the same time it contains a very personal comment: The Marranos, who concealed their Jewish identity living as Christians among the Gentiles in Spain in order to escape persecution, considered the story of Queen Esther a justification of nominal apostasy when life was at stake. Fuchs's sculpture and a number of his other works, including his paintings, allude to his survival during the Nazi era and pay homage to the Jewish tradition.¹⁰

No less splendorous and idiosyncratic is the colorful, odd-shaped Hundertwasser House in the midst of the monotonous lower-middle-class tenement blocks of Vienna's Third District. The striking building with its golden domes, turrets, and crescent-shaped ornaments is, strangely enough, a social housing project, but its arabesques remind the onlooker of Middle Eastern imagination. Hundertwasser designed the structure without rectangles or straight lines and it stands out as an oddity next to the straight-lined prewar and minimalist post-1945 architecture. The building is a fairy-tale-like reminder of the luxurious designs of some of the destroyed Viennese synagogues, particularly the Turkish and Polish *Shuls* in Leopoldstadt.

Hundertwasser's architecture as well as Fuchs's paintings and sculptures are deliberately subversive, contradicting the ideology of efficiency and functionality at all cost that dominated Nazi philosophy and was perpetuated in the postwar era. At the same time they question the dictate of uniformity in modern Western, i.e. secularized Christian, civilization. His critical statements about his contemporary society have become legendary. It is no coincidence that formal charges were brought against Fuchs because of his alleged attacks on the Catholic Church (Grunfeld, p. 131).

From the start a discreet subversiveness has been characteristic of the prose and poetry of Ilse Aichinger who, like Fuchs and Hundertwasser, survived the Holocaust classified as a *Mischling*. Both the plot and the form of her postwar novel *Herod's Children* (*Die größere Hoffnung*, 1948) express dissent and distance from the war experience of the Austrian and German mainstream. Aichinger focused on the fate of Jewish children in Nazi Austria, reflecting in the decision of her protagonist, a "half-Jewish" girl, her own resolve of solidarity with the persecuted people and to live as one of them. Aichinger's musical language, rich with mystical and spiritual allusions, and her style reminiscent of the Bible, Romanticism, and Expressionism are in direct opposition to the terse "Point Zero Literature" of the German mainstream. While young German authors maintained that it was necessary to construct the German language anew since it had become infested with Nazi concepts and vocabulary, Holocaust survivors and potential Nazi victims such as Aichinger never had identified with the ideas and language of their oppressors. Therefore they had no reason to denounce literary tradition, Romanticism, and Expressionism. They were at liberty to appropriate them and use them for their own purposes. Aichinger's identification with the persecuted Jews and her mourning for the dead were the cause of her increasing detachment from Catholicism and the Austrians, as she made explicit in her later texts.

The journalist and author Friedrich Torberg, who returned from his Swiss exile to Vienna in 1951, wrote consistently about Jewish topics. His literary and essayistic works were often viciously attacked, be it because of his controversial approach to his subject matter, his conservative style or his supposedly bourgeois mentality, or, most likely, because he kept the memory of Jewish Vienna alive and became a mentor and an inspiration for Jewish intellectuals born after the war, such as Ruth Beckermann. Several other journalists, critics, and editors of Leftist papers such as *Die Volksstimme* and

*Arbeiter-Zeitung*, for example Heinz Sichrovski and Franz Weintraub/West, played an equally important role in postwar Vienna. Their concern was to insure the correctness of the historical record and ensure cultural continuity.

The work of Elfriede Jelinek, the Jewish-identified feminist novelist and playwright, frequently sparks controversy. It is firmly anchored in Vienna as her intellectual territory. Jelinek identifies with her father's legacy, Vienna's coffee-house culture and Socialism. Her social criticism, satire, and political feminism perpetuate the tradition of the satirists and cultural critics Karl Kraus, Hugo Bettauer, and Elias and Veza Canetti. She described her own work as an oddity within the contemporary scene where satire is rare and often misunderstood, "because the Jews are dead." [11]

Jelinek's career has its roots in Vienna's first experimental literary circle, the *Wiener Gruppe*, and the Viennese Actionists, whose often bloody and sadomasochist performances can be seen as forerunners of the "Happening." Jelinek's philosophical basis is the Marxism and anti-Fascism of the 1960s' Student Movement, as is evident from her novels *Die Liebhaberinnen* (1975), *Die Ausgesperrten* (1980), *Die Klavierlehrerin* (1983), and *Lust* (1989).

The Holocaust made the position of Jewish intellectuals in Vienna highly problematic. Artists and writers of the exile community were ignored and often not welcome in Vienna. Unrelenting Jewish voices like Torberg's were frequently attacked and sneered at. Others, who established a connection between their work and the destroyed literary traditions, were purposely misinterpreted. Authors who returned from exile and assimilated in the mainstream had the least difficulty in reestablishing themselves, while those who focused on Jewish topics and their experience in Nazi Austria remained marginalized. Axel Corti's film *Welcome in Vienna* aptly expresses the difficulties faced by returning exiles.

There can be no doubt about the willingness on the part of Hans J. Thalberg to coexist with his former persecutors and to work for the Second Austrian Republic. However, in his memoirs *Von der Kunst, Österreicher zu sein* (1984), he characterizes the political and social reorganization after World War II as superficial. As late as the 1980s he felt alienated from his Gentile fellow-Austrians, including his wife's family, as if separated from them by a deep moat—as deep as the ancient moat that separated the ghetto from the Inner City.[12]

At the present time, there is an increased interest in Jewish themes, as indicated by the large number of publications on Vienna's Jewish history and community. There are even attempts by Gentile authors to record Jewish oral history in a literary fashion, for instance Brigitte Schwaiger, *Eva Deutsch: Die Galizianerin* (1982). The novelist Peter Henisch made a literary assessment of the psychological plight of a Jew living in Vienna in *Steins Paranoia* (1988), describing his assimilated protagonist's ever-growing alienation from his environment. Works like Henisch's novel reflect on different levels the brutal anti-Semitism that motivated the attacks on the Stadttempel and the vandalism in 1979 and 1981, the bombing of the Schöps department stores in 1982, culminating in the unabashed anti-Semitic outbursts during and after the Waldheim campaign 1986. A point had been reached when it was no longer possible to avoid the debate of the concerns of Vienna's Jewish communities, past and present.

An increasing number of intellectuals born after 1945 have as their goal to live as unassimilated Jews in Austria, however, also outside of the framework of the Orthodox religious community. Young intellectuals who claim Austria as their rightful place are searching for alternatives to Zionism, religious orthodoxy, and assimilation. This is, for example, the unmistakable message of the film *Kieselsteine* [Pebbles] (1982) by the Prague-born Austrian writer Nadja Seelich. The setting and local flavor make Seelich's film emphatically Viennese: Vienna is shown as the place of a Jewish biography. Seelich's protagonist Hannah Stern has left the confines of her community and explores life with Austrian and German Gentiles. While the assimilation of a child of Holocaust survivors into a society of children of Nazi perpetrators and anti-Semites proves impossible, Hannah's quest leads to a real adventure. By necessity she embarks on a search for a *modus vivendi* that suits her values as a Jewish woman without the traditional constraints, but distinctly separate from Austrian Gentile society.

The search for a secular Jewish existence is also expressed by Ruth Beckermann, the author of the documentary about Jewish life in Vienna's Second District, *Die Mazzesinsel. Juden in der Wiener Leopoldstadt* (1984). In her more recent essay, *Unzugehörig. Österreicher und Juden nach 1945* [Not Belonging. Austrians and Jews after 1945] (1989), Beckermann abandoned her earlier posture of objectivity. She integrates her own childhood memories, accepting them as her point of departure to the problems of Jewish life in Vienna. There are, according to Beckermann, no rational reasons why her parents lived in post-Holocaust Austria, only historical explanations. Without harboring illusions about Austria's past and present, Beckermann, like Seelich, opts for an existence in Vienna as a critical, assertive Jewish intellectual. "The children of the survivors do not want to be quiet any longer, discuss with anti-Semites, or solicit compassion."[13]

Beckermann's film *Wien Retour* (1983), a screen interview of the anti-Fascist journalist and Communist activist Franz Weintraub/West who for a number of years was the editor of Vienna's Communist paper *Die Volksstimme*,[14] defines the context in which Beckermann situates herself: setting herself apart from a Vienna that is traditionally associated with the bourgeoisie, she emphasizes "Red" Vienna, which was a Socialist model city during the 1920s until its decline after the burning of the Houses of Justice (*Justizpalast*) in 1927.

The film *Die papierene Brücke* (1987) deals with Beckermann's quest for her father's lost culture in Jewish Czernowitz. It indirectly motivates Ruth

Beckermann's resolve to persist in debating and fighting with her hometown, Vienna, rather than leaving it: neither Israel, her childhood vacation country, nor Eastern Europe offer her a viable alternative. Aware of the political reality of the one, and having come face to face with the destruction of the other, Waldheim's Vienna remains her place to assert herself.

## NOTES

1. Walther Pichler, *Von der Synagoge zur Kirche. Zur Entstehungsgeschichte der Pfarre St. Leopold, Wien II* (Vienna: Wiener Dom-Verlag, 1974), p. 23.
2. Joseph Roth, *Juden auf Wanderschaft* (Berlin: Schmiede, 1927); Veza Canetti, *Die Gelbe Straße* (Munich: Hanser, 1990).
3. Ruth Beckermann, *Die Mazzesinsel* (Vienna and Munich: Löcker, 1984).
4. Ruth Beckermann; Josef Aichholzer. *Wien Retour* (Vienna: filmladen, 1983).
5. Cf. Claudio Magris, *Der habsburgische Mythos in der österreichischen Literatur* (Salzburg: Müller, 1966), and Friedrich Torberg, *Die Tante Jolesch* (Munich: dtv, 1977).
6. Wiesenthal does not "hunt" anyone, but documents and researches Nazi crimes and attempts to convince the countries where the perpetrators reside to bring the guilty to justice.
7. Ruth V. Gross, *Plan and the Austrian Rebirth. Portrait of a Journal* (Columbia: Camden House, 1982).
8. Bruno Kreisky had difficulty saying the word "Jew." In his address in honor of Erich Fried ("Fest für Erich Fried," 29 April 1986) he used descriptive terms such as "the religion of my fathers," "the background he and Fried share," the "religious community," "the community of fate."
9. Frederic V. Grunfeld, *Vienna* (New York: Newsweek, 1981), pp. 130ff.
10. Gershom G. Scholem, *Major Trends in Jewish Mysticism* (New York: Schocken, 1961), p. 95: To "don the garments of a Marrano" was also justified among Jewish Sabbatians, the followers of the "false" Messiah, Shabbata Zwi. In the context of the "defense story of Queen Esther" formal apostasy is not considered to represent a break with their mother faith. Galit Hasan–Rokem, R. Edelmann, "Ahasuerus, the Wandering Jew: Origin and Background," Alan Dundes, ed., *The Wandering Jew. Essays in the Interpretation of a Christian Legend* (Bloomington: Indiana University Press, 1986), pp. 1–10. The Black Queen Esther who emerges triumphant in front of one of Vienna's prized edifices reminds the viewer of Fuchs and those who like him went underground and denied their identity for the sake of survival. Ironically, the name of Ahasver, the Biblical Esther's non-Jewish royal husband, not that of the Jewish Queen, attached itself to the legend of the *Wandering Jew*, the most persistent European anti-Jewish legend.
11. Sigrid Löffler, "Spezialistin für den Haß," *Die Zeit* (4 November 1983), p. 18.
12. Hans Thalberg, *Von der Kunst, Österreicher zu sein* (Vienna: Böhlau, 1984).
13. Ruth Beckermann, *Unzugehörig. Österreicher und Juden nach 1945* (Vienna: Löcker, 1989), pp. 10–11,
14. The paper ceased to exist after the reorganization of Eastern Europe.

# Beyond the Bridges

## Ruth Beckermann

The river invites no one to cross it. Neither the Danube with its artificial island nor the Danube Canal. The latter, still an unregulated arm of the river, was a factor in the founding of the Roman city of Vindobona. To this day it is located in the center and at the same time on the margins.

I spent my childhood years on this side of the canal. I do not remember ever having walked across into the Second District. We took the streetcar for excursions to the Prater[1] and the Danube beaches, otherwise there was no reason to cross over the bridges. On the contrary, without knowing what had actually happened there, we were afraid of that miserable part of town which smelled of war.

We did not know that in the Second District of Vienna roughly one-third of the approximately 180,000 Vienna Jews had lived, that on 9 November 1938 five synagogues had gone up in flames and thirty prayer houses been destroyed. We, the children of survivors, knew nothing at all. In conversations with Jews born after World War II in Vienna, you can frequently hear statements like "My childhood was spent in a no-man's-land" or "We did and did not live here."

These memories do not capture the truth, although they do describe a perception of the truth. We lived in a provisional Vienna, a place where we socialized almost exclusively with Jews and talked about our imminent departure. It was as if, in the midst of Austria of the 1950s, we were acculturated to the image of a distant Austria, one that emerged in the literature of yesteryear[2] and had nothing to do with the immediate past and present. Until the 1980s we discussed our experiences and observations discreetly and only with our closest friends. Even the word "Jew" was taboo. We were students of the "Mosaic faith," staring at the crucifix where our supposed victim languished, a crucifix that hangs on the wall of every classroom to this day.

But let us go across the bridges.

Let us take along an old photograph of that part of town from the time Joseph Roth, Elias Canetti, Manès Sperber, and many others described so aptly.[3] You can see the Schweden Bridge. And there, where insurance and bank buildings tower over the city today, the photograph shows the two large coffee houses—Fetzer and Stierböck. From the Danube Canal well into the Prater, coffee houses covered this entire district, which is popularly referred to as *Mazzesinsel*, Matzo Island, because it was both an island and the most Jewish district of Vienna. These coffee houses were less elegant than the famous literary and social spots in the inner city, but they fulfilled many functions. Business was conducted here, people played Tarock and chess and read all the papers of the monarchy. Here political assemblies were held, and on the Jewish high holy days prayer meetings. One such coffee house on Tabor Street was called the "American Spot." At this place, unemployed people and potential emigrants could obtain information about the "country of unlimited possibilities," addresses, and immigration law. After the pogrom of November 1938, many people saved valuable months of desperate searching because they knew these facts and could find badly-needed asylum.

The fact that not one genuine old coffee house can be found in today's Leopoldstadt speaks louder than words. After 1938 the coffee houses had to close one by one because the world of which they had been a vital part began to vanish, along with their predominantly Jewish clientele. Today McDonald's tries to imitate the elegance of a substitute coffee house with the help of chairs à la Thonet. There are other attempts to adapt this district to the nearby city. However, the sweeping broom of those eager to embellish the city is not really effective, and the Second District remains less bourgeois than the other nine districts inside the outer belt.

It feels good to step out of the city, which has come to resemble an extension of the petty bourgeois living room. As a tourist favorite, Vienna is loaded with nostalgic public telephone booths, rustic benches, tacky street lights, and potted plants. Already the "bunglers" have worked their way across the Danube Canal, where a "Johann Strauß-Schiffscafé" [Riverboat Café] and a flea market have been established to lure Viennese and visitors alike. At the present time blueprints are being developed for the homey decoration and efficient use of the canal banks.

Despite the fact that two or three fashionable restaurants have already opened, offering "Nouvelle Viennese Cuisine" as their specialty, the district still belongs to the underground "milieu" after sundown. This is the time of day when shady figures emerge that the Nazis were unable to eliminate as thoroughly as the Jews through their cleansing: vagrants, smugglers, whores, and pimps. They crowd the espresso bars, wine halls, and the hotels that rent their rooms by the hour as well as the red-light district for child prostitutes behind Venedigerau. Mexico Square, close to the Danube River, is the center of cigarette smuggling and illicit trade in all kinds of goods. This is the meeting place of Central Europe. The Poles have become the object of the populist anger, raging not only in the "golden Viennese hearts," but also in those of most other Eastern Europeans. It hardly comes as a surprise that, albeit by only one point of a percent, even in this traditionally "red" district,

Jörg Haider's supposedly "Liberal Party" defeated the Socialists for the first time, using as its slogan for the 1990 election: "Vienna must not become Chicago." This victory occurred despite the fact that the predominantly socialist government (paradoxically after the fall of the "Iron Curtain") had passed a visa requirement for Polish citizens entering Austria and even encouraged the Austrian military to hunt for illegal immigrants at the supposedly open Hungarian border. It appears that a small country like Austria can get away with activities for which Germany was criticized, for example sending weapons to Iraq (Austrian distributors were in third place) or making visas for Poles mandatory.

Despite all this, Leopoldstadt continues to attract foreigners. Since the 1970s even Jews began to arrive. The majority came from different parts of the Soviet Union and some from Israel. The Lubavich Hassids opened daycare centers and schools for new immigrants of whom the local Jewish communities were suspicious for a long time. By now the approximately 6,000 members of the over-aged community have begun to consider the positive aspects of the population increase, and the newly opened Jewish middle school in the second district now accepts Russian children. In the Tempelgasse, where the largest synagogue of Vienna used to be located, a Sephardic Center, including an apartment building and a prayer house, is being constructed.

Jewish people are no longer hiding. The massive onslaught of anti-Semitism caused by the Waldheim affair proved that even in the "City without Jews"[5] ethnic prejudice continues to survive. Jews have recognized that prudence and assimilation were not in their best interest. During that time the illusionary nature of the compromises they had made became clear. In order to live in Vienna, they had to accept conditions that demanded they repress their own history, make a new start at Point Zero, and act as if that were, in fact, possible.

In order to legitimate their existence in Austria, the Jews themselves bought into the popular stereotype of the "evil German" and the "roly-poly" Austrian. They managed to cope by projecting fanciful images of a Jewish–Austrian symbiosis into the past, glorifying an era of only one lifetime (1867–1938, the time during which Jews had been citizens and endowed with equal rights). In retrospect both parties of the "symbiosis" were fashioned into equal partners who gave life to psychoanalysis and modern music in an exemplary cooperative effort. What is forgotten is that the Jews achieved their accomplishments despite the pettiness of their Viennese environment and against its resistance. One forgets that the Jews conducted a "one-sided dialogue," trying in every imaginable way to make themselves understood. But who except for the anti-Semites answered them? What Gershom Scholem said about the German–Jewish symbiosis is equally true for Austria. He termed such a symbiosis a myth because a dialogue needs two people "who listen to one another, who are ready to see the other person for what he is and what he represents and to respond to him."[6]

The longing for a symbiosis brought about great works of art by severing actual experience from the desired image that was supposed to remain intact. Contradictory emotions had to exist side by side because their fusion would have shattered the tenuous identity. Bitter and painful anti-Semitic experiences had to be repressed time and again and considered a private matter, while those signs that reinforced the desired image were underscored. However, the Viennese Jews have become more skeptical and recognize the shabbiness of a city administration that tried to compensate for the loss of face incurred during the Waldheim debacle by offering charity toward its "Jewish Fellow Citizens," granting a little money to establish a Jewish vocational school in two dilapidated rooms close to the Praterstern and a Jewish museum in a building completely unsuited for the purpose.

Despite its "new" Jews, the streets of Leopoldstadt do not lend themselves to imagining the former character of this part of town. The Leopoldstadt of the prewar era must have been unique, very different from the rest of Vienna, and at the same time it was so much a part of the city that it did not seem exotic. This is why hardly anyone considered it worthwhile to describe and photograph it during the time of its existence. Only after normal communal life had been destroyed and its particular atmosphere was lost, did it become an object of contemplation. For example, Sigmund Freud, Theodor Herzl, Alfred Polgar, and Arnold Schönberg grew up here, but they never discussed this district as a phenomenon because they did not consider it one. The Leopoldstadt of the 1920s was a phenomenon only for someone who was passing through, like Joseph Roth.

At that time a Jewish rhythm of life influenced the district just as much as the Christian rhythm. Not only different religions, but also different social classes lived here side by side—the population of Leopoldstadt could not be forced sociologically or ethnically into the corset of uniformity. The principle was diversity. It was possible, for example, to be a Jewish socialist, a communist, a hassid at one of the "courts" that had moved from Eastern Europe to Vienna during World War I, a member of the small Sephardic community, or a Zionist. Some people were Zionists and at the same time adherents of social democracy; others considered themselves assimilated Viennese Jews, distancing themselves from East European Jewry; yet others abandoned their Jewish religion or did not even remember that they were Jews at all. By the 1920s the Jews had become a multilevel community. Some were more committed to their affiliation with a class, a profession, or a political group than to their Jewishness. This astonishing development had taken place within one or two generations. Only after the revolution of 1848 had the Jews been allowed to move freely within the Habsburg monarchy, to settle in Vienna, and to conduct different trades. Vienna became a magnet for the Jews in Bohemia,

Moravia, Hungary, and Galicia. The new northern railroad carried thousands of them into the capital city. While the Jewish bourgeoisie moved into the formidable residences of Praterstraße, Jewish craftsmen, merchants, and workers mingled with the native population in the side streets.

"In those days Leopoldstadt was still a fashionable and distinguished district," Arthur Schnitzler reminisced about his childhood in the 1860s. "And the main thoroughfare, on which the Carl Theater stood, managed to preserve some of its festiveness even during the quieter hours when an elegant and carefree world came tearing back from the races or flower shows in their equipages and fiacres. During my childhood I often enjoyed the exciting sight from the windows of my grandparents' apartment."[7]

At that time the representational great Jewish temples were erected in the vicinity of this luxurious and vivacious Praterstraße. Industrialists, major businessmen, and intellectuals, despite all their professed liberalism and enlightenment, had them built to promote their own glory rather than that of the Lord. At the corner of Rotensterngasse their Christian counterpart was built— the Johannes von Nepomuk Church, now gray and worn like everything else in this district today. During the turn-of-the-century *Gründerzeit* when representation and religion went hand in hand, it was the Sunday meeting place. Nearby two large synagogues were erected in conformity with the predominantly ornamental piety of liberalism—seeing and being seen were a higher social obligation.

On the right-hand side of Praterstraße the Great Temple (*Großer Tempel*) was located. Earlier than the architecture of the Ring Boulevard (*Ringstraße*), and even more vividly than the nearby Nepomuk Church, its Arabic motifs expressed how the extravagant but confused, intellectually repressed but economically expanding Viennese upper middle class wished to represent itself. On the left side of Praterstraße one could find the "Turkish Temple" as the complement and counterpart of the Ashkenasic "Great Temple." It was an octagonal miracle of pseudo-Ottoman architecture, imitating patterns of the Alhambra. However, there were also other synagogues in Leopoldstadt where Viennese Jews attempted to reconcile their traditional spirituality with their newly-gained status as "genuine Austrians"—the Polish Temple and the Emperor Franz Joseph Memorial Temple (Kaiser Franz Joseph-Huldigungstempel). Aside from these buildings there was the Schiffschul, the synagogue of the orthodox Hungarian Jews. At the time of the Republic all these places, including the more than thirty prayer houses of the most pious and the poor, were the ceremonial centers of their respective communities. All of them were destroyed during a single November night in 1938.

There were already visible danger signals after World War I when Vienna had changed from the cosmopolitan center of a multination empire into the oversized capital of a starving republic. At the very place where the tradition of integrating other groups and individuals was upheld, Karl Lueger's anti-Semitism grew into a mass movement and foreigners became the object of hatred. At precisely the same time approximately 350,000 people were moving westward in an unprecedented flow of refugees. At the end of the war roughly 25,000 Jews from Poland remained in Vienna, most of them in Leopoldstadt where they found cheap places to live and form a social network. Perhaps half of the 120 Jewish associations after the war were charitable associations. For example, there was a Verein zur Bekleidung und Unterstützung alter Männer israelitischer Konfession [Association for the Clothing and Support of Old Men of Israelitic Faith] and the Verein zur Unterstützung armer Talmudschüler [Association for the Support of Poor Talmud Students].

Joseph Roth wrote about the Eastern Jews living in Vienna in the 1920s: "The Leopoldstadt is a voluntary ghetto. Many bridges connect it with the other districts of the city. During the daytime merchants, peddlers, stock-exchange brokers, businessmen, in other words all the unproductive elements of the East European Jewish immigration, cross over the bridges. But in the early morning hours also the progeny of the selfsame unproductive elements cross over these bridges; the sons and daughters of the merchants who work in the factories, offices, banks, press agencies, and industrial workshops. The sons and daughters of the Eastern Jews are productive. While their parents barter and peddle, their children are the most talented lawyers, doctors, bankers, journalists, and actors" (Roth, "Wanderschaft," p. 657).

In the interwar period they contributed to the unique ambiance of "Red Vienna" as the most enthusiastic adherents of the intellectual and messianic Austro-Marxist movement, which (like psychoanalysis and Zionism) had evolved at the time of a specifically Viennese Jewish identity crisis of the fin de siècle. The radical changes of the year 1918 had led to a departure from the old. The hoped-for result was a new epoch that could be conquered through human labor and technology. To this day the erect, muscular statues of this period with their broad chests and their hollow spines stand everywhere in the midst of a decor symbolizing technology, streamlining, and faith in progress. Also the Jewish youth of that time, even if they dreamed of socialism or Palestine, possessed an optimism that in retrospect seems incomprehensible.

But not everything then was as delightful as it is made to appear to this day in the euphoric recollections of many who witnessed those years. The Eastern Jews were the first targets of the anti-Semites, who tested their weapons on them. As early as 1919 anti-Semites armed with canes promenaded along the bridges of the Danube Canal and were an everyday phenomenon. In the course of one of their spectacular forays in December of 1929, Nazi hoodlums devastated the elegant Café Produktenbörse on Taborstraße because it had the reputation of being a "Jewish" coffee house. Three years later, at the Jewish New Year's celebration, they ravaged Café Sperl where a temporary prayer house had been established. They battered the praying people with metal sheaves and demolished the furniture. The photographs of Jews on their knees who had to scrub the streets with tooth brushes after the invasion of Austria, euphemistically referred to as *Anschluß* [annexation], were seen all over the world. They document the end of the "Matzo Island."

After my stroll through the Second District, I have arrived in the Große Schiffgasse, once again, close to the bridges across the Danube Canal. On summer evenings the singsong of Jews at prayer emanates from the open windows of an apartment. Every once in a while someone looks down on the large empty space between buildings covered with vegetation growing wild—it was here that the synagogue, the Schiffschul, used to stand. It continues to be a monument of extermination. The history of this gap has not yet been marked by one of the little plates with the red and white Austrian flag that are used to explain historic sites all over Vienna. This gap is as transitory as the memory of the victims. Already it is covered with grass. Soon a new house will take its place.

*Translated by Dagmar C. G. Lorenz*

## Notes

1. The metropolitan recreation and amusement park with the famous Ferris wheel.

2. Beckermann uses the term "Literatur der Welt von gestern," evoking Stefan Zweig's novel by the same title. Cf. Luke Springman, this volume.

3. Joseph Roth, *Juden auf Wanderschaft: Wien*, in *Werke in drei Bänden*, vol. III (Cologne: Kiepenheuer & Witsch, 1956), pp. 625–685. Manès Sperber, *All das Vergangene* . . . (Vienna: Europa, 1983), especially "Die Wasserträger Gottes," "Die vergebliche Warnung," and "Bis man mir Scherben auf die Augen legt." Elias Canetti, *Das Augenspiel* (Munich: Hanser, 1985); *Die Fackel im Ohr* (Munich: Hanser, 1980); *Die gerettete Zunge* (Munich: Hanser, 1977; Frankfurt: Fischer, 1979).

4. Leopoldstad, or the City of the Emperor Leopold, is the popular name of the Second District. Under Leopold, Vienna's second official ghetto was raided and destroyed. A new "Christian" quarter was established on the site; it later became one of the most important centers of Jewish immigration in the twentieth century.

5. Allusion to Huger Bettauer's novel by the same title. Bettauer became the victim of a right-wing fanatic in the 1920s.

6. Gershom Scholem, "Vom Mythos deutsch–jüdischer Symbiose," *Judaica* 2 (Frankfurt: Suhrkamp, 1970), p. 7.

7. Arthur Schnitzler, *My Youth in Vienna*, translated by Catherine Hutter (New York: Holt, Rinehart & Winston, 1970), p. 14.

# Identity Problems of Postwar Generation Jews in Germany: A Historical Perspective

## Lea Fleischmann

In the following essay I shall discuss the situation of Jews in the Federal Republic of Germany, the former West Germany. The number of Jews who lived in what was previously the German Democratic Republic was so minimal that their presence was hardly noticeable.

On 8 May 1945, after the defeat of Nazi Germany and the liberation of Jewish prisoners from the concentration camps by the Allied Forces, a new era began for the Jewish communities in Germany. At that time most Jews did not envision staying in Germany for any length of time. Robert Welsch expressed this opinion in 1946 during his visit to conquered and occupied Germany: "We cannot assume that there are Jews who feel drawn to Germany. It smells here of corpses—of gas chambers and of torture cells."[1]

In spite of such predictions, Jewish communities did in fact establish themselves in Germany. One of the reasons was that the federal government of West Germany wished to reintegrate itself from a moral point of view into the *Völkerfamilie*, the family or community of nations, and it had to prove that the new Germany had undergone a complete metamorphosis. Many former top Nazi officials remained in office—the best example was Adenauer's first Secretary of State, Globke, who had been one of the creators of the Nuremberg *Rassengesetze*, the infamous racial laws of 1935. However, the system of government *had* changed for the better, from a dictatorship into a democracy, and newly-established Jewish communities could serve as evidence of this transformation in Germany. The Jewish communities received generous financial support. Anti-Semitism in any form was outlawed and in the media Jews were portrayed predominantly as innocently suffering, morally upstanding people. The blatant anti-Semitism of the Nazi years was replaced by equally blatant philo-Semitism at the time of Germany's occupation by the Allied Forces.

Dan Diner addressed this phenomenon as follows:

> The presence of Jews in this country was of great importance for the Germans' moral 'rehabilitation'—the existence of a Jewish community within the Federal

Republic of Germany fulfilled the purpose of lending credibility on an international scale to the new state. Nationwide a re-identification of Germans with Germany was taking place. In order to accommodate the Germans' desire for *Normalität*—"normal life"—the continued presence of Jews in Germany was necessary.[2]

The majority of Jews in postwar Germany were refugees from East European countries, so-called "Displaced Persons" (DPs). The majority of this group emigrated to the United States, Canada, Australia, and Israel. However, among these refugees were also people who were either physically or psychologically too weak to emigrate, as well as those who had built an existence in Germany while waiting for permission to enter other countries and therefore remained here. Yet another group consisted of Jewish anti-Fascists—politically motivated intellectuals who after their liberation from concentration camps or their return from their countries of exile wished to take part in the creation of a democratic Germany. In the 1950s, many Jews who had emigrated to Israel at the beginning of the Hitler era returned to Germany. They had adjusted poorly to Israel and, moreover, the economic conditions in the newly-formed Federal Republic of Germany were incomparably better than those in Israel. In addition to the Jews returning from Israel, others immigrated to Germany, for example the Hungarian Jews after the anti-Soviet uprising in Hungary, Czech Jews after the Prague Spring, as well as Polish Jews in the aftermath of the anti-Zionist campaign in Poland in 1967. The Jewish community had 30,000 officially listed members in 1992. However, because a part of the Jewish immigrants do not register as Jews, the number of Jews in Germany can be estimated to be approximately 50,000.

Ambivalence toward Germany is characteristic of the Jewish postwar generations, along with a keen historical perspective, an awareness of continuity. Almost without exception every family can claim at least one Nazi victim. In many families, all relatives were murdered. The young generation was directly confronted with mourning and sorrow. Whether their parents discussed freely their experiences during the time of persecution and in the concentration camps or whether they remained silent, sparing their children the psychological burden, the past could always be sensed: "The Third Reich was constantly present. When I went to the butcher on Saturday and stood in line with a sixty-year-old woman ahead of me and a sixty-five-year-old woman behind me, it would suddenly occur to me: What did you do back then? Did you scream 'Heil Hitler,' break windows, denounce people—who are you?"[3]

The other ever-present questions asked by the postwar generation were: How could it have come about, this annihilation of the Jews, this barbaric conduct of a civilized society? Why did the parents come back to Germany, or never even leave in the first place, how could all this have even been possible? Those were questions to which there were no answers. The German mainstream cloaked itself in silence. History instruction in the schools of the

1960s and 1970s was more than deficient in this respect. In general, the lesson plans ended with the introduction of the Weimar Republic. If a younger Jew entered into a conversation with an older German about the 'Third Reich' at all, the latter would advance the well-known clichés: "We knew nothing," "We didn't want 'it,'" "We saved some Jews." The appearance of normalcy that marked everyday life in Germany made the recent history even less comprehensible.

I described this contradiction between past and present, between normalcy and absurdity, as follows:

> Just as my past lay in darkness, there was also a black haze over the past of other young Jews. Having grandparents was out of the ordinary. We could not penetrate into this past, because the way this past had ended was so difficult to imagine: 'They were gassed.' What does that mean? We lived in an enlightened new era. Equal rights, emancipation, *these* were, after all, the words of our new era. 'They were gassed' simply did not fit this scheme. Our grandparents, our dead aunts and uncles seemed to us like ghosts, like volatile, transparent spirits, but not like people of flesh and blood.[4]

Because of this history, Jews in Germany are unable to construct for themselves a German identity. They are state citizens with German passports, but they do not feel 'German.' Now as much as ever before do they consider themselves at risk—they are foreigners and victims who in most situations do not trust the country in which they live. As the psychoanalyst Samy Speyer elaborated:

> Trusting one's own surroundings, even the most immediate surroundings! Despite many years of awareness, perhaps because of it, I have not succeeded in building up such a confidence, and I am certain that the reason cannot be traced back to my early childhood experiences, but rather to the vigilance with which I routinely scrutinize my immediate environment. I wish to emphasize that I have problems with neither my close nor my extended surroundings as I evaluate these [German] people—provided they do not, as did Kohl, take the easy way out, claiming that because they belong to a new generation they have nothing to do with the past. They have to be honest about the fact that everyone at least to some degree carries this horrible inheritance within themselves. The decisive factor is precisely this supposed ignorance, this wished-for objectivity, which even among my colleagues has come to be viewed frequently as the 'new' ideal of health.[5]

The sociologist Cilly Kugelmann advanced the following psychological reasons for Jews remaining in Germany:

> The act of establishing oneself in Germany seemed to offer a kind of paradoxical advantage. It was precisely the proximity to the country and society which was responsible for the destruction of one's own life that allowed a fictitious new beginning, something like a Jewish 'Point Zero,' although ultimately it

would probably be impossible to circumvent the psychological effort necessary to affirm one's own experience as the basis of this existence. Life among the Germans worked as an insurance against forgetting the past.[6]

In spite of all the reservations, fears, and resentments typical of the generations of Jews reared in Germany after World War II, one must accept the fact that Jewish communities *did* establish themselves here and it has to be assumed that they will not be transitory. The grandchildren of the concentration camp survivors are now reaching adulthood. Despite their mistrust in their language, in their culture, and above all in their economic security, these Jews stay in Germany.

However, even for the second postwar generation the 'Third Reich' is ever-present. Every anti-Semitic utterance, every verbal attack upon Jews, takes on historical dimensions and is instantly interpreted in the context of the 'Final Solution.' There is no Jewish publication in which the Nazis, persecution, and fear are not addressed, and Jewish intellectuals remain unswervingly preoccupied with the Holocaust. I still consider Hanna Vogt's observations, which were written thirty years ago, completely accurate and to the point:

> The temporal distance of historical events has the following effect: the distance continues to grow larger, but it does not, as some would like to believe, cause the dimensions of the atrocities to diminish. In my opinion, exactly the opposite is the case. Future generations will not judge more mildly, but rather more harshly, because—at least according to the experiences up until now—the development of human rights legislature is irreversible and the human race cannot return to a legal consciousness that allowed for greater privileges and more exceptions.[7]

With Germans the situation is quite different. After the war there was silence regarding the monstrous crimes against the Jews. The Nazi trials, which finally began, albeit sluggishly, in the 1960s, were degraded to a farce, and it took the American film *Holocaust* in the late 1970s to instigate an official coming-to-terms with the 'Final Solution' politics of the 'Third Reich.' For years there have been attempts to minimize the crimes in the death camps by comparing Israel to Nazi Germany and the Israeli military to the Nazis. "In the chasms of German history, false equations are greedily fabricated that place the draconic Israeli military actions in the occupied territories on the same level with the industrialized mass murder of the victims."[8]

Or, let us for instance consider the historical argument unleashed by a book written by the renowned historian Ernst Nolte, which makes the concentration camps appear harmless and questions the numbers of persons who died in the Holocaust. The Germans are in the process of discounting the 'Final Solution' chapter of their history in order to integrate the 'Third Reich' into their history. As far as the Germans are concerned, this resolution is too convincing as to even mention the crimes of the Nazis in the Treaty of

'Reunification,' despite massive Jewish protests. A newly awakened nationalism accompanied the unification of Germany. No one wanted to engage in a critical reflection upon one's native country, traditions, and history. Those Jewish voices which refused to be silenced and continued to remind the German public of the crimes of the older generation were not heeded.

The new German self-confidence—the result of economic and political power—no longer tolerates being reproached with Auschwitz. The way Jews and Germans have come to look at 9 November can be taken as symbolic of the situation at large. For the former, 9 November is the memorial day of *Kristallnacht*, the 'Night of Broken Glass,' and the beginning of the 'Final Solution.' For the latter, the majority, it is a day of rejoicing. It is the day the Berlin Wall came down.

## NOTES

1. Monika Richarz, *Jüdisches Leben in Deutschland seit 1945* (Königstein CZ: Jüdischer Verlag bei Athenäum, 1986), p. 14.
2. Dan Diner, "Negative Symbiose. Deutsche und Juden nach Auschwitz," *Babylon, Beiträge zur jüdischen Gegenwart* 1 (1988), p. 18.
3. Sarah Haffner in *Fremd im eigenen Land*, ed. Henryk Broder and Michael R. Lang (Frankfurt: Fischer, 1979), p. 226.
4. Lea Fleischmann, *Dies ist nicht mein Land* (Hamburg: Hoffmann und Campe, 1980), p. 53.
5. Samy Speyer, "Von der Pubertät zum Erwachsenendasein." In Micha Brumlik, ed., *Jüdisches Leben in Deutschland seit 1945* (Frankfurt am Main: Jüdischer Verlag bei Athenäum, 1986), p. 190.
6. Cilly Kugelmann, "Zur Identität osteuropäischer Juden in der Bundesrepublik" in *Jüdisches Leben in Deutschland seit 1945*, p. 180.
7. Hanna Vogt, *Die Darstellung des Judentums in der pädagogischen Praxis* (Ner Tamid Verlag, 1960), p. 44.
8. Otto Schily in *Tribüne. Zeitschrift zum Verständnis des Judentums* 27/106 (1988), p. 121.

# Lea Fleischmann and Wolf Biermann:
# Like Strangers in Their Own House

## Peter Werres

Lea Fleischmann and Wolf Biermann, contemporary German-speaking authors of Jewish descent born a decade apart, can be described as polar opposites in biography, emotional makeup, political background, and in the way in which they tend to express themselves. At the same time, they appear to share feelings of marginality as outsiders in an almost exclusively Gentile country or have, at times, even seemed united in their concerns, as in their outcry in unison over a reemergence of blatantly racist sentiment in Germany or over the recent threat to Israel caused by poison gas—the collective trauma of the Jewish people. This essay intends to examine their work so as to outline some obvious differences as well as some striking similarities.

Fleischmann, who was born in Ulm in 1947 to Polish parents whose families had been decimated[1] in the course of industrial,[2] systematic genocide of East European Jewry, rose in 1980 to the forefront of German literary discussion with her first book, *Dies ist nicht mein Land. Eine Jüdin verläßt die Bundesrepublik* [This Is Not My Country. A Jewish Woman Leaves the Federal Republic].[3] It contains a succession of images and reflections, formatted as a sequence of autobiographical sketches, anecdotal material, and quotations, and is an unusual array of rational and sometimes nearly clairvoyant observations on what the author perceives to be the crux of the German psyche.

It is, however, a book also marked by some highly emotional outcries and the occasional blanket statements[4] such as: "The Jews were killed mainly because of money. Everything else was disguise and distortion" (*Land*, p. 39). In any case, Fleischmann's "powerful autobiographical statement"[5] constituted a breakthrough for post-Holocaust Jewish literature in Germany: "Lea Fleischmann in her witty, wrathful *Dies ist nicht mein Land* represented a kind of coming out for a postwar generation of Jews."[6] This young woman wrote a book that hit a raw nerve in Germany because of its frontal assault on the German self-image, a book by a child of the Holocaust who, while living in Germany, always took pains to avoid calling herself German and, stressing her outsider status, reminded her readers that she merely traveled with a German passport (Grossmann, p. 21).[7]

It was simple everyday life in Germany which convinced Fleischmann that they are a weak people—and have long been weak—not strong, as always claimed. In her view, the Germans are a collection of timid and well-behaved individuals, burghers who often find pleasure in regulating their own humiliation. According to Fleischmann—who is hardly the only observer to make such a remark[8]—the apparent strength of the Germans is an authoritarian façade that rarely cracks because certain rules of the game are usually observed, and authority goes unquestioned. Minorities and outsiders, who do not have an easy time anywhere, find it especially difficult to handle everyday life in Germany. They are frequently marginalized because they inadvertently question the façade, i.e. they threaten to knock a delicate national consensus off balance.[9] Instead of trying to understand and appreciate the heterogeneous identities of minorities as an enhancement to mainstream culture, Germans tend to consider them a hinderance or a threat to supposedly preestablished harmony. As Herbert Marcuse observes, multiculturalism has been and still is a sensitive subject in this "one-dimensional society."[10]

When Fleischmann was a child, her displaced family felt like the living dead described by Jurek Becker, another child of the Holocaust, himself a death camp survivor, or by Nobel Peace Laureate Elie Wiesel, according to whom such survivors were "neither alive nor fully dead."[11] The author remembers: "We were too weak to leave, to establish ourselves in a different country" (*Land*, p. 203). Fleischmann spent her early years in a camp for displaced persons[12] in Upper Bavaria, a camp that during World War II had served as a German ammunition dump and was still heavily secured with barbed wire—but now, however, was crowned by a huge metal Star of David—not an altogether encouraging environment: "In the early 1950s no Jew could imagine not emigrating from Germany" (*Land*, p. 22).

Yet over time, Fleischmann became more resolute: "Later I asked myself why I should leave at all. They would have liked just that" (*Land*, p. 203). As a result, Fleischmann appears to have been on the path toward a life of marginality early on, in the position of the outsider "with the view from the enclave of negation,"[13] as Horkheimer called such a role. During the course of the book, the reader witnesses how "a Jewish woman of the younger generation sought to develop her identity as someone who was other and wanted to be other" (*Land*, p. 44). After failed Jewish attempts at assimilation, after the experience of deadly difference, the need to fall back on one's particularity was felt, not just by many older Jewish survivors, but particularly by several children of the Holocaust, among them Fleischmann.

For a time, however, the author did try to fit in, hoping that a new and different generation of Germans would evolve. She lived in relative isolation in the small, two-block Jewish ghetto of Frankfurt, completed her schooling, and then spent five years teaching German adolescents. In those schools—the sector of German life with which the teacher Fleischmann was most familiar—she found no reason to hope for a future improvement in German ways, as long as symptoms of neurotic perfectionism abounded: "It appears to me that the Germans developed from their fear of turning a mistake into a philosophy of life" (*Land*, p. 131).

The author often sees reflections of the bureaucratic machinery of the Nazi past in the narrow-mindedness of present-day German educational practices. While the term *Befehl* [order] has been euphemistically replaced by the more palatable *Anweisung* [directive], the effects seem the same. What kind of people, Fleischmann asks, can consider an order unjust and yet still carry it out, and, worst of all, do not even feel personally responsible for what they have done? According to Zipes, "Fleischmann's depiction of the German school system resembles a training camp for the banality of evil" (Zipes, p. 44). The author sees children confronted with a "Reiß-dich-zusammen-Pädagogik und die Laß-dich-nicht-gehen-Erziehung" [a pull-yourself-together pedagogy and a don't-let-yourself-go education] (*Land*, p. 93), which leave little or no room for feelings: "They are not allowed to show their pain because rather than comfort they encounter contempt" (*Land*, p. 95).[14] As a result, Fleischmann notes, feelings are considered a weakness in Germany, lack of feeling is synonymous with strength. At night, in her dreams, the past and present flow together; her headmaster appears in an SS uniform;[15] and her pupils goose-step: "Directives" have once again become "orders" (*Land*, p. 82). Fleischmann grows increasingly convinced that the Holocaust was more than a *Betriebsunfall* [job-related accident] of history (*Land*, p. 77).

Overwhelmed by alienating experiences with mainstream German society and by the pressures of the bureaucratic apparatus, Fleischmann resigns in the end: "Today I resigned. I terminated my service to the German people. My career as a German civil servant has come to an end. . . . My mother lived under the Germans for five years, and I lived with them for five years. That's enough" (*Land*, p. 205).[16] The author came to view the Germans as frequently driven by detached, noncommittal, and thus potentially criminal perfectionism. In her first book, she analyzes the infamous Wannsee Conference as an example.[17]

Dealing with insensitivity and pettiness on a daily basis had ultimately become too frustrating, too tiresome for Fleischmann. In mid 1979, having reverted to the outsider she was in her childhood, she moved to Israel. "The intolerant way Germans treat each other . . . ultimately drove her to make the decision," observed Zipes (p. 44). "What kind of a people is that? What kind of a race?" (*Land*, p. 96) she cries out, boldly turning the race ideology of the Nazis on its head.

In her broadsides against German ways, Fleischmann is at times simply not interested in, and perhaps emotionally incapable of, writing objectively. In her first book, she did not seem to realize that a great many of her complaints perhaps had as much to do with her status of marginality—being a

Jewish woman professional—as with the intrinsic aspects of the German psyche.

It was not until Fleischmann had lived in Israel for some time that she also wrote, in her considerably toned-down second book, of the possibility that some of her disaffections with Teutonic ways were in part rooted in the idiosyncrasies not just of German, but of typical Western modes of socialization. The author came to the conclusion that in other European nations as well minorities deviating from dominant value systems become living proof of the inability of society to tolerate difference and otherness. This is not to say that Fleischmann just happened to experience stigmatization and marginalization in one of several European nations with similar problems: in her eyes, Germany is a country with an especially horrible past and, at present, still a nation eerily preoccupied with purity and, as a result, an impossibly 'clean' place. Such cleanliness,[18] in the author's view, is yet another symptom of the German compulsion for perfection and thus for potential elimination and extermination.

Living in the Middle East and turning her sights on Europe in general, the author in *Ich bin Israelin. Erfahrungen in einem orientalischen Land* [I Am an Israeli. Experiences in a Middle Eastern Country] observes: "Perfection was sacrificed to being human. I no longer want to learn any lessons from Europe..." (*Israelin*, p. 217). In her latest book *Gas. Tagebuch einer Bedrohung* [Gas. Diary of a Threat], Fleischmann goes even further: "Western man only sees his own image.... Those who do not place limits on their intelligence, will be killed by this very intelligence in the end."[19] At the time of her first book, however, Fleischmann simply drew the conclusion, "This is Not My Country"[20] about Germany, moved to Israel, and made a special point of returning her German passport[21]—ironically encountering further bureaucratic complications with German authorities in the process (*Israelin*, p. 25).

Among the numerous callous bureaucratic terms that have irritated a number of critics, the appallingly insensitive *Wiedergutmachung* [restitution] has especially enraged some German postwar authors, among them Enzensberger, who coined the harrowing term *Niewiedergutmachung* [never-restitution].[22] Fleischmann observes: "There was an entire chapter on reparation in my history reader, but nothing on the plundering of the Jews" (*Land*, p. 62).

Similar, yet painfully more personal, observations were made by the songwriter, poet, essayist, and playwright Wolf Biermann, Fleischmann's senior by a decade, and in 1991 the recipient of Germany's most prestigious literary award, the Büchner Prize[23]: "Nobody can make restitution and nothing compensates for the wrongs suffered." Beyond this, however, Biermann has more personal reasons to ponder this issue:

> I knew gypsies in East Berlin, who could not even
> turn the Auschwitz number on their arm into a VdN pension.
> Nothing enjoys more credibility than a document stamped
> with an eagle and a Swastika.[24]

Precisely such an eerie document describing the fate of Biermann's father is in the possession of the writer's mother:

> The death certificate arrived by mail. Auschwitz registry. Hitler's head on the postage stamp.... Nonetheless, this rare document proved advantageous to my mother after '45.... She was immediately granted a widow's pension for which other survivors had to wait until doomsday. (*Klartexte*, pp. 230–231)

Fleischmann and Biermann not only have shared complaints about always perfect and hence inhumanly unrelenting adherence to procedure. Cases of stubborn bureaucratic behavior that caused, or very nearly caused, ironic, unanticipated consequences, even bizarre twists, within the Nazi death machine are also reported by both authors. Fleischmann quotes a Mrs. Stein, who survived Auschwitz because the Block Commander in charge was a stickler for procedure. Sentenced to twenty-one days of hard labor for a minor infraction, she was kept there to finish her full sentence while everyone else in her block was gassed to make room for new arrivals: "Formaljuristisch unanfechtbar" [legally indisputable] (*Land*, p. 183).

Biermann's account of his father's fate hints at the same ironic twist but lacks the fortunate ending. His father Dagobert, a Jewish Communist and dock worker at the Hamburg harbor, was serving a six-year sentence for his political activities and therefore out of reach when the Jews of his hometown were rounded up: "But apparently even the Nazis were people with a sense of justice. In 1943 they also purged their prisons of Jews" (*Klartexte*, p. 34). In his paradoxically condensed style, Biermann notes with bitter sarcasm: "My father had fought against injustice. This way he lived one year longer."[25] For Biermann it is simply absurd that his politically involved father in the end met the fate of his entire family—over twenty relatives had been murdered—not before them, but *after* them, and not on account of his anti-Fascist activities, but for the same reason his family had been killed: simply for being Jewish.

In similar accounts and with inevitable feelings of alienation, Fleischmann and Biermann describe the same strange and often absurd German reality of bureaucracies, formalities, procedures—and of little people[26] who willingly, callously, and often blindly, comply in their *Kadavergehorsam* [blind obedience] and *Stempelgläubigkeit* [unquestioning faith in the authorities]. Just as Fleischmann cites examples of cold-hearted behavior, Biermann shares several such experiences, especially with German bureaucrats, the most heart-wrenching one again related to the circumstances surrounding his father's murder. His mother was finally told about her husband's fate in the following way:

> A civil servant... standing in the doorway told my mother: On February 22 your husband died of heart failure at seven o'clock in the morning. My mother screamed, then she lost consciousness... then my mother screamed again and cried holding on to the banister with the one hand—with the other she held me.

> The man repeatedly tore her hand off the banister gasping: 'Stop being so sentimental!' (*Klartexte*, p. 229)

Despite such obvious parallels in their assessments of life and human interaction in Germany, the two writers' responses to the numerous unpleasant aspects of daily reality there vary greatly. When Fleischmann felt too much like the outsider of her childhood days, she simply moved to Israel to start a new life, looking back at Germany: "These are not my people ... let them live whichever way they like. I am neither a revolutionary nor a fighter" (*Land*, p. 201). Unlike so many Jewish intellectuals at the time, Fleischmann did not identify with the Left in Germany, thus abandoning the longstanding historic affinity between Socialism and secular Judaism.[27] In contrast, Biermann has always believed that the memory of his murdered father is best served by trying to actively change in Germany what Fleischmann might consider unchangeable—trying to confront the *Bürokratensau* [the bureaucrat sow] (M, p. 57).

Beyond chastising the "homunculus buerocraticus" (*Klartexte*, p. 117), the usually pugnacious Biermann is especially quick to detect traces of residual or, more recently, renewed Fascistoid (and also plain Fascist) behavior patterns in cozy everyday German life, and readily speaks out whenever racism rears its ugly head—something he did in no uncertain terms in his highly publicized and much-discussed speech when accepting the Büchner Prize. In the past, the *Liedermacher* or songwriter had not been overly concerned with occasional racist utterances, such as "Juuda verrekke [sic]" ("Die Jew Die," P, pp. 109, 127, 131), or hate-mail warning him: "Also right-wingers own rifle telescopes,"[28] "we will gas you and burn you like your father" (P, p. 109).

For Biermann, the real problem has always had deeper roots: "The little everyday Fascism/ appears so very cozy."[29] This line constitutes the moral and the refrain of a chilling ballad set in Lower Bavaria, entitled "Gemütlicher Faschismus" [Cozy Fascism] (V, p. 83), in which a forester plays games with his faithful German Shepherd dog, taunting him with what he claims to be Jewish flesh. Rarely in the past did the author see the Germans owning up to their recent history, and rarely does he now see them stand up for marginalized members of society and foreigners mistreated or even persecuted in Germany. Biermann readily takes up the cause of several minorities. Long before Germany's constitutional obligation to grant asylum became a hotly contested political issue in 1991 and 1992, Biermann, in his "Asyl für den Türken" [Asylum for the Turk], bitterly questioned bureaucratic intent altogether:

> they suicided him
> now he has asylum forever
> on German ground and soil

> now he gets his little piece of land
> like every dead dog
> ...
> the liberties are wasting away
> and I know all too well why it is
> that I am so sad [30]

While he was still living in the GDR, Biermann published a song on behalf of the Gypsies—Roma—, "Stillepan–Schlufflied" [Stillepan's Lullaby] (G, p. 67)[31] and in 1982 he wrote as a pendant "Schlaflied für Tanepen" [Lullaby for Tanepen] containing the haunting verse:

> The dead cannot sleep
> under the ground there is yelling and screaming
> that is because the killers up here
> are loose and enjoy life.[32]

On the outside looking in, Biermann, paraphrasing Broder in his own sinister, biting, and paradoxical way, sums up a situation of grotesque role reversal of victim and oppressor[33] in the German psyche: "The Germans have forgiven the Jews/ but they have not yet forgiven the Gypsies."[34] Ever since 1945, it has been noted, Germans have by and large been exercising the "politics of forgetting" (Yago–Jung, p. 138), bristling at the mere suggestion of any historical continuity between Nazism and post-World War II Germany. At the same time, until recently—and with notable exceptions—they embraced a decidedly philo-Semitic stance. Yet critics have held that this newly-found love has a dishonest, hollow ring to it, whether they describe this philo-Semitism as "silent,"[35] "conscientious,"[36] "open,"[37] or, as Biermann does, plainly hypocritical in nature. "The official philo-Semitic treatment of the Jews, ... this obsequious civility had something more basic to conceal," Dan Diner (p. 130) could also not avoid observing.

Some Germans—especially those seemingly omnipresent beefy adolescents to whom Biermann refers as "mordsgemütliche Jungs"[38]—have in the meantime, "mangels Juden" [in the absence of Jews], resorted to other scapegoats, some new, namely the Turks, some old, such as the Roma, to act out what can only be described as their displaced self-aggression (*Dädalus*, p. 58). Even in the once officially anti-Fascist former GDR, individuals started ganging up on these minority groups as early as 1989.[39] Neo Nazis began preying on arriving refugees, especially those from Eastern Europe—among them, so far, twelve thousand Jewish asylum seekers, who now, in a strange twist of bureaucratic history, have to prove their Jewishness in order to be admitted.[40] Ever since the fall of the wall, aggressive East German youth, after frustrating years as docile GDR citizens, finally appear to see a chance to vent their long-repressed anger:

> Skinheads at Lichtenberg station
> Wearing shining bomber jackets
> They guarantee German cleanliness
> Until the gypsies get out.[41]

After his initial euphoria over the cultural explosion in the GDR and the historic political reorientation of Eastern Europe—the intoxication of people deciding their own destiny—Biermann has come to resign himself, in this sober age of pragmatic post-communism marked by the absence of utopian vision and a reemergence of racial violence, to continued marginality. No love lost, he seems to be saying: "You more-than-German Germans. . . . I know you can get along very well without me. But also I can manage without you."[42] Pondering his renewed minority status, however, the poet does admit to some pain: "I would have liked so much to have been part of the majority only once."[43] Not unlike Fleischmann at the end of her residence in Germany, Biermann, feeling left out in the cold, sees a circle coming to a close: "For me, this is a déja vu of my early childhood years in this country ignorant of history. I am arriving, once again, in the cold climate of a hostility I know all too well."[44] As early as 1972, in his "Hölderlin Lied" [Hölderlin Song] (G, p. 19), Biermann had used that poet's line "This is how I ended up among the Germans"[45]—to which Fleischmann alluded in order to express her feelings of marginality—to set the tone for a poem starting with yet another line borrowed from the same author: "We live in this country/ like strangers in our own house."[46]

The frequently surfacing[47] melancholic side of the author,[48] for which he claims to be indebted to Jewish heritage,[49] stresses the paradoxical aspects of an existence on the outside. Even the devastating Allied air raids on his neighborhood in Hamburg in July 1943, disastrous as they were, had unexpected side effects, as they worked in favor of the remaining members of the Biermann family: these raids brought the Nazi machinery of annihilation temporarily to a halt.[50] Biermann was evacuated to Bavaria with his mother, where they managed to avoid further persecution:

> And because I was born under the yellow star
> In Germany
> We received the English bombs
> Like gifts from heaven
>     (*Die Zeit* 6, p. 17)

Biermann, for himself, rarely stresses his Jewish ancestry. "I remain what I have been all along/ Half Jew boy and half Goy."[51] Seeing Jewishness not so much as a question of heritage, but rather in Sartrean terms, as a sociohistorical construct, he even goes so far as to claim: "I am not a Jew. Those who could have made me a Jew, have all been murdered" (*Die Zeit* 6, p. 18).[52] It is mainly the haunting memory of his Jewish father's fate that finds expression throughout his work. Even here, Biermann regards his father less as a Jewish victim of the Holocaust than as a casualty of the class struggle and an ongoing war to liberate mankind.[53] For the songwriter, his father ranks as an immortal among those numerous fallen fighters for the cause who happen to be Jewish:[54]

> I sing for my comrade Dagobert Biermann
> who became smoke rising from the chimneys
> whose stench was resurrected from Auschwitz.[55]

Elsewhere, in prose, Biermann has added the following multilayered, twisting comment to Adorno's much discussed remark concerning Auschwitz: "And perhaps the chimney of the crematorium in Auschwitz is the only thing about which a barbarian like myself can still write a poem."[56]

The combative side of Biermann follows both the politically conscious bohemian tradition and the radical anti-bureaucratic spontaneity of Rosa Luxemburg and other critical spirits and visionaries of a secular Jewish utopia along Socialist lines. Yet in his version of the anthem of the *Bund*, the union and political party of the Jewish proletariat of Poland and Russia at the turn of the century, a song entitled "Mag sein, daß ich irre" [Perhaps I'm Wrong] (P, p. 226), he resigns himself to more modest goals. In the paradoxical style of antithetical expression that has become his trademark, Biermann sizes up the present situation: "These days it is difficult not to be a prophet of darkness."[57]

The author's concerns were long focused on Germany, where he had become an outspoken agent of political change for three decades. Early on, in the stolid equality of the GDR, he had been unwilling to mouth Socialist homilies and was therefore soon considered "the supersinner among the 'skeptics,'"[58] his lyrics often communicating an "increasing sense of despair at the ability of the bureaucracy to reform."[59] Later, in the West, Biermann chastised for many years the barbaric oversimplifications of the Cold War waged with particular intensity by the erstwhile two Germanies.[60] He continues to protest the politics of forgetting, democratic conformism, and the tyranny of the profit motive. Globally, the poet had frequently commented on political oppression from Chile to Alabama, interestingly so, however, not on confrontations in the Middle East until the outbreak of the 1991 Gulf War. In the past, Biermann had not been an apologist for Israel and had frequently even shown ambivalence in his feelings toward that country.[61]

At the same time, the author had been closely following recent political developments that could have constituted the very existence of the Jewish State—especially those developments in which some Germans had a hand. As a result, Biermann, alluding to the haunting leitmotif of the well-known poem "Todesfuge" [Death Fugue] by another German-speaking Jewish poet of this century, Paul Celan, wrote in the autumn of 1990 lines that were certain not to endear him to mainstream German society:

> Far away in Iraq with German gas
> And jet bombers from France
> the Master from Germany, Death
> has a chance against Israel.[62]

Earlier it had, understandably so, only been the extreme Right in Germany that threatened Biermann with retaliation for perceived *Nestbeschmutzung* [soiling one's own nest], but subsequently when he publicly (*Die Zeit* 6, 1991, p. 18) supported action against Iraq to protect Israel, he received death threats—ironically—from the fringes of the extreme German Left[63] he had helped nurture into existence in the mid 1960s and for which he had served as an acclaimed rallying figure for so long. By late 1992, things had somewhat reverted to the *status quo ante*, as any leftist hostility toward Biermann was gravely overshadowed by increasing death threats from neo-Nazi groups. Other writers and journalists of Jewish descent came to share this fate with Biermann, as anti-foreigner and anti-Semitic violence appeared to peak in what could only be described as an *annus horribilis* for Germany's self-image.

As much as Fleischmann and Biermann might disagree on an array of political topics and issues past or current, the prospect of a chemical war against the Jewish State, carried out with gas made available to Israel's enemy by Germans,[64] mobilized in both writers emotional resources that surprised them and others. "The collective trauma of the Jewish people is activated," Fleischmann ponders, sitting with her gas mask[65] in her sealed room in Jerusalem. "The fear of the present is coupled with the terror of the past; tomorrow's potential misfortune conjures up immediately yesterday's terrible catastrophe" (*Gas*, p. 18); "Once again gas made in Germany threatens us" (p. 107). Compared to the outrage ringing from Fleischmann's latest book, Biermann's comment on the unthinkable is marked by a sarcasm so bitter that it seems to border on insensitivity:

> Forty-five years after Auschwitz Jews sit in their cozy little gas chambers behind plastic wrappers and adhesive tape, that is progress. In Tel Aviv and Jerusalem they are expecting behind German gas masks on their Jewish noses the moment when the poison gas will be dropped inside from above. (*Die Zeit* 6, 1991, p. 17)

In Fleischmann, the threat of poison gas triggered the realization that cold profit motives, those of German as well as other merchants of death, were responsible for an insane global arms buildup.[66] This insight finally made her somewhat of the Cassandra and political activist (*Gas*, pp. 135–162) that Biermann has been for so many years.[67] "Where will tomorrow's great fire take place? We know for certain that it will come" (*Gas*, p. 122) seems to echo Biermann's warnings of the last decade, warnings, however, that go beyond the threat of war: "Humankind has to change fast or it will croak even without a war" (*Über das Geld*, p. 42).

From their recent writings it would thus seem that both authors, sensitized by their own feelings of marginality as well as the bitter personal lessons of the Holocaust, have, in sight of man-made disasters everywhere, come to embrace in their writings urgent concerns that transcend all ethnic roots and political alliances and appear truly global in nature.

## NOTES

1. Fleischmann's mother had eleven siblings and her father seven; only her parents and one of their eighteen siblings survived the death camps. Her father later died in a mental institution.
2. See Jean-Paul Bier, *Auschwitz et les nouvelles littératures allemandes* (Brussels: Editions de l' Université Bruxelles, 1979).
3. The edition quoted here is: Lea Fleischmann, *Dies ist nicht mein Land. Eine Jüdin verläßt die Bundesrepublik* (Munich: Heyne, 1989). The translations are by the editors.
4. Jack Zipes seems to share this assessment: "Perhaps there are too many generalizations and stereotypes in her description of . . . the Germans." "The Vicissitudes of Being Jewish in West Germany," *Germans and Jews since the Holocaust*, ed. Anson Rabinbach and Jack Zipes (New York: Holmes & Meier, 1986), p. 44.
5. Anson Rabinbach, "Reflections on Germans and Jews since Auschwitz," *Germans and Jews since the Holocaust*, p. 10.
6. Atina Grossmann, "Questions of Jewish Identity," *Germans and Jews since the Holocaust*, p. 172.
7. Also in Fleischmann's second book, *Ich bin Israelin. Erfahrungen in einem orientalischen Land* (Hamburg: Hoffmann und Campe, 1982), p. 23.
8. Still, Fleischmann seems to have been capable of verbalizing something others could often only sense: "Fleischmann . . . recognized the underlying reasons for my fear during my youth in Germany—the worship of anonymous and constraining authority, the flight from the past, and the rejection of everything that is different, spontaneous, humane, and therefore potentially chaotic." Yudit Yago–Jung, "Growing up in Germany: After the War—After Hitler—Afterwards," *Germans and Jews since the Holocaust*, p. 144.
9. Fleischmann, *Land*, p. 200. Henryk Broder had made the similar observation that Germans like to steer clear of dispute because it disturbs the existing harmony. In *Fremd im eigenen Land*, ed. Henryk Broder and Michael R. Lang (Frankfurt am Main: 1979), p. 90, a volume to which Fleischmann had also been a contributor. Broder, after publishing *Deutschland erwacht* (Cologne: Kiepenheuer & Witsch, 1978) and a virtual barrage of articles, e.g. "Für Juden gibt es hier keine Normalität," *Der Spiegel* 17 (1981), pp. 39–55; "Gegen meinen Willen in die Geschichte verknotet," *Konkret* (April 1981), pp. 55–57, bid Germany a polemic farewell in the early 1980s with "Ihr bleibt die Kinder Eurer Eltern," *Die Zeit* 10 (1981), p. 9. Broder continues to write for the German press.
10. Cf. Herbert Marcuse, *One Dimensional Man: Studies in the Ideology of Advanced Industrial Society* (Boston: Beacon Press, 1966).
11. Elie Wiesel, *A Beggar in Jerusalem* (New York: Random, 1970), p. 19.

12. For details of such an existence, see Wolfgang Jacobmeyer, "Jüdische Überlebende als 'Displaced Persons,'" *Geschichte und Gesellschaft* 9 (1983), pp. 429–444.

13. Similarly, Leslie A. Adelson, in her discussion of Jeannette Lander, describes "the curious paradox of finding one's grounding in . . . foreignness" in "There's No Place Like Home: Jeannette Lander and Ronnith Neumann's Utopian Quests for Jewish Identity in the Contemporary West German Context," *New German Critique* 50 (1990), p. 117. See also earlier, Paul Piccone and Russell Berman, "Recycling the 'Jewish Question,'" *New German Critique* 21 (1980), pp. 113–127, as well as Cily Kugelmann, "Was heißt jüdische Identität?" *Alternative* 140/41 (December 1981), pp. 234–240.

14. During childbirth, Fleischmann, then Rosenzweig, encountered the same coldness: "Pull yourself together Mrs. Rosenzweig, don't let yourself go like that" (p. 94). It was, incidentally, a non-German woman that showed sympathy: "Later a cleaning woman entered the room, a woman who knew only a few words of German, but who understood my pain" (p. 95).

15. While growing up in West Germany, Israeli-born Dan Diner made similar observations: "In the closet of a schoolmate's father the black SS uniform could still be found hanging among garments of everyday life as a matter of fact" ("Fragments of an Uncompleted Journey: On Jewish Socialization and Political Identity in West Germany," *Germans and Jews since the Holocaust*, p. 123).

16. Fleischmann's phrasing reminds us of Hölderlin who, nearly two centuries earlier, had voiced his feelings of alienation from his fellow countrymen in a strikingly similar manner: "So kam ich unter die Deutschen" [That is how I ended up among the Germans], Friedrich Beißner, ed., *Friedrich Hölderlin. Sämtliche Werke* (Frankfurt: Insel, 1965), p. 636.

17. The later film *Die Wannseekonferenz* highlighted this very aspect of the banality of evil, two decades after the original shock of Rudolf Höss, *Kommandant in Auschwitz* (Frankfurt am Main: Fischer, 1958).

18. In this regard, Fleischmann honestly admits that her German upbringing has left its traces. In her new home in Jerusalem, she seriously considers posting a *Hausordnung* [house rules] to improve her neighbor's sloppy habits of refuse disposal (*Israelin*, p. 158).

19. *Gas. Tagebuch einer Bedrohung* (Göttingen: Steidl, 1991), pp. 123–124.

20. The American critic Atina Grossmann muses: "When my friends and I read Lea Fleischmann's book here in New York, it was only half a joke to say that we could hardly wait for her next book from Israel, 'This is Not My Country, Either'" (p. 182). Fleischmann, of course, never wrote anything by this title, even though her second book *Ich bin Israelin* shows that her critical spirit remained alive, even where she dealt with her country of choice.

21. Fleischmann wanted to make a clean break with Germany. Even though eligible for reimbursement of her mandatory payments into German pension funds after her move to Israel, the author never considered applying—something worth mentioning that she has not personally publicized.

22. Hans Magnus Enzensberger, *Landessprache* (Frankfurt am Main: Suhrkamp, 1960), p. 38.

23. Through use of the bracketed abbreviations indicated, the following collections of poems and songs by Wolf Biermann are cited and referenced parenthetically in the text, including page numbers: *Mit Marx- und Engelszungen* (Berlin: Wagenbach, 1968) [M]; *Für meine Genossen* (Berlin: Wagenbach, 1972) [G]; *Preußischer*

*Ikarus* (Cologne: Kiepenheuer & Witsch, 1978) [P]; *Verdrehte Welt—das seh' ich gerne* (Cologne: K & W, 1982) [V]; *Affenfels und Barrikade* (Cologne: K & W, 1986) [A].

24. Wolf Biermann, "À la laterne! À la laterne!" *Der Sturz des Dädalus* (Cologne: Kiepenheuer & Witsch, 1992), p. 259. Hannes Stein, ed., *Wolf Biermann. Klartexte im Getümmel* (Cologne: Kiepenheuer & Witsch, 1990), p. 231:

> "Ich kannte Zigeuner in Ostberlin, die schafften es
> nicht mal, ihre Auschwitznummer auf dem Unterarm in
> eine VdN-Rente umzumünzen. [Alles] nicht so
> glaubwürdig wie ein Dokument mit dem Hakenkreuzadlerstempel drauf.
> VdN—Verfolgte des Nazi-Regimes [Persecuted by the Nazi regime].

25. Wolf Biermann, "Kriegshetze. Friedenshetze," *Die Zeit* 6 (1991), p. 18.

26. Surveying the German security build-up during the terrorist scare of the late 1970s, Biermann, catching the tone of Heine, wryly observes: "Und Straßen voll Uniformen / Und Blaulicht. Und Sichtvermerk / Es rüstet sich auf zum Riesen / Der deutsche Gartenzwerg" (P, p. 152). [The streets full of uniforms / blue light. And visa / the German garden gnome rearms himself to turn into a giant]. References to Heinrich Heine as regards mood, mode, and diction are obvious throughout the work of Biermann, who also went to great length comparing his own situation in exile to that of his "frecher Cousin" [fresh cousin] in Paris. Cf. A, pp. 105, 107, 110.

27. Whether Fleischmann in doing so actually set an example or simply followed an already emerging trend is up to debate; the rift, however, that began to open in the early 1980s between the (West) German Left and German-speaking writers of Jewish descent can simply not be overlooked.

28. Biermann showed me such a letter during an interview on 5 August 1980 in Hamburg.

29. "Der tägliche kleine Faschismus sieht/ So urgemütlich aus."

30. . . .
> geselbstmordet haben sie ihn
> jetzt hat er Asyl und für ewig
> auf deutschem Boden und Grund
> jetzt kriegt er sein Fleckchen Erde
> wie jeder tote Hund
> . . .
> die Freiheiten siechen dahin
> und ich weiß ja, was es bedeutet
> daß ich so traurig bin (A, p. 135)

31. The same volume also contains "Die Lebenden und die Toten," with the telling verse: "Wer uns immer noch Mörder nennt/ Macht uns am Ende zu Mördern, denn/ Sowas muß ja mundtot gemacht werden!" (G, p. 61).

32. "Die Toten können nicht schlafen/ Tief unter der Erd ein Geschrei/ Das kommt weil die Mörder hier oben/ So lustig leben und frei" (V, p. 44).

33. In this context, see also Ruth Angress, "A 'Jewish Problem' in German Postwar Fiction," *Modern Judaism* 5 (1985), pp. 215–233.

34. "Die Deutschen haben den Juden verziehn/— und bloß den Zigeunern noch nicht" (A, p. 29). See also "Vergasen I" (V, p. 45), "Vergasen II" (V, p. 46). As late as December 1992, the Jewish journalist Ralph Giordano, in recent years himself a fre-

quent target of not merely anonymous death threats (which prompted him to send a furious telegram to the German Chancellor), addressed this particular problem in the post-World War II German psyche: "The terrible thing about it is that in this country there are privileged victims—the Jews—victims of a second and even lower order. The Roma are, of course, considered the lowest." In "Wir sind die Stärkeren," *Der Spiegel* 52 (1992), p. 41.

35. Andrei S. Markovits, "Germans and Jews: An Uneasy Relationship Continues," *Jewish Frontier* 51 (April 1984), p. 17.

36. Detlev Claussen, "In the House of the Hangman," *Germans and Jews since the Holocaust*, p. 63.

37. Lea Fleischmann, "Identity Problems of the Jewish Post-War Generation," paper read at the 1991 International Symposium on Germanic Languages and Literatures: Cultural and Linguistic Diversity, Ohio State University (English-language handout).

38. Biermann, in his acceptance speech of the Büchner Prize on 19 October 1991, recently published as "Lichtblick im gräßlichen Fatalismus der Geschichte," *Der Sturz des Dädalus*, p. 58.

39. The kind that by the end of 1992 had desecrated dozens of Jewish cemeteries all over Germany, and had as early as 1990 defaced Bertolt Brecht's grave in Berlin's Hugenottenfriedhof with anti-Semitic graffiti. In 1972, Biermann had written a lengthy song about this very graveyard and, ironically, this very graveside of Bertolt Brecht and his Jewish wife, Helene Weigel.

40. The Berlin counseling office for Jewish refugees from the Soviet Union explained, with appalling insensitivity, "live" on German television, a bizarre situation of German bureaucrats once again deciding who is Jewish: "According to Soviet law it is illegal for a tourist to carry birth certificates across the border.... They come here anyhow and have no government documents to prove that they are Jewish. Now we have to make the decision, are they Jews or are they not" (*ZDF* "Heute," 28 December 1990). Biermann had his own comment on these developments: "The panic flight of the Jews from hungry Pamjat-Russia, which is eager to lynch people—to Germany of all places—that is a terrible omen" (*Zeit* 35 [1990], p. 17). By late 1992, it would seem, a number of these Jewish refugees had second thoughts about having come to Germany, of all places. See "Dann bin ich weg über Nacht. Die Jüdischen Gemeinden und der wachsende Antisemitismus in Deutschland," *Der Spiegel* 51 (1992), p. 56.

41. Wolf Biermann, "Ich halt's gut aus," *Die Zeit* 43 (1990), p. 15:

> Skins auf dem Bahnhof Lichtenberg
> In glänzenden Bomberjacken
> Sie sorgen für deutsche Sauberkeit
> Bis die Zigeuner sich packen.

42. *Die Zeit* 6 (1991), p. 18.

43. Wolf Biermann, "Duftmarke setzen," *Über das Geld und andere Herzensdinge* (Cologne: Kiepenheuer & Witsch, 1991), p. 23.

44. *Die Zeit* 6 (1991), p. 18. See also Wolf Biermann, "Am Tatort," *Die Zeit* 24 (1991): "Nun schließt sich ein Lebenskreis," p. 16. As regards the recent reemergence of anti-Semitism in Germany, see Günter B. Ginzel, ed., *Antisemitismus. Erscheinungsformen der Judenfeindschaft gestern und heute* (Cologne: Wissenschaft und Politik, 1992).

45. "So kam ich unter die Deutschen." Five years later, Erich Fried used the very

same line as a title for one of his volumes of poetry. Biermann himself has frequently made reference to this line, e.g. "so kamt Ihr unter die Deutschen" (P, p. 211).

46. "In diesem Lande leben wir/ wie Fremdlinge im eigenen Haus" (*Hölderlin*, p. 638). This line, in turn, was used in 1980 as title and theme of an anthology of contemporary German poetry by Hans Bender who, in his introduction, attributed it to Biermann in its entirety, seemingly unaware that part of what he was using is merely intertext. Latest among many spirited attempts to reclaim Hölderlin from nationalistic misrepresentation—attempts dating back to Peter Weiss and Peter Härtling in the early 1970s—stands Biermann's "Vaterlandsphrasen oder schwäbische Marseillaise?" *Frankfurter Allgemeine Zeitung*, 7 September 1991.

47. Biermann, in an interview with me on 13 June 1990 in Hamburg, talked about his "lebenslängliche [!] Seelenschiefheit" [a lifelong [!] crookedness of the soul]: "There are times when rather than feeling sad, sadness takes me prisoner."

48. On the subject of Jewish optimism, pessimism, and melancholy see Fritz J. Raddatz, *Revolte und Melancholie* (Frankfurt am Main: Fischer, 1982).

49. Biermann often feels that is his politically working through his 'Jewish anxiety': "My Jewish fear, which I claim to own—of which, however, I am certain that one day it will own me," G, p. 8. Similarly, Grossmann talks about her Jewish "hypersensitivity" (p. 179) and her "overdeveloped antennae," using the same term Biermann did when describing himself during an interview with me on 20 June 1978 in Hamburg.

50. At the same time, Biermann does not deny the traumatic impact of these raids and sheds some light on his psychological makeup in the process: "Do you know the melted clock of Hiroshima? My little life clock stopped in Hammerbrook. Since that night under the British bomb carpet I have remained six-and-a-half years old." *Die Zeit* 6 (1990), p. 17.

51. Wolf Biermann, *Alle Lieder* (Cologne: Kiepenheuer & Witsch, 1992), p. 352.

52. In contrast, Biermann told me in the course of an interview on 13 June 1990: "I have become somewhat more Jewish. I have a friend who 'infects' me with Jewishness." Jay Rosellini simply doubts that Biermann actually meant what he wrote in the *Zeit* article: "Although [he] ... writes that he was not impartial during the Gulf War, but 'not a Jew,' the readers have to come to the conclusion that he means the opposite." In Jay Roselini, *Wolf Biermann* (Munich: Beck, 1992), p. 152.

53. In this context, Biermann again refers to Heine: "In the war of liberation of mankind/ there are no dead" (P, p. 43).

54. *Die Zeit* 6 (1991), p. 18: "My father's exhilarating experience in the 1920s was not that he was a Jew, but that he was a human being. As a Communist and a dock worker he repressed the Jewishness of his childhood." At the same time, Biermann was quick to honor, in his own way, the memory of the three young victims, one of them Jewish, of the 1992 Moscow *putsch* in an Aramaic elegy entitled "Kaddisch":

> Ein Judenjunge ist unter den Drein
> Ich Träumer bild mir wahrhaftig ein
> das könnte den russischen Pöbel noch rühren beim nächsten Pogrom
>
> [A young Jew is among the three
> I am enough of a dreamer to imagine
> that this might move the Russian mob/ during the next pogrom.]

In Wolf Biermann, *Ein deutsch-deutscher Liedermacher. Bilingual Edition of Selected Songs for Biermann's 1992 North American Tour* (organized by the Goethe-Institut and the German Cultural Center), p. 48.

55. G., p. 7. Regarding the allusion to Adorno, cf. Theodor W. Adorno: "Nach Auschwitz ein Gedicht zu schreiben, ist barbarisch." "Auferstehung der Kultur in Deutschland?" *Frankfurter Hefte* 5 (1950), p. 469.

56. *Die Zeit* 10 (1990), p. 14. See also: "Gräber" (V, p. 41), "Nach Auschwitz" (V, p. 47), and "Heimspiel" (V, p. 78).

57. *Die Zeit* 35 (1991), p. 17. For similar statements, see also "Zwei Tage danach," *Frankfurter Allgemeine Zeitung* (23 August 1991).

58. Peter Demetz, *After the Fires* (San Diego: Harcourt Brace Jovanovich, 1986), p. 140. See also Jack Zipes, "Wolf Biermann's Double Allegiance and Double Bind," *New German Critique* 10 (1977), pp. 191–198.

59. David Bathrick et al., "Wolf Biermann's Lyric I," *New German Critique* 10 (1977), p. 4.

60. Biermann had been quick to point out that this was done with unmistakably Teutonic determination.

> We [!] Germans are in East and West
> The most faithful legions
> of the generals residing in the Pentagon
> or in the Kremlin

*Deutschland. Ein Wintermärchen* (Berlin: Wagenbach, 1972), p. 25.

61. Biermann in conversations with me as early as 10 July 1974 in then East Berlin and as recent as 9 November 1992 in Washington.

62. *Die Zeit* 43 (1990), p. 15:

> Fern im Irak mit deutschen Gas
> Und Düsenbombern aus France
> Hat nun der Meister aus Deutschland, der Tod
> Gegen Israel seine Chance

Already in 1982 Biermann had referred to Celan's poem: "Der Tod ist ein rechter Meister/ aus Deutschland" [Death Is a Real Master from Germany] (V, p. 73).

63. The often militant anti-philo-Semitism of the German Left was perceived to develop decidedly anti-Semitic overtones as early as 1983. See Mischa Brumlik, "Antisemitismus wieder salonfähig," *Jüdischer Pressedienst* 1/2 (1984), p. 35, Jessica Benjamin and Anson Rabinbach, "Germans, Leftists, Jews," *New German Critique* 31 (1984), pp. 183–193.

64. As it turned out, at the time both West German firms and East German military advisers had been involved, the former selling production sites, the latter supplying the know-how for application.

65. Fleischmann speculates about the death of four elderly Israeli women, who suffocated under their gas masks during a missile attack: "Perhaps they escaped the gas chambers in World War II, and now, so many years later, German gas has, once again, caught up with them" (*Gas*, p. 82).

66. Described by Biermann in many forms, e.g. as "Waffenwälder" [Forests of Arms] (V, p. 92).

67. According to Fleischmann (conversation with me on 15 March 1991 in Columbus, Ohio), she had sought Biermann's contribution to her volume *Gas*. He declined after his article of 8 February 1991 in *Die Zeit*.

# Barbara Honigmann:
# A Preliminary Assessment

## Guy Stern

Barbara Honigmann's literary texts and canvasses—she stands in the tradition of Germany's *Doppelbegabungen* [dual talents]—are sparse at present and will not, as she has given her public to understand, increase rapidly.[1] She will continue to work, she has said, with painstaking care and will, at least in the years ahead, to balance her commitment to art with her responsibilities to her family, which includes two sons still attending high school. She also feels committed to establishing a new life in Strasbourg, her home of choice, especially within its Jewish community.[2] To emphasize her own stance she has repeatedly satirized the practitioners of a cultish devotion to art and literature.[3]

Yet despite her sparseness, Honigmann's compact texts command early scholarly attention because of their high literary quality and their standing as paradigms. They can be read as paradigmatic for post-exile writings by German Jewish authors, as an example of the literary reactions to the demise of the GDR by its decamped intellectuals, and as the articulations of a new generation of women writers. Honigmann's prose fiction itself, however, defies an easy categorization. She has labeled both her earlier text, *Roman von einem Kinde* [A Child's Novel] (1986), and the more recent one, *Eine Liebe aus Nichts* [A Love Consisting of Nothing] (1991), as novels.[4] The designation has not gone unchallenged. Marcel Reich–Ranicki would prefer to call the earlier work "sketches and études"; Joachim Kaiser is tempted to call the earlier work "a documentation of an inescapable (*ausweglos*) situation."[5] Yet at a time when the boundaries of genres have become fluid, labels matter less than the basic structure of a given text. Both books are in essence pastiches of fictionalized autobiography,[6] consisting of *Dichtung und Wahrheit*—in which a goodly variety of narrative devices interlink. Epistolary passages, anecdotes, diary excerpts, quotes of lyric poetry, factual reportage, and musings and reflections of the narrator accommodate the authorial intention of shuffling between time frames and of creating continuity out of fragmentation. In the service of the last-named purpose Honigmann has recourse to an entirely original fictional building block. The narrator, finding her father's diary among his bequeathed papers, continues the diaristic account with entries of her own. She updates the obsolete calendar, just as her father had done with this same outdated calendar of his exile years (*Liebe*, pp. 100–106). Symbolically and structurally exile extends into homecoming—both for father and daughter.

*Roman von einem Kinde* is a composite of six narratives. It begins with the title story in which the "I" of the work writes an extended letter to her former lover, mentioning the latest events in her life, including the birth of her son. It also clarifies the ambiguous title of the work, an obvious variation of Bettina von Arnim's title.[7] The work, as the letter makes clear, is both about a child and by a child—birth and rebirth. "I could no longer tell whether I was giving birth or being born," (*Kinde* p. 15)[8] the narrator observes in a key passage. Beyond the recall of a shared intimacy, now lost, between the letter writer and the intended recipient, the narrator also introduces two recurring themes: her need to leave the former German Democratic Republic and to cope, as a postwar German Jewish writer, with the second-generation trauma of the Holocaust and the indefinable guilt feelings it induces.

Guilt of a more personal nature sustains the next vignette, "Eine Postkarte für Herrn Altkirch" [A Postcard for Mr. Altkirch], in which the narrator blames herself for not repaying the kindness of the father-figure of the title. Guilt, in fact, surfaces time and again in the novel; often it is unmotivated. There is guilt about leaving her East German friends or a vague guilt while passing a group of prostitutes, unresponsive to her mute signal of solidarity (*Kinde*, pp. 113–117).

In the next story, "Wanderung," the narrator describes a hike on foot through Czechoslovakia, where she and a mildly oppositional "in-group" from East Berlin are vacationing. The story revives the motif of a return to childhood: when the narrator falls ill during the exhausting hike, she is sheltered by a friendly Slovak couple, and she dreams that she has reverted to childhood. But the story also constitutes a picaresque interlude within the narrative. Heated discussions about Rilke, Benn, Hitler, Stalin, East–West relations, and about the parents of the hikers cause them to lose their way; a group of smugglers succeeds in literally drinking the male vacationers under the table, and the liaisons among the hikers permutate in breathtaking profusion.

In the next two stories, the most chronicle-like of the collection, the narrator prepares the reader for the novel's denouement. In "Doppeltes Grab" she details the visit of the German-born Israeli scholar Gershom Scholem and his wife to the graves of his ancestors in East Berlin. He advises the narrator that a practicing Jew cannot live in Germany. But upon his death shortly afterwards, a gravestone at the ancestral burial site in East Berlin, coupled with his actual grave in Jerusalem, leads the narrator to conclude that Scholem probably lived his entire life in both cities. And in "Marina Roža" the narrator recreates her protagonist's visit to a dilapidated Hasidic synagogue in the environs of Moscow and his neophyte participation in a service. Without pathos she tells of the Communist suppression of Jewish activities; some of the rituals must be conducted clandestinely, and the community leader is ultimately exiled to Siberia. Peter, the hero of the story, in a way signaling Honigmann's own drift toward traditional Judaism, takes part in all the extensive observances except for the ceremonial bath in the Russian lake.

The last story, "Bonsoir, Madame Benhamou," provides the logical conclusion to the narrator's search for self-realization through a new identity. She has taken the triple "death-defying leap without a safety net": from East to West, from Germany to France, and from assimilated to traditional Judaism. She has come to the end of a new beginning; the integration into the life of Strasbourg and into its Jewish community has started.

Honigmann's second novel, *Eine Liebe aus Nichts*, more tightly woven, supplements and deepens the quest of the same narrator. But this time it is principally confined to the relationship of father–daughter and narrator–lover. In a way the protagonist has been the captive of both relationships. The decision of her father and mother to return, out of a sense of mission, to East rather than West Germany, determines the early career of their daughter. After studying theater arts, she is employed (and exploited) as a year-to-year dramaturge at various East Berlin theaters and starts to write theater commentaries and to paint her first sketches. Her sporadic encounters with her father, both during her childhood and when he moves from Berlin to Weimar as a result of a fourth marriage, lack intimacy: "Perhaps there was never any intimacy between us because again and again, at every new encounter, the husks of estrangement superimposed themselves" (*Liebe*, p. 28). The same insubstantiality marks her relationship to a lover with the despised German name Alfried, a director at the same East Berlin theater. He precedes her in her departure from the GDR, writes her occasionally, but without revealing his new address. A chance encounter in Paris, after the narrator's immigration, finally reveals to her that it was "eine Liebe aus Nichts" [a love consisting of nothing]. The death and burial of her father in Castle Belvedere, where his fourth wife was the curator of the never-completed museum, frame the novel; the evocation of Germany's cultural icons—e.g., a performance of *Egmont*, the gathering of leaves from Goethe's Ginkgo Biloba tree—punctuate it. The narrator, deprived of father and lover, tries to force a sense of continuity into her life by visiting her parents' waystations in life, by joining her father's diary notes with hers, and by finding a new lover in Paris. But he, too, fades from her life when she refuses his offer of marriage and he returns to America.

Is a new beginning possible? Alfried, during their last encounter, denies that one can start *ad ovum*. But the narrator balances her pessimism by breaking with her past as a theater or publishing employee and by enrolling and attaining a scholarship at the École des Beaux Arts. "Instead of simply letting the wave of a new life roll across me, allowing myself to be exhausted or even thrown to the ground by it, I wanted to use its movement and change positions on my own" (*Liebe*, p. 52). Honigmann leaves it open whether Alfried's or the narrator's prognosis will prevail.

Both novels, as observed, are autobiographical. The narrator and the author are children of refugees returned from England. They are of approximately equal age, grow up in the former GDR, and have careers as dramaturges. They give birth to sons in the absence of the father, become playwrights and painters, defect from the GDR and seek new roots, not in West Germany, but in France, trying to discover meaning behind their inherited Judaism.

But there are dissimilarities as well between author and narrator. Honigmann's identification with traditional (let alone orthodox) Judaism, for example, is not as unconditional as that of her protagonist[9]; the author's mother, unlike the narrator's, is not a native of Bulgaria. But congruencies or incongruencies are really not central to an analysis of Honigmann's prose fiction. More important is the sure-handed, subtle, and conscious process of selection that went into her pastiches. Her novels, she told a journalist, underwent several processes of distillation.[10]

The selection of episodes and details accounts in large part for Honigmann's success as a storyteller. All, or virtually all of them, are borrowed from precise observations of ordinary occurrences rather than from the large sweep of history. To put it another way, they fit one of the characteristics of postmodern writing. Decades before the term was employed on behalf of literary periodization, Siegfried Kracauer demanded of fiction that it describe a period of culture by its surface manifestations (*Oberflächenäußerungen*).[11] The basic substance of an era, he maintained, is ascertainable by its neglected motions. "On hand of the trivial and everyday occurrences he [Kracauer] develops the peculiarities [of a period]."[12]

In that sense Honigmann's texts are postmodern. For example, she has maintained, rightly so, that she is not a "political writer."[13] And, in fact, she does not, as did many other defectors from Communism, spell out the flaws of the former Iron Curtain countries and their leaders in broad terms. Yet her narrator's skepticism vis-à-vis an oppressive and dysfunctional system emerges from her snapshots of everyday life. The room allocated to her as a dramaturge in Brandenburg is miserably cold. "And even this is not the right word for it: miserable. I had no coal; for a myriad of reasons I had no coal and could not get any either" (*Kinde*, p. 45). Her father, freely choosing the GDR as a returned exile, must run the gauntlet of investigations. Why didn't he, for example, opt for the Soviet Union rather than a Western nation, as his country of asylum (*Liebe*, pp. 95–98). The harassment of the Jewish worshippers of Moscow consists not only of the dire threat of deportation, but also of such petty accusations as the crime of nude bathing when taking their ritual bath (*Kinde*, p. 104). Her knocking superstitiously three times on a mailbox to assure the safe arrival of a letter from the GDR does not testify to great confidence in its postal system (*Kinde*, p. 28). Finally, in the most direct and scatological attack on a Communist leader, the narrator and her fellow hikers find themselves confronted by a difficult choice, when they are forced to spend the night in the filthy meeting hall of a Czech village dive. Should they bed down facing a randomly deposited pile of human feces or in full view of a picture of Georg Husak, the despised, Soviet-imposed head-of-state of Czechoslovakia (*Kinde*, p. 60)?

The technique of portraying her semi-fictional world through revelatory but utterly commonplace details marks Honigmann's narrative method throughout, even when she deals with literature, the theater, or aesthetics. While she has claimed in some of her essays her rootedness in a German and European matrix, this claimed inheritance is mentioned quite casually and unobtrusively in her belletristic texts. Her implicit commitment to the German cultural heritage might almost go unnoticed. Yet its appearance is pervasive.[14] One of the actors at the theater recites a Rilke poem, provoking an argument about the merits of his poetry (*Liebe*, p. 42); the narrator's father will quote Hölderlin's lyrics (*Liebe*, p. 52), shifting its emphasis by underlining a single word; the evocation of Kleist's stoicism helps describe the narrator's acceptance of a painful birth (*Kinde*, p. 15). Honigmann is equally steeped in non-German European literature. No narratological theory accompanies the heroine's admiring nod to Marcel Proust, but she makes very clear, nonetheless, why he is her favorite author (*Kinde*, p. 22).

Similarly, her academic training in theater arts does not obtrude upon her novels. But in the description of her heroine's growing love for the theater there is a most graphic rendering of an alienation effect, not created by the play's author but imposed upon the spectator by the situation. She and her father, who is married to a famous actress, routinely watch performances from backstage. As city and stage noises reach the narrator simultaneously and intermingle she examines her reaction: "Only the two of us were standing between the dark auditorium and the artificial stage world and the world behind the big world outside, which, however, in some way did not seem to be the real world either" (*Liebe*, p. 26). In short, literature and the theater are woven as unobtrusively into the everyday world of the protagonist as her other understated experiences. That kind of restraint and modesty in the face of thorough knowledge also marks Honigmann's personal demeanor. During my interview of 17 June 1992 she faulted her university study of theater arts with lacking the exacting demands of *Germanistics*. Yet time and again our day-long conversation produced evidence of her erudition, buried beneath an ingenious casualness (and heavy Berlin accent); references to some less frequently read works of German literature, e.g., Wilhelm Heinse's *Ardinghello*—"a book I have wanted to read for a long time"—and Kleist's *Robert Guiscard*, emerged spontaneously.

But most pertinent to her own novels are Honigmann's and her narrator's references to Goethe's *Wilhelm Meister* and Gottfried Keller's *Der grüne Heinrich*. Read as intertexts, they not only set a mood, but reveal a purpose. The narrator puzzles why she feels so close to these two title heroines in the days following her hospital stay. *Der grüne Heinrich*, she surmises, is because of his impossibly high aspirations and his inevitable failure (*Kinde*, p. 19). But she is sure of what Goethe's hero means to her: her identification with his love and dedication to his son Felix. Wilhelm's famous invocation of the fates on behalf of his son constitutes the lengthiest quote within the two novels (*Kinde*, p. 15). She again quotes from *Wilhelm Meister* in the same work and within a related context. One of the hikers carries Goethe's novel in his backpack and reads to the group, reunited after the narrator's illness, about the world's emptiness without kindred spirits (*Kinde*, p. 85). The two passages illuminate the deeper structure of Honigmann's novels. Her and Goethe's protagonists, as one standard interpretation of *Wilhelm Meister* posits,[15] are in quest of a bond to family and community. Honigmann's heroines, but particularly the one in *Roman von einem Kinde*, are sent forth on their peregrinations to find a community of kindred minds, and through them a new identity. As in *Wilhelm Meister*, the quest does not end with complete fulfillment, but with the goal clearly in sight.

Even though Honigmann has disavowed any intentions of writing dramas in the future, saying that playwriting is not really her métier,[16] a word about her plays or rather short dramas appears in order. One of her first ones, a children's play loosely based on the Grimm's fairy tale of the *Löweneckerchen* [skylark], has been repeatedly performed both in the Federal Republic of Germany and the former GDR.[17] It appears to have enjoyed both critical and popular success and will be discussed below in a different context. Her thesis play, *Der Schneider von Ulm*, received far more mixed reviews.[18] Unlike Brecht's poem of the same name, which juxtaposes the myopic views of an arch-conservative bishop with those of a visionary inventor,[19] Honigmann's dramatic retelling of the story of the adventurous tailor Berblinger and his self-propelled flying machine has a far more pointed political implication. With an unmistakable applicability to the artists and writers of the former GDR, the tailor is far less fearful of state interference than of the state "coopting" his individual achievement and claiming it to be a national accomplishment. When the tailor hears that his experimental flight is to be part of a program celebrating a royal visit to Ulm, he expostulates: "It must not be that those people also want to have as their own what I truly need for myself. In the end I will be doing all this for the king's smile. It can't be, that they will take me over, even including my last gasp" (p. 12). In the same spirit Berblinger's wife denies the dictatorial state their child by intentionally carrying it beyond term, thereby bringing forth a stillborn baby.

*Der Schneider von Ulm* was repeatedly performed in tandem with Honigmann's equally short play, *Don Juan*.[20] In her treatment of the archetypal myth, the banished Don Juan returns illegally to Donna Anna. She is a lonely woman now, still in love with him; she will flee with him, but refuses to shelter the travel-weary exile who is intent on surcease from wandering. He only represents to her, as Don Juan comes to realize, the Romantic "elsewhere" ("Wandern," *Don Juan*, p. 66). He breaks the impasse by killing her; the ultimate "elsewhere" is death. In the last scene he is wooing her statue at the cemetery.

Finally, Honigmann has written a monologue in poetic prose, *Die Schöpfung*.[21] A mother describes her unceasing love for her son since birth; she retreats with him to a subterranean cave during a nuclear disaster. But as death approaches her, she sends her son back to the surface, confident that the earth will renew itself.

To my mind the wealth and originality of Honigmann's ideas run ahead of their integration into dramatic form. In a similar vein Pavel Kohout called *Don Juan* "an étude and an advance payment [*Vorschuß*] on the good plays that . . . [she] surely ought to write."[22] Rudolf Krämer–Badoni, reviewing both works, summarized: "Barbara Honigmann needs someone who will teach her how one breathes dramatic life into profound thoughts."[23] Honigmann, despite her abjuration of writing dramas, may still live up to the expectations of her critics. She told me in the course of our interview that she is working on a radio play based on the last years of Else Lasker–Schüler.

Looking at Honigmann's prose fiction and dramas collectively, one is struck by the consistency of her style. With the possible exception of *Die Schöpfung* her language is marked by a self-imposed simplicity that is entirely consistent with her postmodern symbols and images. Her language is, in fact, that feature of her writing which immediately, upon her first West German publication, all but mesmerized her reviewers. Marcel Reich–Ranicki, not known for the charitableness of his reviews, admiringly defined her style as follows:

> Whence comes the magic of this astonishingly simple prose whose tone seems almost childlike at times? From her naiveté? From the charm of her naturalness? Or from her unpretentiousness? If all this is true, we are dealing in fact with a naiveté of a higher order, a naturalness acquired via detours, an unpretentiousness that suggests a tacit, discreet, or restrained control.[24]

Reich–Ranicki's analysis is, to my mind, entirely valid. In her conversation with me, Honigmann told me that she consciously eschews the political jargon of the former GDR and likewise the trendy neologisms of the West. Her remark betokens a highly conscious stylistic control. The result is, oxymoron aside, a sophisticated naiveté, the elegance of a simple dress enveloping her fastidiously selected composites. Honigmann's style, I suspect, is dictated by an ingrained need to be honest, to discover and expand upon her own horizons and to communicate unambiguously.

The same motivations characterize her paintings. Viewing many of them at a recent exhibit at the Gallery Hasenclever in Munich (28 April to 6 June 1992, subsequently extended) and several additional ones at Honigmann's studio in Strasbourg, I was startled by the reckless frankness of her self-portrait and the stark contrasts separating her human figures from their surroundings. For example, a geometric nude, her skin-color dampened, lies on a bluish-white bed, framed by a black wall and an equally black exterior glimpsed through a single, partially obscured window frame. Michael Hasenclever, the art expert and gallery owner, believes that the representations are so arresting in their directness that questions such as their classifications as to school or movement, even their *locus standi* as art, never arise.[25] One reviewer likened one of her canvasses, upon a first viewing, to naive paintings, "powerful and direct."[26] Honigmann agrees that her pictures are autobiographical, but extend beyond mere self-analysis. A reporter for *Die Zeit* paraphrased her as follows: "Working with the moveable scenery of her biography—not in order to descend into self-analysis, but to ascend into flights of imagination."[27]

In the same interview she likened her writings and paintings to two sides of the same coin, as a way "to express an inner concept of form in different ways" (Schneider). And in an earlier interview she termed her ways of writing and painting as being similar.[28] She also quoted to me the observation of Heinrich Bethke, an East German painter: "You write the way you paint." I asked her about her routine of alternating between the two forms of artistic expression. "First comes the word. When I am exhausted from writing, I take up the brush as a form of release. And after a while I return to the desk."

Given this nearly simultaneous genesis of her writings and paintings it is scarcely surprising that the subjects depicted in the two artistic media are often identical. Her evocation and quotation of a Kleist letter (*Liebe*, p. 15) recurs in her oil painting of Kleist of the same period, as she superimposes the title page of a Kleist volume, complete with the only known portrait of him, over a recreated letter (*Catalogue*, ill. 6) Her reminiscences of her last look at the Ginkgo Biloba tree from a window of Schloss Belvedere after her father's funeral (*Liebe*, p. 9) finds its pictorial correspondence in an oil painting of a funereally black window on whose inner crosslike frame a view of Goethe's tree and his garden house seems to be nailed, while an actual yellowing copy of his famous poem has been glued, collage-fashion, on the painted window cross (*Catalogue*, ill. 7).

Even when there is a time gap between the crafting of texts and paintings there are close contextual similarities. Her character analysis of her father "who, after all had left [us]" (*Liebe*, pp. 23–28) is anticipated by her posthumous portrait of him from the year 1987, in which his eyes are averted from the beholder. In her radio play about Else Lasker–Schüler, now in the process of being written, she will probably borrow from her 1991 self-portrait, stylized to resemble the poet's features and from another oil painting of 1988, entitled "Else Lasker–Schülers Jerusalemer Tagebuch" [Else Lasker–Schüler's Jerusalem Diary], which shows a scraggly, slightly bent woman, painted in a grayish-green color on a torn-out piece of notebook paper with only the open mouth suggesting retained animation (*Catalogue*, ill. 9 and 5). "My radio play veers away now from an exact representation of Lasker–Schüler; it is turning into the portrait of an aging woman," Honigmann told me. "It is so difficult to intuit the personality of such a poet." The *artist* Honigmann might have said the same about her painting of Else Lasker–Schüler.

Barbara Honigmann, despite her highly individualistic talents, belongs to several clearly definable subgroups of postwar writers, an identification she, too, readily concurs with. In a previous article I have observed that many of the children of exiles, once they became writers, discovered the exilic existence of the parent generation as a rewarding subject matter. Even when they do not (or no longer) have command of German as a literary language, they have become a successor generation to the exiles by vicariously reliving and fictionally recreating the experiences of their elders.[29] This holds particularly true for those among them who live in and around Germany. Several critics concur: Dieter Lamping, surveying the new generation of German writers—for example Maxim Biller, Irene Dische, Esther Dischereit, Lea Fleischmann, Matthias Hermann, Barbara Honigmann, Robert Schindel, and Rafael Seligmann—conclude that many of them, especially those born outside Germany, manifest a preoccupation with exiles and Jewish characters in their writings: "In this aspect alone they prove to be a kind of exile literature—a second generational exile literature."[30] Addressing herself specifically to Barbara Honigmann's second novel, Ursula März finds that she has written the continuation to an exile novel ("Fortsetzungsroman des Exils"). "The peripatetic life of the Jewish family is like an heirloom that is passed on to the next generation."[31]

But no one is more eloquent or explicit in the theme of exile in her works than Barbara Honigmann herself. She explains that it was difficult for her generation to escape the history and stories of her youth. After her parents' return to (East) Germany, they and she felt themselves to be an elite class; returned exiles, including the children, consorted only among themselves. Even today, with her parents dead, she is tempted to fall under the spell of these old myths and legends. The suppressed stories—of the victims of the Holocaust, or the fates of survivors—they now fill her thoughts, although she herself was born in Germany. But the sagas, myths, and legends of her parents' disrupted lives continue to reverberate in her mind and find expression in her works as in this poem:

> The routes of exile
> Crossings of tempestuous seas
> Submerged cities
> The loyalty of one's companions
> The disloyalty of one's companions
> The country of rescue
> The island of survival
> A strange language
> Vienna before the war
> Berlin before the war
> Paris until the occupation
> London
> Bombs over London
> The Blitz.[32]

Virtually all the themes struck in this "catalogue poem" also suffuse Honigmann's nonfiction and fiction. In one of her recent columns, she chronicles the waystations of an exile, a Monsieur Levy. Of German descent, he was born in one of the worst slum districts of Berlin, turned Communist, fled Germany at an early date, and fought with Spain's Republican army. Then, after Franco's victory, he joined the Maquis, and finally ended up in Strasbourg. To this date, despite his daughter's exhortations, he is psychologically unable to pay a visit to his hometown Berlin.[33]

We will find additional stories of exiles and the children of exiles throughout Honigmann's fiction and dramas. These are, of course, primarily the experiences of the parents of the narrator, of herself, and of her friend Peter in the "Marina Roža" section of *Roman von einem Kinde*. But occasionally there are glimpses of other returned exiles, of Johannes R. Becher and Hans Schoeps (*Liebe*, pp. 95, 100f.) and, by implication, of the mother in *Die Schöpfung* (p. 16). But, as Honigmann's texts illustrate, there has been a subtle shift of perspective in the depiction of the *return from exile*, if compared with the writings of the exiles themselves. While the problem of return with all its ambivalence does occur in the fictional works of the earlier generation—in novels, for example, by Hilde Domin, Oskar Maria Graf, Hermann Kesten, and Fritz von Unruh[34]—some members of the successor generation question the wisdom of return with greater vehemence and finality. "Am I supposed to be grateful to you for having taken me from Israel into this land of the Nazis?" asks the protagonist of a novel by Rafael Seligmann.[35] Barbara Honigmann, in the above-quoted self-appraisal, finds that her parents sat down between two chairs, "that they . . . no longer belonged to the Jews and had not become Germans."[36] In her second novel she shows the dual absurdity of her father's wished-for Jewish funeral in Germany after a lifetime of complete severance from religion and given his feeling of being a stranger in his own country (*Liebe*, pp. 7, 35).

But beyond such subtle differences there is an eerie holdover from earlier exile writings in Honigmann's texts. The tropes and symbols evoking exile are identical to those which suffuse exile literature in the more restricted sense. The narrator, held by the German language as if by a magic spell, is fearful of a severance from it (*Liebe*, p. 56). Time and again she uses Ellis Island as a symbol for a forbidding waystation *en route* to a country of asylum. The former processing center was, of course, a readymade objective correlative of exile for those writers who actually passed through it, but it is a surprising one in Honigmann's fiction, since she visited Ellis Island (as a tourist) only *after* the completion of her two novels.[37] Still more surprising, she applies this symbol not only to the America-bound refugees of earlier times (*Liebe*, p. 14) but—knowing full well that Ellis Island has been stripped of its former function—to her heroine's self-imposed exile in Paris: "[I] was sitting there or was running around like an immigrant, an emigrant, a flaneur, on Ellis Island" (*Liebe*, pp. 57, 20).

Among the numerous other "traditional" exilic symbols and myths employed by Honigmann, the following one is particularly striking. Wolfgang Frühwald, in a compelling article, has illustrated that the exiles frequently mythologized their peripatetic lives by references to the *Odyssey*.[38] Honigmann's protagonist, reminiscing upon the tales of exile of her parents' generation, has recourse to the same narrative strategy:

> Most of the time we talked about our background, about our parents, where they had come from and how they had escaped the Nazis. Their emigration routes and experiences in strange countries were the myths of our childhood and of our lives in general, like the *Odyssey*; legends, told a thousand times. Now we repeated them to each other, sang them almost in chorus, like different strophes of one and the same song. (*Liebe*, p. 55)

Asked about the motivation for this myth-making, Honigmann told me: "Of course I connect up with my parents' fate. There is so much that links me up with my father, particularly language. His letters to me left their mark on my style. Beyond that I consider exile as archetypal, as part of human impermanence —in short, the *condition humaine*."

Honigmann's predilection for the fairy tale, a preference, as Donald Haase has pointed out, that characterizes exile literature,[39] also confirms her position as an exile writer of the second generation.[40] She mentions Grimm's fairy tales in one of her essays but more telling yet, her first venture into writing was her very subjective dramatic adaptation of one of the Grimm's tales.[41] Written in modern, colloquial German, it became a successful play for children. More pertinent to the point under discussion, it introduces among the numerous changes imposed on the original tale at least two that mark Honigmann's version as exilic. Unlike the original tale, the three sisters, the female protagonists of the story are given names in the Honigmann version. But while the two older, stay-at-home sisters receive the fairly common German (or European) names of Bettina and Christine, the youngest daughter, who follows her bewitched husband to the ends of the earth, receives the Old Testament name of Hanna, meaning "grace" or "favor."[42] She is, indeed, the favored one.

Honigmann expands as well on a minor motif of the Grimms. She, who would in a later work equate *Heimweh* [nostalgia] with *Herzweh* [heartache] (*Kinde*, p. 115), introduces the motif in this early drama. The unadorned original line in the Grimm's tale, "she [the youngest daughter] would like to see her father again," leads to the following plaint in Honigmann's version:

> Only it is so difficult. Do not think that I no longer love you. But I feel a great longing for my father and my sisters and the things at home which were so familiar to me for so long. (*Löweneckerchen*, p. 140)

Thus Honigmann, steeped in the exile experience of her parents and already contemplating and anticipating her own, is lending her feelings to her heroine.

In Honigmann's writings the world of the exiles is frequently linked to the Jewish world. In a highly autobiographical writer it could scarcely have been otherwise: one of Honigmann's most important decisions in recent years was her resolution to evolve her nominal Judaism into one of active participation. Beginning with her ceremonial wedding to Peter Honigmann—one of the first traditional weddings to take place in the GDR[43]—she journeyed step-by-step from an areligious attitude to a comfortable embracing of Judaism.

Much erroneous information has been written about her new adherence to an old faith. It was *not* an exchange of a political credo for a religious one (cf. Reich–Ranicki). Her individualism, her commitment to her art and to women's rights, and the feeling of being a permanent outsider, which kept her from being a conforming Communist in the GDR, also prevents her from an unreserved integration into a common faith. In an interview she characterized herself as a "back-bencher in the synagogue" and her route to Judaism as an exploratory trip rather than a highway to a new identity.

> The other text [i.e. *Liebe*] is the one dealing with Strasbourg and tells about my studying books together with other women. First and foremost studying means getting to know and not yet fully identifying with them. I have come to understand that Judaism as pure ethics is not enough, that the core of all of history is—whether one likes it or not—religion. Without it nothing really works.
>
> And since I did not know religion at all, I wanted to find out about it. Now I have become familiar with it only to realize that I cannot truly identify with it, after all.[44]

By Jewish standards she can scarcely be labeled as Orthodox, even though she has adopted a few of the Jewish observances pertaining to diet and to the Sabbath and is sending her sons to Jewish schools. While she has come to realize, after her own first tentative steps, that a return to the faith of the fathers or forefathers is a worldwide trend among Jews, she has taken an individualistic return road. She had started out from the realization that an inherited (and inescapable) Jewish heritage was not enough, but that it had to be supplemented by concrete knowledge of Biblical and post-Biblical writings and of Jewish history and culture—beyond the always recurring themes of anti-Semitism and the Holocaust. As she had intended at the outset, Judaism in all of its aspects has become part of her life—but only one part among many.[45]

That autobiographical development is mirrored in Honigmann's fiction. In fact, it helped sustain her novels as "novels of exploration," just as such probing help sustain Honigmann's admired models, *Wilhelm Meister* and *Der grüne Heinrich*. In *Roman von einem Kinde* the exploration starts with a search for the only synagogue in East Berlin at that time and with the narrator's subsequent participation in a Passover service and a communal seder. Despite the fact that the protagonist meets a childhood acquaintance (who called her by her nickname Babu) she is a stranger in the crowd, "a [separated] Jew among Jews" (*Kinde*, p. 24). Honigmann, describing her heroine's departure from the community house, finds a telling symbol for Babu's first exploration of Jewish services. She is looking down on the darkened courtyard of the community house: "One could see a little lamp shining close to the stairs of the fire escape, a weak Star of David by a rusty heavenly ladder" (*Kinde*, p. 27). A dim Jewish star beckons to the future above the rusty Jewish past. But at the end the heroine has followed the star, her journey described by the metaphor of a *salto mortale* taken "from assimilation into the midst of Torah-Judaism" (*Kinde*, p. 11).

In between lie the exploratory run-ups to that leap, an identification with the dead of Auschwitz in a nightmare, debates about the Jews among the group of hikers, Gershom Scholem's advice to Peter and Babu to leave Germany and instead go to a country where, as the *Pirke Awoth* command, a knowledge of the Torah prevails, and Peter's exploration (and implied rejection) of Hasidic Judaism (*Kinde*, pp. 28, 57–58, 94, 101–108). When the heroine at the end of the novel joins her Torah study group, the experiment is still in progress.

In *Eine Liebe aus Nichts* Honigmann, sometimes by a mere word, phrase, or minor incident, returns to her exploration of the Jewish world. The narrator's relationship to her lover Alfried also spells out symbolically her ambivalent feelings toward Germany. She is in love with him, but detests his Germanic-sounding name. "I could not utter it, because it sounded so Germanic and because I did not want to love a Germanic man, because I could not, did not want to, and had no right to forgive the German people for what they had done to the Jews" (*Liebe*, p. 46). But she is similarly alienated from her American Jewish lover, Jean-Marc, who, a second-generation immigrant, symbolically rejects the German cultural past *in toto* when he refuses to accompany her to Weimar (*Liebe*, p. 56). And once more Honigmann juxtaposes her parents' suppression of the memories of the Holocaust and the Nazis' genocide to her own uninhibited acknowledgment of them, when she has the single word "Buchenwald" drift across the Weimar landscape or has her father insulted behind his back by the pejorative "Itzig" (*Liebe*, pp. 34, 36, 92).

Honigmann occasionally links the discriminatory treatment of the Jews to the discrimination against women. Although feminism is a secondary theme in her texts, her subtle message is by no means inaudible. On a surface level she often sets herself off from male concerns by her choice of subjects: father–daughter relationships, the intense psychological experience of childbearing and child-rearing, the affront of being shut out from the private realm of a lover. But on a deeper structural level the catalyst for her heroine's quest, her departure from the GDR, can be found in the fact that she was underappreciated there, was kept at the theater on a year-to-year contract, and was "not renewed" when she set her opinion against state policy. When the narrator, now in Paris, decides to abandon the theater and attend art school, she comes to realize how her relegation to minor tasks continues to influence her actions: In the GDR she was "nur eine Gehilfin" [merely a (female) helpmate]:

> Actually I no longer wanted this type of work at all because I knew that once again I would remain a helpmate, the same way I had been one at the *Berliner Theater* for much too long, and I could not permit this situation to last all my life. (*Liebe*, p. 52)

In her columns and interviews Honigmann had also voiced concerns about the difficulties of being both a responsible mother and a creative artist. She is convinced that the death of Paula Modersohn–Becker shortly after the birth of her child was caused by the then irresolvable conflict posed by these dual demands.[46] Elsewhere she argues that the Jewish religion, for the sake of its survival, needs attitudinal changes toward women beyond minor and trivial adjustments in the traditional synagogical customs.[47] One of Honigmann's reviewers raises a more fundamental question: Would a male writer have cast his experiences, if they had been parallel to Honigmann's, in quite the same mold? Would he, contrary to Honigmann, have been more explicit in highlighting his work in the theater? "Instead," finds Beth Bjorklund, "she offers a set of personally meaningful tableaux with the implication that this is the stuff of which life is made." She concludes her review, after pondering that Honigmann's admission of vulnerability might presuppose strength, by asking: "Would a male writer do it differently?"[48]

Such a question is fundamental, but cannot be answered, of course, on the sole basis of an analysis of Honigmann's texts. But recent advances in feminist criticism, for example the hypothesis of Kristin Langellier that women employ different narrative strategies than men,[49] might be applied to a new generation of women writers—of which Honigmann is certainly a most gifted representative.

But, to return to the beginning of this analysis of the writer–painter Barbara Honigmann, she is, beyond any categorization, a very individualistic artist and one whose own "novel of development" is far from concluded. She foresees a different life, perhaps a different artistic mode of expression, once her children are grown. She anticipates and fears this new period, "as [one fears] a new freedom and an empty space that one enters for the first time."[50] As so often before in her life, it is safe to predict that her anxieties and fears will spur her creativity.

## NOTES

1. The author wishes to thank Peter Honigmann, archivist of the Jüdisches Zentralarchiv, Heidelberg, and husband of Barbara Honigmann, and Michael Hasenclever, owner of the Hasenclever Gallery, Munich, for their generous assistance during the research phase of this article.

2. See her interview with Christiane Grefe, "Ihr könnt lange warten" in *Süddeutsche Zeitung Magazin* 19 (April 1991), p. 35–37.

3. See her column "Name vergessen" in *Basler Zeitung* (13 February 1992), Beilage, p. 3.

4. *Roman von einem Kinde. Sechs Erzählungen* (Hamburg: Luchterhand, 1986; Sammlung Luchterhand, 1989). Subsequently referred to as *Kinde*; pages refer to the latter, more easily available pocketbook edition. Also *Eine Liebe aus nichts* (Berlin: Rowohlt, 1992), subsequently referred to as *Liebe*. In her radio interview with Ditte Buchmann (Sender Freies Berlin, 11 July 1991, MS p. 9) Honigmann calls both her texts "Romane."

5. See Reich–Ranicki, "Es ist so schön, sich zu fügen," *Frankfurter Allgemeine Zeitung* 25 (25 October 1986), p. 14 and Kaiser, "Sanfter Sog der Apathie," *Süddeutsche Zeitung* 31 (31 March/1 April 1991), p. iv.

6. Honigmann, in an interview with Ariane Thomalla "Von Ost-Berlin nach Straßburg" in *Deutschland Archiv*, Cologne (November 1986), p. 16, pointed out the autobiographical elements in her texts, but added: "Aber irgendwie möchte ich das nicht so autobiographisch verstanden wissen. . . . Was mich am Schreiben interessiert, daß ich mich von meiner eigenen Biographie auch lösen kann."

7. In my interview with her of 17 June 1992, Honigmann referred to the parallel between her title and Bettina von Arnim's *Goethe's Briefwechsel mit einem Kinde*. A similar observation appears in Anon., "Über dieses Buch," preceding the title page of the paperback edition.

8. The translations are those of the editors.

9. In an interview with Ina Boesch of Radio DRS (= Deutsche und Rätoromanische Schweiz), reprinted in *Allgemeine Jüdische Wochenzeitung* (25 August and 1 September 1989), Honigmann distances herself from traditional Judaism: "Since I will continue to insist, must insist, on writing, painting, being an independent woman . . . I cannot assume the role of a truly religious, traditional Jewish woman."

10. In her interview with Leonore Schwartz, "Zu Hause im ewigen Widerstreit leben," *Kölner Stadt-Anzeiger* (21 August 1992), p. 6: "Like in a poem, the ballast of superfluous words had to be dropped."

11. See Karsten Witte, "Nachwort," in Siegfried Kracauer, *Das Ornament der Masse. Essays* (Frankfurt: Suhrkamp Taschenbuch, 1971), p. 341.

12. See Jörg Bundschuh, "*Ginster* von Siegfried Kracauer. Historisches Erzählen am Beispiel eines Romans über den ersten Weltkrieg." Master's Thesis, University of Munich, 1979, unpublished, MS p. 42.

13. In an interview with Doris Mack, "Schriftstellerin zwischen den Kulturen," *Archer-Rench Zeitung: Mittelbadische Presse* (17 June 1991), p. 6, Honigmann states unambiguously: "The political book is not my genre."

14. Most clearly so in the afterword to the Catalogue of her 1992 exhibit, entitled "Selbstporträt einer Jüdin" [Self Portrait of a Jewish Woman] (Munich: Galerie Michael Hasenclever, unpaginated): "It sounds paradoxical, but I am a German writer despite the fact that I do not feel German and have not lived for years in Germany. However, I believe that an author is what he writes, and he is particularly the language in which he writes. Not only do I write German, but the literature which formed and molded me is the German literature. I refer to it in everything I write." The same essay also appears as "Nicht von einander loskommen können," *Wochenpost* 20 (7 May 1992), p. 31.

15. See, for example, Albert Berger, *Ästhetik und Bildungsroman Goethes "Wilhelm Meisters Lehrjahre"* (Vienna: Braumüller, 1977), p. 152: "if to confirm his final consent Wilhelm asks the Abbé the most intimate, most personal question about Felix . . . , he is ready to accept the arcanum of society as his fate."

16. Interview with Ariane Thomalla, p. 16 (see note 6).

17. *Das singende, springende Löweneckerchen. Märchen nach den Gebrüdern Grimm*, written in 1981, was published in 1991 as part of an anthology of dramas for children. See Marion Victor, ed., *Spielplatz 3. Fünf Theaterstücke für Kinder* (Frankfurt am Main: Verlag der Autoren, 1991), pp. 125–160. To date it has been performed in Zwickau (1981), Zittau (1982), Leipzig (1984), Münster (1984), and Aachen (1987).

18. *Der Schneider von Ulm und Don Juan* (East Berlin: Henschelverlag, 1981), printed as stage MS. Copyright and remaining copies acquired by Verlag der Autoren, Frankfurt am Main. *Schneider* premiered in 1984 at the *Theater am Turm*, Frankfurt.

19. Brecht, "Der Schneider von Ulm," *Gedichte II* in his *Gesammelte Werke XI* (Frankfurt am Main: Suhrkamp, 1967), pp. 645f.

20. *Don Juan* has been reprinted in West Germany as part of an anthology. See Manfred Dierks and Alfred Mensak, *Literatur im Kreienhoop. Bericht aus einer Schriftstellerwerkstatt* (Munich and Hamburg: Albrecht Knaus, 1986), pp. 59–68.

21. Printed together with *Don Juan*, pp. 52–68.

22. See "Aus der Diskussion," pp. 68–69, which is appended to *Literatur im Kreienhoop*.

23. See Krämer–Badoni, "Dreißig Zeilen Lyrik hätten hier auch genügt," *Die Welt* 24 (24 March 1984), p. 15.

24. Reich–Ranicki, see note 5. For the only disapproving criticism to come to my attention see Harold Wieser, "Träume vom märchenhaften Frieden," *Der Spiegel* 23 (December 1986), pp. 185–186.

25. My interview with Michael Hasenclever took place on 12 June 1992 at his Munich gallery.

26. See Hans Jansen, "Magie des Einfachen," *Westdeutsche Allgemeine Zeitung*, Essen (27 September 1986).
27. See Richard Cham Schneider, "Barbara Honigmann. Keine Lust auf deutsche Fragen," *Die Zeit* (12 July 1991), p. 63.
28. Interview with Ariane Thomalla, see note 6.
29. See Guy Stern, "Das Exil und die amerikanische Gegenwartsliteratur" in his *Literatur im Exil* (Ismaning: Max Hueber, 1989), p. 399.
30. Dieter Lamping, "Gibt es eine neue deutsch-jüdische Literatur?" *Semitimes* 3/4 (1991), pp. 96–97.
31. Ursula März, "Exil im Souterrain," *Die Tageszeitung (taz)* (19 July 1991), p. 6.
32. The German original is as follows:

Die Routen des Exils
Überfahren auf stürmischer See
Versunkene Städte
Die Treue der Gefährten
Die Untreue der Gefährten
Das rettende Land
Die Insel des Überlebens
Eine fremde Sprache
Wien vor dem Krieg
Berlin vor dem Krieg
Paris bis zur Okkupation
London / Bomben auf London
der Blitz.

Honigmann's self-definition as a latter-day exile and the poem are taken from her "Selbstporträt." See note 17.
33. Honigmann, "Fast ein richtiger Elsässer," *Basler Zeitung* (20 June 1991), Beilage, p. 3.
34. See Domin, *Das zweite Paradies. Roman in Segmenten* (Munich: Piper, 1968); Oskar Maria Graf, *Die Flucht ins Mittelmäßige. New Yorker Roman* (Munich: Süddeutscher Verlag, 1976); Hermann Kesten, *Die fremden Götter* (Amsterdam: Querido, 1949); Fritz von Unruh, *Der Sohn des Generals* in his *Sämtliche Werke XI* (Berlin: Haude und Spener, 1983).
35. *Rubensteins Versteigerung* (Frankfurt am Main: Eichborn, 1989), p. 16.
36. See note 17.
37. See Honigmann, "Brief aus New York," *Basler Zeitung* (20 November 1991), p. 3.
38. Frühwald, "Odysseus wird leben. Zu einem leitenden Thema in der deutschen Literatur des Exils, 1933—1945," *Schriftsteller und Politik in Deutschland* (Dusseldorf. Droste, 1979), pp. 100–113.
39. Donald H. Haase, "'Verzauberung der Seele,' Das Marchen und die Exilanten der NS-Zeit," *Akten des VII. Internationalen Germanisten-Kongresses Tokyo 1990* (Munich: Judicium, 1991), VIII, pp. 44–50.
40. See note 17.
41. For Honigmann's version see note 16; for the original see Brüder Grimm, *Kinder- und Hausmärchen, vergrößerter Nachdruck der zweibändigen Erstausgabe von 1812 und 1815* I (Göttingen: Vandenhoeck, 1986), pp. 7–16.
42. See the entry "Hannah" in J. D. Douglas and Merril C. Tenner, eds., *The New*

*International Dictionary of the Bible* (Grand Rapids: Regency Reference Library–Zondervan Publishing, 1983).

43. See her interview with Ditta Buchmann, note 4, pp. 6–7, which also details that the Honigmanns' wedding in the GDR provided many of the guests, Jewish by heritage, with their first concrete contact with Judaism.

44. Interview with Boesch.

45. The Honigmanns' attitude toward Judaism emerges most clearly from their conversation with Paul Assall, which was awarded the Ernst Reuter Prize of 1987 for best (documentary) radio play. It was subsequently printed; see "Aus der Assimilation mitten hinein ins Thorajudentum," *Frankfurter Jüdische Nachrichten*, September 1987 (Rosch-Haschanah Ausgabe), pp. 25–27. Asked about her feelings of Jewish identity as of that time, Barbara Honigmann answered: "It is a little like with *Schwann* or if one has a lover and marries this lover. It has something of this kind of sobering experience" (p. 27).

46. See her "Selbstporträt als Mutter," which serves as introduction to the *Catalogue*.

47. Interview with Boesch.

48. Beth Bjorklund, "[Review of] Barbara Honigmann, *Roman von einem Kinde*," *World Literature Today* (Spring 1986), pp. 61, 276.

49. See Kristin Langellier, "Performing Women's Personal Narratives," paper presented at Speech Communication Association Convention, Chicago, November 1986. A printed synthesis of the paper in Jacqueline Taylor, *Grace Paley. Illuminating the Dark Lives* (Austin: University of Texas Press, 1990), p. 93.

50. "Selbstporträt als Mutter."

# Conclusion:

# The New Germany

# and the Future of a Negative Symbiosis

### Gabriele Weinberger

> Injustice to any people is a threat to justice to all people.
> Dr. Martin Luther King

Over the centuries the life of Jews in Germany was determined by a cyclical pattern in which Jews were driven out, banned, and readmitted. The coexistence of Jews and Germans has been a "negative symbiosis," as Dan Diner has pointed out,[1] not just since Auschwitz but for ages. Anti-Semitism is usually followed by a philo-Semitic reaction, the more horrible the crimes committed in the name of anti-Semitism, the stronger the philo-Semitic reaction.

Recent German history has given the answer to the question that, in 1977, the writer Edgar Hilsenrath put into the mouth of his Nazi protagonist Max Schulz, as he wandered about Berlin in 1947: "The spirit of the new times is philo-Semitic. A horrible ghost with teary eyes that will dry up some day. When?"[2] The ghost's eyes dried up when the Berlin Wall came down. Ironically, the tears dried up on the day when Germans were reminded of the violence of *Kristallnacht* on the 9th of November 1938, on the one day on which philo-Semitic Germans had mourned the Jewish people and the Shoah during the past forty-three years. The tears of mourning were replaced with tears of joy, excitement and triumph.

Scholars of German studies in the United States and elsewhere in the world are often asked if they think another Holocaust could occur, whether Germany is condemned to relive her past. The future will not bring back the past or repeat it, but new, possibly worse horrors will have to be endured if we forget the old ones and cling to the belief that we have become too civilized at the end of the twentieth century to commit such horrors, that they were part of a distant past.

The immediacy of worldwide satellite connections has given us access to information on the "ethnic cleansing," systematic rape campaigns against non-Christian women, and suffering and death in concentration camps in the former Yugoslavian republic. Our thin emotional costume is protected from the impact of these horrors by the illusion that United Nations or American intervention can prevent them at a time when these horrors have already taken place and are still ongoing.

As Zygmunt Bauman (in his sociological theory) and Edgar Hilsenrath (in his novel *Nacht*) stated, the Holocaust is only another face of the same modern society whose other, more familiar face we so admire.[3] The Holocaust is only another aspect of our world, not a separate sinister world. The difference between our world and the Holocaust is the level to which crime is elevated as a system. We are all more or less capable of these same horrors, and the Christian world will watch these horrors for a long time without a strong enough impulse to stop them if the victims are Jewish or Muslim or other non-Christians. Mass crime and "the most civilized part of the world" are not mutually exclusive but are in fact like two sides of one coin.

After "reunification," the New Germany was very eager to again break with its past, this time the past of the philo-Semitic postwar years, of often opportunistic shows of mourning and Holocaust restitution, and an ostentatious cosmopolitanism to avoid the appearance of nationalism. The unification of the GDR and the FRG under the sociopolitical and economic system of the Federal Republic of Germany has forced upon all Germans the "German question" of national identity, a question that hardly anybody had asked any more. By the end of the 1980s, the two countries had settled into their respective modes of Western (mostly American) and Russian allegiance. While the Bush administration and the United States media, along with their German counterparts, milked the opening of the Berlin Wall for all its value as a sentimental photo opportunity, nobody—least of all the Germans—had an inkling of the far-reaching consequences the whole country would have to bear.

With the tearing down of the Iron Curtain and the collapse of the Communist/Socialist system, the old enemy images disappeared and were replaced with new ones. The radical Left is no longer functional as the only scapegoat. The collapse of Communism occurred at a time when all top Western economies were in varying states of recession, when the Western world was shaken by doubts in consumerism and tried to slow the destruction of the earth's resources by curbing consumption. At the same time, the European countries face the *Kinderkrankheiten* ["growing pains," lit. childhood illnesses] of a borderless, unified Europe. At the turn to the twenty-first century, the world is in an unstable balance and upheaval not unlike that of the turn of the last century. The emancipation of the Jews and increasingly multicultural European societies had led to an extreme reaction guided by Social Darwinist and racist theories during the nineteenth century.

In the 1990s Germany feels threatened by the prospect of becoming a racial and ethnic melting pot. The country had imported a multicultural workforce in the 1960s but was not ready to live as one people with their new Mediterranean coworkers and neighbors. As "guest workers" (*Gastarbeiter*) they were kept at a distance and expected to return home when they were no longer needed. This thinking has prevailed over the last thirty years despite the fact that this workforce of about six million cannot be replaced by Germans, who demand most of the world's best social benefits. The "guest workers" are kept in their restricted status, at the mercy of German officials and subject to laws that were already in effect before World War II. At a time of high unemployment they are regarded as expendable. The social margin in Germany has been further widened by a stream of about 500,000 immigrants annually since 1989, most of them from Eastern Europe, some so-called *Volksdeutsche*, some Jewish and non-Jewish refugees. As in the 1920s, Germany is again faced with a marginalized population that its citizens consider as "surplus people". Whereas over the last forty or so years Germany and its neighbors East Germany and Austria had "anti-Semitism without Jews,"[4] it now has easily identifiable new victims.

In the philo-Semitic era following 1945, the tiny Jewish community of 30,000 in Germany and 250 in East Berlin served an important function (through restitution and other political maneuvers) in allowing Germany to become an equal partner in the world community of Western nations. However, the new East European Jewish immigrants of the 1990s, especially from Russia, face barriers similar to those earlier Eastern Jewish immigrants had encountered. They can easily be targeted both as Jews and foreigners. Initially, the model of the melting pot itself was projected in two competing images: (a) there is a culture into which newcomers may assimilate; (b) the culture itself is the pot into which the ethnic stew is placed. "The reality of a multiracial, multiethnic society has given rise to a myth of national identity torn between the forces of sameness and difference."[5] The events in Germany show that the fear of a new culture, blended from the elements of all and the xenophobic dogmas of the past are still effective in the presently perceived crisis in the wake of unification.

At this time of seeming chaos and disruption one can observe a high degree of continuity in the channeling of individuals in authoritarian social structures. To fill the void left by the dissolution of the Communist organizations (party, armed forces, and youth organizations), the right-wing Republicans offer a safe haven of continuity for *altautoritare Zwangscharaktere* [traditional compulsive-authoritarian characters]. Their Prussian virtues of order, discipline, and punctuality, secondary virtues that the men in the East German National People's Army had still been taught in the 1960s by the veterans of the German *Wehrmacht*, are very much appreciated by the fighters of the former SS officer Schönhuber, the head of the Republican Party. Many of these former Socialist Unity Party (SED) party members stated that they recognized in the Republican platform positions they had always supported—they hardly had to change their thinking and personality. They continue to function smoothly in their new party. Schönhuber tried to win the former SED members by stating that "there should be no second de-Nazification." His choice of words is very fitting, as many Germans who had undergone the process of de-Nazification had retained their authoritarian personalities and Nazi convictions throughout the existence of the German Democratic Republic. A second de-Nazification is as unlikely to be successful as the first one was. Since tens of thousands of former GDR soldiers and officers lost their jobs following unification, the Republican Party and other extreme right-wing organizations could count on masses of potential new members. Some of their propaganda in a former SED publication is directed against the upper class, mobilizing feelings of social injustice. The Fascist, nationalist, authoritarian structures of the GDR system interface directly with contemporary Fascist structures.

As some of the contributions to this anthology document, these theories and ideologies are still productive today, especially so in Germany where a multitude of groupings such as longstanding (neo-)Nazi gangs similar to those of the 1920s, racist clubs and organizations (of more or less international scope), as well as newly formed extreme right-wing branches of the established conservative Christian parties in Germany (for example the *Deutsches Forum*) enjoy a broad-based but tacit popular support and/or parliamentary representation.

The Germany of 1993 looks back at a wave of violent crimes against foreigners and Jews with the same icons flashed daily on news programs worldwide. The membership of extreme right-wing parties and associations totals about 100,000 and their followers and tacit supporters are numbered much higher. Polls indicate that about a quarter of the German population backs the slogan "Foreigners Out" and 37 percent of the population believes that Germans have reached the point where they have to "defend themselves against foreigners in their own country."[6] While university students in Bavaria have to complete a questionnaire about membership in extremist organizations, what is being defined as such is up to the Secretary of the Interior who included the communist PDS (successor to the SED) but excluded the Republicans from this list.[7]

In 1993 German Jewish community organizations and institutions are heavily guarded by police against an onslaught of anti-Semitic hate crimes. While the German media focus on the shameful increase of publicly displayed xenophobia (which had long been kept private) and of incidents of violence against foreigners, the rising number of anti-Semitic crimes is being played down both by the media and cultural and political representatives.[8] The seriousness of present-day anti-Semitism is not acknowledged. Expressions of anti-Semitism are often represented as individual cases rather than as a syndrome. Thus the mistakes of the past are repeated: claiming that anti-Semitism and xenophobia are isolated problems and identifying them in the "Other," i.e. in social minorities, rather than acknowledging the fact that it is a problem underlying most people's thinking.

The present discourse of national identity has not originated all of a sudden, but was prepared during the 1980s: both the print media and television played a major part in allowing Germans to identify with their roles of heros and victims. Since the mid 1980s, the reactionary discourse of the 1930s through the 1960s was spread through old bestsellers, such as Josef Martin Bauer's popular war novel *So weit die Füße tragen* (1955), celebrating the heroic survival of a German soldier who escaped from a Russian POW camp, as well as the regular broadcast of Nazi film productions on German television, which were often hard to identify since the production year was altered in the program guide. This old investment is put to good use again, as extreme right-wing followers have plenty of old paraphernalia to worship.

When the wording of the *Grundgesetz* [Constitution] was changed to delete passages about the Holocaust, the German constitution was only made to catch up with a process that *de facto* had already been completed. In 1989, fifty years after the beginning of World War II, the German people started a new era and do not want to be reminded of the shameful events in what they have come to regard "ancient history." The collapse of East German Socialism and the reunification terminate the postwar period, which dictated and taught more or less successfully shame and remorse.

## NOTES

1. Dan Diner, "Negative Symbiose. Deutsche und Juden nach Auschwitz," *Babylon, Beiträge zur jüdischen Gegenwart* 1 (1988), pp. 243–257.

2. Edgar Hilsenrath, "Berlin 1947," *Der Nazi und der Friseur* (Frankfurt: Fischer, 1986), p. 161. First published in 1977.

3. Zygmunt Bauman, *Modernity and the Holocaust* (Cambridge: Polity Press, 1989), p. 7.

4. See Egon Schwarz in this anthology.

5. Cf. David Desser, "The Cinematic Melting Pot: Ethnicity, Jews, and Psychoanalysis," in Lester Friedman, ed., *Unspeakable Images. Ethnicity and the American Cinema* (Chicago: University of Illinois Press: 1991), p. 389.

6. "Die Seele des Volkes verbogen," *Der Spiegel* 49 (1992), p. 17.

7. "Gesinnungstest an bayerischen Universitäten," *Der Spiegel* 49 (1992), p. 12.

8. For example the CDU Member of Parliament, Professor Renate Möhrmann at a conference on German Women Writers at the University of Maryland, College Park, February 1993.

# Index of Names

Ackermann, Lieutenant, 146
Adenauer, Konrad, 308
Adler, Alfred, 56
Adler, Max, 57
Adler, Viktor, 57, 295
Adorno, Theodor, 21, 28n., 39, 166, 167, 169, 248n., 267, 321, 328
Agoston, Gerty, 228, 229
Aichinger, Ilse, 5, 216, 295, 296, 297
Aleichem, Sholem, 26, 103, 121, 122
Aloni, Jenny, 127, 128, 129
Altenberg, Peter, 8, 9, 57, 295
Altmann, Nathan, 117
Améry, Jean, 9, 73–86, 216, 237, 295
Anders, Günter, 77
Andersch, Alfred, 230
Apitz, Bruno, 10, 230, 237
Arendt, Hannah, 38n., 163, 215, 230
Arnim, Achim von, 4
Arnim, Bettina von, 330
Arnsberg, Paul, 227
Arnstein, Fanny von, 5
Asch, Scholem, 121
Athanasius, 19

Bachmann, Ingeborg, 78
Bang, Hermann, 80
Bara, Theda, 289n.
Bauer, Ida, 22–23
Bauer, Otto, 57
Baum, Vicki, 295
Bauman, Zygmunt, 11n., 214, 221, 348
Becher, Johannes R., 338
Becker, Jurek, 230, 237, 314
Beckermann, Ruth, 5, 7, 237, 293, 294, 297, 299–300

Beer–Hofmann, Richard, 57
Beethoven, Ludwig van, 63
Behrend, Rahel, 237
Bellow, Saul, 25
Ben-Chorin, Schalom Ben, 128
Benedikt, Moritz, 57
Benjamin, Walter, 4, 9, 11n., 161, 167
Benn, Gottfried, 330
Ber Rybak, Issacher, 117, 118
Berber, Anita, 280, 282–284, 288, 289n., 290n.
Bergammer, Friedrich, 82
Bergelson, Dovid, 116, 117, 118, 121, 122
Bergner, Elisabeth, 281
Bermann, Heinrich, 60–61
Bernhard, Thomas, 78, 82
Bertram, Ernst, 141
Bethke, Heinrich, 336
Bettauer, Hugo, 295, 298
Bettelheim, Bruno, 9, 217, 243
Bienenstock, M. 119
Biermann, Dagobert, 317, 321
Biermann, Wolf, 6, 237, 313, 316–323, 325–326n.
Biller, Maxim, 337
Birkenser, Karl, 245–246
Birnbaum, Nathan, 111
Bismarck, Otto von, 7, 146, 158, 166
Bjorklund, Beth, 342
Blitzer, Hanna, 129
Blum, Ina, 284, 287, 286, 289n.
Bock, Hans Bertram, 243f.
Boleslav, Netti, 127, 129
Bollag Kahn, Léon, 100, 102
Börne, Ludwig, 5

## INDEX OF NAMES

Borowski, Tadeusz, 183, 218
Brandauer, Klaus Maria, 263, 275n.
Brandes, Georg, 117
Brecht, Bertolt, 231, 326n., 334
Brill, A. A., 24
Broch, Hermann, 57, 82, 295
Brod, Max, 121, 125, 126
Broder, Henryk, 237, 259, 319, 323n.
Bronner, Gerhard, 258
Brunner, Alois, 78
Buber, Martin, 8, 18, 27, 56, 111, 121, 235, 236, 239
Buch, Hans Christoph, 66
Buchmann, Ditta, 346n.
Bugmann, Urs, 239
Burger, Friedrich, 182
Burger, Hilde, 175–186
Busch, Wilhelm, 7
Bush, George, 348

Cahun, Léon, 100
Camus, Albert, 73, 74
Canetti, Elias, 5, 6, 12n., 75, 264, 295, 298, 301
Canetti, Veza, 5, 293, 295, 298
Cassels, Lavender, 268
Celan, Paul, 9, 130, 248n., 295, 296, 321–322
Cézanne, 117
Chagall, Marc, 118
Chamberlin, Houston Stewart, 7, 137, 139, 140, 141
Chaplin, Charlie, 284
Charcot, Jean, 140
Chsamowitsch, Leon, 112
Clare, George, 77
Cohen, Hermann, 151
Corti, Axel, 298
Czerski, Alexander, 128

Dahn, Felix, 136
Darwin, Charles, 7, 51
Davis, Bette, 285
Dawidowicz, Lucy, S., 178
Dehmel, Richard, 138f.

Deutsch, Eva, 246
Dick, Eisik Meir, 104
Dietschreit, Frank, 244
Diner, Dan, 144, 145, 152, 308–309, 319, 324n., 347
Dinkins, David N., 16
Dinter, Arthur, 7
Dische, Irene, 337
Dischereit, Esther, 337
Dix, Otto, 287
Döblin, Alfred, 8, 236
Dohm, Christian Wilhelm von, 4, 30, 32–33, 35–36, 36n., 37n.
Domin, Hilde, 338
Dora (patient of S. Freud), 22–23
Dostoyevski, Feodor, 156, 157
Dreyfus, Alfred, 51, 265, 266–267, 277
Droste, Sebastian, 284–286, 290
Drumont, Edouard, 51
Dubnow, Simon, 116
Duke, David, 190
Dyer, Richard, 265

Eckart, Dietrich, 63
Eckhardt, Guido, 96
Edel, Peter, 237, 242, 287
Edvardson, Cordelia, 175
Ehrenburg, Ilja, 117
Eichmann, Adolf, 78
Elbot, Hugh, 225
Elias, Ruth, 175
Eliasberg, Alexander, 121
Elisabeth (Empress of Austria), 273, 279n.
Engels, Eduard, 18
Engels, Friedrich, 216
Enslin, Morton Scott, 20, 28n.
Enzensberger, Hans Magnus, 316
Erhard, Ludwig, 228
Esterhazy, Major, 266
Esther (Queen), 101, 296
Ettinger, Shloyme, 104
Eugen (Prince of Savoyen), 279
Eulenberg, Herbert, 138
Eusebius, 19

Ezrahi, Sidra, 217

Falcke, Eberhard, 244–245
Falkenberg, Hans-Geert, 225, 230
Fassbinder, Werner Rainer, 280, 281, 288
Fechner, Eberhard, 78
Fetz, Berhnard, 243
Feuchtwanger, Lion, 6, 8, 9
Fichte, Friedrich Gottlieb, 4
Figl, Julius, 77
Figl, Leopold, 252
Fischer, Alfred Joachim, 230
Fischer, Ernst, 253, 254
Fischer, Lothar, 282, 283
Fishberg, Maurice, 140
Fisher, Terence, 289n.
fjg (book reviewer), 238, 239
Fleischmann, Lea, 6, 10, 237, 259, 313–318, 320, 322, 325n., 329, 337
Fluss, Emil, 17, 22–23
Fontane, Theodor, 4
Foreman, Milos, 263
Foucault, Michel, 267
Franco, Francisco, 338
Francois, Jean, 241
Frank, Anne, 243
Frank, Leonhard, 287
Franz Ferdinand (Austrian Heir Apparent), 264, 266–268, 271–274, 278n., 279n.
Franz Joseph (Austrian Emperor), 267, 272, 273, 279n.
Franzos, Karl Emil, 103
Freedman, Paul 229
Freud, Sigmund, 8, 17, 22, 23, 27, 28n., 56, 79, 140, 151, 163, 164, 258, 269, 294, 295, 304
Freytag, Gustav, 4, 7, 136
Fried, Erich, 5, 295
Friedell, Egon, 9
Friedlaender, Salomo 145, 147, 149–151, 152
Friedman, Maurice, 112

Friedrich III, 165
Frings, Joseph, 21
Frisch, Max, 103
Frischmuth, Barbara, 78
Fruchtmann, Benno, 128
Frühwald, Wolfgang, 339
Fuchs, Ernst, 296, 297
Fuhrman, P. Matthias, 293
Fürnberg, Louis, 125

Gates, Jr., Henry L., 15, 27n.
Geiger, Abraham, 122
Geiger, Ludwig, 121, 139
Gid, Marion, 225, 227, 228, 231,232
Gilman, Charlotte Perkins, 17, 28n.
Gilman, Sander, 3, 10, 12n., 28n., 135, 169, 232
Giordano, Ralph, 178, 325–326n.
Giuliani, Rudolf, 16
Glahn, Thomas, 80
Globocnik, Odilo, 78
Gobineau, Joseph Arthur de, 7
Goes, Albrecht, 230, 237
Goethe, Johann Wolfgang von, 40, 100, 120, 156, 157, 158, 166, 264, 331, 334, 336
Golan, Menachem, 263, 274n.
Goldfaden, Abraham, 104
Goll, Claire, 5
Göring, Hermann, 264, 265, 277n.
Gorki, Maxim, 117, 225
Gottlober, Abraham Ber, 104
Gottsched, Johann Christoph, 31, 36n.
Goverts, Henry, 241
Graf, Oskar Maria, 338
Graubard, B., 224f., 226, 230
Grenz, Albert Wilhelm, 146
Grillparzer, Franz, 4
Gringhaus, Samuel, 229
Grossman, Kurt, 227, 228, 229
Grosz, Paul, 255f.
Grouchy, Marshal, 156
Grünbaum, Max, 102
Gründgens, Gustav, 264, 266, 275n.
Gurewitsch, Vonnie, 191

INDEX OF NAMES 355

Gutzkow, Karl, 5

Ha-Am, Ahad, 109
Haase, Donald, 339
Habsburgs, 47, 52, 53, 77, 111, 304
Haider, Jörg, 303
Hakel, Hermann, 82, 296
Handke, Peter, 78
Harden, Maximilian, 145f.
Hartl, Edwin, 232
Hartmann, Eduard von, 138
Hasenclever, Michael, 336, 344n.
Hausner, Rudolf, 296
Havelka, Leopold, 296
Hebel, Frida, 128
Hecht, Ingeborg, 175, 178
Heine, Heinrich, 5, 6, 39, 40–45, 102, 119, 151, 325n., 327n.
Heinse, Wilhelm, 333
Heller, Agnes, 157, 158
Henisch, Peter, 298
Herder, Johann Gottfried, 4, 100, 166
Hermann, Matthias, 337
Hermlin, Stephan, 230
Hertzka, Theodor, 57
Herzl, Theodor, 6, 8, 55, 57, 60, 162, 304, 110, 111, 162
Herzog, Marvin, 89
Herzog, Walter, 232
Hess, Moses, 5, 11n.
Heydrich, Reinhard, 49
Hilberg, Raul, 178, 242
Hille, Peter, 80
Hilsenrath, Edgar, 5, 214–223, 224–232, 237, 241, 247, 347, 348
Hirschfeld, Magnus, 282, 289n.
Hitler, Adolf, 7, 9, 25, 53, 54, 63, 75, 77, 78, 150, 161, 162, 164, 178, 211n., 229, 241, 264, 285, 309, 317, 330
Hofmannsthal, Hugo von, 6, 57, 295
Hofshteyn, Dovid, 116, 117, 118
Hölderlin, Friedrich, 324n., 327n., 333
Holz, Arno, 117
Honigmann, Barbara, 237, 329–343

Honigmann, Peter, 340, 341, 344n.
Horkheimer, Max, 167, 169, 314
Huber, Lotti, 281, 282–288, 290n.
Hugo, Victor, 102
Humboldt, Wilhelm von, 32, 35, 37n., 38n., 100
Hundertwasser, Friedensreich [Friedrich Stowasser], 296–297
Husak, George, 333
Husserl, Edmund, 56
Hutmacher, Rahel, 237

Illies, Florian, 238f.

Jacobsen, Jens Peter, 80
Jakob, Emil, 226
James, Henry, 25, 29n.
Jansen, Hans, 239
Jelinek, Elfriede, 7, 298
Jesus, 19, 20, 27, 163
John (Ev.), 20
John II (Portugal), 34
Jokostra, Peter, 227–228, 229, 241
Joseph II, 4

K. K. (book reviewer), 245
Kafka, Franz, 5, 6, 73
Kafka, Hermann, 135
Kaiser, Joachim, 329
Kallenbach, Albert, 177
Kalmanovitsch, Zelig, 89, 90, 91, 92, 93
Kalmar, Magda, 274n.
Kalmar, Rudolf, 242
Kalmus, Dora, 289n.
Kant, Immanuel, 120, 152
Karniuk, Yoram, 241
Kastein, Josef, 125
Katz, Jacob, 138
Kaufmann, Fritz Mordechai, 121
Kautsky, Benedikt, 8, 242
Keller, Gottfried, 334
Kelsen, Hans, 57
Kesten, Hermann, 227, 338
Keyserling, Eduard, 120

Kindler, Helmut, 224, 225
Kisch, Egon Erwin, 57, 264, 295
Kittner, Alfred, 130
Klein, Hillel, 195–198, 204, 205, 211n.
Kleinmann, Moyshe, 118
Kleist, Heirich von, 66, 67, 68, 69, 70, 71, 333, 336
Klemperer, Victor, 242
Klimt, Gustav, 287
Kline, Dana, 199–204, 207–208, 209n., 212n.
Kluger Herbert, 236, 238, 241, 244
Klüger, Ruth, 237
Koelbl, Herlinde, 59
Koeppen, Wolfgang, 236–247
Kogon, Eugen, 241, 242
Kohout, Pavel, 335
Kokoschka, Oskar, 283
Kolmar, Gertrud, 5, 9, 236, 237
Kompert, Leopold, 100
König, A. J., 9
Kosinski, Jerzy, 9, 183, 217
Kracauer, Siegfried, 332
Krafft–Ebing, Richard, 25, 28n.
Kraft, Werner, 127
Kramer, Theodor, 295
Krämer–Badoni, Rudolf, 335
Kraus, Karl, 5, 8, 9, 27, 39, 57, 62, 63, 295, 296, 298
Kraus, Wolfgang, 75, 79
Kreisky, Bruno, 57, 296
Kreisler, Fritz, 295
Kreisler, Georg, 296
Kugelmann, Cilly, 310–311
Kulbak, Moyshe, 116, 118, 119, 120
Kutowski, Madame, 284
Kvitko, Leyb, 115

Labov, William, 211n.
Lagarde, Paul de, 52
Lamping, Dieter, 337
Lampl, Rusia, 128
Landau, Ernest, 225–227, 228, 229–231
Landau–Wegner, Lola, 126
Landauer, Gustav, 9

Lander, Jeannette, 237, 324n.
Landsberger, Arthur, 139
Lang, Fritz, 282
Langbein, Hermann, 218
Langellier, Kristin, 342
Langer, Lawrence, 191
Langgässer, Elisabeth, 237
Langhammer, Leopold, 75
Lanzmann, Claude, 74, 190
Lasalle, Ferdinand, 151
Lasker–Schüler, Else, 5, 9, 120, 121, 125, 126, 236, 281, 335, 336–337
Laub, Dori, 191, 195, 197, 205–206
Lawrence, D. H., 73
Lazarsfeld, Paul, 57
Lazius, Wolfgang, 293
Lee, Christopher, 289n.
Leer, Eugen, 228
Leinsdorf, Erich, 59
Lemke, Fritz, 145, 149
Lenin, Vladimir Ilycih, 82
Lenz, Jakob Michael, 4
Lessing, Gotthold Ephraim, 3, 4, 30, 31, 32, 35, 36, 37n.
Lessing, Theodor, 3, 9, 11n., 147, 151–152n., 159, 166, 169
Leven, Maria Christiana, 281
Levetzov, Ulrike von, 157
Levi, Primo, 183, 189, 190, 192, 202, 204, 213n.,
Levy, Hanna, 175
Lewald, Fanny, 5, 136
Lewy, Hermann, 226
Liebermann, Max, 117
Lietz, Hermann, 158, 159, 160
Lind, Jakov, 295, 296
Liptzin, Sol, 3
Lissauer, Ernst, 163
Littner, Jakob, 235–247
Locke, John, 31, 33, 35
Löhndorf, Marion, 239
Lopate, Philip, 26
Löwenthal, Ernst,G., 225, 226, 227
Löwenthal, Leo, 151
Lubowski, Bernd, 232

## INDEX OF NAMES

Lueger, Karl, 7, 53, 54, 162, 279n., 305n.
Lukatsky, Debbie, 25, 29n.
Luke (Ev.), 20
Lustig, Moses, 227
Luther, Martin, 9, 50
Luxemburg, Rosa, 9, 321

Mahler, Gustav, 57, 295
Maimon, Salomon, 151
Mann, Erika, 264
Mann, Heinrich, 139, 265
Mann, Klaus, 263, 264, 265–266, 277n.
Mann, Thomas, 7, 59, 82, 135–143
Manthey, Jürgen, 246
Marc, Franc, 286
Marcuse, Herbert, 314
Marcuse, Max, 138
Mark (Ev.), 19
Markish, Perets, 118, 119
Marr, Wilhelm, 7
Marx, Henry, 225, 228, 229
Marx, Karl and Lilly (publishers), 227
Marx, Karl, 5, 75, 151, 216
März, Ursula, 337
Mason, Jackie, 15, 16, 18
Matthew (Ev.), 19
Mauthner, Fritz, 57
Maybaum, Siegmund, 139
Mayer, Ernst, 82
Mayer, Hanns (ps. Jean Améry), 73, 75, 81
Mayr, Richard, 35
Mendel, Gregor, 7
Mendelssohn, Moses, 3, 4, 5, 32, 35, 36n., 115, 116, 151
Menninger, Karl A., 23–24
Merkin, Daphne, 24–26
Meyer, Thomas, 242
Meyer, Martin, 240
Michaelis, Johann David, 34–35, 37n.
Miegel, Agnes, 79
Mikesch, Elfi, 283
Miller, Alice, 169

Millöcker, Karl, 274n.
Modersohn–Becker, Paul, 342
Mommsen, Theodor, 137f.
Mosse, George, 140
Müller, Andreas, 242–243
Münchhausen, Börries von, 79
Murnau, Friedrich Wilhelm, 289n.
Mussolini, Benito, 264
Mynona. *See* Salomo Friedlaender

Nabokov, Vladimir, 117
Nachtsheim, Hubert, 224
Nadherny, Sidie, 55
Napoleon, 156, 159
Nashitz, Fritz, 127
Nasser, Abdel, 264
Neumann, Franz, 242
Nicodemus, 19
Nilus, Sergeij, 7
Nister, Der, 116, 117,
Nolte, Ernst, 311
Nordau, Max, 57, 140
Nordhausen, Richard, 138
Nordmann, Moses, 105

Osborne, John, 263–266, 270, 276
Oswald, Richard, 282

Paepcke, Lotte, 175
Panizza, Oskar, 150
Pappenheim, Bertha, 6, 8
Pasmanik, David, 111
Pavel, Lilith, 129
Perets, Izchak Leib, 121, 122
Peter (Ev.), 20
Piccolomini, Max, 159
Platen–Hallermunde, August Count von, 40
Pohlmann, Margareta, 177
Polgar, Alfred, 57, 304
Poore, Carol, 45
Praunheim, Rosa von, 280–290
Pringsheim, Alfred, 135, 138, 141
Pringsheim, Katja, 135, 141, 264
Proust, Marcel, 333

Pulzer, Peter, 53

Raabe, Wilhelm, 4, 7
Rabin, Ester, 128
Ramseger, Georg, 227f.
Rathenau, Walther, 9, 145, 146–148, 151, 163
Raven–Kindler, Nina, 230
Rawicz, Melekh (Ravitsch), 115, 118
Reagan, Ronald, 10
Redl, Alfred, 264–266, 268–273, 276n.
Redlich, Josef, 57
Reich–Ranicki, Marcel, 329, 335, 340
Reiling, Netty. *See* Anna Seghers
Reinhardt, Max, 57, 295
Resnais, Alain, 267
Rilke, Rainer Maria, 55ff., 330, 333
Ringelheim, Joan, 180–181, 217, 219
Rinser, Luise, 237
Robert, Marthe, 258
Roden, Johanna, W. 169n.
Rooy, Piet de, 214, 218
Rose, William, 40
Roskies, David, 191
Rosselini, Roberto, 84
Roth, Joseph, 8, 9, 57, 293, 295, 301, 304, 306
Rubenstein, Richard, 215, 219, 221
Rudnicki, Adolf, 228
Ruppin, Arthur, 140

Sacher–Masoch, Leopold von, 105
Sachs, Nelly, 5, 236
Salten, Felix, 57
Sartre, Jean-Paul, 49, 62, 73, 74, 320
Schiller, Friedrich von, 172, 182
Schindel, Robert, 337
Schlodder, Holger, 240, 242
Schneider, Richard Cham, 336
Schnitzler, Arthur, 5, 6, 8, 16, 55, 57, 60, 61, 62, 73f., 79, 117, 270, 271, 295, 305
Schoeps, Hans, 338
Scholem, Gershom, 121, 144, 145, 236, 237, 303, 330, 341

Schönberg, Arnold, 57, 294, 295, 304
Schönerer, Georg von, 7, 53
Schönerer, Karl, 7
Schönhuber, Franz, 349–350
Schopenhauer, Arthur, 120
Schorske, Carl, 53
Schwaiger, Brigitte, 246, 298
Schwarz, Alice, 127, 129
Schwarz, Egon, 295
Schwarzkoppen, Max von, 266
Scott, Robert, 156, 157
Seelich, Nadja, 299
Seghers, Anna, 66–72, 287
Seligmann, Rafael, 337, 338
Seyss–Inquart, Dr. A., 78
Sforim, Mendele Mocher, 122
Shmendrik. *See* Abraham Goldfaden
Shtif, Nokhem, 116
Sichrovski, Heinz, 298
Sichrovsky, Peter, 191
Silcher, Friedrich, 44
Singer, Isaac Bashevis, 274
Singer, Israel Joshua, 8
Soyfer, Jura, 9, 295
Sparr, Thomas, 240
Spengler, Oswald, 120, 140
Sperber, Manès, 301
Speyer, Samy, 310
Speyer, Wilhelm, 155, 158–161, 165f., 167–169, 310
Spiel, Hilde, 295
Spies, Gerty, 237
Spinoza, Baruch, 120
Stahr, Adolf, 136
Stalin, Josef, 120, 264, 330
Stauben, Daniel, 100, 101
Steuermann, Manfred, 128
Stifter, Adalbert, 4
Stöcker, Adolf, 166, 168
Stowasser, Friedrich. *See* Friedensreich Hundertwasser
Strauß, Johann, 57, 274n., 295
Strauß, Richard, 57
Streicher, Julius, 7
Struck, Hermann, 117

Sullivan, Ed, 15
Sulzberger, Arthur, 23–24
Suter, Johann August, 156
Szabó, István, 263–279
Szeps, Moritz, 57

Tandler, Julius, 57
Tchaikov, Joseph, 117
Tendlau, Abraham, 102
Thalberg, Hans, 295, 296, 298
Theilhaber, Felix, 5
Themistocles, 160
Theweleit, Klaus, 265, 267, 275n., 277n.
Thiemann, Andreas, 240
Thurn und Taxis, Marie von, 55
Thuswaldner, Werner, 240, 243
Toback, Sandy Barnett, 25
Torberg, Friedrich, 230, 247, 297, 298
Toussenel, Alphonse, 51ff.
Treitschke, Heinrich von, 137,138, 165, 166, 168
Troller, Georg Stefan, 59
Troller Norbert, 248n.
Tsherikover, Elias, 116
Tucholsky, Kurt, 9, 130, 146–152
Twain, Mark, 47

Ulbricht, Walter, 228
Unruh, Fritz von 338
Unseld, Siegfried, 239, 240
Uris, Leon, 228

Vaget, Hans, 135
Valentino, Rudolph, 284, 289n.
Varnhagen, Rahel Levin, 5
Vegh, Claudine, 190
Veit Schlegel, Dorothea, 5
Verosta, Stephan, 268
Vidal, August. *See* Daniel Stauben
Vigée, Claude, 101
Vischer, Friedrich Theodor, 39
Vogt, Hanna, 311
Volkov, Shulamith, 30, 36n.

Waggerl, Karl Heinrich, 79

Wagner, Otto, 296
Wagner, Richard, 4, 135
Waldheim, Kurt ,10, 54, 251, 253, 254, 258, 259, 299, 300, 303
Wallraff, Günter, 232
Walser, Martin, 190
Walter, Marie, 141
Wassermann, Jakob, 5, 6, 151, 238, 296
Weichardt, Herbert, 146
Weigel, Hans, 296
Weigel, Helene, 326n.
Weil, Grete, 237
Weill, Alexandre, 100–102, 104
Weininger, Otto, 6, 9, 17, 28n., 56, 62–63, 277n.
Weinreich, Max, 89, 90, 91, 93, 94, 95, 116
Weinreich, Uriel, 94, 95
Weintraub/West, Franz, 294, 298, 299
Weiss, Peter, 190
Weissenberg, Heinz, 128
Weizmann, Chaim, 235
Welsch, Robert, 308
Werfel, Franz, 55ff., 295
Wertheimstein family (Vienna), 57
Werthmüller, Lina, 217
Wichner, Ernest, 243
Wieckhorst, Karin, 246
Wiesel, Elie, 183, 190, 228, 314
Wiesenthal, Simon, 258, 295
Wiesner, Herbert, 241f., 243, 246
Wiggershaus, Renate, 175
Wigman, Mary, 281
Wilde, Oscar, 278n.
Wilder, Billy, 294
Wilhelm II, 137, 146, 165, 268
Wilson, E. O., 221
Wischnitzer–Bernstein, Rachel, 117, 118, 123n.
Witkowski, Felix Ernst. *See* Maximilian Harden
Wittgenstein, Ludwig von, 7, 56, 82
Wolf, Friedrich, 151
Woog, Mayer, 101, 103, 104–107
Wormser, Simon, 101, 102

Wulf, Joseph, 225

Yago–Jung, Yudit, 319

Zipes, Jack, 229, 259, 315, 323n.
Zivy, Arthur, 105
Zollschan, Ignaz, 5, 139, 140

Zuckmann, Julie, 183
Zweig, Arnold, 5, 8, 9, 27, 125, 126, 130, 145, 149, 151
Zweig, Max, 128
Zweig, Stefan, 5, 8, 9, 121, 155–158, 160–165, 295
Zwillinger, Frank, 295

# Index of Titles

*Affengeil* (Rosa von Praunheim), 282
*The Age of Daydreaming* (István Szabó), 263, 267
*Albatross* (journal), 118, 121
*Als unsichtbare Mauern wuchsen* (Ingeborg Hecht), 178
*Amadeus* (Milos Foreman), 263
*Der Angriff*, 9
*Anita, Dances of Vice* (Rosa von Praunheim), 280–288
*Anmerkungen zum aufhaltsamen Aufstieg des Arturo Ui* (Bertolt Brecht), 231
*Ardinghello* (Wilhelm Heinse), 333
*Aufzeichnungen aus einem Erdloch* (Wolfgang Koeppen), 236–247
*Aufzeichnungen eines Überwältigten* (Jean Améry), 84
*Aus dem nahen Osten* (Sholem Aleichem), 122
*Die Ausgesperrten* (Elfriede Jelinek), 298

*Die Bäder von Lucca* (Heinrich Heine), 41
*The Bajazzo* (Karl Emil Franzos), 103
*Behemot. The Structure and Practice of National Socialism* (Franz Neumann), 242
*Berlin Alexanderplatz* (Alfred Döblin), 8, 280
*Die Bertinis* (Ralph Giordano), 178
*Bezwingt des Herzens Bitterkeit* (Hilde Burger), 176–177, 181–183
Bible, 19, 124, 129, 297

*Bilanz der deutschen Judenheit* (Arnold Zweig), 9, 151
*Das Brandopfer* (Albrecht Goes), 230
*The Brothers Karamazov* (Feodor Dostoyevski), 157
*Buch der Lieder* (Heinrich Heine), 39, 40, 41–44
*Buddenbrooks* (Thomas Mann), 59, 164

*Chicken Soup* (television series), 15f.
*Colonel Redl* (István Szabó), 263, 266–274
*Communist Manifesto* (Karl Marx, Friedrich Engels), 216
*Concert* (István Szabó), 275n.

*Degeneration* (Max Nordau), 140
*Der Dektuch* (Abraham Ber Gottlober), 104
*The Destruction of the European Jews* (Raul Hilberg), 178
*Deutschland, ein Wintermärchen* (Heinrich Heine), 119
*Deutschland, Stunde Null* (Roberto Rosselini), 84
*Dialectic of Enlightenment* (Max Horkheimer and Theodor Adorno), 169
*Dies ist nicht mein Land* (Lea Fleischmann), 313–315
*Different from the Others* (Magnus Hirschfeld), 282
*Diskussion: Kultur-Parlament* (Hans Oswald, ed.), 138

*Disner Tshayld Harold* (Moyshe Kulbak), 120
*Doktor Faust* (Mayer Woog), 103
*Dolly, Lotte, and Maria* (Rosa von Praunheim), 282
*Don Juan* (Barbara Honigmann), 334f.
*Donna Clara* (Heinrich Heine), 41
*Dr. Mabuse* (Fritz Lang), 282

*Efraim* (Alfred Andersch), 230
*Egmont* (Johann Wolfgang von Goethe), 331
*Else Lasker–Schülers Jerusalemer Tagebuch* (Barbara Honigmann), 338
*Emperor Waltz* (Johann Strauß), 274n.
*Epistola de Tolerantia* (John Locke), 31
*Die Ermittlung* (Peter Weiss), 190
*Die Erziehung des Menschengeschlechts* (Gotthold Ephraim Lessin), 31
*Essai sur l'inégalité des races humaines* (Joseph Arthur de Gobineau), 7
*Es war einmal in Masuren* (Wolfgang Koeppen), 239
*Eva Deutsch: Die Galizianerin* (Brigitte Schwaiger), 246, 298

*Die Fackel* (Karl Kraus), 62
*The Family Carnovsky* (Israel Joshua Singer), 8
*Father* (István Szabó), 263
*Faust* (Johann Wolfgang von Goethe), 264, 275n.
*Fishke der Krumer* (Mendele Mocher Sforim), 122
*The Foundations of the Nineteenth Century* (Houston Stewart Chamberlain), 7, 137, 139
*La France Juive* (Edouard Drumont), 51

*Gas. Tagebuch einer Bedrohung* (Lea Fleischmann), 316, 322
*Die Gelbe Straße* (Veza Canetti), 293
*Der Gershing Narr* (Alexandre Weill), 104
*Die Geschichte der 1002. Nacht* (Joseph Roth), 8
*Geschlecht und Charakter* (Otto Weininger), 17, 56, 62–63, 277n.
*Die Geschwister Oppenheim* (Lion Feuchtwanger), 8, 9
*Das Glück der Andernachs* (Wilhelm Speyer), 155, 160, 164, 165–167
*Die goldene Kette* (Jizchak Leib Perets), 122
*Die größere Hoffnung* (Ilse Aichinger), 297
*Der grüne Heinrich* (Gottfried Keller), 334, 341

*Hanussen* (István Szabó), 263
*Hebräische Melodien* (Heinrich Heine), 5
*Hier bin ich mein Vater* (Friedrich Torberg), 230
*Hiob* (Joseph Roth), 8
*Die Hochzeit von Haiti* (Anna Seghers), 66–71
*Die Hochzeit von Port-au-Prince* (Hans Christoph Buch), 66
*Holocaust* (television series), 10, 259, 311
*Holocaust Testimonies: Ruins of Memory* (Lawrence Langer), 191
*Horror vacui* (Rosa von Praunheim), 281, 282, 283, 284, 287

*Ich bin Israelin* (Lea Fleischmann), 316
*Ich bin meine eigene Frau* (Rosa von Praunheim), 282
*Im Hof der schönen Damen* (Wilhelm Speyer), 165

*Jakob der Lügner* (Jurek Becker), 230

# INDEX OF TITLES

*Je ne lui ai pas dit au revoir* (Claudine Vegh), 191
*Jenny* (Fanny Lewald), 136
*Jenseits von Schuld und Sühne* (Jean Améry), 73, 75
*Jeremias* (Stefan Zweig), 164
*Jewish American Princess Handbook* (Debbie Lukatsky and Sandy Barnett Toback), 25
*Jewish Self-Hatred* (Sander Gilman), 19
*On Jews and Judaism in Crisis* (Gershom Sholem), 144
*The Jews: A Study of Race and Environment* (Maurice Fishberg), 140
*Der Jude* (Martin Buber), 121
*Juden auf Wanderschaft* (Joseph Roth), 293
*Der Judenstaat* (Theodor Herzl), 8, 110
*Judentaufen* (Walter Sombart, ed.), 138, 139
*Die Juden und die Kreuzfahrer* (Riesport), 6
*Jüdische Portraits* (Herlinde Koelbl), 59
*Der jüdische Selbsthaß* (Theodor Lessing), 147, 159
*Jüdisches Leben* (Leopold von Sacher–Masoch), 105
*Der Jud' ist Schuld* (Theodor Lessing), 152
*Jud Süß* (Lion Feuchtwanger), 9
*Jugend in Wien* (Arthur Schnitzler), 55
*Les juifs, rois de l'époque* (Alphonse Toussenel), 51

*Das Kabinett des Dr. Caligari* (Robert Weine), 287
*Der Kampf der Tertia* (Wilhelm Speyer), 155, 158–160, 169
*Ein Kampf um Rom* (Felix Dahn), 136
*Karibische Geschichten* (Anna Seghers), 66
*Kieselsteine* (Nadja Seelich), 299

*Die Klavierlehrerin* (Elfriede Jelinek), 298
*Von der Kunst, Österreicher zu sein* (Hans Thalberg), 298
*KZ Manager* (video game), 190

"Der lachende Hiob" (Mynona, ps. Salomo Friedlaender), 145, 150
*Lady Chatterly's Lover* (D. H. Lawrence), 73
*Language and Culture Atlas of Ashkenazic Jewry*, 90
*Die letzten Tage der Menschheit* (Karl Kraus), 62
*Leutnant Gustl* (Arthur Schnitzler), 8
*Eine Liebe aus Nichts* (Barbara Honigmann), 329, 330, 331, 332, 333, 339, 341–342
*Die Liebhaberinnen* (Elfriede Jelinek), 298
*Littners Aufzeichnungen* (Wolfgang Koeppen), 245
*Lorelei* (Heinrich Heine), 39, 43, 44
*Love Film* (István Szabó), 263
*Lust* (Elfriede Jelinek), 298

*The Magician of Lublin* (Menachem Golan), 263
*Manhattan Transfer* (Max Frisch), 103
*Männerphantasien II* (Klaus Theweleit), 275n., 276n.
*Das Märchen vom letzten Gedanken* (Edgar Hilsenrath), 214
*Marienbader Elegie* (Johann Wolfgang von Goethe), 156
*Die Mazzesinsel. Juden in der Wiener Leopoldstadt* (Ruth Beckermann), 293, 299
*Mein blaues Klavier* (Else Lasker–Schüler), 125
*Mein Kampf* (Adolf Hitler), 9, 54
*Mein Leben als Deutscher und Jude* (Jakob Wassermann), 151, 238
*Mephisto* (Klaus Mann), 275n.

*Mephisto* (István Szabó), 263–268, 271, 274
*Milgroym* (journal), 117–118, 119, 121
*Mr. Sammler's Planet* (Saul Bellow), 25

*Nacht* (Edgar Hilsenrath), 214, 215–221, 224–232, 237, 241, 348
*Nachtasyl* (Maxim Gorki), 225
*Nackt unter Wölfen* (Bruno Apitz), 10, 237
*Nathan der Weise* (Gotthold Ephraim Lessing), 4, 30, 32
New Testament, 19f., 36
*Nosferatu* (Friedrich Murnau), 289n.

"The Operated Jew" (Oskar Panizza), 150
"Der operierte Goy" (Mynona, ps. Salomo Friedlaender) 145
*The Origins of Totalitarianism* (Hannah Arendt), 215
*Örtlichkeiten* (Jean Améry), 80
*Our Corpses Are Still Alive* (Rosa von Praunheim), 281

*The Painted Bird* (Jerzy Kosinsky), 217
*Die papierene Brücke* (Ruth Beckermann), 299
*A Patriot for Me* (John Osborne), 263, 265, 270
*La Peste* (Albert Camus), 73
*Professor Bernhardi* (Arthur Schnitzler), 74
*Professor Mamlock* (Friedrich Wolf), 151, 152
*Professor Unrat* (Heinrich Mann), 265
*Protocols of the Elders of Zion* (Sergeij Nilus), 7
*Der Prozeß* (Eberhard Fechner), 78
*Der Prozeß* (Franz Kafka), 73

*Querelle* (Rainer Werner Fassbinder), 280

*Der Rabbi von Bacharach* (Heinrich Heine), 5, 6
*Radetzky March* (Johann Strauß), 271, 274n.
*Das Rassenproblem* (Ignaz Zollschan), 139
*Reigen* (Arthur Schnitzler), 73
*Robert Guiscard* (Heinrich von Kleist), 333
*Roman von einem Kinde* (Barbara Honigmann), 329, 330, 332–333, 334, 338, 341
*Romancero* (Heinrich Heine), 39
*Der romantische Ödipus* (August von Platen–Hallermünde), 40
*Der Rosenkavalier* (Richard Strauß), 57

*Schadchen Johle* (Meier Woog), 103
*Die Scheidung von San Domingo* (Hans Christoph Buch), 66
*Die Schiffbrüchigen* (Jean Améry), 82
*Der Schneider von Ulm* (Barbara Honigmann), 334
*Die Schöpfung* (Barbara Honigmann), 335, 338
*Schuldig geboren: Kinder aus Nazifamilien* (Peter Sichrovsky), 191
*Schwester der Nacht* (Peter Edel), 237, 242
*Serkele* (Shloyme Ettinger), 104
*Seven Beauties* (Lina Werthmüller), 217
*Shmendrik* (Abraham Goldfaden), 104
*Shoah* (Claude Lanzmann), 190
*Der Sieg des Judenthums über das Germanenthum* (Wilhelm Marr), 7
*Das singende, springende Löweneckerchen* (Barbara Honigmann), 334, 344n.
*Soll und Haben* (Gustav Freytag), 136
*The Sound of Music*, 251
*So weit die Füße tragen* (Josef Martin Bauer), 351

# INDEX OF TITLES

*Der SS-Staat* (Eugen Kogon), 242
*Steins Paranoia* (Peter Henisch), 298
*Sternstunden der Menschheit* (Stefan Zweig), 155-158, 164
*Der Stürmer*, 9
*Survival in Auschwitz* (Primo Levi), 189
*Surviving in New York* (Rosa von Praunheim), 282
*Susanna* (Gertrud Kolmar), 237

*Teufel und Verdammte* (Benedikt Kautsky), 242
"Todesfuge" (Paul Celan), 130, 321
*Trappistenstreik* (Mynona, ps. Salomo Friedlaender), 145
*Treblinka* (Jean Francois), 241
*The 24th Floor* (Rosa von Praunheim), 281

*Über die bürgerliche Verbesserung der Juden* (Christian von Dohm), 4, 30
"Die Unlösbarkeit der Judenfrage" (Theodor Lessing), 151
*Unheimliche Geschichten* (film), 282
*Unmeisterliche Wanderjahre* (Jean Améry), 80, 82
*Unzugehörig* (Ruth Beckermann), 299

*Die Verlobung in St. Domingo* (Heinrich von Kleist), 66
*Di vog* (journal), 116, 118
*Der völkische Beobachter* (Dietrich Eckart), 9, 63

*Die Walküre* (Richard Wagner), 135
*Wally die Zweiflerin* (Karl Gutzkow), 5
*Wälsungenblut* (Thomas Mann), 135–136, 141
*The War against the Jews* (Lucy Dawidowicz), 178
*Der Weg ins Freie* (Arthur Schnitzler), 60, 74
*Welcome in Vienna* (Axel Corti), 298
*Die Welt von Gestern* (Stefan Zweig), 155, 161–163, 164
*Whereto and Back* (Georg Stefan Troller), 59
*Wien Retour* (Ruth Beckermann), 299
*Wilhelm Meister* (Johann Wolfgang von Goethe), 335, 341
*Wir wissen nicht was Morgen wird* (Peter Sichrovsky), 191

*Youthful Sorrows* (Heinrich Heine), 43

*Zeit ohne Gnade* (Rudolf Kalmar), 242